A Free Grace Primer

A Free Grace Primer:

The Hungry Inherit
The Gospel Under Siege
Grace in Eclipse

by Zane C. Hodges

Grace Evangelical Society
Denton, TX

A Free Grace Primer
Copyright © 2011 by Grace Evangelical Society
Printed in the United States of America

The Hungry Inherit © 1972, 1980, 1997 by Zane C. Hodges
The Gospel Under Siege © 1981, 1992 by Zane C. Hodges
Grace in Eclipse © 1985, 2007 by Zane C. Hodges

Requests for information should be addressed to: ges@faithalone.org

Editor: Robert N. Wilkin
Cover Design: Rachel Goss
Production Design: Kyle Kaumeyer
Typesetting: Holly Melton

Library of Congress Cataloging-in-Publication Data

Hodges, Zane C., 1932-2008
A Free Grace Primer: The Hungry Inherit, The Gospel Under Siege, Grace in Eclipse/ by Zane C. Hodges
Includes bibliographical references
ISBN 978-0-9788773-9-2

Unless otherwise indicated, Scripture quotations are from *The New King James Version*, Copyright © 1979, 1980, 1982 by Thomas Nelson, Inc.

All rights reserved. No part of this book may be reproduced in any form without the prior permission of the publisher, except as provided by USA copyright law.

Contents

Introduction to A Free Grace Primer   7

Book One: The Hungry Inherit

   Prologue   15

   1. Discovering the Gift of God   17

   2. True Spiritual Food   25

   3. We Are God's Workmanship   33

   4. The Life-Giving Word   41

   5. Born from Above   51

   6. The Seed Is the Word   63

   7. Discipleship: Saving the Life We Lose   75

   8. The Faith That Lives   91

   9. The Riches of the World to Come   107

   10. For the One Who Is Thirsty   119

Book Two: The Gospel Under Siege

   Prologue   143

   1. The Gospel Under Siege   145

   2. John's Gospel: Can I Really Be Sure?   151

   3. James 2: What Is Dead Faith?   165

   4. Luke 14: The Cost of Discipleship   189

   5. First John: Tests of Life?   201

   6. The Christian and Apostasy   231

   7. Problem Passages in Paul   249

   8. Faith and Water Baptism   293

9. Who Are the Heirs?	307
10. Grace Triumphant	325
Postscript: The Sufficiency of the Cross	329
Appendices	335

Book Three: Grace in Eclipse

Prologue	381
1. Grace In Eclipse	383
2. False Professors	391
3. The Sermon on the Mount	399
4. The Indestructible Life	407
5. The Rich Young Ruler	415
6. Judged According to Works	429
7. Ten Cities	441
8. To Receive a Kingdom	453
9. The Darkness Outside	473
10. The Overcomers	487
Epilogue	507

Scripture Index — 509

Subject Index — 521

Introduction

About the Author

The author, Zane C. Hodges, went to be with the Lord in November of 2008 after suffering a major heart attack. He was 76.

Zane, which is what everyone called him, never married, though he came close a few times. His devotion to God and God's Word was so consuming that Zane reasoned he could serve the Lord better as a single man. And he did.

As a young boy of around ten in Pennsylvania, Zane came to faith in Christ through the witness of his own mother. He showed a zeal for the Word of God that led him to Wheaton College where he majored in New Testament Greek.

From Wheaton Zane was accepted at Dallas Theological Seminary (DTS), where he once again majored in New Testament Greek. Up until the mid-eighties a DTS student had to write a 40 to 60 page master's thesis to graduate. Typically students picked safe topics. Not Zane. He wrote on textual variants in the Book of Revelation. Textual criticism was a relatively new discipline. And the Book of Revelation is the one book of the New Testament with the most textual variants.

A few months after graduation in the summer of 1958, Zane was hired to work in the library. Less than a year later, he was hired to teach Greek. For 27 years Zane taught Greek (as well as Hebrew one year). He loved to teach the elements of Greek, which we called *baby Greek* or *first year Greek*. But each semester in addition to teaching two sections of baby Greek, he also would teach one elective, always on a tough New Testament book. Over the years he taught Acts, the Pastoral Epistles (1-2 Timothy and Titus),

Hebrews, James, 1-2 Peter and Jude, and 1-3 John. He also taught a doctoral course on textual criticism.

While teaching at DTS, Zane wrote and published the three books which are united in this volume: *The Hungry Inherit, The Gospel Under Siege,* and *Grace in Eclipse*. During those 27 years he also released his work on textual criticism, *The Greek New Testament According to the Majority Text*, which he co-edited with the late Dr. Art Farstad.

In 1986, at the age of 54, Zane quit his teaching position at DTS. He went to the Academic Dean, Dr. Roy Zuck, and to the President, Dr. Don Campbell, and told them each of his plans to step down at the end of the 1985-1986 school year. Both men wished him well. By 1986 Zane's views on evangelism and discipleship were different from those of most of the faculty. After resigning his teaching position, Zane pursued a full-time ministry of writing.

It was brave to leave. Faculty at leading schools did not simply quit. The prestige was too great.

Zane lived another 22 years after leaving DTS. During that time he wrote many more books including *Six Secrets of the Christian Life, Harmony with God, Jesus: God's Prophet, Power to Make War*, and commentaries on James, Second Peter, and the Johannine Epistles. He had nearly completed a commentary on Romans by the time of his death. We are currently completing the editing of that work and it should be in print, *Deo Volente*, within one year.

About These Three Books

The three books included in this collection were the first three written by Zane.

The Hungry Inherit was first published by Moody Press in 1972. Later it was re-released by Multnomah Press and still later by a publishing company Zane and his friend Luis Rodriguez established, Redención Viva (Spanish for *Living Redemption*).

Introduction

The thesis of *The Hungry Inherit* is that there is a distinction between inheriting riches in the life to come and receiving everlasting life. The latter is a free gift received by faith alone. The former is a reward for work done. Thus those who are hungry to please the Lord Jesus Christ and to have His approval will inherit a life of richer service for Him in the Kingdom to come.

Sales of *The Hungry Inherit* marked it as Zane's most influential and popular book. This book was written in a very simple style and with little detailed exegetical discussion.

Nine years later Zane came out with *The Gospel Under Siege* (1981). That was during my third year at DTS. I recall that Dr. S. Lewis Johnson came on campus and gave a critique of it to students gathered during the lunch break. One week later Zane responded to a packed Lamb Auditorium. Zane and Lewis were good friends, and Zane's response showed that. Of course, Lewis held to five-point Calvinism and a mild form of Lordship Salvation and Zane clearly was opposing those views in this book. But the great respect that they had for each other led to a discussion that fascinated the students.

The thesis of *The Gospel Under Siege* is that the message of life which Jesus and His apostles preached is under attack by theologians today. No longer is justification by faith alone truly by faith alone. Theologians go to great lengths to define faith in such a way as to introduce commitment and obedience and perseverance as conditions for everlasting life.

Ultimately it was likely this book that led to Zane's departure from DTS five years later. I recall other faculty critiquing Zane and his views in class. This was highly unusual for seminary faculty. The prevailing practice in scholarly circles was that faculty did not criticize their colleagues publicly. Say a student asked a question like, "What do you think of Professor Hodges's view that the Parable of the Four Soils represents one unbeliever and three different types of believers?" The normal response from a faculty member about a colleague would be, "Well, I don't comment specifically on the views of my colleague. In the future if you wish to discuss a passage, just ask about the passage. Do not attach your question to the view of a fellow faculty member whom I greatly respect."

In his third book Zane returned to the theme of eternal rewards which he introduced in *The Hungry Inherit* (and which he touched on somewhat in *The Gospel Under Siege*). This book was published in 1986, Zane's last year at DTS.

The thesis of *Grace in Eclipse* is that there is widespread failure in Evangelical circles to understand passages dealing with rewards. In this book Zane is not so much defending the message of life as he is championing the power and majesty of the doctrine of eternal rewards. Zane's passion for Christ's approval comes across loud and clear in this book. He longed to hear his Lord and Savior say to him, "Well done, good servant" (Luke 19:17).

I recall hearing him teach us in class that friendship with the world is enmity with God (Jas 4:4). He said something like this to us: *Men, do not seek to be well-respected scholars in the Evangelical world. If you ever achieve that, you will do so at a great price. You will not be able to be a friend of God and a friend of the scholarly world.*

He followed his own advice. Many scholars ridiculed Zane and his views in journal articles, books, conference messages, classroom lectures, and sermons. Zane was criticized in a book called *Exegetical Fallacies* as one who adopted views that were obviously wrong since they not only did not agree with the Evangelical consensus, and in some cases were views not represented at all in the scholarly literature. Attacks like that especially annoyed Zane. Rather than discuss his exegetical arguments, scholars would resort to counting noses and reject his views ex cathedra. By the wave of a hand they would reject his views without even interacting with his reasoning.

Introduction

I founded Grace Evangelical Society in 1986 while on the faculty of Multnomah Bible College in Portland, OR. It is more than coincidence that I founded GES on the year that Zane released the third of these books and the year that he left DTS. Zane's three books paved the way for GES and for schools and other organizations that promote the grace message. It is not a stretch to suggest that the Lord raised up Zane to be a leader in the modern grace movement and that these three books were pivotal in the birth and growth of that movement.

The Hungry Inherit went out of print in 2009 and *The Gospel Under Siege* and *Grace in Eclipse* in 2010. (There is a Spanish translation of *The Gospel Under Siege* which remains in print.) With this 2011 release we not only get all of these books back in print, but we are doing so in a handy three-books-in-one volume.

We have set a very low price for such a large and influential collection for two reasons. First, we are able to do so because donors underwrite our ministry and make it possible to sell books for far less than the normal retail price. Second, we wish to get this book into as many hands as possible. A lower price makes greater distribution possible.

We have added Scripture and subject indexes to make this collection a very handy reference work. We also plan to have it placed in many forms of electronic publishing within the next year. The message of these books is a message that needs to be heard.

—Bob Wilkin, January 2011

The Hungry Inherit

Prologue

Come with me to Palestine, a tiny land only a trifle larger than the state of Vermont, and join me at the site of an ancient well near the little village of Sychar. An important conversation, which has affected the lives of untold multitudes down through the ages, is about to take place there.

In fact, Palestine is the world's greatest stage. For on that stage there has been enacted history's most significant drama. And though it happened long ago, its relevance to men in these days is as great as—and greater than—the headlines in tomorrow morning's papers. There is not a man alive who can escape the crucial questions with which that drama—right here and now—confronts him.

I don't want to just tell you about the drama. I want you to be a part of it. I want you to meet its actors and to hear their voices. Above all, I want you to think their thoughts and feel their feelings. Only in this way perhaps, can the momentous issues which are involved be clothed with flesh and blood. For the people in this story are made of flesh and blood. They lived and breathed, and talked and ate, and felt and believed. They are real people in a real world facing real questions which we must face today as well.

Of course, you will not find *all* the scenes of this drama unfolded within the pages of this book. For that, you must consult the Bible itself. But if you look closely you will find here two great themes which run like interwoven threads throughout the entirety of the drama and give color and character even to the parts of it which are not herein described. It would be impossible to exaggerate the importance of these kindred themes. They are central to man's search for the meaning of his life.

You will need a little imagination as you read this book, for the pictures painted here are not only those of an ancient land and culture, but more especially of the hearts and minds of men and women who wrestled with staggering realities. No one can paint such pictures perfectly, and I have only done the best I could. Yet if there are details of the portrait which another might draw with somewhat different strokes, the twin truths which the portrait is designed to set off are sure and certain. And it is to these that I am calling the reader's attention.

What are these truths? To answer that here would be to get ahead of my story. We must take one step at a time. So for now, it is on to Sychar.

1
Discovering the Gift of God
John 4:1-29

> Jesus answered and said to her, "If you knew the gift of God, and who it is who says to you, 'Give Me a drink,' you would have asked Him, and He would have given you living water" (John 4:10).

The setting sun beat down warmly as a road-weary traveler stopped to rest at a small well. To the west, Mount Gerizim loomed over the land of the Samaritan people, in whose territory the traveler now found Himself. To the east rose the even higher peak of Mount Ebal, sheltering the tiny village of Sychar. The mountains formed a valley which opened to a vast plain covered with fertile fields of grain, south of where the traveller now sat.

Though exhausted by the long journey from Judea in the south, the traveler scanned the landscape to His north as though searching for someone or something. His attentive gaze was rewarded by the lone figure of a woman, water jar mounted securely on her head, making her way toward the well. His eyes followed her approaching steps and the flicker of compassion passed briefly over His sweat-streaked countenance.

At length she arrived and stood before Him. To her surprise, He addressed her. "Give me a drink," Jesus said (John 4:7).

"How is it," the woman replied, "that You, being a Jew, ask a drink from me, a Samaritan woman?" (John 4:9).

Her question was no idle one, for she knew well the deep scorn with which the women of Samaria were regarded by the typical Jewish man. The features of the man before her and His Galilean accent marked Him plainly as a Jew. Why then this request? A scrupulous man of His race would not think of using the same drinking vessel as a woman of hers.

But the social question she had raised was of no moment on this occasion. That was an external consideration only, for it was with matters deeper and far more penetrating than this that the man before her was concerned. He did not even pause to answer her question.

He continued, "If you knew the gift of God, and who it is who says to you, 'Give Me a drink,' you would have asked Him, and He would have given you living water" (John 4:10).

The woman was not so sure she agreed with that. What could induce her to ask Him for a drink? After all, she had her own water pot and came daily to this well. She had not needed assistance before and felt she did not need it now. Furthermore it seemed quite irrelevant at the moment to talk about some gift from God. Whatever that might be, it had nothing to do with the problem of filling her water pot.

Of course, the woman did not understand Him. In the language they were using, the words "living water" signified *flowing* water such as that which supplied the deep well on which Jesus was sitting.

"Sir," she responded quizzically, "You have nothing to draw with, and the well is deep. Where then do You get that living water? Are You greater than our father Jacob, who gave us the well, and drank from it himself, as well as his sons and his livestock?" (John 4:11-12).

There was a note of sarcasm in her voice now. To dig a well to which supplies of water would be both copious and long-lasting in the arid East was no small accomplishment. Jacob's well met both these conditions for its resources had been adequate not only for his sizable household and for his numerous flocks and herds, but more than this, its waters had continued to flow through the centuries right down to this very day. And that was why the woman was here. "He gave us this well," she said. "Are You great enough to do better?"

He was great enough. But this was not the moment to tell her so. True, a basic datum which He must shortly impart to her involved His divine identity, and the revelation of that identity would make it as pointless to compare Jacob with Him as it is pointless to compare a candle with the sun. But first, she must know the gift of God. This well was Jacob's gift. The gift of God, however, was of an entirely different order, and this fact must be stated at once.

"Whoever drinks of this water will thirst again," replied the Savior, ignoring the reference to Jacob entirely. "But whoever drinks of the water that I shall give him will never thirst. But the water that I shall give him will become in him a fountain of water springing up into everlasting life" (John 4:13-14).

The offer was staggering. No water from this or any other earthly well could produce such a result. In fact, every drink of whatever kind that the world offered to a thirsty man could have only the most fleeting and transient effect. And if that was true of all the literal waters used to temporarily quench man's physical thirst, it was much more poignantly true of the worldly fountains at which they sought to quench their thirst of heart.

Love, success, wealth, fame; these were but a few of the countless springs at which men had stooped to drink, only to rise from them to find that they offered no lasting inward satisfaction, no enduring personal fulfillment. "Whoever drinks of this water will thirst again," was a statement as broad as the innumerable means by which men had sought their ultimate contentment.

But His water was different. His water could accomplish a miracle. The one who drank it was secure from thirst, not merely for this time but for eternity as well. "Whoever drinks of the water that I shall give him will *never* thirst" (John 4:14). The need that His water was designed to meet and for which men were to appropriate it, was a need that could never recur. Thus, in its infinitely satisfying qualities, it exceeded the value of any earthly drink as much as the value of an ingot of pure gold exceeds the value of a speck of sand.

But how could it do this? The answer was both simple and mysterious. This water, when appropriated, became something within the one who appropriated it. "The water that I shall give him will become in him a fountain of water springing up into everlasting life" (John 4:14). So vital, so transforming was such a drink that in the innermost being of the man who drank it there was created an inexhaustible fountain of life. The waters of that hidden inner spring could not run dry; they could not be stanched; they virtually leaped up to produce the surpassing experience of eternal life. There could be no question, then, of needing more than a single drink. Deep though Jacob's well was, and though its waters had flowed continuously for many centuries, the drinker of that water must return again and again. For Jacob's spring was in the earth, external to the one who sought it. But the Savior's spring was within the heart, continuously meeting the need of one who drank but a single time.

"Are You greater than our father Jacob, who gave us the well?" (John 4:12). He *had* to be. Man might dig wells in the earth. Only God could dig one in the human heart. But the woman once more missed the point. "Sir," she replied, "give me this water, that I may not thirst, nor come here to draw" (John 4:15).

It was as much a challenge as a request. It would be easy enough to test this fantastic offer. Let Him give her a drink. It wouldn't be long before she discovered whether His water had the staying powers He claimed for it. And after all, it *would* be nice to eliminate this well from her daily itinerary. Life would at least be a trifle more simple.

But Jesus had not offered her that. The elimination of physical and temporal needs was not the purpose of His coming nor the goal of this conversation. He had never said she would not have to come back here to draw water. His offer dealt with her spiritual and eternal need. And until she could think with Him in those terms, she could not make her request aright. Clearly, the conversation needed a new focus.

"Go, call your husband, and come here" (John 4:16), said Jesus. An embarrassed moment of silence ensued. "I have no husband," she blurted out.

"You have well said, 'I have no husband'" (John 4:17), continued Jesus calmly. "For you have had five husbands, and the one whom you now have is not your husband; in that you spoke truly" (John 4:18).

This was quite unexpected. Also quite unwelcome. How did He know all this? She'd never seen Him before in her life. She was both curious and uncomfortable. How could she pursue the conversation in a manner less painful to her sensibilities? Then a thought struck her.

"Sir, I perceive that You are a prophet. Our fathers worshiped on this mountain," she nodded toward Gerizim behind Him, "and you Jews say that in Jerusalem is the place where one ought to worship" (John 4:19-20).

It was skillfully done. If He were nothing more than an ordinary Jew, He would only give her the ordinary Jewish answer, perhaps even a religious tirade, for she knew how explosive the subject was. Yet she could no longer resist the feeling that His answer to this question might be just as striking as His comment on her life. This was no ordinary man. Might He not have an unlooked-for wisdom on the very point she had raised? Her expectation was not disappointed. She had raised the subject of worship and the Savior's reply was as pregnant a statement on this theme as had ever escaped the lips of man. Indeed, once He had uttered it, it would be impossible thereafter for any man to intelligently ponder this theme without returning to consider those priceless words. As an utterance on worship they were timeless and absolutely definitive.

"Woman," said Jesus, "believe Me, the hour is coming when you will neither on this mountain," He too nodded toward Gerizim, "nor in Jerusalem, worship the Father. You worship what you do not know; we know what we worship, for salvation is of the Jews" (John 4:21-22). *Here is a new approach,* the woman could not help thinking. A Jew who was willing to dismiss Jerusalem along with Gerizim? That was novel. Yet He insisted on the Jewish origin of salvation, and that was *not* novel. Still, she was intrigued.

Jesus was continuing. "But the hour is coming, and now is, when the true worshipers will worship the Father in spirit and truth; for the Father is seeking such to worship Him" (John 4:23). *So that's it,* she thought. This man was telling her that God was not satisfied with the worship either of Gerizim *or* Jerusalem. He looked for *real* worshipers, not the kind whose pious prayers and religious platitudes hypocritically cloaked the pride and covetousness of their hearts. There was all too much of that at Gerizim, she knew, and there must be a great deal more in Jerusalem as well. At least she was quite ready to believe there was.

"God is Spirit," the Savior's answer went on, "and those who worship Him must worship in spirit and truth" (John 4:24). He paused, and so did she. It seemed that a new vista of truth had been opened up before her eyes, though just now she could but dimly see some of its terrain. Yet His words had the ring of self-evident truth. God, she knew, was indeed a spiritual being. How then could a material mountain like Gerizim or a lavishly adorned structure like the temple at Jerusalem, have any real or enduring importance to such a being? Was it not the heart of man that God searched? Was it not truth that He sought in man's inward parts? Was it not with the spirit of man, which He Himself had made, that the Creator sought communion? And was it not plain that if He were to be worshiped at all, He *must* be worshiped "in spirit and truth"?

Yes, it was plain. But so was something else. The prophet-like person before her, who knew so well, *too well* about her five failed marriages and that she was now living in adultery with a sixth, spoke of worship as though it pertained to her and her fellow Samaritans.

"The hour is coming when you will neither on this mountain, nor in Jerusalem, worship the Father" (John 4:21), He had said. Indeed, the hour was here already, He had affirmed. Might it not be, after all, that He Himself was an emissary of the Father-God about whom He spoke, whose mission it was to seek worshipers for this God? And might it not be as well (the thought staggered her) that *she* was one of those whom He thus sought?

But how could she ever approach the infinite and eternal Spirit who desired her worship? Her own spirit it seemed, was irrevocably soiled by the baseness of her life, hopelessly dried up by the emptiness of an existence strewn with the wreckage of marriage upon marriage. She could find nothing in her heart or life that might serve as a viable point of contact with a living God.

Then she remembered it. The *water*. "Flowing" water she had thought at first, but the word He had used meant "living" as well. *Living* water. Water gushing up to eternal life. Life producing life throughout all ages; one drink, therefore, satisfying her need for such life once and for all; bringing her into living contact with God; washing away the barrenness of her heart, granting her the capacity to *worship*. The thoughts rushed in upon her all at once. She could not quite sort them out. But now she *had* to ask Him a question.

"Salvation is of the Jews" (John 4:22), He had said. And *He* was a Jew. He had also offered her life, eternal life, were she but to ask for it. Could He be?—Was He?

"I know," replied the woman, "that Messiah is coming." She hesitated to put the question directly, but it *was* a question. "When He comes, He will tell us all things" (John 4:25). *And,* she thought, *could He tell us more than this man about worship?*

She was ready for the answer and the Savior spoke it with climactic succinctness. "I," He said, "who speak to you am He" (John 4:26).

Not one further word was spoken. Like the sun bursting forth from behind the clouds, the light of truth had flooded her soul. She turned from Him, the water jar she had come to fill standing empty upon the ground, but the heart she had not come to fill was now overflowing with living water. She must tell the people of her city who was here before He passed from them. She must go back. And so she quickly retreated along the path by which she had come, while the Son of God, still seated upon the well, watched her go.

"If you knew the gift of God, and who it is who says to you, 'Give me a drink,' you would have asked Him, and He would have given you living water." Ignorant she had come; enlightened she had left. Empty she had arrived; full she had departed. The gift of God? She knew it now—eternal life inexhaustibly welling up within the heart. She knew *Him* now, the Christ, the Savior of the world.

She knew these two things. They were all she needed to know, deftly led to them by the skill of the Savior. Then a transaction had occurred. Without a word, without a prayer, her heart had asked and He had given.

2
True Spiritual Food
John 4:27-39

> In the meantime His disciples urged Him, saying, "Rabbi, eat." But He said to them, "I have food to eat of which you do not know" (John 4:31-32).

The water jar stood there perfectly empty and completely forgotten. The woman who had carried it to this spot was now gone, excitedly announcing her startling discovery to the incredulous villagers of Sychar. Often before, on innumerable days just like this one, she had drawn out the water of Jacob's well, and by now its taste and appearance were so familiar to her that she no longer really noticed them. But on *this* day she had found at that well, though not *in* it, a new kind of water totally unfamiliar to her before.

The same well was now surrounded by Jesus' disciples. The foodstuffs which they had gone off into Sychar to purchase were rapidly emerging from the bulging traveler's sacks of leather which they wore at their left hip, fastened by a strap over the right shoulder. They were eager to eat. Only momentarily had they been deflected from this purpose. For, a few moments before, they had managed to arrive just as their Master was concluding His interview with the woman of Sychar, and they had had difficulty concealing their shock.

They knew quite well that no respectable Jewish rabbi allowed himself to engage in public conversation with a woman, and they had been astounded by the obvious impropriety of the situation they had found. Yet their respect for their teacher was too deep to permit them to voice any word of censure. They had been sorely tempted to ask some question like, "What do You seek?" or, "Why are You talking with her?" (John 4:27), but that would have sounded critical and so they had kept silent. Nevertheless, their puzzlement had been real.

Just now, however, they could almost forget that. The long day's journey had left them all hungry and the provisions over which they had haggled with the Samaritan merchants looked at this moment as if they were worth every penny of their exorbitant price.

It was not for themselves alone they had bought however, but for their teacher as well. By now they knew His tastes and these they had kept in mind while they negotiated in Sychar's marketplace. Moreover, deference to Him as their rabbi forbade them to eat their own food before He should begin to partake of His. It was, therefore, with a mixture of true consideration and of self-concern that they now offered Him some of their choicest purchases.

"Rabbi, eat" (John 4:31), they said. They were not prepared for the reply.

Only a short time before, a woman had discovered on this very spot the *water* that she knew not of. Now it was the disciples' turn to make a different discovery. What the woman had learned at the well that day, the disciples had learned a number of months before. The one to whom they now offered physical nourishment was already known to them as He had not been known to the woman. He was the Christ, the Son of the living God, and from the moment they had recognized this fact they had possessed the same gift of God as that which had just been bestowed on the sinful citizen of Sychar. Therefore, they were no strangers to life eternal. Deep within their inner selves there had been opened up some time ago the same limitless fountain of life that had sprung into being in that other heart right where they now stood. And no more could that experience be repeated for them than it could be repeated for the woman. But of another matter they remained quite ignorant.

Jesus answered them, "I have food to eat of which you do not know" (John 4:32).

How could that be? He carried no provisions of His own. Had He had some other encounter while they were gone, with someone other than the woman? So far as they had observed, she had given Him nothing. "Has anyone brought Him anything to eat?" (John 4:33) they inquired dubiously of each other. Obviously, on one point there could be no debate. Whatever food it was their Master spoke about, it was food they *did not know*. As surely as the woman had been ignorant of His water, *they* were ignorant of His food.

Their teacher had paused to allow them to puzzle over His statement. When He saw that they had exhausted the limited explanations they could conceive, He was ready to instruct them further.

"My food," said Jesus, "is to do the will of Him who sent Me, and to finish His work" (John 4:34).

Here indeed was a new theme altogether. Doing the will of God, finishing His work? Not a word of these matters had been spoken to the woman. Clearly the life she had lived up until she met Jesus had done shameful and inexcusable violence to the will of God for her. Yet Jesus had said nothing about the repair of her life which, plainly, was so urgently needed.

It was not that He did not care; no one cared more than He. But He knew He would see her again. There would be time for further instruction, just as now He was instructing His disciples. But in those moments when she stood before Him at the well, He had said nothing of her obligations to God's will for a very simple reason: He was there to offer her a *gift*. "*If* you knew the gift of God" had been His theme. And she could not have comprehended the dazzling splendor of that gift, its sublime and total freeness, had He encumbered His offer with a call to reform her life.

Indeed, in that interview before the well, it was not the moment for Jesus to be concerned that *she* should do the will of God. Rather it was the moment to be concerned that *He* should do the will of God. And if the Father longed for worshipers who would worship Him in spirit and in truth, the Son must seek them in order for Him to do the Father's will. It was God's will that the parched and arid ground of a guilty woman's heart should taste that day the refreshing streams of life eternal. The universe has no greater gift for man than this, nor any greater impulse to thankful worship than that which reception of this gift imparts. And so, at Jacob's well, Jesus did the will of God.

But what did the disciples know of this? Nothing, really. That the need of their souls had been satisfied was true enough. But to satisfy God? To find worshipers for Him? To eat and enjoy that task, as one eats and enjoys food? *That* was food that they knew not of.

Strangely enough, the woman herself seemed almost intuitively to have begun to learn the lesson on which the disciples required such specific instruction. No sooner had she abandoned her unfilled water jar and rushed back into the village from which she had come, than she began to proclaim her experience to others.

"Come," she said to the men of Sychar, "see a Man who told me all things that I ever did. Could this be the Christ?" (John 4:29).

"Could this be the Christ?" Her caution was instinctively judicious. Had she frontally asserted the truth about which she had become convinced, she might have repelled them. Her notorious life was common knowledge in that city. So they had not mistaken her cautious approach for a lack of conviction. Oblique though it had been, it was effective. The curiosity of the village was aroused. And while the Lord Jesus was preparing His disciples to partake of His food, a company of the men of Sychar was making their way back to the well to partake of His water.

The Son of God was still sitting on the stone which covered the shaft of Jacob's well. Before Him stretched a vast expanse of waving grain, its ripening ears gently moved by an evening breeze. But the keen eyes of the Savior saw other movement as well. The company from Sychar had begun to leave the village, making its way rapidly toward the well. Visually, the harvest of men and the harvest of God, for a few moments at least, had merged.

Jesus continued speaking to His disciples. "Do you not say, 'There are still four months and then comes the harvest'? Behold, I say to you, lift up your eyes and look at the fields, for they are already white for harvest!" (John 4:35).

In the fertile plain of Samaria on which the eyes of Jesus rested, the four months between seedtime and harvest had already elapsed. The patience with which the Palestinian farmer resigned himself to the cycle of nature, expressed so aptly at sowing time by the observation that four months must pass before the fruit, was now once again about to be rewarded. The fields were white and ready to harvest.

Yet, in the harvest field of God, no such lapse of time was needed. The good seed of the Savior's word had already brought forth fruit in the heart of a sinful woman. And now, in turn, the seed of her words to the villagers of Sychar was about to bear even more abundant fruit. The approaching company of men, after only the briefest cultivation, was ready to be reaped into God's barn.

But harvesting is not done without work. Effort must be expended by the reaper to gather in the crop. If the divine harvest field was ripe, the divine will was that it should be reaped. And reaped completely. Not merely one needy woman must be brought into God's barn, but many more from the village where she lived. "My food," Jesus had said, "is to do the will of Him who sent Me, and *to finish* His work" (John 4:34).[1]

The soul of the Savior had already tasted the spiritual nourishment which came as He imparted the gift of life to one sinner. That was the will of God for Him. But the

---

[1] Editor's note: See also John 17:4 ("I have *finished* the work which You have given Me to do") and John 19:30 ("It is *finished*"). Jesus accomplished the Father's will for Him.

work must be completed, the field of Sychar thoroughly harvested. And Jesus is now prepared to invite the disciples to share that task with Him, and thus to partake of the food which, until now, they knew not of.

"And," Jesus continued, "he who reaps receives wages, and gathers fruit for eternal life, that both he who sows and he who reaps may rejoice together" (John 4:36).

So that was it. A glimmer of light now began to filter its way into the darkened recesses of the disciples' minds. Fruit gathered in to eternal life. Clearly their teacher was not thinking of an ordinary harvest, though instinctively they had glanced at the ripening grain fields when He first mentioned them. But eternal life was a spiritual reality, not a natural one. It was, they knew, a surpassing experience enjoyed not merely in time but throughout all eternity as well. And the imagery Jesus used suggested to them a new figure for that life. Eternal life, it seemed, was like a vast and spacious barn into which men, like harvested grain, could be gathered for their own eternal preservation. And for this task God wanted reapers. Might He, therefore, want them?

He did. "For in this," said Jesus, "the saying is true: 'One sows and another reaps.' I sent you to reap that for which you have not labored; others have labored, and you have entered into their labors" (John 4:37-38).

Yes, they knew it was so. In the natural world a reaper was not usually the one who had sowed the seed. Indeed, while one man alone might sow an entire field, the handfuls of seed from his seed sack being hurled over the terrain, one man alone could scarcely reap that field once the crop was ripe. The sower, therefore, looked for help at harvest time, and thus the joys and reward of the harvest were distributed to a wider circle than those who had planted the field.

And now Jesus had said plainly that they had a commission from Him to reap what others alone had sowed. Not that the sowers themselves would cease to be active. But rather the disciples would then participate in the continuing labor.

By now the crowd from Sychar was clearly visible even to the disciples. The woman they had seen earlier was leading them. Clearly the conversation Jesus had held with her was responsible for their approach. What had been obscure to Jesus' disciples before, even shocking, was now becoming plain. Of course. They should have guessed. Jesus had obviously been talking to this woman about eternal life, just as they had seen Him talk to so many others on the same sublime theme. Indeed, there was nothing He talked about so frequently as that, and they should have known how deeply He felt that such conversation was His way of doing the will of the One who sent Him. But evidently the woman had been talking as well, or these Samaritan men would not be coming to this well. Drawing water was a woman's job in that culture and these Samaritan men had not come to do that.

The disciples knew what would happen. They would have to forget about supper. They must get ready to talk to these villagers just as Jesus had done with this woman. So they must try to forget how hungry they were.

And then it was all so perfectly clear. "I have food to eat of which you do not know...My food is to do the will of Him who sent Me, and to finish His work" (John 4:32, 34). He could easily forget His earthly food, if only He could partake of this spiritual food. If only He could be in God's harvest field, reaping souls into eternal life, He could forget anything. And so could they, if they chose to. He had sowed, the woman had sowed, and now it was the disciples' opportunity to enter into those labors. Thus, they too, could do the will of God and do it till God's work was finished.

"And he who reaps receives wages" (John 4:36), Jesus had said. Their effort would be well repaid. The kingdom of God toward which they looked would be a richer place for them if just now they could make some small sacrifice for the will of God. And what after all did their modest supper count for, when weighed against the honors and glories of that kingdom? Already, they were beginning to sense the exhilaration of the task to which they had been called.

No wonder He could forget to eat. This was better than food! No, that was wrong. This was a *better* food. He had had food to eat that they knew not of. But the crowd from Sychar had just arrived. The inevitable conversation was now beginning. And so also was their opportunity to taste that food.

3

We Are God's Workmanship

John 4:40; Ephesians 2:8-10

> For by grace you have been saved through faith, and that not of yourselves; it is the gift of God, not of works, lest anyone should boast. For we are His workmanship, created in Christ Jesus for good works, which God prepared beforehand that we should walk in them (Eph 2:8-10).

The sun had now disappeared beneath the horizon, and the shadows of the approaching darkness spread rapidly over the Samaritan landscape. The conversation at the well had had a predictable outcome. The villagers of Sychar had been deeply impressed with this Jewish traveler and had entreated Him to lodge that night in their city. And so Jesus and His disciples were now making their way toward the town in the company of their new-found hosts.

Jacob's well was being left behind, deserted for the first time in hours. The stone which covered its shaft remained unmoved. What a pity that that stone could not speak. What words had been uttered over it that day? Indeed, the words that had been spoken there that day had been of such magnitude and significance that, for those who comprehend them, they are a key which unlocks the Bible.

But only the stone had heard *all* those words. When Jesus had spoken of living water, only the woman had been present. And when He had spoken of unknown food, only the disciples had been present. The water was what the woman needed and the food was what the disciples needed. The Savior carefully segregated His audiences.

Nothing happened by chance in the life of the Son of God. All of the circumstances in which He moved were as perfect as He was Himself. The woman was a sinner, never having experienced that salvation which was "of the Jews." *She* needed the water of life. The disciples had already come to know the Savior and the salvation He gave. *They* needed the food of obedience to God's will.

The two must never be confused. Water is water and food is food.[2] And an unsaved sinner is an unsaved sinner, but a disciple is a disciple. Thus, the thirst of a disciple has already been quenched forever. He needs food. Doing the will of God. Finishing His work.

Here then, is found the very embodiment of the message of life and the very essence of the Christian experience. Here too, are found the differing audiences for which they are each designed. The message of life is the offer of the gift of everlasting life directed toward the unregenerate. Fullness of life is the experience of the loyal disciple. The former is water, the latter is food. The former guarantees eternal life, throughout all ages, to any who will take it. The latter promises reward and superlative joy, like the joy of a great harvest, to all who are willing to expend their labor. The former is a gift. The latter involves work.

Years after the events at Jacob's well, a short, slightly balding man slowly paced the floor of his private quarters. A Roman sentry dozed intermittently in one corner of the room, while a professional scribe sat alertly at his desk, a large parchment sheet spread open before him and a pen poised in his hand.

The short man pacing the floor frowned slightly as he struggled for words. *How shall I phrase the next utterance? It has to be just right.*

He must make clear to the Christians who would read this letter the exact relationship between the wondrous kindness God had showed in saving them and their

---

[2] Editor's note: Zane is referring to Jesus' references to water (message of everlasting life) and food (message of finishing the Father's work) in John 4. He is not denying that in John 6 Jesus refers to Himself as "the bread of life" in an evangelistic sense (cf. John 6:35).

unrivaled privilege in serving Him. Not that he had never made it clear before. For two years he had preached and taught in Ephesus, that bustling metropolis of Asia Minor. Those in that place to whom he now wrote had heard him state such truths many times (Acts 19:10; 20:20-21, 27). Yet he knew from long experience in the harvest fields of God that those who were reaped into the divine barn often became confused on these very points. Moreover, there were always the sinister agents of Satan, posing as ministers of the gospel, who cultivated and encouraged such confusion. The facts, therefore, could never be stated too often or too well.

Now the words were beginning to come. He began again to dictate and the scribe began again to write. "For," said Paul, "by grace you have been saved through faith" (Eph 2:8).

Grace? It was one of his favorite words. Kindness, goodness, mercy, generosity; grace signified all these things to him. What a rebel he had been before he knew what that word was all about. Stubbornly rejecting the claim that Jesus of Nazareth was the Son of God. Viciously hounding and persecuting all who had trusted in Jesus as the Giver of life, the Savior. Some he had had imprisoned; others he had had killed. He had believed, of course, that salvation was of the Jews, but not of the man called Jesus. Then Paul had met Him in one blazing, brilliant moment on a highway leading into Damascus. And out of the splendor of a light which exceeded the brightness of the noonday sun, he had heard the answer to his question, "Who are You, Lord?" (Acts 9:5).

The answer had crushed him, but it had revolutionized his life. "I am Jesus, whom you are persecuting" (Acts 9:5, cf. 26:9-20). And now he was a Christian missionary and an apostle as well. Was any man ever less deserving of such privileges?

He did not think so. But that was what *grace* meant to him. The superlative goodness of God to the utterly undeserving, and every one of the readers of his letter must be reminded that they too were the beneficiaries of grace. The salvation which they had and the eternal life which they had received had become theirs simply by believing.

"By grace you have been saved through faith, and that not of yourselves;" Paul continued, "it is the gift of God."

The gift of God. How perfect the expression was. How fully in the Spirit of the One Paul had met outside Damascus. For after all, it was not Paul who had first used such a phrase but the Savior Himself. "If you knew *the gift of God*" (John 4:10), Jesus had said to the woman. And unworthy though her life had been, she, like the Ephesians to whom Paul now wrote, had taken God's gift by faith. They had all been saved in the same way. Indeed, there is no other way to be saved. "Not of works," Paul went on, "lest anyone should boast" (Eph 2:9).

Boast? How was that possible for one who received this gift? Could the woman of Sychar boast that God had singled her out, the first in all her village to possess eternal life, when in the very next breath she must say, "He told me all things that I ever did"? Now, if she had promised to *work* for it or if she had guaranteed to *make up* for her sordid, wasted life with *good works,* then, she *might* have boasted. But how could she boast about things as they actually were? She hadn't worked for it, and she couldn't pay for it. It was the *gift* of God. *Not* of works. And why? Just so that all the glory might be God's and no one might usurp that glory.

The woman could not boast. Paul, the one-time persecutor, could not boast. The Ephesian Christians could not boast. No man in all the ages of an endless future will ever be able to boast, for salvation cannot be earned. It is never deserved. It is always the gift of God. That was the water. What about the food? Paul continued to dictate.

"For we are His workmanship, created in Christ Jesus for good works, which God prepared beforehand that we should walk in them" (Eph 2:10).[3]

Often Paul had seen a potter sitting before the wheel on which he painstakingly shaped vessels of every size and description, carefully molding some object he held firmly but lovingly in his hands. Then he had watched the artisan, when the work on the wheel was done, take a shell or a shard or an instrument of bone, with which he might smooth and burnish or decorate its surface.

The final product of his work, a pitcher, a jar, a cup, or platter, was always an object of pride to a conscientious craftsman, the product of his skill and genius. That vessel, whatever its intended use, was his *workmanship. And so, thought Paul, is every person who has been saved by grace.*

"For we are *His* workmanship, created in Christ Jesus."

We were most surely not our own workmanship, Paul was thinking. *Our* works had nothing to do with our salvation.

Rather, we were, by means of the gift of God, the product of the master Potter. Sinners He had found us, a miserable, misshapen mass of earthly clay, and when the transforming touch of His grace had been applied to us, we had a new life in Christ Jesus. We were, in short, a new creation, a product of the skill and craft of the eternal Artisan.

But every vessel wrought by an earthly potter has a purpose and function for which it is designed. And so it is with every vessel wrought by the heavenly Father. "For we are His workmanship, created in Christ Jesus *for good works.*" Good works, then, are *our* function, the purpose for which He made us.

---

[3] Editor's note: There is a change from the second person plural, *you*, in vv 8-9, to the first person plural, *we*, in v 10. In the entire epistle and in the rest of chap. 2, the first person plural refers to the Church, Jews and Gentiles together in one body. It is possible that Paul shifted to the first person plural to emphasize the fact that the Church, corporately, is to do good works. Of course, as Zane suggests, this has individual application.

They have nothing to do with the bestowal of God's gift, but they have everything to do with the life which should follow. The water is always *given*. The food is always *worked for*. So God has created us, Paul was saying, for good works.

But, he adds, He has also created good works for us. "For we are His workmanship, created in Christ Jesus for good works, which God *prepared beforehand* that we should walk in them." Nothing is left to chance. The person is designed for the work, and the work is designed for the person. When the water of life has been tasted, divine food will be ready at hand.

"Lift up your eyes and look at the fields," Jesus had said to His disciples, "for they are already white for harvest!" (John 4:35). There it was—God's will for them, right before their eyes, if only they were willing to see it. There it was—God's work for them, ready at hand, if only they were willing to do it.

Life eternal the disciples possessed already. They, too, were God's workmanship. Now the vessel must be employed in the task it was formed for, and in the task that was formed for it. Thus the disciples entered God's harvest field, joining their Master in order to do the will of God and to finish His work. And that was a disciple's special privilege, as it was also his special joy, to be guided by his teacher into the realization of every splendid goal which God has prepared for him to achieve.

* * * * *

The company that left Jacob's well had now entered the village of Sychar. Darkness had fallen, but the conversation continued long into the night. The disciples were weary when at last they were able to throw themselves down on pallets in the home where they were lodged. Tomorrow was likely to be just as busy, for the thirst of that village for the water of life had not yet been quenched. Still more souls were ready to be harvested into God's barn. The morning would come all too quickly.

It was work, to be sure. But ultimately those men would become superbly skilled in doing it. And why not? Was it not one of the very tasks they had been called to perform? And whether it was this good work or any of the countless other good works their Savior had designed, the disciples' responsibility was simply "to walk in them."

4

The Life-Giving Word

John 4:39-54

And many more believed because of His own word. Then they said to the woman, "Now we believe, not because of what you said, for we ourselves have heard Him and we know that this is indeed the Christ, the Savior of the world" (John 4:41-42).

The disciples spent two days walking with their Master in the good work being done in Sychar. That was how long it took to complete God's harvest in that Samaritan village. The interest of the villagers had been intense; the disciples had not seen anything like it among the Jews, and they seemed to hang on every statement Jesus uttered. There were no miracles performed in Sychar, and no one asked for any. All that the Samaritans needed to convince them was His word.

That was, after all, what had convinced the woman at Jacob's well. "Come, see a man who told me all things that I ever did" (John 4:29), she had exclaimed, upon rushing back to her village. She had been amazed that this perfect stranger had unrolled before her the entire scroll of her unhappy life. "You have well said, 'I have no husband,'" Jesus had told her, "for you have had five husbands, and the one whom you now have is not your husband" (John 4:17-18). That was her whole life in a nutshell. For nothing else had really mattered to this woman but her vain pursuit of happiness in wedlock, just as nothing else had so thoroughly made her what she was. She did not need a supporting miracle. His word to her was miracle enough. And when He had added those unforgettable pronouncements on the theme of worship, she had been prepared to believe that He was exactly who He claimed to be: God's Christ.

Many of the villagers of Sychar had been equally impressed with His word to her. And when she had explained how "He told me all things that I ever did" (John 4:39), many of them had believed in Him, agreeing that this must be the Christ. But some preferred to defer their decision until they had heard Him firsthand. And during those two days in Sychar they had had ample opportunity to do just that. Like the woman at the well, they plied Him with questions and were continually amazed by the wisdom and insight in His answers. Often, it seemed, He did more than answer the questions they had asked. He seemed to be answering the questions they had *not* asked but had wanted to, as though He was reading their hearts. The impact was irresistible. Many more from that village believed in Him.

Then they did an unkind thing. The woman who had aroused their interest in the first place had completely forfeited the respect of her fellow townspeople by the wanton life she had lived. They hated to let her think that, despite her base character, she had led them to the greatest discovery of their lives. Indeed, she might prove intolerable if they permitted her to build up her self-esteem on this point. Better to quash her pride before it had a chance to appear. So now they undertook to do just that.

Those who had previously believed when she had told them Jesus' words to her, and those who had just now believed after having personal audience with Him, were united in their attitude toward the woman. "Now we believe," they assured her, "not because of what you said, for we ourselves have heard Him and we know that this is indeed the Christ, the Savior of the world" (John 4:42).

The words stung, but it was all right. Her own heart was too full of the joy of the water of life for her to brood over this rejection. After all, it was not really *her* word that had convinced any of them, but *Jesus'* word to her. She had simply reported it. Whether they heard His words through her or heard them from His own lips personally, it was *His* word that had produced new life in them.

Already, after only two days in His presence, it was as evident to her, as it was to every believer in that city, that the word of Jesus was a life-giving word. It could not be otherwise. For here at last was the promised one, whose coming mankind had long awaited. Here indeed was the Savior of the world, the Christ. Such was the discovery of that tiny village during two unforgettable days.

The departure from Sychar was a touching one with so many well-wishers seeing them off and so many entreaties to return that way again. The disciples had never suspected that Samaritans could feel so warmly toward a little band of Jews. More than that, they had never suspected the warmth that could be born in their own hearts toward members of so despised a race. They actually would not mind coming back to Sychar someday.

Up the northward road they went now, the peaks of Gerizim and Ebal gradually receding into the background as they made their way past row upon row of waving grain. Yes, they noted, those fields certainly were ripe for harvesting. Could they, in fact, ever again look at nature's harvest without recalling the harvest of God? They doubted it. And so, absorbed with such thoughts, they left that memorable little village behind.

In due course their journey had led them into Galilee, native soil both for them and for their Master. True, He had not actually been born there, though this fact was not generally known, but He had been reared in the village of Nazareth and now made His home in the lake side town of Capernaum (Matt 4:13; John 2:12). Both Nazareth and Capernaum were Galilean cities, as was Cana which they now approached.

When they crossed into Galilee, they were surprised by the cordiality of the Galileans toward their Teacher. They had observed well that He received no honor in His own country. In Nazareth especially, He had been held in no special esteem. Trained at home in the trade of a carpenter, without formal theological instruction, He had never seemed to the villagers of Nazareth to deserve recognition as a qualified rabbi, much less as a prophet of God. After all, He was simply a well-known, hometown product, a young man barely thirty, whose claims to fame rested on no special achievements in the city where He grew up (Mark 6:1-6; Luke 3:23; 4:16-24; John 7:15). But this spirit, which to a greater or lesser extent pervaded the whole Galilean attitude toward Jesus, now seemed to be sharply diminished, and in its place there was a new-found atmosphere of respect.

The reason for this was not hard to find. As was their custom, the Galileans had recently fulfilled their religious obligations by going south to Jerusalem for Passover. Jesus had been there too and had astounded the many Jewish pilgrims who thronged that city by the miracles He had performed. The Galileans had had opportunity at that feast to observe these miracles, and they were duly impressed. Now they were welcoming Jesus as the miracle-worker that He was.

But He was more than that. He was a prophet who spoke the word of God. Above all, He was the Christ whose word could create an inexhaustible well of life in every heart that trusted Him. This, at least, the Samaritans had learned simply by listening to Him talk. The Galileans had not learned it even by seeing the miracles He did. But those very miracles were now conditioning some of them for just such a realization as that.

They were entering Cana now and making their way toward the marketplace to buy supplies. The welcome here seemed unusually warm, and well it might have been. For this was the city where the Savior had performed one of His most striking deeds of power. Six large stone pots had been filled with water at the instructions of Jesus, while the festivities of a local marriage had swirled around them. Then the servants who had filled them (the pots altogether held nearly 120 gallons) had been told to dip smaller vessels into these water jars and to carry what they drew out to the master of ceremonies. But instead of water, what they drew out was superb wine, which abundantly supplied the embarrassing shortage the wedding hosts had suddenly encountered (John 2:1-11). Thus it was nothing less than the power of the Creator that Jesus had displayed in this city.

Of course, at first only the servants who had drawn the water were privy to the secret of its transformation. But in the days that followed they talked and talked about what their eyes had seen. Naturally they were not always believed, but now their report seemed to be confirmed by the miracles the Galileans had recently witnessed in Jerusalem. Cana, therefore, was like an open city to Jesus and to the group of men who followed Him.

Suddenly, through the crowd that was rapidly gathering around Jesus and His disciples, came a man whose costly looking garments clearly marked him as different from the rest of the villagers in Cana. The practiced eye could tell by a glance at the robe he wore that he belonged to the royal retinue which served in the court of Herod Antipas, the luxury-loving tetrarch of Galilee. As he approached Jesus, his drawn and haggard countenance betrayed alike the weariness of a journey and the deep anxiety within him. In a moment he was before the Savior pouring out the trouble which had brought him here.

He was indeed a courtier of Herod's as his expensive clothing had revealed. His home was the village of Capernaum on the shores of lake Gennesaret, to which Jesus not long ago had moved. There in Capernaum at this very moment his son lay desperately sick and the father was full of fear that death was imminent. So as soon as word had reached him that Jesus had returned from Judea and had entered Galilee, this nobleman had set out, hoping to encounter Him on His northward route. How rapidly Jesus might travel through Galilee, or when He might intend to be in Capernaum, the father had had no way of knowing.

But now he implored Him, without delay, to commence His journey there. Though the entire journey of some twenty miles could not be completed that day, they might still make a start. Haste seemed urgently called for and the courtier's pleas for this were plaintively insistent.

Jesus' answer startled him and sounded at first like a cold rebuff. "Unless you people see signs and wonders, you will by no means believe" (John 4:48).

It was true, of course. These Galileans were not like the Samaritans at all. The word of Jesus, unadorned by any visible display of the miraculous, did not seem to be sufficient for them. In Sychar it had been enough, but not here. A prophet speaking simply as a prophet had no honor in his own country.

"Sir, come down before my child dies!" (John 4:49). He almost wept the words. This Man had the power to help him, he knew. How could He withhold it? The father could not bear to think of the tragedy that would follow.

The next words he heard were more startling than the first. "Go your way; your son lives" (John 4:50), said Jesus.

My son lives? the nobleman thought. Then recovery was guaranteed. His boy would return once again from death's door. A wonderful promise, but could he believe it? Yes. Yes, he could. He had no proof, there was nothing visible to rely upon, just the naked word of Jesus. That was all he had. But there was a solemnity in that word. The one who spoke it spoke in tones of absolute, unwavering authority. "Your son lives." Believe it? Yes, he could, and he did.

Jesus and His disciples remained that night in Cana. The nobleman did not. The journey which, just a short time before, he had insisted that Jesus make with him, he now made alone. Back to the North and East he went, across the Galilean hills, as far as he was able to go until night interrupted his travels. The next morning he arose, and was soon on his way. But it was not long before he observed some travelers on the same road moving rapidly toward him from the opposite direction. The nearer they came, the more familiar they looked, until at length he could recognize in them his own servants. It was evident that they had news; nothing else could have brought them out. As soon as they met, they wasted not a moment in telling it.

"Your son lives!" (John 4:51), they announced to him. The words left him momentarily shaken. They were nearly identical to the words that Jesus Himself had spoken the evening before. At least, the crucial word was there, he *lives*.

Recovering his composure, the nobleman thought of a question. Perhaps, after all, the whole affair was simply one supreme coincidence. Perhaps, when he had left on his journey, his boy had begun to get better by himself. In that case the trip to see Jesus had been needless, and the words "Your son lives" had not had the decisive effect he at first imagined. There was one way to find out. He would ask these servants what time it had been when his son began to get better. Obviously, the answer to that question was crucial to him and would determine his whole view of what had transpired. So he posed it.

The reply was a bolt of lightning. "Yesterday at the seventh hour the fever left him" (John 4:52), they reported. The fever *left* him? Why then, it was not at all a matter of *beginning* to get better, but instead, of getting well all at once. Jesus had said to him, "Your son lives," but he had grossly underestimated those words. They were *not*, as he had originally believed, the point at which recovery commenced. That would have been wonderful enough, and it was all he had at first been capable of accepting. But they were more than that.

They were the point at which health had been restored completely. Those words started no process; they accomplished the whole work. They had healed his boy completely and instantaneously.

"Your son lives." There was *life* in that utterance, and the nobleman could not resist the next conclusion. A person who could speak those words with such a result, unhindered by the hills and valleys which separated Him from the one about whom He spoke, must be more than a mortal man. After all, had it not been the *word* of the Creator God that had caused all things to leap from nothingness into being? Did not the psalmist say of old, "By the word of the LORD the heavens were made, and all the host of them by the breath of His mouth… For He spoke, and it was done; He commanded, and it stood fast" (Ps 33:6, 9). The question that now framed itself in the nobleman's soul was no different than that which the woman at the well had posed to the villagers of Sychar. "Could this be the Christ?" (John 4:29). And the answer which his heart gave to it was identical to the woman's own—the nobleman believed.

In Cana of Galilee, Jesus made the water into wine; the Maker's power had transformed one element of His creation into another. How appropriate that here, too, those words, "Your son lives!" should transform sickness into health, imminent death into continuing life. But this was not all those words had accomplished in their creative potency. For by their means, Herod's courtier had been brought to believe that the One who uttered them was the Christ of God. And in the moment when that faith was born, an even greater act of creation transpired. For in that moment, there sprang into being in the heart of the nobleman an eternal fountain, "a fountain of water springing up into everlasting life" (John 4:14). The *father* lived as well.

So the nobleman became God's workmanship, specially formed for particular good works. And for him too, as also for the woman of Sychar, those works began in a harvest field near at hand. In his case, the harvest field was found in his own home in the village of Capernaum. For no sooner did he arrive there than he reported to his entire household, servants and family alike, the discovery he had made about Jesus. His testimony was compelling, his conviction transparent, and fruit was gathered into eternal life. Everyone under his roof now agreed with him. This man called Jesus was indeed the Christ, the Savior of the world.

The Life-Giving Word

Thus, from Samaria to Galilee, from Sychar to Capernaum, the power of Jesus' word was still the same. It created life in every believing heart. True, in Galilee the desire to see miracles had furnished at first a barrier to that creative work, while in Samaria it had not. But even in Galilee there was now one household at least where that word had won its total victory.

The entire family of the nobleman now believed. But a tragedy remained. For in the very city where the nobleman lived, Capernaum, Jesus' own family had also recently come to reside. And in *that* household His quickening word was still resisted. By an incomparable irony, some who had dwelt for years under the same roof with the Prince of Life knew nothing of that life nor of the power of His word which could impart it. Yet there was hope. For if the Creator's life-giving utterance had opened springs of living water within His own city, might it not also open them in like manner within the circle of His own family?

5

Born from Above

James 1:1-18

> Do not be deceived, my beloved brethren.
> Every good gift and every perfect gift is
> from above, and comes down from the Father
> of lights, with whom there is no variation
> or shadow of turning. Of His own will He
> brought us forth by the word of truth, that we
> might be a kind of firstfruits of His creatures
> (Jas 1:16-18).

"A prophet has no honor in his own country" had been the testimony of Jesus, and it was amply verified by the Galileans craving for miraculous proofs. Later the Savior was to elaborate that testimony in an even more pointed way. "A prophet is not without honor except in his own country, among his own relatives, *and in his own house*" (Mark 6:4). It was in His own house that the Son of God had tasted most deeply the bitter dregs of rejection and unbelief.

Jesus was the oldest of five brothers (Mark 6:3). Half-brothers, perhaps they should have been called, for though they were sons of the carpenter Joseph and his wife Mary, He was the son of Mary alone, conceived by the power of God while she was yet a virgin (Luke 1:27-35).

It had not been easy, of course, for Joseph to adjust to the discovery that the woman betrothed to him was pregnant before their marriage was consummated. The explanation she gave, that the Spirit of God had produced this pregnancy, was more than he could accept. Indeed, he had made up his mind to formally annul their engagement with a minimum of public embarrassment to her, when his plans were interrupted by a divinely given dream. Reassured by this dream, Joseph went ahead with the marriage though he carefully refrained from fulfilling his physical desire until after the birth of Jesus (Matt 1:18-25).

Subsequently, however, their union became complete; and they had the joy of bringing sons and daughters into the world. The four boys whom they bore were named James and Joses and Jude and Simon (Matt 13:55). James was the oldest of the four; and as he grew to manhood, he soon displayed striking qualities of character and mind for leadership.

It was inevitable that questions about the birth of Jesus should linger on in the tiny village of Nazareth for many years. Apparently, the rumor circulated far beyond that little town once Jesus had become well known. Even in Jerusalem it was such common knowledge that, in a moment of controversy, the Savior had to hear the cutting words, "*We* were not born of fornication" (John 8:41). It was, therefore, quite unavoidable that Jesus' four brothers should hear what the townspeople sometimes said about His birth. Without doubt, they vehemently denied it and were ready to argue with anyone who cast aspersions on their mother. Still, they could not deny that in subtle ways both of their parents treated Jesus differently. Worse yet, they sensed that Jesus on His part regarded Himself as in some way different from them. They had to acknowledge that His conduct toward them was always exemplary and His attitude one of utmost graciousness. Still, there was something about Him they resented; and the fires of this resentment were periodically stoked by the ugly gossip in their village.

The situation worsened when Jesus began to preach. The irritation He aroused in them became greater than ever. At times it seemed to them He was almost prepared to admit the truth of those sordid speculations about His ancestry with which they had had to contend. Only *He* made a virtue out of it. For now, people had begun to speculate about their brother in terms of the nation's Messianic expectations. And, both implicitly and explicitly, Jesus seemed to encourage such speculation, and worse, to encourage the conclusion toward which it pointed—to claim to be the Son of God. How could He trade so crassly on the shadows that still hovered over His birth, as though to suggest that He had no merely mortal origin but had come down from above. Who did He think He was? After all, they grew up with Him.

None of the brothers felt these things more deeply than James. After all, the rights of first birth were his if Jesus were actually illegitimate. But he tried never to dwell consciously on this thought, though at times it was difficult to suppress. And then, when Jesus began to perform miracles, as His fame spread and His popularity grew, the tension inside James seemed to rise also. Whenever he thought about his brother and the things his brother did and said, it was as if a storm had arisen in his soul. He knew about storms, in particular the sudden squalls that so often and so unexpectedly churned the Sea of Galilee into a frothing fury. And that was what his heart was like at times. Who *was* his brother really? An imposter? A man gone out of his mind? (Mark 3:21). Or, was He really what many had already come to believe, the Son of God? How deeply James yearned for the wisdom that would answer this question.

It was now hard for James and his brothers to get along with Him. Whenever He came home, the tension between them was electric. They rejected His claims, but at the same time they prodded Him to prove them. If You do these things, they said on one occasion, show Yourself to the world (John 7:3-5). Give the world a spectacular and decisive demonstration of Your claims, they were saying. Settle the question once and for all. It was a taunt, but it was also a cry for help. Deep in their souls, *they* wanted to be sure.

And then tragedy came. For while they were in Jerusalem at one of the annual Passover celebrations, their brother's career was abruptly brought to a ruinous end. He had aroused the jealousy and enmity of the religious aristocracy in that city, and, conspiring with one of his own professed disciples, the leaders had managed both to arrest Him and to bring Him under an indictment of death.

They knew the Roman mode of execution, crucifixion on a wooden cross, was horribly painful, and they were not so far past brotherly feeling as to be unmoved by that.

Worst of all was the agony they knew their mother must pass through because of this. It would be like a sharp sword piercing her very soul, bringing anguish such as only a mother can feel. Indeed, from a distance they watched her standing desolate beneath Jesus' cross, with one of His most loyal disciples standing beside her (Luke 2:35; John 19:26-27).

They did not know till later that Jesus had committed the care of His mother to that disciple. Not to them, His brothers, but to a disciple. That touched them, too, as though their eldest brother felt nearer to this follower of His than to them. But, of course, they understood why. After all, they had made their rejection plain to Him. They could not resent this dying act of His. It did, however, prick their hearts.

That happened on a Friday. On the Sunday that followed, a discovery was made that was to shake the entire city of Jerusalem. The tomb of Jesus was found empty, and the report began to circulate in the ensuing days that some of His followers had seen Him alive. Naturally, the rumor reached Jesus' family and it astounded them. Mary seemed ready to believe it at once; that was quite natural for a mother, the brothers thought. But *they* were skeptical; not as before, however, with the skepticism that is born of hostility. Their feelings now were different, tinged with sorrow and a hope they dared not hope. If their brother *could* rise from the dead, then that would settle all their questions. Then they would have no trouble concluding that He truly was the Messiah; but that was foolish. They had seen Him die.

Then it happened. James saw Him (1 Cor 15:7). Face to face they met and talked. And from that moment on, James became a loyal and devoted bondservant of the very one who had grown up with him in the home at Nazareth (Acts 1:14; Jas 1:1).

James never denied their earthly brotherhood, but neither did he ever stress it. For now the relationship had been drastically transformed and his brother was also his Lord. Now, too, he understood the mystery of Jesus' birth as he learned from his mother the miracle that had been wrought in the days of her virginity. It was that miracle which made possible the most momentous of all events—God became a man and lived on earth. His brother was the Lord of glory. He had come down from the Father of lights above.

"James, a bondservant of God and of the Lord Jesus Christ" (Jas 1:1) were the words that opened a pastoral letter he wrote years later. Much had happened in those years. The Christian church had been founded at Jerusalem, and many of its members had been scattered by persecution throughout the regions of Judea and Samaria (Acts 8:1). James himself had risen to the place of leadership in the Jerusalem congregation, for which his basic instincts so aptly fitted him (Acts 15:13-21).

More than that, it seemed to those early Christian believers that James was very much like the brother he now called Lord. There was a moral integrity in James coupled with a practical wisdom that was unmistakably familiar to many who had seen and listened to Jesus. There was also a spirit of compassion, especially expressed in sympathy for the poor, the orphaned, and the widowed, that had in like manner marked the Savior (Jas 1:27). Moreover, the Christians valued those intimate glimpses of their Master which, from time to time, they managed to pry out of James. But as much as anything, they valued his rich conception of God as the unrivaled Giver.

Some of the Christians to whom he wrote his pastoral letter were among the ones who had been scattered by that early persecution. Since that time, in all too many ways, they and their fellow believers had been sorely tried both by their circumstances and by the opposition and enmity of men. So James wrote to encourage them and to urge them to profit fully from every trial that came their way.

"Count it all joy," James said, "when you fall into various trials" (Jas 1:2). James went on to assure them, "God will use that trouble—of whatever kind—to supply you with the very thing you lack to make you a well-rounded Christian" (Jas 1:3-4 [paraphrase]). Suppose, for example, the trouble reveals your lack of wisdom. The solution is simple. "If any of you lacks wisdom, let him ask of God, who gives to all liberally and without reproach, and it will be given to him. But let him ask in faith, with no doubting, for he who doubts is like a wave of the sea driven and tossed by the wind. For let not that man suppose that he will receive anything from the Lord" (Jas 1:5-7).

Be calm in your time of trouble, James was telling these Christians. Quiet the storm in your soul, and let the waves of inward debate subside. Let there be a calm in your spirit, like the calm of a motionless sea, so that the voice of God may speak wisdom to your needy heart. You need only ask for it in faith. For He gives, oh how liberally, and He never chides the ignorance which made it necessary to ask. Had not James himself been ignorant once, his soul wracked by the violence of his inward uncertainty about Jesus? Yet that tempest had been stilled for him by a generous Lord who had granted the wisdom of faith. And now he was sure that whatever lesser wisdom his readers might need would be bounteously bestowed by that same graciously giving God.

It was not long after these words were penned that James returned again to the theme of giving. If the Christians to whom he wrote felt, in their time of trouble, some solicitation to do evil, let them never blame their temptation on God. The inclination to sin arose from within themselves, he insisted, and the ultimate fruit of sin was death. Nothing like this, therefore, could originate with God. But what did originate with Him? The soul of James was now filled to overflowing as he dipped his pen and readied it to write the words that followed.

Don't go astray, my beloved brothers. The words conveyed the tenderness of spirit with which he sought to instruct these fellow Christians, so dear to him. "Every good gift and every perfect gift is from above, and comes down from the Father of lights" (Jas 1:17).

It was a sweeping statement, much more than merely saying that if God gave a gift, it would be good and perfect. That was true, of course, but James meant something more. If a gift was good and perfect, then God had given it. Every good gift and every perfect gift is from above. Man cannot give such gifts, encompassed as he always is by the limitations and weaknesses of human nature, and every gift he gives will always have clinging to it some trace of his frailty; some hint of his own mortality. At their very best, man's gifts cannot last forever. At their very worst, they may be utterly unwise and unsuited for their intended recipients. No, if a gift were ever good and perfect in the truest sense of those words, it had to originate with God.

"Every good gift and every perfect gift is from above, and comes down from the Father of lights, with whom there is no variation or shadow of turning" (Jas 1:17).

James was thinking now of those heavenly lights: the sun, the moon, and the stars of which God had become the Father by creating them. "Oh, give thanks to the Lord of lords!" the psalmist of old had said, "To Him who made great lights" (Ps 136:3, 7). Nevertheless, James was saying, the Creator is greater than His creation. The Father of lights is more wonderful than the lights themselves. For in Him there is not a trace of the variableness that is so clearly visible in the luminaries of heaven. The moon passes regularly through its phases as it waxes and wanes from month to month. Similarly, the sun as it travels its appointed round from dawn to dusk, causes the shadows of earth to lengthen or contract according to its location.

All is change; nothing is without variation in the lights that illumine mankind. Not so with God. When He gives those good and perfect gifts that He alone can give, they possess for all who take them the mark of their immutable Giver. As gifts they never fail to be all that a gift should be; the surpassing excellence that is theirs never fades or grows dim, and they never cast a shadow upon the life they bless.

God is ever at the zenith of His glory, blazing forth like a noonday sun for which there can be no evening and no twilight. Good and perfect gifts He gives, these alone and these always. He is the Father of Lights, with whom there is no variation, nor any shadow cast by turning.

But how could James illustrate this truth? What gift shall he speak of, out of the countless gifts God gives, which could furnish the supreme demonstration of the principle he has just declared? The answer was obvious: "Of His own will He brought us forth by the word of truth" (Jas 1:18).

That was it. The gift par excellence. The very gift the Savior had spoken of at Jacob's well, imparted by His word alone. The gift of life. God has given us *life,* James was saying, for He brought us forth. And the seed which brought that life into being was the seed of His Word. It was so because He *willed* it to be so. There was no effort on our part, no work, no labor; it was simply an act of the divine volition.

"Your son lives!" (John 4:51). Such had been the utterance by which the life-imparting power of the Savior's word had been displayed.

And though during those long years of painful rejection James had been a stranger to that power, he knew it now. The word that declared eternal life to be freely available to man, that word, he knew, was the word of truth. And by means of it God could beget spiritual children, individual souls, like the woman at Sychar or James himself, who would then possess His very life.

"Of His own will He brought us forth by the word of truth, that we might be a kind of firstfruits of His creatures" (Jas 1:18).

We are His workmanship, James thought, though the image he used to convey it was his own. The Father of lights, whose creative word had called the natural world into being, would someday remake that world so that all His creatures, every created thing, would be made anew. The Christian hope was clear and definite on this point: "We, according to His promise, look for new heavens and a new earth in which righteousness dwells" (2 Pet 3:13).

But Christians had looked for that new world from the very first. And James was looking for it too, and in doing so, pronouncing those whom God begot, to be the first tokens of its coming. We are a kind of first fruits in relation to all creation, he affirms. What the first product of a season's harvest is to the harvest itself. Like it in kind and a promise of more, such are we to the world to come. Remade by the vitalizing Word of God, imbued with the life of the coming age, we are a fore-gleam of the new creation which is yet to be.

Could any gift be greater? Could any be more perfect? Clearly not. For this is eternal life. And as that life can never fail the one who has it, as it becomes within him a spring whose supply of water can never be exhausted, just so it is the gift best suited to display the unchanging character of Him with whom no variation is found, nor shadow cast by turning.

* * * * *

The Creator had walked on earth. In Cana He had turned the water into wine, and He had transformed the sickness of a little boy into exuberant health. Most amazing of all, it seemed to James, He had actually condescended to dwell in that home at Nazareth, an insignificant village of Galilee. The problem of His presence there had once caused a storm in the heart of James; but now that storm was stilled, and the wisdom of God was in its place. James knew now that this One had not originated in that home, but had come down from above. And with Him He had brought His most good and perfect gift, eternal life. Therefore, wherever He went, preaching and teaching, it was the word of truth He proclaimed and the gift of life He offered.

More than once James wished he could go back and relive those eventful years. Instead of staying behind at home, blinded by unbelief, he would have followed his heaven-sent brother about, and he would have hung on every vital word the Savior uttered. How much he might have learned that way. How much the disciples who actually did follow Him about had learned. Indeed, it seemed to James that these disciples possessed so rich and varied an understanding of God's thoughts, to which he could attend for hours upon end to the things they had heard in the company of Jesus. Now that James had been begotten by God's word of truth, he could never learn enough about the vitality of that truth in the hearts of those to whom it had given life. And it was precisely about this that the disciples seemed to be able to say so much. Naturally when the disciples talked, James listened.

But James was far from complaining. Everything was according to God's sovereign plan. If he had never known what it was to follow the Son of God about as He proclaimed His word along the highways and byways of their native land, neither had the disciples known what it was to grow up with Him. How favored he had been. How unspeakably favored, to live under the same roof with the one who came down from heaven.

But there was one favor even greater than that. It was a favor he shared now with the woman of Sychar, with the nobleman of Capernaum, and with the disciples themselves. And on this subject he could speak every bit as eloquently as they. Indeed, none of these ever described this favor with any greater beauty than did James himself. "Every good gift and every perfect gift is from above, and comes down from the Father of lights," and, "Of His own will He brought us forth by the word of truth" (Jas 1:17-18).

6

The Seed Is the Word

Luke 8:1-15

"Now the parable is this: The seed is the word of God. Those by the wayside are the ones who hear; then the devil comes and takes away the word out of their hearts, lest they should believe and be saved. But the ones on the rock are those who, when they hear, receive the word with joy; and these have no root, who believe for a while and in time of temptation fall away. Now the ones that fell among thorns are those who, when they have heard, go out and are choked with cares, riches, and pleasures of life, and bring no fruit to maturity. But the ones that fell on the good ground are those who, having heard the word with a noble and good heart, keep it and bear fruit with patience" (Luke 8:11-15).

"Of His own will He brought us forth with the word of truth" (Jas 1:18). Thus had James identified the vehicle through which the gift of life was communicated to men. So, too, the villagers of Sychar had, in effect, confessed their indebtedness to that same word. "Now we believe," they insisted to the woman, "not because of what you said, for we ourselves have heard Him, and we know that this is indeed the Christ, the Savior of the world" (John 4:42).

The power of life, therefore, was resident in the words of Jesus, and His *"your son lives"* conveyed it on a physical plane in precisely the way His message of life did on the spiritual plane. His word, therefore, was like a seed, imparting the germ of eternal life to every believing heart.

James now knew the truth of the seed-like character of the Word of God, but he always regretted that he had not been present when the wondrous ramifications of that truth were first unfolded by the Son of God. That privilege had been granted to the disciples who had followed Him about while James stayed at home in his unbelief. Thus, in later years, James depended on these disciples to recount the simple but memorable narrative in which the Savior had forever enshrined this truth.

And they could recount it well. Indeed, the parable of the seed and the soils had been indelibly etched on their minds and hearts, for of all the vivid stories the disciples had heard Jesus tell, there was none they had heard Him tell more often than this. Repeating it time and again as He did, their Master seemed also to signify thereby the importance He attached to it. Nor was He unwilling to explain more than once to them its inner meaning.

On one occasion in particular, they recalled in later years, they had been traveling with Him through numerous Palestinian villages and cities, followed by that loyal band of women who so faithfully served them in the mundane needs of their ordinary life. The journey they were taking with Jesus seemed to be attracting even greater crowds than usual. It appeared that every town and village through which they passed augmented the numbers who swarmed about them. The audience, therefore, was immense when Jesus paused one morning to teach.

The place He chose to stop was situated along a Galilean roadside. (It was quite impossible to accommodate so large a following inside a village or town.) In order that He might be visible to all to whom He spoke, their Master had chosen an elevated area dotted with rocks jutting sharply out of the ground. On one of the stones atop this eminence He sat down.

It seemed fortunate to the disciples that at the base of this rise of ground there should be a tangled cluster of thorns, for this bramble thicket thus formed a natural barrier between Jesus and His audience, and furnished Him with much needed breathing room. In the road in front of Jesus, and in the farmer's field on its opposite side, the people followed His lead and began to sit down. When all had finally found a place which looked reasonably comfortable at least, the Savior began to speak.

"A sower went out to sow his seed." The words sounded so natural in this agricultural setting, some of the crowd glanced instinctively at the field behind them, almost expecting to see a farmer engaged in his work.

"And as he sowed, some fell by the wayside; and it was trampled down, and the birds of the air devoured it" (Luke 8:5). Now some of the people, who had managed to find a seat on the road just in front of Jesus, looked down. *Yes,* they thought, *the farmer who sowed the field beside us might easily have let some seed fall right here.* For when he reached his hand into the large sack that he carried suspended from his shoulder, and when he hurled a handful of seed across his land, several of those tiny grains might land on this very roadside. But here the seeds could find no permanent lodging. They would soon be spied by the ever-present birds and be completely devoured by them. It was useless to look for any seed here now, or even any sprout. It had all long since been snatched away.

"Some fell on rock; and as soon as it sprang up, it withered away because it lacked moisture" (Luke 8:6). *That too could easily happen right here,* the audience thought. If the farmer was near the roadside when he let fly a handful of seed, some of it might land across the road, right there on the rocky hillside where Jesus was sitting. Into the cracks and crevices of the stones which thrust their way above the surface of the ground, some of it might go, finding there a permanent home safe from the birds which so easily cleared off the roadside. But that was of little value to the farmer. Out of those cracks and crevices, the sprouts of would-be grain might soon appear, only to be withered and ruined by the heat to which they were then exposed. And because the seed could not penetrate its rocky home with roots capable of drawing moisture from the soil below, its fruit was doomed never to be produced.

"And some fell among thorns, and the thorns sprang up with it and choked it" (Luke 8:7). And, of course, the thorns were right there before their eyes. No one would have wished to thrust his hand into that jagged, tangled mass of brambles. What an uncongenial home the thorn bushes would make for a life-bearing grain of wheat. How could its shoots ever hope to emerge to maturity from that wretched environment? Surely, as Jesus said, they would be choked.

"But others fell on good ground, sprang up, and yielded a crop a hundredfold" (Luke 8:8). The point was clear. The fruitfulness of the seed depended on the character of the ground on which it fell. It was always the same seed, but not always the same soil. On the roadside, it lay exposed to the birds. On the rock, it could not penetrate its stony bed. In the thorns, it was crushed by the thicket. But on good ground, well-plowed and furrowed to receive it, the final crop could be marvelous indeed.

This much was clear. But the audience wondered why Jesus had told the story. So did the disciples. After all, its truths were self-evident in nature, and in a region dotted with farmlands the story's informational content seemed negligible indeed. Everyone, therefore, was a little surprised when Jesus moved on into a new line of teaching and offered no light upon the parable He had told.

But a parable it was, the disciples were sure. They were familiar by this time with their Master's technique. And one of the best privileges of discipleship was the special information they often acquired from Him over and above what He disclosed to the crowds. So at their earliest opportunity later that day, the disciples asked for an explanation. What might this parable mean?

His reply revealed the reason for His reticence with the multitudes. "To you it has been given," said Jesus, "to know the mysteries of the kingdom of God, but to the rest it is given in parables, that 'Seeing they may not see, and hearing they may not understand'" (Luke 8:10).

Their Master, they knew, did not regard God's truth as cheap or common. Neither did He feel that His audiences ought to have it cast before them without any challenge to their desire to penetrate its meaning. And this was especially true of anything which He regarded as a *mystery* of the kingdom of God. Indeed, when any of these divine secrets were expounded by Him, He always sought an audience deeply sympathetic to His instruction. Such an audience the disciples were, as were also the devoted women who followed Him. To them, but not to the fickle masses outside, the hidden realities which characterized God's kingdom were disclosed.

The Lord Jesus continued. "Now the parable is this: the seed is the word of God" (Luke 8:11).

Of course. What light that shed on the parable already, before anything else was said. The word of God. This was the life-bearing seed of which He spoke, the word that had opened a spring of living water in hearts at Sychar and had done the same in their hearts as well. He was referring to the word of truth by means of which they were begotten to eternal life, as was everyone who received that word in faith.

What marvelous potential for fruitage was latent in that word. Who could begin to estimate the capacity for good which it conveyed to the heart in which it found its lodging? Who could measure the fruit which it ought to produce for the glory of God? We are His workmanship, created for good works, and those works ought to be as abundant as the vital source of life within could make them.

"Those by the wayside," Jesus explained, "are the ones who hear; then the devil comes and takes away the word out of their hearts, lest they should believe and be saved" (Luke 8:12).

That was clear enough, the disciples felt. There was a life imparting power in God's word which stirred the animosity of man's adversary. As surely as an effort was made to gain a home for that vital seed, by faith in some human heart, so surely would Satan seek to prevent it. Above all, he could not allow God's word to lodge in that heart. He must somehow devour it and thus remove it before faith occurred. For if faith occurred, so would salvation. It was a matter of urgency for him, lest they should believe and be saved.

In later years, if not at that moment, the disciples were also to consider the appropriateness of a roadside to describe the heart out of which the enemy retrieved God's word. For a road, in contrast to a field or to ground containing rocks or thorns, was a thoroughfare for travel. The seed, Jesus had said, was trampled on and *then* the birds had snatched it away. And this suggested the kind of heart which was, so to speak, a roadway for many thoughts. Distracted by its own concerns, its own ideas, its own ambitions, such a heart became a place where the word of God was trodden down, smothered as it were, and crushed by the multiplied preoccupations that made that heart their highway. Hence with his consummate skill and masterly insight into man's psychology, the devil could fan that heart into irrelevant or confused activity at the very moment it was hearing the word of truth. Thus the word was not heard in faith, its simplicity not discerned or appreciated, and its bearing and relevance very shortly forgotten. And so the enemy had effectively snatched it away. Salvation did not take place.

Before Jesus had said anything else, however, one fact was intuitively obvious to the disciples about the rest of His parable. From the roadside, *and from the roadside alone*, the Word of God had been retrieved. By the Savior's own explicit observation this retrieval was for the purpose that salvation might not occur. Here, and here alone, Satan had triumphed completely. The birds had devoured the seed. But from the rocky ground, from the ground with thorns, and from the furrowed field, the vital seed had never been removed. Whatever the fruit produced, whether none or much, the seed had found its home in the soil into which it fell, and the malignant birds had never touched it.

The inference from this was plain. Into all of the remaining hearts, whatever the character of their soil, new life had come. The quickening seed, the living utterance of a living God who of His own will begot men with the word of truth, it was this that had fallen permanently into those hearts. But how different the results. The disciples waited eagerly for further light.

"But the ones on the rock are those who, when they hear, receive the word with joy; and these have no root, who believe for a while and in time of temptation fall away" (Luke 8:13).

Yes, the disciples had been right. Faith *had* occurred in the heart the Savior now described, and not mere passive faith, adequate though that would be, but *joyous* faith. When they hear, they receive the word *with joy*. But alas, the faith by which they appropriated the gift of life had not endured. These were they who for a while believe and in time of testing turn away.

The *faith* had not endured. God's *gift* had. Indeed, that gift always endures, for "whoever drinks of the water that I shall give him," Jesus had insisted, "will never thirst. But the water that I shall give him will become in him a fountain of water springing up into everlasting life" (John 4:13).

Man, to be sure, was changeable; the God who gifted him is not. And the gift of life, like every other good and perfect gift, had its origin and source in an immutable giver. It came down from above, from the Father of lights with whom there is neither variation nor any shadow of turning. No, their Master's meaning was plain. The living seed remained in the heart. The faith that received it did not.

The disciples had seen individuals in some of the many cities through which they passed, who had heard their Master's word with almost boundless enthusiasm. Openly and boldly they had acknowledged Him as God's Christ and rejoiced in the salvation they had received from Him. So stirring, in fact, had been their initial response that others in their village had been aroused by it and brought to share their faith. Thus, with startling quickness, the living seed within them was shooting forth its sprouts.

Yet sadly, after a lapse of months, when next the Savior passed that way, it had been hard to get in touch with these individuals. And when they were found, the coldness of their greeting, the averted eye, the transparent excuse to be going all told the same somber tale. Their attitude had changed, their faith was gone. Often, when the disciples made inquiries in those places, there emerged a tangled web of circumstances prominently woven with the dark threads of trouble and persecution. The initial enthusiasm they had felt had collapsed under the burden of trials and testings. And with it, so had their faith.

But how helpful was their teacher's parable in understanding such cases. The ground in those hearts was *rocky* ground. The terrain on which the seed had fallen was hard, tough, and resistant. And for this very reason it was shallow as well, for the seed could not penetrate its stony barrier to send its roots deep into the moisture-laden soil. Hence, all the sooner it sprouted upward, but all the sooner too it withered away when exposed to the remorseless heat. Without the opportunity to probe the very depths of its home, the seed could produce no crop.

So now they understood. Henceforth they would not assume that initial enthusiasm was invariably a sign that the heart was fertile. Indeed, it might indicate the very reverse, for it might mark a shallowness of spirit through which the truth of God could scarcely penetrate. Only time and testing could reveal the sort of soil God's word had found. Better by far, for the shoots to delay their appearance while the truth sent roots deep into the soul it had entered, so that in the end the fruit might be abundant and the presence of the seed unmistakably displayed.

For once the little sprigs upon the rocks had died, who could guess that hidden within its cracks was a life-giving seed? Who would suppose that a man who turned away from his faith had ever had life at all? But if it had been there once, it remained there still. And that was one of the mysteries of the kingdom of God.

But what about the thorns? The Savior continued. "Now the ones that fell among thorns are those who, when they have heard, go out and are choked with cares, riches, and pleasures of life, and bring no fruit to maturity" (Luke 8:14).

It was getting easier now. There was progression in the Master's figures. The seed on the roadside vanished completely, never displaying its vitality at all by as much as a single sprig. The seed on the rocks shot forth a few sprouts, evidence of the life that produced them, but these were soon gone. But the seed among thorns did better. The vital life that seed contained was working once again, but the stalk of grain it produced was stunted and never became fully ripe. The thorns among which it found its home had stifled its maturation and were dooming it to become perpetually undersized.

The disciples knew all too well the type of person to whom the thorns applied. More than once, in their presence, Jesus had invited some person to follow Him (Luke 9:59-62). That person, perhaps, had newly come to believe in Him, and now the Savior was setting before him the pathway of discipleship. Having bestowed on that heart the water of life, He now invited that heart to eat His food.

His call was a challenge to do the will of God and to finish His work. But all too often the invitation was politely declined. There were family responsibilities; there were business interests; life with Jesus would be too hard; there were a thousand excuses, but they all came down to the same things. The cares of life, the pleasures of life, the love of money; these then were the thorns. Searing, jagged thorns, deeply entrenched in the same heart into which the word of God had come in life-bestowing power.

It was not a question of losing one's faith, as with those whose hearts were rocky ground, but a question of finding room for the truth of God to flourish. It was a question of allowing the life of God within to grow to its full expression and to produce the luxuriant harvest of works for which the seed was sown. But the thorns prevented this and grew up along with God's Word and choked it back.

Fortunately, the disciples thought, *there was another kind of soil.* "But the ones that fell on the good ground," concluded Jesus, "are those who, having heard the word with a noble and good heart, keep it and bear fruit with patience" (Luke 8:15).

The disciples could not help thinking of the women who traveled with them. Mary Magdalene was one of them; and Joanna, the wife of a responsible Herodian official named Chuza; and a woman called Susanna, as well as many others. What a help they had been in so many ways. They had cooked; they had sewed; they had expended time, energy, and their own money—all that the Savior's tours to preach God's word might, by their efforts, be made a little more comfortable for Him.

Joanna, in particular, had left the comfortable life at the court of Herod Antipas to follow Jesus on this grueling journey. They had lost track of the money she had spent; probably she herself had lost track, for she was extremely well-to-do.

What made them different from others who heard God's word and believed it? Was it not the attitude of their hearts? Was it not the spirit of gratitude that imbued them? Surely they had hearts which, like a thoroughly furrowed field, were good soil on which God's seed had fallen. No wonder they persisted in following the Savior month after month along the wearisome paths He trod.

The disciples marveled at the loyalty of the women, but they also understood it. Their own hearts furnished them an explanation they were confident they could apply to others. It seemed to them that devotion to the Savior was the only sensible, honest course they had. After all, had He not granted to them that gift of life by which they could be assured a place with Him in the world to come? Were they not, by virtue of possessing that gift, forever preserved from the damnation of hell? It was a glorious gift, and one so good and perfect as to inspire the utmost gratitude toward its giver. No task was too large to do, no sacrifice too great to be made for Him. The disciples believed the women felt that way too.

There was not a trace in them of that hardness and shallowness of heart which, like stony ground, allowed God's truth to dwell only on the surface. Already the roots of the new life they had received had penetrated their souls most deeply, drawing up the moisture of devotedness and love to God.

Nor were they bothered by thorns. They all could have stayed at home, pleading the pressing concerns of daily living, but they had not done so. Would their fruit reach maturity? Would the harvest of their lives for God be truly abundant? The disciples felt confident they knew the answer. They could only wish their own hearts to be as honest and good as they believed these women's to be.

What insight they had gained from this simple parable. The seed was the Word of God. And only the heart from which it could be snatched at once, before it had been grasped by faith, only a heart like that would fail to partake of life. But the measure of life, the extent of its fullness and blessing—this depended on the kind of soil into which the seed had taken root.

It was always the same vital seed, vibrant with eternal life and all of the divine potential of that life. But if it could not put down deep roots into its new-found home, the evidences of its presence would be brief and passing, little more than a few weak shoots quickly withered in the heat of testing. And if it must grow on the same ground with a worldly spirit, with a love for money or for pleasure, or simply grow in a heart pervaded by earthly cares, it could never reach the real limits of its promise or attain the full stature toward which it strove.

No, the full harvest of good works in the life of one who had tasted the water of life depended on the heart possessing a sincerity that could lay a firm hold on God's Word and hold fast its truth as a most prized possession. It depended on a dedication of spirit capable of endurance under trial and testing. The life within the seed was the gift of God. But the fruit of that life depended on the spirit of the man in whose heart the seed now dwelt.

The disciples thought they had heard this before. In fact they were sure of it. One could freely take of the water of life and possess it forever. But one must labor to do the will of God and to finish His work. And unless a man did, that might always remain food which he knew not of.

7

Discipleship: Saving the Life We Lose
Luke 9:18-26

> Then He said to them all, "If anyone desires to come after Me, let him deny himself, and take up his cross daily, and follow Me. For whoever desires to save his life will lose it, but whoever loses his life for My sake will save it. For what profit is it to a man if he gains the whole world, and is himself destroyed or lost? For whoever is ashamed of Me and My words, of him the Son of Man will be ashamed when He comes in His own glory, and in His Father's, and of the holy angels" (Luke 9:23-26).

Following the Lord Jesus around through the towns and villages of Palestine could be very exhausting. Sometimes the disciples were almost tempted to ask if it was really worth it all. Occasionally, in some rare moment when they could escape the crowds, they would simply sit in silence, each thinking his own thoughts. And in those times of reflection, it was natural that their minds should wander back to home and family and friends.

It almost seemed that life was passing them by. Instead of traveling these dusty highways, trying to communicate with mobs of people who often seemed so unappreciative and uncomprehending, they should be back with their wives, earning a solid living, and rearing their children. That was what everybody else seemed to be doing, even many who believed in their Master and had accepted His gift of life. And if others, why not them? As things were now, they sometimes thought, they were losing their lives. In the very prime of their years, they were missing out on life's basic satisfactions.

Such reflections, however, were usually very fleeting. They knew why they were doing what they did. The Savior in whom they so deeply believed had called them to this life. Had He been just another man they would have left Him in a moment. But He was more than a man, more indeed than the greatest of men, more than the greatest spokesmen for God in Jewish history. He was the world's Redeemer. That's why they followed Him. Let others' hearts be stony ground. Let others be choked by the thorns of worldly cares. *They* would follow Jesus.

Some of them glanced in His direction. He was praying. There were few things that moved them more than seeing Jesus pray. That was a side of Him the crowds never saw. For when Jesus wanted to pray, He always tried to get away from the multitudes that thronged Him. But He didn't mind having *them* around and how glad they were He didn't. They had never seen anyone pray like He did. His words were not usually audible to them, His habit being to go off from them a little distance. But they didn't need to hear the words. It was evident that, for Jesus, prayer was the richest form of communion with His heavenly Father that anyone could imagine. They watched His face, if they could, and if they were close enough, His eyes, upturned toward heaven. What simplicity of spirit (they thought they could detect), what trust, what love. They wished *they* could pray like that. Perhaps He would be willing to teach them someday (Luke 11:1). He was finished now, and, rising from His knees, He walked back toward them. His face was thoughtful as He sat down with them, and presently He posed a question.

"Who do the crowds say that I am?" (Luke 9:18), He asked. There was no single answer to that question. The disciples had heard many conjectures as they had mingled with Jesus' audiences. Most people agreed that Jesus was someone of great importance in the plan of God. But here the consensus ended, and diversity of opinion began.

"John the Baptist," they began, offering a highly popular suggestion, "but some say Elijah; and others say that one of the old prophets has risen again" (Luke 9:19).

"But who do you say that I am?" Jesus continued. Of course, He knew already who they thought He was. But, as was often His custom, He preferred to draw the assertion from them rather than simply to make it Himself. Master instructor that He was, He knew full well that a truth clearly stated once by a pupil was worth ten such statements from his teacher.

And their answer *was* clear, as it was also most emphatic. Peter spoke it for the rest. "[You are] the Christ of God" (Luke 9:20), he asserted. It was a crucial affirmation. Had Jesus been simply some reappearing prophet of old, or John the Baptist recently beheaded but now returned to life, or even Elijah come back from the heavens into which he had been miraculously taken, that would have been a marvelous thing. And the crowds were prepared to believe that something marvelous was taking place in those days. But there was no salvation in such conjectures. Even the greatest of prophets could not give the gift of eternal life. The woman of Sychar had learned that. No, to give men living water Jesus must be who the disciples said He was, the Christ of God. They were surprised by the reaction that Peter's confession drew from their Master. For no sooner was it made, than He began to charge them quite sternly to tell no man this fact. They understood, of course, what He meant; He wished them to do precisely what He had just done to them. The truth about His person was something they should seek to elicit from men as a conclusion of their own, rather than a fact to be forced on them by direct assertion. This had been the Savior's method from the first.

At Jacob's well, for example, He had not mentioned His Messianic title until first it had been mentioned by the woman. "I know," she had said, "that Messiah is coming... When He comes, He will tell us all things" (John 4:25). That, of course, was the conclusion He had wanted her to reach, and He was ready at once to confirm it. "I, who speak to you, am He" (John 4:26), He had said. But it was *her* conclusion really, to which Jesus had deftly led her by the insight and wisdom in His words. It was thus that He frequently preferred to lead men, step by step, to faith and to salvation. In that respect, there was nothing particularly new in this stern command.

But it seemed to them that there was a new urgency in what He said. There was also a new reason.

"The Son of Man," said Jesus, "must suffer many things, and be rejected by the elders and chief priests and scribes, and be killed, and be raised the third day" (Luke 9:22).

They found this hard to assimilate. As the Christ of God, they thought then, He must surely enter very soon upon a glorious reign in the kingdom He was destined to establish. It was only after the events He now described had actually transpired that the disciples came to understand how necessary those events had been. He might indeed have founded His kingdom at once—no human power could have stood against Him had He chosen to do so—but it would have been a kingdom empty of men. Holy angels, of whom there were myriads, could have entered that kingdom, but not guilty men made of flesh. The gift of eternal life itself, a gift which guaranteed mankind's access to that kingdom, could not have been given to any heart apart from the fateful events of which Jesus was now speaking.

A gift is free to one who receives it, but it may be immeasurably costly to its giver. And so it is with the gift of eternal life. Freely offered to any who might ask for it ("If you knew the gift of God... you would have asked" [John 4:10]) it was nevertheless a present for which a terrible price was paid. And Jesus, its giver, must pay it. He must suffer; He must die. He must bear the sins of those to whom He gave His gift, yes, and even of those who, to their eternal sorrow, rejected it.

This the disciples did not yet understand. But when they did, they made it a part of the message they proclaimed

Discipleship: Saving the Life We Lose 79

to men. Then they fully subscribed to the words yet to be uttered by another apostle named Paul, "that Christ died for our sins according to the Scriptures, and that He was buried, and that He rose again the third day according to the Scriptures" (1 Cor 15:3-4).

It was of these necessary events that Jesus now spoke to them. "The Son of Man <u>must</u> suffer many things," He was saying, "and be killed, and be raised the third day" (Luke 9:22, emphasis added). And the necessity for this seemed to be the reason He now insisted on a greater reticence on their part in divulging that He was "the Christ of God." The blindness of the crowds, their misguided guesses about who He was, would soon play into the hands of Jesus' enemies. The elders of the nation, the chief priests of the temple, the scribes of the Jewish law—all these hostile forces would find that a blind and unbelieving mob was easy to manipulate during the tragic events which lay ahead (Matt 27:20-25). Though the disciples were only dimly aware of what it all meant, from now on they were walking with Jesus in the shadow of His cross.

Little wonder, they were later to think, that the next time He spoke to all the people His words were shaped by this new theme He had just introduced and about which He had no doubt been praying.

"If anyone desires to come after Me," the Savior said to all His hearers, "let him deny himself, and take up his cross daily,[4] and follow Me" (Luke 9:23).

It was the first time He had mentioned the word *cross*. To the audience at large the expression might seem scarcely intelligible. To the disciples, against the background of His private remarks to them, the word had powerful meaning. Clearly, it signified death. And such a death—slow, lingering, and agonizing. The thought chilled them. Moreover, His words brought to life in their minds the familiar image of

---

[4] Editor's note: Though the word *daily* is not found in the majority of manuscripts, the Lord clearly was calling for ongoing obedience, even in the face of suffering.

a convicted criminal carrying his own wooden plank to the spot chosen for his execution. Thus their Master was saying (they could hardly believe He was saying it) that they, like an assortment of guilty malefactors, should take up their own crosses and fall in line with Him. He had told them He must die. Now He was telling them to get in step behind Him.

Obviously, this was no way to attract disciples from that crowd. Indeed, it was a good way to repel them. Surely, when experience showed how many there often were whose hearts had rocky or thorny soul, this was no way to surmount the impediment which the living seed of God's word encountered in such lives. But, on second thought, He probably knew that. Undoubtedly He did. It was not at all a question of appealing to the heart that was hard or worldly, but an effort to sort out from them all the heart that was honest and good. It was, therefore, an effort to shake down His following and to appeal only to those whose devotion was real.

Jesus was reluctant to force upon men the conclusion that He was the "Christ of God" when they were satisfied to think that He was only a prophet. So too was Jesus reluctant to call men into discipleship without the most stringent warning of its cost.

In the former case, the gift of the water of life would be missed by those who were content to remain in their blindness. In the latter case, the food of doing God's will would be missed by those who were content to remain in a life of ease. As the hour of His rejection approached, with all of its tragic sorrow for those who were nearest to Him, the Savior was weeding out the unmotivated and the insincere.

Did He really mean for them *all* to die? Maybe, but that was by no means clear. It was evident to the disciples that there was a symbolic content in this utterance. They were to take up their crosses daily. Obviously, it was not a question of picking up a literal piece of wood and lugging it around each day. Their trips were wearisome enough as it was. No, it must rather be a matter of principle, a matter of accepting, on a daily basis, all that a cross might mean. And with this He had coupled a call for self-denial.

Later, when they had more opportunity to reflect, they realized that this was what discipleship was all about. Whenever they dreamed of home, loved ones, or comforts left behind, yet persisted in following Jesus wherever He led them, this was the self-denial of which He spoke. And when each day seemed to them a day when their personal lives were lost in the interests of God's work and the spread of the gospel, this surely was a kind of dying in which they took up a cross *day by day*.

To follow Jesus then, was to resign one's personal interests, to say no to the natural desire to realize one's full potential for earthly satisfaction, and to accept a cross in its place. It sounded rather stern when it was put that way. There was no mention of the deep joy that only those who tasted that splendid food of doing God's will could know. But that was their Master's purpose at this point. He was going to a cross, with all its stark reality and suffering. No one who truly wished to give his or her life to Him should be under any delusion that the way was soft and easy. Rewards, even here and now, there undoubtedly were in such a life. But there was deprivation and suffering too, perhaps even death, and the true disciple should accept that premise daily.

==How fortunate that one's entrance into the kingdom of God did not depend on his discipleship.== If it did, how few would ever enter that kingdom. Indeed, the disciples themselves could not help wondering if they could really measure up to such standards in the long run. If eternal life had depended on doing so, the disciples could have felt no assurance that they really possessed it or ever would. They could only have hoped that they might make it in the end.

But how sweet, how incomparably sweet, to know that life was truly theirs, right now, as the gift of God. They had not earned it, they could not lose it. They had drunk the living water and would never thirst for it again; they had been given eternal life. And they were amazed, when they pondered it, how this assurance actually undergirded and strengthened their determination to go on being disciples. They might have thought that it would do the reverse, that it would make them careless, knowing that their eternal destiny was secure. But it didn't at all. In fact, it gave to them that basic inner security in their relationship to Jesus which was their best protection against discouragement and failure.

Discipleship was hard and, if their Master's words meant anything, it was destined to get harder. It would have been psychologically intolerable if they had thought that failure somewhere down the road would destroy their whole experience with God. But it couldn't.[5] Whatever lay ahead, exhilarating or depressing, the living spring within them would keep on gushing up into eternal life. And that thought was like a spiritual Gibraltar, against which the waves of self-doubt and discouragement could spend their force in vain.

The next words of Jesus were as solemn and sobering as the ones they had just heard. They also confirmed the impressions those previous ones had made on them.

"For whoever desires to save his life will lose it, but whoever loses his life for My sake will will save it" (Luke 9:24).

Yes, they had been quite right in interpreting those earlier words as they had done. The cross they must take up daily in order to follow Jesus spoke to them of losing their life. The very life they so often felt they really *were* losing during endless days on the road with the Savior. They still breathed and ate and slept, of course. But in terms of earthly joy and the realization of worldly ambitions, such

---

[5] Editor's note: After this Jesus sent out seventy of His disciples (Luke 10:1). When they returned after the ministry trip with great rejoicing, Jesus said, "Do not rejoice in this, that the spirits are subject to you, but rather rejoice because your names are written in heaven" (Luke 10:20).

an experience was a gigantic zero. It was life minus all that men of the world call "life." It was, in its essence, the loss of "life."

Yet Jesus was saying, when men try to preserve their lives they actually end up losing them. And when they lost them for Him, as the disciples were doing day by day, they were really saving them. It was a striking paradox. And though it required much more thought than the disciples could give it just then, its general significance was clear. It would be easy enough for a man to decline the rigors and deprivations of discipleship in order to cling to his home, family, business, and pleasures. It was natural to want to live one's life here and now to the fullest, but to do so was to sacrifice its eternal value. Living like that was selfish living and could really have no enduring significance or worth. Such a life was gone as soon as it was lived. Thus in seeking to preserve it, a man actually lost it.

Conversely, the Master's paradox asserted, to lose one's life for His sake was to save it. To find in Jesus a focus for living, which superficially seemed to sacrifice so much that men hold dear, was to discover the secret of extending the value of that life into an eternal future. The disciples were not so obtuse to the spiritual realities which their teacher proclaimed that they could not sense the truth of this.

Take only the basic matter of offering the water of life to thirsty sinners. There, beyond a doubt, was an activity fraught with timeless consequences. To labor in God's harvest fields, to do His will, and to finish His work—this was, they had learned, a process by which fruit was gathered in to eternal life. However hard and frustrating these preaching tours with Jesus might seem at times, one immutable fact remained—God's barn was being filled with sinners saved by grace. And as reapers, when the entire harvest was finally in, their joy would be immense. Then they could look back over their lives from the vantage point of God's future kingdom, and they could be satisfied that those lives had been well spent.

In that day they could look around them at the men and women they had helped to reach and win, and they could know that their temporal experience of human life had not been wasted or annulled by selfish and self-serving pursuits. The life they thought they had lost for Jesus had in fact been saved. Their self-denial in the present would be more than compensated for by their joy and fulfillment in the future.

Of course, there was also the possibility of actual loss of life in the service of God. By His own admission, their Master was heading for just such an experience. And of course, the words He spoke would be fully as true in that case as they were on any other level of meaning.

If a man sought to preserve his physical life, when the service of God called on him to lay it down, such self-preservation would involve incalculable loss. On the other hand, to literally die for Jesus' sake was to enhance supremely the eternal worth of the life thus surrendered for God.

The principle was always the same. Selfishness sought to protect life for one's own use and gratification. Discipleship yielded it up, if need be, in the ultimate sense of that idea for the accomplishment of God's will and work. The former way in the light of eternal future was to lose one's life. The latter way was the saving thereof. But it was not a once-for-all sacrifice of which the Master spoke, except in the final act of martyrdom itself, but a daily submission to the principle of self-giving for the glory of God. Let him "take up his cross daily," Jesus had said, "and follow Me" (Luke 9:23).

The Savior continued to speak. "For what profit is it to a man if he gains the whole world, and is himself destroyed or lost?" (Luke 9:25). The world of commerce was now before their teacher's mind. The balance sheets were being totaled. Suppose, on the positive side of life's ledger, one could set down the entire world as a gain. This would be selfishness magnified to the nth power.

All the world's pleasures and possessions, every jot and tittle, fully experienced by man during his days on earth. What a "profit," it might seem. Such a life should show how profitable our days here on earth can be.

Not so, said Jesus. For on the negative side of the same ledger, one must enter "myself." In the process of gaining all that the world had to offer, the price for this was a man's own self, which he had thoughtlessly cast away and lost. It would be a massive forfeiture, indeed. So massive, in fact, that when measured against the gain recorded in the opposite column, the total profit would stand at zero. "For what profit is it to a man?" the Savior had asked. And the answer was obvious, absolutely nothing.

When the present world, with all its potential for enjoyment and material gain, had passed away, the man who had realized that potential to the limit would have nothing left. Naked he had come into the world, and naked he would leave it again. For nothing that he had selfishly experienced or acquired in that world could be extended into the kingdom of God. The age to come would obliterate the fulfillments of earth-bound living as completely as a new day obliterates the nighttime that precedes it.

Nothing in a man's present human experience is eternal, except the man himself. Thus it is imperative that a man cultivate *himself*, rather than the world in which he lives. It is indispensable that he learns the lessons of life and enters into its most precious secrets if he wishes to become a fully developed personality, prepared to enjoy the kingdom of God, and only thus would his life show a genuine and enduring profit.

Not all of the ramifications of their Savior's thoughts were evident just now to the disciples. Later they were able to penetrate them more deeply.

And when they did, they realized that the premise of all which He now uttered was a simple one—*suffering and self-sacrifice are what truly make a man*. The man who lives an easy, self-indulgent life is a hollow shell, too weak to resist the slightest pressure, too unworthy to deserve the slightest honor. Years later one of the disciples, Peter was to write glowingly of the significance of suffering in the lives of the followers of Jesus. "But may the God of all grace," he was to say to his fellow Christians, "who called us to His eternal glory by Christ Jesus, *after you have suffered a while,* perfect [complete], establish, strengthen, and settle you" (1 Pet 5:10, emphasis added). God, therefore, said Peter, desires to mold you in the crucible of affliction and thereby to make you all you ought to be. May the God of all grace make you *complete.*

The "complete" man, the fully developed person, which was what the Master was training those who followed Him to become. It requires self-denial; it requires the daily acceptance of a cross; it entails coming to know what it means to lose life in order to save it; but it is also profitable. Selfhood, fully realized in all its grand potential for the age to come—this was what He offered. Over and against it stands the whole world, and men must choose. They cannot have both. If you gain one, you must lose the other. And in truth, "what profit is it to a man if he gains the whole world, and is himself destroyed or lost?" (Luke 9:25).

What does it mean for the future if a man really does lose himself? What, in particular, does it mean for one who has accepted the gift of life? What lies in store for those whose hearts prove to be rocky ground, or full of thorns? The next words of Jesus cast a flood of light upon it all.

"For whoever is ashamed of Me and My words," the Lord Jesus now affirmed, "of him the Son of Man will be ashamed when He comes in His *own* glory, and in *His* Father's, and of the holy angels" (Luke 9:26).

It was a splendid panorama that their Master had opened up before them, a scene filled with light and wonder, the day of His coming to reign. Though they did not yet clearly perceive that He must go away, they sensed from His words that somehow He would appear to men in that day with a glory which was now veiled from their eyes. It was, of course, the kingdom of God, the kingdom about which they dreamed and for which they longed. All the glorious angels of God would be there amidst the splendor as well, and the brilliant effulgence of the Father Himself.

No mortal, they realized instinctively, could stand in that awesome light. No mere human being could enter that luminous realm, unless he had been divinely prepared for it. Indeed, the disciples knew that the Savior had said, "unless one is born again, he cannot see the kingdom of God" (John 3:3). And they knew it was true. Unless the Father of lights, from whom proceeded every good and perfect gift, should of His own will beget a man with the word of truth, that man must be banished forever from the divine presence and from the glory of the divine kingdom. But if He brought them forth, then they became a sort of first fruits of all His creatures, ready ahead of time for the new age which was someday to dawn. The gift of eternal life must be possessed by all who would find a place in that radiant scene.

But some *were* there of whom *He* was ashamed. He said nothing of casting them out, nothing of banishing them from Him, only that He was ashamed of them amidst the splendor all around. If they were there, they had to possess the gift of life. But there was something they now tragically failed to possess. For it was clear that they lacked the worthiness of character which would have made Him proud to acknowledge them. In a day when He Himself was so highly honored, He could not honor them at all.

Why was He ashamed of them? Because *they* had been ashamed of *Him*. Not that they rejected Him, not that they did not believe, it was simply that He was an embarrassment to them. Instead of exhibiting the loyalty of true discipleship, instead of picking up their cross of self-denial day by day and clearly walking before men as followers of Him, they had been ashamed to do so. They were ashamed of Him personally, and equally sad, ashamed of His words.

Thus, the life-giving message that had reached them had not been vigorously spread by them. Into the harvest fields of God they had not entered unreservedly to gather fruit to life eternal. While others, like the women for example, followed Him faithfully about, if only they might in some measure make Him a little more comfortable as He preached God's Word, *they* had stayed at home. To bear a cross behind Him had been to them a scandal, not an honor. And whether the soil of their hearts had been stony or marred by thorns, they had still failed dismally and disastrously to become worthy of His praise in the presence of His Father and in the presence of His holy angels.

So that was what it meant to lose oneself. It was the utter forfeiture of personal merit and worth in the very moment when it counted most. For now, in that day, no longer did the tinseled sham of a temporal world delude the eye or beguile the heart. No longer could the unworthy among men be exalted, while the worthy were disdained. Reality had now banished mere pretense, and devastating truth shattered men's miserable hypocrisy. Now, at last, if the life a man had lived had *really* mattered, the universe was ready to behold it. The holy angels were there to observe, the Father was prepared to approve, but *Jesus* must commend. And if He could not, if He would not, that was the ultimate personal shame. Indeed, if a man had possessed all the world right up to that very instant of time, it would have mattered no more. For all that mattered now was what he was, the man himself, in the eyes of his eternal Maker and Redeemer.

"For what profit is it to a man if he gains the whole world, and is himself destroyed or lost?" (Luke 9:25).

The divine accounting said "zero," and eternity would verify that total. For if the man himself was nothing, having lived for self and not for God, his possessions amounted to nothing as well. For *they* would then be gone, and *he* alone would remain. The question about life which the Son of God was addressing to His hearers was profoundly searching. It was not, "What did you *have*?" but, "What did you *become*?" And if a man *became* a true disciple to the Master, he would be acknowledged and honored in the kingdom of God. And if not, the Savior would be ashamed.

It seemed to the disciples when they considered it, that they were almost overwhelmed by the solemnity of such thoughts. Rugged as their itinerant experience with Jesus often was, to glimpse reality in this light was to gain from it a new measure of purpose and determination. No longer could they envy those who, though believing in their Master, had shunned the pathway to which He invited them in order to avoid the hardships which it entailed. Indeed, they could only pity them and feel a touch of sorrow at the shame which one day awaited these who had chosen their course so poorly.

In later years it was to be the disciples' privilege to teach such precepts to many in the fledgling Christian Church. Men like James who had not even been believers during the Savior's career on earth would be deeply challenged and profoundly motivated by these truths. The conscience of Jesus' followers was to be permanently colored by this very wisdom that the disciples were gleaning along the dusty roads of Galilee and Judea. Of course, just now, the disciples could not sense how richly profitable their growing insight would be to believers in all future time. But for the moment they could sense how richly profitable it could be for them. Indeed, they made up their minds they would stop complaining to themselves about their wearisome journeys with Jesus. The next day their crosses seemed remarkably lighter.

8
The Faith That Lives
James 1:19–2:26

> Therefore lay aside all filthiness and overflow of wickedness, and receive with meekness the implanted word, which is able to save your souls. But be doers of the word, and not hearers only, deceiving yourselves (Jas 1:21-22).
>
> For as the body without the spirit is dead, so faith without works is dead also (Jas 2:26).

Eventually the Savior's instructions about the way of the cross became fully fruitful in the lives of His disciples. Having learned for themselves what it meant to *save their lives* through selfless submission to their Master, they proclaimed this principle wherever they taught the Word of God. Particularly in Jerusalem, after the Lord Jesus had returned to the heavenly glory from which He had come, the disciples assisted in the formation of a Christian community for which this truth was of transcendent importance.

Indeed, in that infant fellowship of believers, self-sacrifice in the name of Jesus was a way of life (Acts 2:44-45). And it was there that James was nurtured in the early days of his faith, listening with all eagerness and hunger of heart to the teaching of the original followers of his Lord. He could not hear soon enough, nor be told often enough, all that his brother had laid down on this surpassing theme, and the concept of *saving one's life* soon passed into the very fiber of his being. Though he had not personally heard the Savior's public pronouncements of this truth, by the time James became a teacher in the church it was a part of the warp and woof of his own ministry.

There had been, of course, certain occasions when he *had* heard his brother preach. And even then, in his unbelief, he had not failed to be impressed. Take Jesus' Sermon on the Mount, for example. That had been delivered in Galilee early in the Savior's ministry, and James happened to have been there. He never really forgot much of what his brother had said that day. Though he had not yet accepted from Jesus the "good and perfect" gift of life, his memory was marked by some of the striking phrases and unforgettable images that Jesus had employed.

Years later, after he had come to believe in his brother and had willingly become His "bondservant," James recalled a large number of those memorable utterances and put them to use. If he spoke to his fellow Christians of the joy that could be theirs in the time of trial, it was not without remembering that Jesus had said, "Blessed are you when they revile and persecute you, and say all kinds of evil against you falsely for My sake. Rejoice and be exceedingly glad, for great is your reward in heaven, for so they persecuted the prophets who were before you" (Matt 5:11-12). And if he spoke of the Father as One who gave every good and perfect gift, there was yet another recollection from that sermon lodged deep in his heart. "If you then, being evil, know how to give good gifts to your children," Jesus had affirmed, "how much more will your Father who is in heaven give good things to those who ask Him" (Matt 7:11).

There were many other memories that James had from that mountain-top message, but few that more completely shaped his thinking than Jesus' final words that day. As long as he lived, he could recall them clearly. "Therefore," said Jesus, "whoever hears these sayings of Mine, and does them, I will liken him to a wise man who built his house upon the rock: and the rain descended, the floods came, and the winds blew and beat on that house; and it did not fall, for it was founded on the rock. But everyone who hears these sayings of Mine, and does not do them, will be like a foolish man who built his house on the sand: and the rain descended, the floods came, and the winds blew and beat on that house; and it fell. And great was its fall" (Matt 7:24-27).

And with that, Jesus had stopped speaking. It was an impressive conclusion, and the huge audience that had heard Him buzzed with comment. James remembered some of that comment and above all the frequently repeated observation that Jesus taught differently than the Jewish scribes (Matt 7:28-29). For whereas those men were constantly appealing to the decisions and interpretations of Israel's greatest rabbis, Jesus appealed to no authority beyond Himself. He spoke as an oracle of God, and He asserted unequivocally the demands that His words placed on all who heard them. That was what the conclusion of His message had been all about. A man who heard *and did* His words was like a prudent builder whose house was secure from storm, but the man who heard and did them not was, by contrast, a foolish man whose building was destined for ruin.

James could recall, in later years, that he had thought at the time how logical the demand of Jesus actually was. It was not as a mere scribe of the Jewish law that his brother was presenting Himself to men, but instead as the Christ of God. Perhaps He did not usually make that claim explicit, but it was plainly implicit in all He said and did. Already there were many who claimed to have found eternal life through Him, and were boldly confessing Him as their Savior. And it was evident that Jesus welcomed such faith and encouraged it. It followed, therefore, James had realized, that if that was who his brother really was, though he could not for a moment believe it, then His words *did* carry all the weight He claimed for them.

In that case, the words of Jesus were the words of God with all of the supreme and holy authority which that fact implied.

Consequently, it was obvious that the figure of the two builders made good sense if one granted the premise that Jesus spoke the Word of God. The "house" which each of them built must signify their life, for a man *lives* in his house. It followed that if Jesus' words were indeed the timeless truth of God, there was no other secure foundation on which a man could build his life.

Hearing those words was not enough. One must by all means *do* them. For, the parable asserted emphatically, whenever a man's life was smitten by the storms and misfortunes which inevitably come to human experience, that life could only withstand the tests if it was firmly grounded on *doing* what Jesus said.

Obedience was the key to endurance. A mere hearing, where Jesus' words were concerned, was dangerous. It was like building a house on sand without any consideration of what might happen in one good storm. As soon as the storm struck that house it would collapse, leaving the life of the man who built it in irreparable shambles. That life might even be terminated altogether if the storm which struck it was the ultimate one of death itself. This much had been clear to James even then.

James could remember thinking at the time also that if he ever *did* believe in his brother, he would most certainly also become His disciple. In fact, at the very start of that unforgettable sermon, Jesus had deliberately and conspicuously singled His disciples out of the crowd, allowing them to come to Him and sit around Him while He spoke (Matt 5:1-2). Clearly He intended His audience to perceive that it was through discipleship to Him that His utterances could be realized in their lives.

This, of course, implied that they must have faith in Him, but it implied more as well. It implied a willingness on their part to yield their lives to the redirection He would give them. In short, the house they lived in was to be built upon the foundation of His word and in obedience to His specifications. Only thus could they be secure in the storm. Later James was to realize that faith in Jesus brought to men the gift of life. Discipleship introduced them to doing God's will and work. By the former, they were begotten of

God. By the latter, their lives were built up and preserved from ruin and loss.

Much time had now passed. James had become a leading figure in the Christian church at Jerusalem, with pastoral concerns that stretched far beyond that city. These were difficult days for the followers of Jesus, and persecution and testing of all kinds and descriptions seemed to afflict them frequently. And because these believers in God's Son were often materially poor, they were particularly exposed to the oppression of rich men who happened to reject the Savior. More than once, some defenseless Christian had been hauled into court on trumped up charges by some blasphemous man of wealth. Such experiences were like violent storms sweeping down on their lives, and they desperately needed the advice and counsel of a spiritual shepherd.

Such a shepherd James had now become. Believing in Jesus, his brother after the flesh but also the Lord of glory, he now served Him as a "bondservant." The Savior's interests were now James's interests, the Savior's concerns his concerns as well. In writing to a widely scattered collection of Christian churches, James sought to give advice to his troubled readers like the advice he felt his Lord would give had He been here to do it. Thus the words that he inscribed were saturated with principles drawn from the teachings of Jesus, especially those He had laid down in His Sermon on the Mount.

Following the salutation of his letter, James came right to the point. Were his readers burdened by various trials? "Count it all joy," James said (Jas 1:2), just as the Savior would have said.

Were they in need of wisdom in their time of trial? Let them ask for it from God, the Father whom Jesus said knew how to give good gifts to those who asked Him. But if, in their troubles, they felt tempted to do evil, let them be careful not to blame such feelings on a generous God. From the urge to sin, only death could come. From the Father of lights, only good and perfect gifts (Jas 1:18).

"Let no one say when he is tempted, 'I am tempted by God,'" wrote James, "for God cannot be tempted by evil, nor does He Himself tempt anyone. But each one is tempted when he is drawn away by his own desires and enticed. Then, when desire has conceived, it gives birth to sin; and sin, when it is full-grown, brings forth death. Do not be deceived, my beloved brethren. Every good gift and every perfect gift is from above, and comes down from the Father of lights, with whom there is no variation or shadow of turning. Of His own will He brought us forth by the word of truth" (Jas 1:13-18).

Never blame God for your temptations to sin, James was saying. To do so is to misunderstand the very character of God, who cannot be tempted with evil, and to misjudge His activity. God never tempts a man to sin. A man's own inward lust does that. Rather, God gives good and perfect gifts. Moreover, lust is like a wicked woman of the streets which, through forming an affinity with our hearts, becomes pregnant with a sinful act. When that act is born—in short, when we do what lust prompts us to do—that act becomes the daughter of our wrong desire, capable of growing in its consequences until maturity is attained and a new child is born. And *that* child is death. But that is the offspring of our lust, through sin, and not in any way the offspring of the Father of lights. We, however, *are* His offspring, for "of His own will He brought us forth by the word of truth" (Jas 1:18).

And there it stood in language as plain as James could make it. We have indeed received the good and perfect gift of life eternal, and by its means we have become God's children.

But that fact, wonderful though it is, does not annul the capacity of the heart to sin. Our divine birth is by the word of truth, a living seed implanted in our being. But the fruit of that seed depends altogether on what is allowed to go on in the heart into which it now has entered.

Jesus had taught that if rocky soil was in the heart, the seed could attain no depth. If thorns were there, it could attain no maturity. And, says James, if *lust* is there, the individual who fulfills that lust may *die!* Never confuse the two, James insisted. By the Father's gift, we have eternal life. As the consequence of sin, we may experience physical death.

The principle James was enunciating was as old as the ancient scriptures on which he had been reared in that godly home at Nazareth. Long ago Solomon, the wisest of men, had observed:

> The fear of the Lord prolongs days,
> But the years of the wicked will be shortened
> (Prov 10:27).

And:

> As righteousness leads to life,
> So he who pursues evil *pursues it* to his own death (Prov 11:19).

And also:

> The law of the wise is a fountain of life,
> To turn one away from the snares of death
> (Prov 13:14).

There was no question about it. The prolongation of one's days on earth was facilitated by a righteous life. Their premature termination was the all too frequent consequence of sin. James's statement, therefore, was undeniably true. "Sin, when it is full-grown, brings forth death."

Having contrasted God's gift of life with sin's "gift" of death, James is now ready in his letter to drive home a practical piece of advice. He wants his Christian readers, begotten as they are by the word of truth, to avoid the death-dealing consequences of any unrighteous behavior that they were tempted to indulge in under the pressure of their troubles. He wants, in short, to save their lives. The avoidance of sin alone could, in a real sense, accomplish this end. But James also realized that the concept of saving the life had received a new dimension in the teaching of Jesus.

By means of paradox, which the Savior was so fond of using, Jesus had taught that a man's life could be saved even when it was lost. Of course He demanded righteousness to achieve this end, just as the Old Testament demanded it for the prolonging of one's days. But the righteousness Jesus insisted on was worked out in discipleship, by which men were called to take up their cross and follow Him. And even if that path led to a martyr's death, still the life was saved.

In a real sense the life might be lost *day by day* as one sacrificed personal interests to do the will of God, but in the process his eternal preservation was being worked out. For such a life could never really end even when, paradoxically, it did, because its value and worth would last forever.

Thus, the Old Testament concept of extending one's life had been transformed in the teaching of Jesus. According to the Old Testament doctrine, righteousness extended one's life and postponed the grave. According to Jesus' doctrine, discipleship extended one's life *beyond* the grave. In both cases, the life was saved, but the richer and deeper sense belonged to the precepts of Jesus. As James prepares to write his practical counsel, he has both concepts in mind.

"Of His own will He brought us forth by the word of truth, that we might be a kind of firstfruits of His creatures" (Jas 1:18), James had just written. Now he proceeds, "So then, my beloved brethren, let every man be swift to hear, slow to speak, slow to wrath; for the wrath of man does not produce the righteousness of God. Therefore lay aside all filthiness and overflow of wickedness, and receive with meekness the implanted word, which is able to save your souls" (Jas 1:19-21).

How practical James's words were for his readers in the midst of their testings. Under the pressure of trial and difficulty, they were sometimes tempted to blame God for an insidious inward desire to do evil. After all, He allowed them to have trouble. Yet, the desire to sin came from the lust in their hearts, while the God they felt like blaming was the very One whose good and perfect gift of life they had so freely received. By the word of truth He had actually begotten them.

What then should they do? Blame so generous a God for their sin? Perish the thought! Now, if ever, was the time to listen to the Word of God. It was a time for hearing, not for speaking, and certainly not for impatient anger. God's righteousness would never be worked out in their lives by anger. No, they must lay aside their tendencies to evil, and humbly receive instruction from the very word by which they had been born anew. That word of truth had already made them a sort of firstfruits of God's creatures. Now it could save their souls.

For one who read the words, *save your souls*, in Greek, the language in which James was now writing, the words meant equally well, "Save your *lives*." Indeed, the expression was verbally the same as Jesus' own when He said, "Whoever wants to save his life..." Thus, in the Greek tongue the words *soul* and *life* were one. There were, of course, other words for life, but this one in particular suggested the intrinsic, inner self which was *alive* and capable of experiencing all that human existence could offer. It was "life," conceived of as inseparable from selfhood.

What did James mean when he said that application of God's Word was necessary to "save your lives"? Clearly, at the very least, he meant that the deadly consequences of sin would be averted if they gave true heed to God's Word. Physical life could be extended by humble submission to God's truth, as one laid aside his own filthiness and rejected wickedness as a worthless superfluity of his experience. But saving the life was more than that, as Jesus Himself had taught. It was the capacity of a man's life to withstand every storm, every test, every trouble, even death itself, so that the basic structure and value of that life endured beyond the grave.

And it was just here that James's mind inevitably worked its way back to the parable of the two builders which he had heard in that sermon on the mountain so many years ago (Matt 7:24-27). From that parable it was clear that the life lived in discipleship to Jesus had a resilience in time of trouble that was totally lacking in a life that was not so lived. The disciple was nothing less than a prudent builder who founded his life—his house—on solid bedrock. And that rock, Jesus had made clear, was His *word*.

The parable of Jesus did not merely teach that the house upon the rock lasted *longer* than the house upon the sand. Rather, it taught that the former *lasted,* while the other did not. Thus it taught that a man whose life is built on the words of the Savior is a man whose life nothing, not even death, can destroy, while a man whose life is not so built is a man whose life many things, but *especially* death, can overturn in ruins. The word of Jesus was the secret of saving one's life in the ultimate sense of that truth.

"Receive with meekness the implanted word which is able to save your lives." How James's readers needed to hear that. Buffeted as they were by troubles, tempted often to sin, they needed to know where to find real bedrock for their lives. They needed to learn how to give to their lives a security and solidity which none of the vicissitudes of their stormy experience could touch. The word of truth is your secret, says James. The implanted word can preserve your life, be it for a time or eternity.

The *implanted* word. The term evoked an image from nature, but in general use it signified "innate." The word that saves the life is "innate" to you, James was saying. You are no strangers to that word, for through it you were begotten by the Father of lights. Hence it is an *inborn* word because by it you were *born in* to the family of God. Like a seed planted in the soil of your heart, God's Word is now native to your being. It is something which it is most natural for you to respond to.

Yet be sure you do respond, James continued to write:

> But be doers of the word, and not hearers only, deceiving yourselves. For if anyone is a hearer of the word, and not a doer, he is like a man observing his natural face in a mirror; for he observes himself, goes away, and immediately forgets what kind of man he was. But he who looks into the perfect law of liberty and continues in it, and is not a forgetful hearer but a doer of the work, this one will be blessed in what he does (Jas 1:22-25).

The parable of Jesus was now ringing in James's ears. "Whoever hears these sayings of mine, and does them, I will liken him to a wise man" (Matt 7:24). And, "Everyone who hears these sayings of mine, and does not do them, will be like a foolish man" (Matt 7:26). The one who hears and does versus the one who only hears had been the contrast presented by the Savior, and it was now the contrast set forth by James. How foolish it was to be merely a hearer of the Word and not a doer of it also. So foolish, in fact, that it was comparable to a man who studied himself in a mirror and then immediately forgot what he looked like. Obviously a piece of sheer stupidity.

But there was more to James's new imagery than that. In an ordinary mirror a man might see the face he had by natural birth, "his natural face" (Jas 1:23). But in the word of truth a man might see the face he received by his birth from above. There he might discern "what kind of man he was" (Jas 1:24), now that he was born of God. Indeed the Word of God into which he was to look was an *innate* word, native to his inner being, because with it he had been begotten by the Father of lights. It was an excellent mirror in which to see what the grace of God had made him.

In the natural world of men, a single glance into a mirror might suffice to hopelessly enamor a man with the appearance of his natural face. It was, in any case, an appearance he was not likely to soon forget. Why then, in spiritual matters, should a man not be enamored by the wondrous visage that was his as a child of God? "Of His own will He brought us forth…that we might be a kind of firstfruits of His creatures" (Jas 1:18). A firstfruits of His creatures? What a vision to catch sight of in the divine looking glass. To discern that by our birth from above we are men possessing the capacity to reflect the purity and holiness of the world to come. To discover that we are God's workmanship created for the good works He has prepared for us to walk in. What a radiant spiritual countenance to behold in the mirror of God's Word. The very likeness of Jesus is there, and that's what manner of men we are because the Savior's life is in us. How could we behold and then forget? Yet that was precisely what we did every time we heard and did not do His word. It was the height of folly.

But conversely, James was saying, if we are wise enough to peer attentively into the mirror of God's Word and persevere in that word by doing it and not just hearing it only, then true blessing will be ours. After all, the Word into which we are to look with obedient hearts is not a law of bondage but a law of freedom. Had not Jesus once said to some who believed in Him, "If you abide in My word, you are My disciples indeed. And you shall know the truth, and the truth shall make you free" (John 8:31-32)? Yes, these had been His words, to which He had then added, "Whoever commits sin is a slave of sin" (John 8:34). So it was sin that robbed men of their truest freedom. But it was discipleship to Jesus, persisting obediently in His word, that gave it back.[6]

Such then was the only true course of wisdom. As those who have been born from above, James was saying, you must each set it as your unflinching purpose to be, not a forgetful hearer, but a *doer* of God's Word.

---

[6] Editor's note: *Experiential* freedom from sin's enslaving power comes by abiding in Jesus' words. However, all believers have *positional* freedom from slavery to sin as Paul says in Rom 6:18: "And having been set free from sin, you became slaves of righteousness."

And so it happened that in the letter he was writing, James was teaching the same truth that Jesus Himself had taught in His Sermon on the Mount. In the midst of the troubles and storms of human experience, the life of a man was saved by God's Word *if* the man heard *and did it.* Thus it had an eternal worth that not even death could shake. But if he was a hearer only, he was risking a colossal disaster. He was consigning his earthly experience to tragic ruins.

There it was again. The water and the food. The gift of God on the one hand, freely bestowed and eternally unfailing. And on the other hand, the call of discipleship to do the will of God and to finish His work. Jesus had spoken of both things at the well of Sychar. And in the hands of James these twin truths found fresh and vital exposition. Birth from above was utterly without human effort. "Of His own will He brought us forth" (Jas 1:18). But the preservation of one's life required works.

"But he who looks into the perfect law of liberty and continues in it, and is not a forgetful hearer but a doer of the work, this one will be blessed in what he does" (Jas 1:25). If the blessing of God was to rest truly and fully on the life of any whom He had begotten, that person must by all means be a worker. Only thus could the life be saved.

Presently, as his letter continued, James went on to spell out some of the works which the Christian conscience commended. One such work was realized by practical, down-to-earth generosity to those in need, particularly the fatherless and the widows. Another good work involved an even-handed, impartial treatment of rich and poor alike in the local Christian church, so that the rich man was not favored nor the poor man despised. In short, mercy in all its forms and expressions was to be assiduously cultivated, for the merciful man was ever the recipient of the mercy of God.

And mercy was what man needed most in his hour of trouble and storm. If the judgment of God fell, unrelieved by any mercy, upon the house a man had built, upon his life, how could it survive? What could save him from the disaster and ruin which *that* would bring? Could mere faith, unaccompanied by works, save him? Some of James's readers evidently thought so. Simply because they were believers in the one true God and in His Son the Lord Jesus Christ, they expected God to vindicate them in their troubles, to justify them before men in their time of testing. When the storms came, they expected God's mercy and deliverance from trouble to be theirs automatically because they were people of faith.

That was a great mistake, James went on to point out. In the hour of testing, a man needs more than faith to come through successfully. He needs works. Think of the patriarch Abraham. How did he pass his supreme test when he was called upon to sacrifice his very own son? How was he vindicated in his trial so that he earned the title "friend of God" (Jas 2:23)?

By faith alone? No. But by a faith that worked, producing obedience to the Word of God which had come to him.

And consider Rahab, whose story James's readers knew from the book of Joshua. How did she pass *her* test when Jericho, her city, was about to be reduced to ruins and all its people killed? Was *her life* saved by faith alone? Once again, no.

Rather by her works—the help she actually furnished the messengers who came to her—she survived. And thus she too was justified by works, vindicated in an hour of potential calamity.

Do you wish to be vindicated as truly righteous people in your troubles, James was asking. If so, you will be justified by works. Faith alone is not enough for *this kind* of justification. For the only kind of faith that can save a life is the kind of faith which is itself *alive* and *working*. "For as the body without the spirit is dead, so faith without works is dead also" (Jas 2:26).

James's readers were not dead. At least, not yet. But "sin, when it is full-grown, brings forth death" (Jas 1:15).

That was a solemn thought. And obedience to God's implanted word was the only preventative for that. Not mere affirmation that that word was true. Not mere hearing. But *doing*. Faith that responded obediently to the truth of God was truly vital and alive. Faith was like a body which required the animation of an inward spirit. Without the quickening influence of good works in one's life, faith died and became a mere corpse in a man's experience. Real enough it might be, tangible like a lifeless body was tangible, but equally inactive and dormant. And a dead faith could certainly not save one's life.

Years before James wrote these words, the Lord Jesus had spoken of the seed which fell on stony ground. Little shoots had sprung up at once, then died. In interpreting His own figure, the Savior had explained how those transient shoots exposed a temporary faith in the individuals He described. These were people "who [believed] for a while and in time of temptation [fell] away" (Luke 8:13). Their troubles as believers in Him had been too much for them, and their faith had withered away and died. Pretty soon it was gone altogether, blown away, as it were, by the violent winds of adversity. Of course, the life of God within them had not vanished, for the spring of living water continued to gush up into eternal life, just as Jesus had promised. But the vital seed of that life was now fruitless, hidden from view in some crack or crevice of its rocky home.

And such was the real and present danger to every believer in the Savior who confronted the storms of life. Unless he saw to it that the vitality of his faith was maintained by the constant reanimation of a life of good works, a life securely built on obedience to God, that faith could wither and die. And if it died, it might disappear altogether, decomposing, so to speak, like a corpse, and buried for good beneath a barren and wasted experience.

So, James insisted, keep your faith alive by working at it. Build your house securely on the will and Word of God.

9

The Riches of the World to Come

James 2:5

And seeing the multitudes, He went up on a mountain, and when He was seated His disciples came to Him. Then He opened His mouth and taught them, saying: "Blessed are the poor in spirit, for theirs is the kingdom of heaven" (Matt 5:1-3).

Then He lifted up His eyes toward His disciples, and said: "Blessed are you poor, for yours is the kingdom of God" (Luke 6:20).

Listen, my beloved brethren: Has God not chosen the poor of this world to be rich in faith and heirs of the kingdom which He promised to those who love Him? (Jas 2:5).

Both Jesus and James had grown up in a home that was poor. A little less than six weeks after Jesus was born, Joseph and Mary had presented Him before God in the temple at Jerusalem in accordance with the Jewish law. But they had been unable to afford the lamb which was prescribed as a sacrifice on that occasion, so they had taken advantage of Moses' provision for the poor. They had offered a pigeon instead (Lev 12:6-8; Luke 2:21-24). Joseph himself was a humble carpenter. Later, when God blessed him and Mary with more sons and daughters, it was not easy for him to provide for the large family which they were raising. Jesus and James had learned from childhood how to be satisfied with little more than the basic necessities of life. Yet, though there was poverty in their home, there was dignity as well, and they had never felt ashamed.

In later years, after he had come to believe in Jesus, James had often pondered the astounding reality that the Son of God had left the undimmed splendor of heaven to live in a home like that. He might have chosen some richer dwelling, a royal palace had He so desired, but instead He had chosen James's home with all its material lacks and needs, and there He had been content to grow up. James could not help but think what a comment that was upon the low esteem in which God held the wealth of earth. How clearly it suggested that whatever might be truly riches in the eyes of the heavenly Father, they were not the riches of this age.

And whenever he thought that way, he always remembered once more that unforgettable Sermon on the Mount. How full his mind was of recollections from that message. Little had he dreamed at the time that the brother in whom he could not then believe was nevertheless powerfully shaping his convictions by the words He uttered on that occasion. Only now did James perceive what vital and transforming words they had proved to be. And among those words James could not forget were these:

> "Do not lay up for yourselves treasures on earth, where moth and rust destroy and where thieves break in and steal; but lay up for yourselves treasures in heaven, where neither moth nor rust destroys and where thieves do not break in and steal. For where your treasure is, there your heart will be also" (Matt 6:19-21).

As much or more than any other words he ever heard, these had molded James's concept of genuine wealth. The true riches were not those which men store up here, but those which they store up for the hereafter.

"For where your treasure is, there your heart will be also." *How true,* James had thought even then. A man lived for what was truly valuable to him. If the things he valued most were those he could store up in this life, he lived for them. But if his most treasured hopes were such as could be realized only in the age to come, he would fix his heart on that unseen world and live for it. But it took *faith* to reject the former kind of riches and to prefer the latter. For the riches of Earth were visible, tangible, and accessible in the here and now, while those of heaven were presently unseen and inexperienced. From the very first, James had sensed that to become a man of wealth in the kingdom of God required much faith, for it required the capacity to grasp the realities of a future world and to set one's heart on them unswervingly.

This, of course, was much more than the faith by which men appropriated God's gift of life eternal. For that, a single moment of simple, childlike trust was all that God required. It took but a single drink of the Savior's living water to forever fix the destiny of the drinker who could never thirst again. But far more than a moment of faith was required if one were determined to lay up treasures in heaven, while rejecting the allurements of the treasures of earth. To make a choice like that, and to maintain that choice to the end of life, clearly required a faith that was both robust and very abundant. Thus, as James came eventually to perceive, the wealth of that future age would surely belong to those who possessed a wealth of faith right here and now.

But what of those, like some Christians James knew, who had little more than the faith they started with when first they believed in the Savior? Suppose through lack of a rich and luxuriant faith they continued to live largely for the satisfactions of this life, rather than for those of the life to come? Did it not follow, with irresistible logic, that if wealth in God's kingdom depended on fulfilling the Savior's command to lay it up, then one who ignored that command would find himself by comparison poor in that day? *Surely it followed,* James knew.

In fact, as James now saw most clearly, in a sense there would be rich and poor in that future age just as there were rich and poor in this present one. All who entered that splendid world would do so by virtue of receiving the gift of God in simple faith. But all who acquired the treasures of that world would do so by virtue of their wealth of faith through which they laid those treasures up. No wonder that Jesus had chosen a home of poverty while here on earth. For here it mattered not if one were poor. That could only matter in the day to come.

Moreover, James now knew, the distinction between "rich" and "poor" in the kingdom of God described precisely the difference in destiny between the disciple and the non-disciple. The disciple was one who, with vitality of faith in Jesus, denied himself, took up his cross daily, and devotedly followed the Savior. It was he who saved his life while seeming to lose it. But the non-disciple was one who, through meagerness of faith, pursued a path of worldly self-indulgence only to hopelessly lose the life he had so desperately sought to preserve. For the former, measureless eternal wealth awaited him at the end of life's road; for the latter, sad loss and embarrassing poverty.

Both would most certainly enter God's kingdom; that was God's gift; but the one would have so much more to enjoy there than the other that no other terms could adequately appraise the qualitative distinction between them than the words *wealth* and *poverty*.

James no longer looked at rich men with that twinge of envy he had sometimes felt when still a boy. How fleeting and transient was the wealth such men possessed. How quickly it was gone, and life itself—impoverishing its proud possessor so that he left the world exactly as he entered it, empty-handed. Who could envy an experience like that? Or even desire it? Was it not so much better to follow the Savior, to experience whatever deprivation that course might entail, and thus to become rich toward God? What did it matter to have riches here, but poverty hereafter? Better by far to be poor now if one could be rich then.

In fact, James realized, there was a sense in which it was essential to be poor now in order to be rich then. And once again, the Master's words in His Sermon on the Mount had been formative in James's perceptions. He remembered clearly the crucial utterance with which that sermon opened: "Blessed are the poor in spirit, for theirs is the kingdom of heaven" (Matt 5:3). And he remembered too that this utterance had been pointedly directed by Jesus at His disciples, who had just come out of the crowds to sit before him. It seemed evident that Jesus had meant to indicate that poverty of spirit was to be a leading feature of His true disciples and that ownership of God's kingdom was its fitting reward.

Later, James had understood this more clearly. A genuine disciple was one who emptied his human spirit of pride and self-will and who meekly submitted his life to the authority of Jesus, following Him wherever He led. Divesting himself of the stubborn self-interest to which men cling as they might cling to a priceless treasure, the disciple was to become truly "poor in spirit." To such people, Jesus declared, the kingdom of heaven belonged.

James had learned much from the Sermon on the Mount. He had not, however, had the privilege of hearing the sermon on the plain. The original disciples had heard it, and from them James was not surprised to learn that the Savior had begun that discourse in a manner very much the same. For then, too, the Lord Jesus had commenced His message by fixing His gaze pointedly on the disciples themselves and saying, "Blessed are you poor, for yours is the kingdom of God" (Luke 6:20). James at first had thought that corresponded exactly to the words he had heard earlier on the mountainside. Yet, upon later reflection, he realized that there was also a difference. On the mountain Jesus had said, "Blessed are the poor *in spirit*," but on the plain He had simply stated, "Blessed are *you poor*."

This distinction deserved some thought. What was the relationship between poverty and poverty of spirit? It was evident that no one could truly possess the kingdom of God unless he were in some sense poor, but did that mean that literal poverty somehow furnished a better environment in which to cultivate spiritual poverty as well?

Then he thought of Jesus and their home in Nazareth. How superlative an example of spiritual meekness and submission to God his own brother had supplied, coming down from resplendent heavenly glory to live in a home like that and then to die for the sins of men. In Jesus, surely, material poverty and sublime poverty of spirit had been perfectly combined. Indeed, no one appreciated better than James the supernal truth that Paul was later to express, "For you know the grace of our Lord Jesus Christ, that though He was rich, yet for your sakes He became poor, that you through His poverty might become rich" (2 Cor 8:9). And thus impressed, James could not help but believe that the example of the Master had a voice for all His followers. True submission to God, true dedication to the wealth of the age to come, was like a rare and exquisite flower. It flourished best in the fertile soil of earthly poverty.

Not of course that the rich could never become "poor in spirit." But they found the becoming so extremely hard. To begin with, it was hard enough for a rich man even to *enter* the kingdom of God, much less to qualify to *possess* it. In fact, James had often heard the disciples tell of a sadly disappointing interview the Savior had had one day with a wealthy young inquirer. And on that occasion Jesus had affirmed emphatically, "How hard it is for those who have riches to enter into the kingdom of God!" (Mark 10:23). Of course at the time the disciples had been shocked by this. Like most of their fellow countrymen, they supposed that if a man was rich, God's blessing must truly rest upon him.

But Jesus answered their amazement with a further statement which they never forgot. "Children," He had said most gently, "how hard it is for *those who trust in riches* to enter into the kingdom of God! It is easier for a camel to go through the eye of a needle than for a rich man to enter into the kingdom of God" (Mark 10:24-25, emphasis added). Naturally that explained it. To gain entrance into the heavenly kingdom God insisted that men should trust, with childlike simplicity, in the gift He could give them through His Son. But the rich man trusted his riches. Whatever he needed he could buy, and it was hard for him to accept so priceless a gift and pay nothing in return. Like an overloaded camel, vainly seeking to slip through the tiniest of holes, the rich man was too big, too confident in the wealth with which he was laden, to pass easily through so restricted, yet so simple, an entrance way into life eternal.

Yet it could happen, of course, and Jesus had assured His disciples of that. "With men it is impossible," He had said, "but not with God; for with God all things are possible" (Mark 10:27). And just as no man could ever push a camel through a needle's eye, no more could human persuasion bring a self-confident rich man to trust in Christ, and Christ alone. But God could do it. And James now knew quite well that everywhere the gospel had been preached there were men of wealth—a few whose eyes God had opened to receive the gift of life. But obviously, if it was so hard for the well-to-do to gain entrance into the kingdom of God by so simple an act of faith, it was immeasurably harder for them by a whole life of faith to gain *possession* of that kingdom. Time and time again experience had shown how rarely the soil in a rich man's heart was truly fertile ground for the life-bestowing seed of the Savior's word. Usually that soil was filled with thorns, the jagged, tearing goads of care and wealth and worldly pleasure. Only seldom did the gospel seed bear full and abundant fruitage in the life of a man of wealth. It could happen—with God all things were possible—but it did not happen often.

Thus an impressive paradox emerged. James could not escape its truth. Clearly, in the very nature of the case, the roles of poverty and wealth tended to be reversed when this age was compared with the age to come. In this world the rich rarely accepted the gift of God, but when they did, their faith tended to remain shriveled and weak. Conversely, the poor, when *they* received that gift had little on earth in which they could put their trust, except in the Savior who had given them life.

Hence, the rich tended to be poor in faith and the poor tended to be rich in faith. And while the rich man was often hindered from a true discipleship by his preoccupation with the treasures of earth, the poor man could devote his whole life to storing away the treasures of heaven. No wonder that Jesus had told His followers on one occasion "Do not fear, little flock, for it is your Father's good pleasure to give you the kingdom. Sell what you have and give alms; provide yourselves money bags which do not grow old, a treasure in the heavens that does not fail, where no thief approaches nor moth destroys. For where your treasure is, there your heart will be also" (Luke 12:32-34).

How much better it would be to divest oneself completely of earthly goods, than to allow those goods to deprive one of so glorious a future possession. It was the Father's good pleasure to *give* the kingdom to those who sacrificially followed His Son. *That* was the priceless treasure men were to invest in for the age to come. And if for any given individual the faith required for this grew better in soil less richly endowed with earthly treasure, that was the soil in which such faith should be most carefully nurtured by him. If to become poor in spirit one needed to become poor, then clearly it was well worth doing. For the utterance of Jesus remained timelessly valid. "Blessed are *you* poor, for yours is the kingdom of God" (Luke 6:20).

Now James was a leader in the Christian church at Jerusalem. In the pastoral letter which he found it necessary to write to his beloved but frequently troubled Christian brothers, he had warned them sternly against playing favorites with the rich men who might come to their church (Jas 2:1-4). It was a real temptation, especially since the patronage of a rich man might stand them in good stead in a moment of crisis. But in the process it was easy to slight some poor man, to steer him to some inferior seat, and to treat him as though he amounted to very little or nothing at all. That, however, might prove to be a disastrous misjudgment, James was careful to point out. Despite the fact that the rich man they honored might be dressed in the most elegant of garments and be sporting on his finger a brilliant golden ring, while the poor man they slighted might be dirty and disheveled, the poor man might actually be the *richer* of the two. "Listen, my beloved brethren:" James penned with emphasis, "Has God not chosen the poor of this world to be rich in faith and heirs of the kingdom which He promised to those who love Him?" (Jas 2:5).

Yes, it was true and it was precisely what James had learned from the humble life and pointed teachings of the brother who was now his Lord. Rich men there might be who had heard and believed the gospel of God's Son, and one might expect them to appear from time to time at the meetings of a Christian church. But too often their faith was miserably small. Though they had accepted the gift of eternal life, beyond that they found it hard to trust God in any deep and consistent way.

Conversely, the poor man who came to faith in Christ seemed somehow to learn very quickly the many lessons of faith which trouble and deprivation could teach him. The rich man could fall back on his prestige and resources in time of testing, but the poor man had little to fall back on but God. Thus that priceless commodity of confidence in God which James's readers urgently needed in their variegated experiences of testing, was the very thing the poor man was very likely to have abundantly acquired, while the rich man remained stunted, a spiritual pauper in the midst of his material plenty.

In fact, it often seemed that the quantity of a man's faith was in inverse proportion to the quantity of his wealth. It was a serious mistake for James's readers to pass a superficial judgment on the basis of what a man wore. It was the poor man, despite his rags, who often was truly rich, "rich in faith."

But those who were "rich in faith" were also "heirs of the kingdom" which God had promised "to those who love Him." *Heirs* of the kingdom. That was something more than merely getting into it. That was to have a prospect of great wealth in that kingdom.

A person might enter the mansion of a rich man, he might survey all its splendid furnishings and appointments, he might even live in it if permitted to do so, but he would own nothing that was there. Unless he had a valid claim in accordance with the established laws of ownership or inheritance, he might personally be a man of poverty even while he dwelt surrounded by priceless abundance. The mansion was where he lived, but it was not truly his.

And so it would be in the kingdom of God. Entrance into that kingdom was assured to all whom the Father of lights had freely begotten with His word of truth. But to inherit that kingdom, to truly possess it, with all its honors and privileges, as one's own, one must become, right now, "rich in faith."

"Unless one is born again, he cannot see the kingdom of God" (John 3:3). Such were the words of Jesus, and since birth from above was a gift from the Father of lights, one could expect to see that kingdom and could expect to enter it on the grounds of God's gracious generosity alone. But *seeing* a thing and *owning* it were two different propositions. And while mere access to God's kingdom was an unspeakable privilege, fraught with wondrous eternal joys, there was incomparably more to be had than that. How splendid it must be to *possess* the kingdom could only be guessed from the fact that those who merely entered it could be thought of as "poor." Blessed poverty, no doubt.

But conversely, its opposite must be unimaginable wealth.

James's own mind was often staggered by that thought as he tried to penetrate the veil through which man can but dimly discern the glistening glories and unspeakable privileges of an eternal world. And even the merest glimpse of them sufficed to cast a pall of sordid cheapness over all that this age described as treasure.

How wondrous then must be the ultimate worth of the Savior's words, "for *yours* is the kingdom of God." How rich such an heirship must be. All of the measureless joys and blessings of Jesus' coming reign upon the earth, all these inherited by those who are poor in spirit and rich in faith. Could there ever be a more clarion call to true discipleship? Could there ever be a more compelling inducement to the pathway of self-denial and bearing the cross? James, at least, could not think of any.

For here was the shining goal that raised one's gratitude to a generous Savior to the level of utter devotion. His gift of life alone was more than enough to inspire a lifetime of loyalty in all who had received it. But to share His kingdom and glory and to be able to call that kingdom yours as well? That was more than mortal man could dare imagine were it not the Son of God Himself who promised it. But promise it He had, and James could not help but love Him for it.

And that was exactly the point. "Heirs of the kingdom which He promised *to those who love Him.*" Not to those who loved earthly wealth or earthly pleasure, but to those who loved *Him*. And again, the words of that mountain sermon were ringing in James's heart. "No one can serve two masters; for either he will hate the one and love the other, or else he will be loyal to the one and despise the other. You cannot serve God and mammon" (Matt 6:24). The choice must be made. No disciple could avoid it. Either the Lord Jesus would be loved, or the world would be loved, but one could not love them both. For those who had little in life to begin with it was easier to choose God and to grow rich in faith. For those who had much, this choice was harder and more rarely made. Thus God had truly chosen the poor of this world to be rich in faith, for He had granted them precisely those circumstances in life in which such faith could grow and flourish.

How thankful James was for the Nazareth home he had shared with the Savior. What a blessing to be poor in the life that is now if it led one to wealth in the life that was coming. It was rather late in life to perceive all this. Some of the original disciples of Jesus, men like Peter and John, had a long head-start along the pathway to eternal riches. But James had now fallen in step behind them. He wished that every Christian would do the same.

10

For the One Who Is Thirsty

Revelation 21:1-8; 22:16-17

Then He who sat on the throne said, "Behold, I make all things new." And He said to me, "Write, for these words are true and faithful." And He said to me, "It is done! I am the Alpha and the Omega, the Beginning and the End. I will give of the fountain of the water of life freely to him who thirsts. He who overcomes shall inherit all things, and I will be his God and he shall be My son. But the cowardly, unbelieving, abominable, murderers, sexually immoral, sorcerers, idolaters, and all liars shall have their part in the lake which burns with fire and brimstone, which is the second death" (Rev 21:5-8).

And the Spirit and the bride say, "Come!" And let him who hears say, "Come!" And let him who thirsts come. Whoever desires, let him take the water of life freely (Rev 22:17).

Peter and John did have a long head start on James. And while James had remained at home, not yet a believer in Jesus, Peter and John and the rest of the twelve disciples had followed the Master about as He sowed the quickening seed of the word of the gospel. And for all but Judas, who had never really received God's gift at all and whose discipleship was the merest pretense (John 6:64, 70-71), every step of the way made them just a little bit richer in the world to come.

But there were none of those twelve men who had traversed the pathway of a disciple longer than the Apostle John. In fact, he was one of the two earliest of Jesus' followers, Andrew, Simon Peter's brother, being the other (John 1:35-40). Thus John had been among the disciples who had traveled with Jesus to Sychar, just as he had been among those who sat before Him as He preached the Sermon on the Mount. Over the years of his companionship with his Lord, he had felt a growing closeness to his Master that was wonderful indeed.

When that fateful night had come and Jesus was eating His last supper with the disciples just before He died, it was John who had reclined right next to Him at the low table on which the Passover meal was spread. Propped up on his left elbow, with feet extending away from the table, John could easily lean his head back on the breast of Jesus who, in identical fashion, was reclining just behind him. And when, during the course of that meal, he had wanted to ask the Savior a question, this is exactly what John did (John 13:23-25).[7] His had been a place of privileged nearness at that memorable dinner.

Moreover, as James and the other brothers were to learn shortly after the crucifixion, John was the disciple to whom Jesus had committed the care of His mother (John 19:26-27). Not to His own brothers, still unbelieving, but to this devoted follower who had been with Him from the beginning. John the son of Zebedee had as intimate a relationship to his Master as anyone else on earth.

Special tasks had been reserved by the Savior for this intimate follower of His. To begin with, he was later to write an account of Jesus' work on earth that was markedly distinct from the other accounts which the Spirit of God inspired.

For one thing, the gospel of John, unlike those of Matthew, Mark, and Luke, stretches its narrative back into

---

[7] Editor's note: The famous picture of the last supper showing Jesus and His disciples siting in chairs is not historically accurate. Each man *reclined* on a sort of dining couch, called a *klinē*. John 13:23-25 shows this to be true. John 13:12 should read "He...*reclined* again," not "He sat again." They reclined as they ate.

the earliest portions of Jesus' activity as a teacher. And among those early segments of His ministry which John alone records, there is the report of the conversations at Sychar's well. The crucial revelations unfolded there about the living water of eternal life and about the supernatural food of the obedient disciple are to be found only on the pages of John's book. Nor could the reader of God's Word afford to be without them, for the remaining three gospels are like giant storerooms, whose abundant supplies of truth are unlocked only by the key that John provides. In short, the later teachings of Jesus, as recorded by Matthew, Mark, and Luke, are only genuinely comprehended if they are read in the light of what the Savior had clearly taught from the beginning. And these foundational teachings of Jesus became John's prerogative to unfold.

But if John's perspective stretched back to the *earliest* revelations which were made by God's Son, at a later time he was to record His *final* revelations as well. For so it happened that John also wrote the last book of the Bible. Accordingly, it might be said that John was granted the privilege of reporting the Alpha and Omega, the A and the Z, the beginning and the end of God's truth as He unveiled it in Jesus Christ, our Lord.

A disciple John had been from the very earliest period of the Savior's ministry, and that discipleship had now spanned more than three decades. Even as he writes the Bible's final book he knows what it means to take up his cross daily to follow Jesus. "I, John," he writes in the opening chapter of that book, "both your brother and companion in the tribulation and kingdom and patience of Jesus Christ, was on the island that is called Patmos for the word of God and for the testimony of Jesus Christ" (Rev 1:9). And so there he was, an exile, banished by Roman authority to a tiny spot of land in the Aegean Sea some thirty-five miles off the coast of Asia Minor. And for what crime? For nothing other than his fearless proclamation of the Word of God and for his ringing testimony to Jesus Christ.

But how could he have done anything else? For over thirty-five years, he had been eating the food of a disciple, the food he had once not known but now had grown to love. Into the harvest fields of God, he had been vigorously entering all this time, sowing the life-bearing seed of the word of truth, and reaping souls into God's barn. That had been the course of John's life for all these years, and it would be still to the very end, whatever might be the cost.

In following the Lord Jesus there was *tribulation* to experience, but there was also a *kingdom* to be possessed, and so there could be *endurance* in time of testing. He bore up under it all because he had so much to gain, so much to *inherit* in the world to come. Whatever the hostile forces of evil arrayed against him, he could *overcome* them through the strength of his Savior and Lord.

Now, at length, John is drawing his last book, God's last book, to its exhilarating conclusion. After a long series of startling visions has been recorded, visions disclosing events which are consummated by the establishment of the Savior's kingdom, John is permitted to glimpse the new, everlasting world that God will finally make:

> Now I saw a new heaven and a new earth, for the first heaven and the first earth had passed away. Also there was no more sea. Then I, John, saw the holy city, New Jerusalem, coming down out of heaven from God, prepared as a bride adorned for her husband. And I heard a loud voice from heaven saying, "Behold, the tabernacle of God is with men, and He will dwell with them, and they shall be His people. God Himself will be with them and be their God. And God will wipe away every tear from their eyes; there shall be no more death, nor sorrow, nor crying. There shall be no more pain, for the former things have passed away" (Rev 21:1-4).

It was a staggering vision. Heaven come down to earth. The God of heaven living among men. And all of the miseries that once marred the world—death and sorrow, tears and pain—were banished, and banished forever. It was almost too good to be true.

But it *was* true. And the next words John heard confirmed it. "Then He who sat on the throne said, 'Behold, I make all things new.' And He said to me, 'Write, for these words are true and faithful'" (Rev 21:5).

John had almost hesitated to record the vision he had seen, so splendid it was. But the divine voice said, "Write. You can depend on it. I *am* making everything new" (Rev 21:5 [paraphrased]). And that voice was the voice of Him who sat on the throne of the universe, whose workmanship the universe was to begin with. And, if He made it once, He could make it over again. In fact, that was the promise His words contained. He would make afresh what He had made before. And those words were "true and faithful."

"And He said to me, 'It is done! I am the Alpha and the Omega, the Beginning and the End'" (Rev 21:6a).

All of the letters of the Greek language, in which the Apostle John was writing, with all of their capacity to express reality, come between alpha and omega. And all of the events of history came between history's beginning and its ending. But *God* is the Alpha and the Omega, and He is the Beginning and the End. *He* stands, as it were, at the beginning of earth's temporal experience, and He stands also at its conclusion. It was He who had made the world, and it was He who would end it that He might make it anew. Thus He sovereignly overshadowed the events of all history, from their beginning to their end, that He might complete His own purposes therein, and all that might accurately be said in man's language about the significance of those events must be said in reference to Him, the Alpha and the Omega.

That too was why John need not hesitate to write the vision he had seen. The eternal One easily spanned all temporal experience, as He also spanned all temporal knowledge. Whatever might be known with certainty about the future could be traced directly to the perfect knowledge of the Alpha and Omega. Whatever guarantees there were that this future would come to pass could be traced to the perfect sovereignty of the Beginning and the End. In short, God, and God alone, could both reveal and guarantee man's destiny.

And every individual man has a destiny, and the voice John heard went on to describe it. "I will give of the fountain of the water of life freely to him who thirsts" (Rev 21:6b).

That was the first category of man whose future was determined, the *thirsty* man who drank at God's spring. John needed no explanation of the meaning of this, for he still remembered Sychar and Jacob's well. Living water was available at God's fountain, and John knew that the vibrant expression *water of life* was to be traced directly to the Savior's words to the Samaritan woman.

She had been among the thirsty that day—so thirsty, in fact, that she was utterly prepared to drink this water if she only knew where it could be found. "If you knew the gift of God, and who it is who says to you, 'Give Me a drink,' you would have asked Him, and He would have given you living water" (John 4:10). And she had satisfied her thirst on that occasion, satisfied it perfectly and forever, for in addition the Lord Jesus had also said, "Whoever drinks of the water that I shall give him will never thirst. But the water that I shall give him will become in him a fountain of water springing up into everlasting life" (John 4:14).

There had been no special conditions attached to that offer, no demands for the reformation of her twisted life, nothing in fact but the simple offer of a wondrous gift. And the offer John had just heard from the Alpha and Omega was the same now at the *end* of God's revelation in Jesus Christ as it had been at the very *beginning*. It was still a gift. "I will give of the fountain of the water of life *freely*[8] to him who thirsts."

But there was a second category of men whose destiny must be described. The voice from the throne went on to do so, as John recorded His words. "He who overcomes shall inherit all things" (Rev 21:7a).

Again, John needed no special instruction. As he had heard his Master offer the gift of life so freely, so he had heard Him offer an inheritance at great cost. Though eternal life was bestowed on any thirsty soul who wished it, the wealth of the future age belonged only to those who lived for God victoriously. To every believer who was born into the family of God there would surely come the storms of testing and the allurements of a gaudy, temporal world. And these the believer in Jesus was summoned to confront and to overcome.

For the call of the Savior was to a life of self-denial and self-sacrifice, in which troubles were endured for Him and the beguilements of this age refused. The one who wished to preserve his earthly life would lose it, while the one who gave it up for Jesus' sake would save it. The pathway of discipleship was the pathway of the cross, and in that pathway there must be self-surrender and poverty of spirit.

Unlike the gift of living water, appropriated once for all, such an experience was a continuing commitment entered into day by day. It was nothing less than a constant participation in the Master's own unrivaled food, to do the will of God and to finish His work.

Eternal life is *free*. Discipleship is immeasurably hard. The former is attained by faith alone; the latter by a faith that *works*. The former brings with it the righteousness of God so that a man is "justified freely by His grace" (Rom 3:24). The latter developed a personal righteousness, based

---

[8] The word translated *freely* in Rev 21:6 and 22:17 is *dōrean*, the normal Greek word for *gift* (cf. John 4:10; Eph 2:8 has the related noun *dōron*). In the accusative it functions as an adverb and means "being freely given, as a gift, without payment" (*BDAG*, 266C).

on good deeds, so that a man was also "justified by works" (Jas 2:24). The former confirmed the believer as God's workmanship; the latter fulfilled the wondrous purpose for which he had been created. The former cost man nothing; the latter could cost him everything, including life itself. Thus the former assured man his entrance into God's kingdom; but the latter assured him of *heirship* there.

"He who *overcomes* shall *inherit* all things." Such was the pronouncement from the throne. There could be no illusions in the matter. God would give living water to a thirsty soul without conditions. But He granted ownership of the world to come only to those who were victorious.

And how splendid was the prospect. New heavens, new earth. A brilliant, celestial city, descending from above, radiant with the exquisite beauty of a bride gorgeously adorned for her husband. Oh, to really *possess* these things. To enjoy them to the limitless fullness of their infinite potential. To be able to say, in that day, not merely, "I am here," but "These are *mine!*"

The price was high. Jesus had never been vague on *that* point. But it was more—unspeakably more—than worth it. In such an inheritance there was *real* worth, and no fleeting treasure on earth could for a moment be compared with it.

"He who overcomes shall inherit all things, and I shall be his God and he shall be My son" (Rev 21:7).

Heirship and sonship. The two concepts were inseparably intertwined, John knew. And the word for "son" which the voice from the throne now called upon the apostle to write, was a word he had never before used in this way. Before, in all of the inspired works that John had written— one Gospel, three letters, and now this book of prophecy— this word, son (*huios*), when used of relationship to God, had been reserved most strictly for the Lord Jesus Christ Himself. *He* was God's Son in a unique and special sense, and believers in Him were never so called in any utterance John had recorded up to now.[9]

Instead, when he wished to designate believers in Jesus as those who had been begotten by God and so possessed everlasting life, he had formerly always availed himself of another Greek word for *son*, a word which simply meant a "child." Thus in the language of John, up to this very moment, Jesus was God's *Son* and Christians were God's *children*. But in the world to come, the divine voice had now announced, the "heirs" would be treated as God's *sons*.

The thought was richly suggestive. John knew that in the temporal world around him a child could not obtain the inheritance that was his until he reached the age of civil responsibility as established by recognized custom and law. He might be *potentially* rich through all the years of his youth, but when the *child* became a full grown "son" his potential wealth could become *actual* wealth, and he could enter into legal possession of his inheritance. Thus the words of the Alpha and Omega, to which John listened, were fraught with meaning.

According to that special concept of things which it was granted to this particular apostle to write down, *sonship* belonged only to the overcomer. All who drank of the water of life John called "children." But the matured, well-rounded experience to which that relationship could lead belonged only to those who overcame. They were the heirs, because they were the full-grown *sons*.

True, John was aware that a beloved fellow apostle named Paul had been in the habit of calling *all* God's children both "heirs" and "sons." And of course John realized that they were, from one point of view. If one thought of salvation itself as an inheritance, freely given to all who believed in Christ, then Paul's conception was valid. But John had not been trained by the Master to think of things

---

[9] Editor's note: John 1:12 uses a different Greek word, *tekna*, which means *children*, not *sons*.

from that point of view. Paul had become a Christian after the Savior had left the earth to return for a time to the glory of heaven and after He had poured out the special gift of the Holy Spirit upon all who believed in Him. Paul had never known what it was to follow the Savior on earth, as John himself had known it. It was natural for Paul's perspective to be different.

God's truth was too large and too grand to be comprehended from only a single vantage point, and John long ago had recognized the enrichment Paul's doctrine had brought to the Christian church. Still, John was a product of the Savior's special training and, for him, heirship was confined to possessing the kingdom and universe over which Christ would reign.

Paul knew about that kind of heirship, too. And although he spoke of an heirship possessed by all believers into whose heart the Spirit of God had come, he spoke also of a *joint heirship* with Christ which is predicated on suffering (Rom 8:16-17). In fact, near the end of his own life so full of affliction for Christ, he could write, "If we endure, we shall also reign with Him. If we deny Him, He also will deny us. If we are faithless, He remains faithful; He cannot deny Himself" (2 Tim 2:12-13). The Apostle John might just as easily have written those words as Paul.

Reigning with Christ, Paul declared, depends on our enduring through suffering for Him. After all, the kingdom He shares with us is His because He Himself suffered to gain it. But the privilege of sharing that reign will be denied to us if we fail Him down here. If we turn from Him in shame in this age, He will turn from us in shame at the Bema. "For whoever is ashamed of Me and of My words," Jesus had said, "of him the Son of Man also will be ashamed when He comes in the glory of His Father with the holy angels" (Mark 8:38). To be *denied* in that day, to be refused recognition and honor, would be a painful experience indeed.

Yet, there was also a word of comfort. "If we are faithless," Paul had added, "He remains faithful; He cannot deny Himself" (2 Tim 2:13). Suppose indeed that instead of bearing up under our trials, our faith collapsed, as in fact it *did* collapse in those whose hearts were like stony ground. What then? Was that the end of our relationship to Him? Far from it. *We* might change; He could not. Whatever promises He had made to us, whatever gifts His grace had bestowed, to these He remained resolutely faithful. To do otherwise would be a denial of His own word, a denial of all that He was; indeed, *it* would be a denial of Himself. And, He could not deny Himself. No, there was no question of retracting the gift of eternal life He had so unconditionally bestowed. Such a thing was unthinkable. As Paul had elsewhere affirmed, "For the gifts and the calling of God are irrevocable" (Rom 11:29).

So Paul and John were in basic harmony, taught as they both were by the same Spirit of God. Yet John, who had been privileged to be so intimate with the earthly Jesus, had always up until this climactic moment reserved the concept of sonship to God for the Savior alone. Now, under the direction of that voice from the throne, he must widen it to include as well the "overcomers," the heirs of the future world. The implications of this were wonderful. To those who lived victoriously on earth, there would be granted as an integral part of their heirship a relationship to God similar in character to the relationship sustained with God by the Lord Jesus Christ Himself.

Even as he penned the words on the sheet before him, John recalled some earlier words his Master had given him to write which were now rich with meaning. "And he who overcomes," the risen Jesus had said to John, "and keeps My works until the end, to him I will give power over the nations—'*He shall rule them with a rod of iron; they shall be dashed to pieces like the potter's vessels*'—as I also have received from My Father" (Rev 2:26-27). And again, the exalted Savior had said, "To him who overcomes I will grant to sit with Me on My throne, *as I also overcame and sat down with My Father on His throne*" (Rev 3:21, emphasis added).

No, there was no mistaking it. The portion of the overcomer was like the portion of the Son of God Himself in relation to His heavenly Father. As the Father had given His victorious Son a throne and authority over mankind, so in a future day that throne and that authority would be shared with other victorious sons as well. *They* were the heirs of God's kingdom or, as Paul had put it, "joint heirs with Christ" (Rom 8:17).

Accordingly, they had fully realized the potential that was latent in taking that priceless drink of the water of life. By means of that drink they had become God's children forever, but they had not stopped there. Feeding on the food of discipleship, facing and overcoming their earthly ordeals of suffering and deprivation, they had grown to full-fledged sonship to the living God. They had entered an experience with Him that was modeled after the experience of Jesus Christ Himself.

Thus they had touched, in a very special way, the ultimate reality of all that God could be to men. Now, in a superlatively deep and meaningful sense, He was *God* to them. He was, of course, the God of all creation, nor could He cease to be at any time the God of every creature. But to the overcomer, He was *God* in a way He could not be to any other thing He had created. For now the overcomer shared the royal privileges of God's own unique, eternal Son. It was a wonderful word that had emanated from the throne. It had conveyed an unforgettable promise: "He who overcomes shall inherit all things, and I will be his God and he will be My son" (Rev 21:7).

The divine voice had previously spoken out the destiny of two classes of men. To those who were thirsty He offered the water of eternal life most freely. That was the gift of God. But to those who did more than drink it, to those who *also* overcame, He offered heirship and sonship in the world to come. And that was *not* a gift. It must be won amidst the struggles and hardships of a life devoted to the Lord Jesus and to doing the will of God. But what of those who belonged to neither of these classes? What of those who not only did not overcome, but did not even drink God's living water? How could *their* fate be appropriately described?

The voice continued. "But the cowardly, unbelieving, abominable, murderers, sexually immoral, sorcerers, idolaters, and all liars shall have their part in the lake which burns with fire and brimstone, which is the second death" (Rev 21:8).

It was an awful pronouncement. For this was hell, the tragic, eternal abode of all who had no true thirst for the living God. Having spurned or neglected the fountain of the water of life, they will find themselves one day in a fiery lake of death. All chance of quenching any kind of thirst at all would then be gone forever. Even the sinful deeds and desires that eternally stamped the character of those who were there could no longer find any kind of realization in a habitat where suffering alone remained. There was no water in *that* lake. Only the fires of God's righteous judgment, and an endless existence so worthless and empty that it did not merit even the *name* of life.

And hence, it must be called "the second death" (Rev 21:8). In the temporal world, John knew, man was always faced with the twin realities of life and death. So it would be also in the eternal world. Life there would be for those who had wisely appropriated it ahead of time; death for those who had not. The former was an endless experience in the presence of a living God. The latter was an endless experience outside of His presence, an existence that had lost all meaning. The former guaranteed man's eternal well-being and, if he overcame, eternal privilege. The latter offered only eternal anguish.

Clearly the fountain of life and the lake of death were the unmistakable alternatives of human destiny. The man who drank of the fountain acquired an inwardly flowing stream which, Jesus had promised, would never cease to gush forth its renewing waters. The man who entered the lake of death entered an abode of dreadful stagnation. It was the ultimate stanching of every vital spring which makes human existence worthwhile. It was the final termination of all usefulness, of all joy, and of all hope. It was hell. And it was also a *second* death.

The roster of those who would find their "part" there, however, included none who were not fully worthy of a destiny so dreadful. And strikingly, John noted, that roster began with "the cowardly" (Rev 21:8). How many there were, John knew from experience, whose hearts and minds cringed with dread from the terrible unknown that lay just beyond the grave. The thought of death and the gloomy mist that shrouded the world to come were torments which they did their best to evade and to forget. The wonderful message of life,[10] the striking revelation of God's love displayed in the death of His Son for sinful men—these were realities that could not penetrate such faltering hearts.

Their blind, unreasoning fear had driven them *away* from God instead of *to* Him. They had submerged themselves in an obviously temporal world, dreading the day of their death but never preparing for it, till at last they found themselves forever in a lake of fire. Who could say they were not worthy of their fate? God's Son had come and had offered them life, and instead of rejoicing in His love and accepting His gift, they simply cowered.

But next on the solemn roll of hell's inhabitants were the "unbelieving." Obviously these were the spiritual brothers of those who were "cowardly." Indeed, the cowardly had been unbelieving, but there was also an unbelief that was separate from cowardice. And whether it arose from a stubborn skepticism that was capable of questioning truth however impressively attested, or from a pride of intellect and

---

[10] Editor's note: Zane loved to emphasize the free gift of everlasting life that can never be lost.

learning which found God's grace too simple or too foolish to accept, or whether it arose from any source, its end was still the same. The unbelieving, as well as the cowardly, had their portion forever in the lake of fire.

So also did the "abominable." It was right that they should be mentioned next. For the cowardice and unbelief which drove man from God, and drove him from God's salvation, were like poisonous roots from which every degrading and disgusting thing in human life could grow. In fact, if a man's character could with any truth be called abominable, it was certain that he in some way lacked confidence and faith in God. A repulsive life was always the misshapen sculpture of a cowardly or unbelieving heart.

The rest of the list was in essence a commentary on the forms which the abominable life may take. Hell will be peopled by those who destroy the lives of others, "murderers"; it will be populated by those who distort the physical drive by which human life is reproduced, "sexually immoral"; it will be inhabited by those who probe beyond life's proper boundaries to seek contact with the unseen powers of evil, "sorcerers"; it will be dwelt in by those who misrepresent the author of life or put some human substitute in the place which belongs alone to Him, "idolaters"; and, in particular, it will be the home of all who distort reality, "all liars."

John knew, even as he transcribed this list, that the voice from the throne was describing to him the character of men as it was finally and unalterably fixed by their rejection of the gift of life. It was true enough that all of the evils that the list contained had been found somewhere, sometime among those who would ultimately enter the kingdom of God, even among those who would ultimately inherit that kingdom. But *their* basic character was not determined by their sin. It was determined rather by the grace of God.

> Do you not know that the unrighteous
> will not inherit the kingdom of God? Do
> not be deceived. Neither fornicators, nor

> idolaters, nor adulterers, nor homosexuals, nor sodomites, nor thieves, nor covetous, nor drunkards, nor revilers, nor extortioners will inherit the kingdom of God. And such were some of you. But you were washed, but you were sanctified, but you were justified in the name of the Lord Jesus and by the Spirit of our God (1 Cor 6:9-11).

The Apostle's meaning was clear. Terms like these could no longer be truly and fully applied to his Christian readers. But it was not that they did not *deserve* to have them applied, even then. Paul knew quite well that the believers to whom he wrote were full of unattractive qualities. There was even a case of incest in the church, for which he had indignantly reproved them (1 Cor 5:1-2). And immediately before penning his catalog of the unrighteous who could not inherit God's kingdom, Paul had charged these believers themselves with unrighteous behavior of their own. He wrote, "No, you yourselves do wrong and cheat, and you do these things to your brethren!" (1 Cor 6:8). Yet in his next breath he could say, "But you were washed, but you were sanctified, but you were justified in the name of the Lord Jesus and by the Spirit of our God" (1 Cor 6:11).

How rich and unfailing was the Apostle's concept of the gift of God! His readers had been "justified freely" by God's grace, and were the privileged possessors of "the righteousness of God" which was "to all and on all who believe" (Rom 3:21-22). Nothing could change that fact, however miserable their failures might be. And it was Paul's manner to challenge his Christian converts, not by dangling them over a hell from which God's grace had saved them, but by an appeal to live in accordance with what they now were through that grace.

So he very soon warns them of the terrible snare of fornication, and he does *not* threaten them with everlasting damnation, but pointedly asks, "Do you not know that your bodies are members of Christ? Shall I then take the members of Christ and make them members of a harlot? Certainly not!" (1 Cor 6:15). And a few sentences on, he says, "Or do you not know that your body is the temple of the Holy Spirit who is in you, whom you have from God, and you are not your own? For you were bought at a price; therefore glorify God in your body and in your spirit, which are God's" (1 Cor 6:19-20).

No higher or more effective appeal could be found. Psychologically a man behaves according to the self-image he seeks to maintain.[11] And in the mirror of the word of truth the believer in Jesus sees the face he was born with (Jas 1:23). He sees in God's Word the outline and reflection of that new personality which is now his as one begotten by the Father of lights. He is God's workmanship, a kind of firstfruits of His creatures, and in accordance with that basic reality alone will he find adequate motivation to live a holy life.

Paul knew this and calls upon his fellow Christians constantly to "walk worthy of the calling" with which they had been called by God's grace (Eph 4:1; see also Col 1:10; 1 Thess 2:12). Would they see fornication in its true light? Let them see it as a thing utterly detestable to one whose body has become the temple of a living God.

And would they know how inappropriate unrighteous behavior was for them now that they were justified in the name of the Lord Jesus? Let them be reminded that those who could properly be called sexually immoral or idolaters or similar things were utterly excluded from an inheritance in God's kingdom. The unbeliever's "part" (inheritance) was in a lake that burned with fire and brimstone; not with those who were washed and sanctified by the Spirit of our God. Inheritance in God's kingdom was a vital, vibrant hope for them. And so, Paul implies, let them live as those who

---

[11] Editor's note: Zane felt that the Scriptures taught that we should see ourselves as holy in our inner selves. He rejected the notion that we should view ourselves as worms. Our eternal selves do not sin (1 John 3:9) and will not sin (1 John 3:2).

wish to acquire that inheritance, not as those who have no hope of it.

Yes, John realized, the catalog of the citizens of hell was a catalog of those unwashed, unsanctified, unjustified by the bountiful gift of God. God saw a man in either one of two ways. Either He saw him as His own workmanship, a kind of first fruits of His creatures, a possessor of righteousness freely given by His grace, or He saw him as cowardly or unbelieving or abominable or whatever else a sinful life had made him. Those who accepted God's gift and thus were His workmanship could inherit the future kingdom. But those who had never accepted that gift could inherit nothing but a lake of fire. "But the cowardly, unbelieving, abominable, murderers, sexually immoral, sorcerers, idolaters, and all liars shall have their part in the lake which burns with fire and brimstone, which is the second death" (Rev 21:8).

If such was the grim reality confronted by those who died in their sins, never having tasted the water of life, it was inevitable that the final book of God's Word should sound one last call to men to partake of that water. And it was fitting that John, who had recorded the initial appeal at Sychar's well, should be chosen to pen this one also. To him, it seemed, belonged the writing of the alpha and the omega, the beginning and the end, of the Savior's offer of living water. John had just reached his last sheet of parchment, and now the voice he heard speaking to him was explicitly that of the same person who had leaned wearily on Jacob's well so many years ago. Its tones and inflections were the same. (John knew them well.) But they now possessed a resonance which they had lacked that day from a tired and thirsty Savior.

He had been a real man down here on earth, just as He was a real man up there in heaven, though partaking now of the vitality of a resurrected life. The Risen One was speaking. "I, Jesus, have sent My angel to testify to you these things in the churches. I am the Root and the Offspring of David, the Bright and Morning Star" (Rev

22:16). He is both the root of David (i.e., David sprang from Him), because He was David's Maker, and also David's offspring (i.e., David was His forefather). In fact, years ago on the occasion of the announcement of His coming birth, the angel of God had said to Mary, "He will be great, and will be called the Son of the Highest; and the Lord God will give Him the throne of His father David. And He will reign over the house of Jacob forever, and of His kingdom there will be no end" (Luke 1:32-33). So this was His destiny as the Offspring of David, and it was this that made Him mankind's greatest hope.

In a world swathed in the darkness of sin and in ignorance of its Maker, He is the Bright and Morning Star, the herald of a new day and a new world, when earth's darkest hours would be relieved at last by His coming and His kingdom. But in the meanwhile there was a message to get out.

The voice of Jesus continued. "And the Spirit and the bride say, 'Come!' And let him who hears say, 'Come!' And let him who thirsts come. Whoever desires, let him take the water of life freely" (Rev 22:17).

John felt a slight lump in his throat as he wrote those words. The years had not dimmed at all his profound appreciation of God's gift, and in his mind's eye he could still see his Master talking with the Samaritan woman as he and his fellow disciples returned with their purchases from Sychar. How shocked they had been at that sight. But it wasn't long before they had realized, through the Savior's skillful instruction about spiritual food, that He had been saying "Come!" to that woman and that He wanted His disciples to say it too. He wanted them to say "Come!" to everyone He sent them to and to broadcast far and wide the availability of His living water. That was the message of God's Holy Spirit. That would be the message of the whole Christian church, Christ's bride (Eph 5:25-32).

And that *should* be the message of anyone at all who heard it. It was a glorious communication. Only the dull of heart could fail to pass it on. And no one could be *that* dull of heart and be a true disciple at the same time.

To say "Come!" to a needy world of men was the disciples' surpassing responsibility. And to say it consistently and faithfully through life often involved toil and sacrifice and suffering. But it was also an unspeakable privilege, a thrilling and invigorating experience, like the eating of some celestial food. And it *was* celestial food. The Lord of glory Himself had eaten it while here on earth, and those who hungered to know more of Him and to possess the eternal world over which He would someday reign, could eat it too. *He* had said "Come!" to them; *they* could say "Come!" to others.

But though discipleship, as taught by the Lord Jesus, was invariably associated with this kind of obedience to God's will and with finishing this kind of work for Him, the water of life was invariably associated with God's unconditional generosity. The poor woman who stood before the Savior and the well that day, so unworthy she might seem even to hear His offer, was precisely the type of person who best exemplified what the grace of God really is. Had her life been in the least degree a worthy one, the lesson might not have been so clear. Moreover, had she been asked to make it worthy, the lesson would not have been clear either. For the lesson involved a gift. And with a gift, there can be no bargaining, only giving and receiving.

And just now, as a resurrected Jesus spoke for the last time of living water, there was no trace of a bargain. "And let him who thirsts come. Whoever desires, let him take the water of life freely." No special, meritorious qualifications were laid down, no binding commitments for the future. Who could take this water? The one who was thirsty. But was even *that* too strong? Well then, simply the one who *wants* to. "Whoever desires, let him take."

Salvation could not be made simpler. Nor clearer. Eternal life is for the taking. And the only ones left out are those who do not want it. It is the perfect bestowal, fulfilling man's highest conception of what a gift should be—totally, unspeakably, utterly *free*.

"If you knew the gift of God, and who it is who says to you, 'Give me a drink,' you would have asked Him, and He would have given you living water" (John 4:10). And she *had* asked Him and He *had* given her that thirst-quenching water.

But then the hunger began. The hunger to go back into that little village and to say to its men, "Come, see a man who told me all things that I ever did. Could this be the Christ?" (John 4:29).

But it was all perfectly natural. Her thirst had led her to eternal life, and her hunger would lead her to eternal heirship. That is the appropriate experience for everyone who believes the Lord Jesus. For after all, the thirsty live, but the hungry inherit.[12]

---

[12] Editor's note: What a beautiful ending. The thirsty live, but the hungry inherit. In one concise sentence Zane expresses the distinction between justification and sanctification.

The Gospel Under Siege

Prologue

Last night Jimmy believed in the Lord Jesus Christ for everlasting life. This morning he is bubbling with a joy he has never experienced before.

On his way to work he meets his friend Bill. Bill has always claimed to be a Christian. He also reads a lot of books on theology. But Jimmy has never been too interested in theology up until now.

"Say, Bill," Jimmy begins, "guess what. I got saved last night! I trusted Christ as my Savior. Now I know I am going to heaven!"

"Hmmm," Bill replies, "maybe you shouldn't quite say it that way. After all, you don't really *know* that you are going to heaven."

"What do you mean?" Jimmy enquires. "The Bible says, 'Believe on the Lord Jesus Christ, and you will be saved,' and that's what I did."

Bill gives Jimmy a wise and knowing look. It is the kind of look all perceptive theologians know how to give the ignorant and the unlearned.

"But did you *really* believe? Maybe you just believed psychologically."

"What do you mean?" Jimmy is feeling a little depressed now.

"I mean," Bill continues sagely, "you can't know yet whether you have *real* saving faith."

"How can I know that?"

"By your works. You'll have to wait and see if you live a real Christian life."

Jimmy is dejected. "You mean that if I sin, I'm not a Christian after all?"

"No, I don't mean that," Bill assures him. "All Christians fail once in a while."

"But how much do they fail? I mean, how bad does it have to get before I find out I'm not saved?"

"Well, it can't get too bad for too long."

"But how bad? For how long?" Jimmy feels desperate.

"I can't tell you exactly. But a true Christian doesn't practice sin. If you find that you are practicing sin, that will show that you didn't have real saving faith to begin with."

"What if I do pretty good for several years and then things start going bad?"

"In that case, maybe you weren't saved to start with."

"Maybe? What do you mean by that?"

"I mean," Bill's tone is solemn, "you'll probably have to wait until the end of your life before you can be sure you are a true Christian. You have to persevere in good works, or your faith wasn't real."

"Do you think I can be sure before I die?"

"Maybe. Listen, Jim, I've got to rush to work. We'll talk about this some other time. Okay?"

"Yeah, okay. See you, Bill"

Bill rushes off. Jimmy is devastated. All the joy he had experienced since last night has suddenly evaporated. He is now filled with questions and doubts.

Jimmy has become a casualty in the siege of the gospel.

1
The Gospel Under Siege

> "Unless you are circumcised according to the custom of Moses, you cannot be saved" (Acts 15:1).

With such words the gospel came under siege during the earliest days of the Christian Church. The claim made by these words created the first theological crisis in the history of Christianity. Nothing less than the unity of the faith was at stake. That unity was preserved only when the Jerusalem Council formally rejected this erroneous doctrine (Acts 15:24).

But the attack has been launched again and again down through the centuries and in no age more often than in our own. The specifics may vary widely, but the attack remains fundamentally the same:

"Unless you are baptized according to the Biblical command, you cannot be saved."

"Unless you persevere in good works, you cannot be saved."

"Unless you yield your life to the Lordship of Christ, you cannot be saved."[1]

But against all such claims, whatever their form or character, the true saving Gospel stands in profound and majestic contrast: "And whoever desires, let him take the water of life freely" (Rev 22:17b).

---

[1] John H. Gerstner, *Wrongly Dividing the Word of Truth: A Critique of Dispensationalism* (Brentwood, TN: Wolgemuth and Hyatt, 1991), 225-26, and 257.

The Claims of the Judaizers

There is no reason to doubt that the Judaizers of Acts 15 claimed to be Christians. They could not have gotten a hearing in the church at Antioch if they had not made this claim. In fact, they probably presented themselves as representatives of the Jerusalem church. The words of the Jerusalem Council, "to whom we gave no such commandment" (Acts 15:24), suggest that the false teachers appealed to the authority of Jerusalem for what they taught.

Naturally this means that they admitted the necessity of faith in Christ. But they insisted on more than that. They claimed that salvation also required submission to the Mosaic law. Circumcision was just the first step in that submission (see Gal 5:3). So the debate at the Council correctly focused on the issue of obedience to the entire law (Acts 15:5; see 15:24).

In the same way, most modern assaults on the gospel do not deny the importance of faith in Christ. On the contrary, they insist on it. But to faith are added other conditions, or provisos, by which the basic nature of the gospel is radically changed.

Often, a distinction is drawn between the kind of faith which saves and the kind which does not save. But the kind of faith which *does* save is said to be the kind that results in some form of outward obedience. But this means a willingness to obey becomes at least an implied part of conversion to Christ. "Saving" faith has thus been subtly redefined in terms of its fruits.[2] In the process, the unconditional freeness of the gospel offer is seriously, if not fatally, compromised.

The Sincerity of the Judaizers

Nowhere in Acts 15 is the sincerity of the Judaizers called into question. No doubt they were genuinely

---

[2] Gerstner, *Wrongly Dividing*, 210. See Appendix 1.

convinced of the truth of their doctrine. In all probability they had grown up in the Jewish faith. They knew that the Mosaic Law was ordained by God. It was easy for them to draw the conclusion that there could be no salvation apart from obedience to that law. But despite all this, they were still tragically wrong.

When the Council wrote that "some who went out from us have troubled you with words, unsettling your souls" (Acts 15:24), they were not necessarily condemning the motives of the Judaizers. But they *were* describing the effects of their doctrine. The believers at Antioch had been troubled by the words these men had spoken, so that their spiritual experience had been "unsettled."

Sincerity is no substitute for truth. It is the truth of God alone that can establish people's souls and give them a genuine stability in holiness. "For it is good," wrote the author of Hebrews, "that the heart be established by grace" (Heb 13:9). And it is truly the grace of God itself, in all its splendid freeness that can establish the hearts of God's people.

The Judaizers probably thought otherwise. Like countless others who have followed them in the Church, they may have feared that to preach a free salvation would lead to lawlessness and sin. To prevent this outcome, insistence on the law seemed to be a moral necessity. But Paul and Barnabas did not agree. And the apostles and elders at Jerusalem sided with them. Peter himself declared: "But we believe that through the grace of the Lord Jesus Christ we have been saved in the same manner as they [the Gentiles]" (Acts 15:11, [trans. from Greek]).

Here lies one of the great truths of the Christian faith. The law could not guarantee life to men (Gal 3:21). It was fundamentally a ministry of condemnation and guilt (Rom 3:19-20; 2 Cor 3:6-9). Only the grace of God in Christ can bring eternal life.

But although the New Testament pronounces the law a failure in producing true holiness (see Rom 8:3-4), people continue to feel that the law's basic principle is the only workable one. From a human perspective, man will not live as God desires him to live unless he is threatened with uncertainty about his eternal destiny.

As popular as this notion is, however, it is false. It reflects a weak view of the power of God's truth to create a new creature at the moment of saving faith. It also underestimates God's capacity to transform the saved individual into the likeness of Christ. It hopelessly misjudges the comparative power of fear and gratitude as motivations for right conduct. And beyond all this, it fails to take into account the powerful inspiration of goals that are centered in eternity itself. That is, it neglects the doctrine of rewards.[3]

The Judaizers and Satan

None of these errors happen by accident. True, they are natural to the soil of the human heart. But their growth is encouraged by the Enemy of souls. Paul understood, as few men have, that blindness to the gospel is fundamentally satanic at its core. He wrote:

> But even if our gospel is veiled, it is veiled to those who are perishing, whose minds the god of this age has blinded, who do not believe, lest the light of the gospel of the glory of Christ, who is the image of God, should shine on them (2 Cor 4:3-4).

There is no mention of Satan in Acts 15. But who can doubt that the Judaizers were serving his interests and aims? Not consciously or wittingly, perhaps, but serving them nonetheless. For if the Devil wishes to blind the unregenerate world to the gospel, could there be a better

---

[3] The sequel and companion volume to *The Gospel Under Siege* is my book *Grace in Eclipse: A Study on Eternal Rewards*, 2nd ed. (Dallas: Redencion Viva, 1987). For an excellent treatment of the role of rewards in Christian motivation, see Charles Stanley, *Eternal Security: Can You Be Sure?* (Nashville: Oliver Nelson, 1990), 106-130.

stratagem than to confuse the Church about its terms? If those who preach the gospel are unclear, or even mistaken, about it, how shall they lead unsaved people to a knowledge of the truth?

The siege of the gospel is not fundamentally a work of man, but a work of man's Adversary. For this purpose Satan can employ his own agents or he can employ well-intentioned, but misguided, Christians. The effect of the siege, wherever real inroads are made, is to dilute the Church's concept of the grace of God, to diminish her power in proclaiming the truth, and to hinder her growth toward real spiritual maturity. It is no accident that Peter wrote: "But grow in the *grace* and knowledge of our Lord and Savior Jesus Christ" (2 Pet 3:18a; emphasis added).

So it is not surprising that the Apostle Paul is never more vigorous than when he is defending the purity of the gospel. In writing to the Galatian Christians, to whom Judaizers also had come, he is completely uncompromising:

> But even if we, or an angel from heaven,
> preach any other gospel to you than what we
> have preached to you, let him be accursed
> (Gal 1:8).

The language is sharp, but it is a measure of Paul's jealousy on behalf of the true grace of God. He knew he was wrestling with supernatural principalities and powers, and not simply with men (Eph 6:12).

Conclusion: The Judaizers and Scripture

Of course, the Judaizers must have appealed to the Scriptures. The authority of the Mosaic Law rested in the written revelation of the Old Testament. But this appeal was misguided. It misunderstood the Old Testament itself as well as the new revelation which had been made through God's Son.

In a similar fashion, modern attacks on the freeness of the Gospel also appeal to Scripture. But these appeals constantly rest on a misunderstanding of the passages in question. There is also often a failure to face the plain meaning of the most direct statements about the way of salvation. The confusion that results is enormous; the consequences are calamitous.

In the pages that follow, attention will be focused first of all upon the absolute simplicity of the offer of eternal life. This offer furnishes the only grounds for real assurance of personal salvation.

Next, consideration will be given to some of the major texts that are thought to teach the necessity for, or the inevitability of, perseverance in good works. In the process, the inconsistency of these views with the real terms of the Gospel will be faced.

Additionally, along the way, some of the true motivations for godly Christian living will be underscored from the teaching of the New Testament.

No study of this sort could accomplish its goals without the ministry of the Holy Spirit in both writer and readers alike. The author prayerfully desires precisely this ministry to the glory of the Lord Jesus Christ.

2

John's Gospel:
Can I Really Be Sure?

Few questions are more fundamental than this one: Can I really be sure of my eternal salvation? Can I know that I belong to Christ and belong to Him forever?

If perseverance in good works is really a condition, or a necessary result, of salvation, the answer to this question must be "no." At least it must be "no" until the hour of one's death. For only then will it be seen (if it can even be seen then) whether the degree to which I have persevered is adequate to justify the conviction that I am saved.

It does not matter how the insistence on perseverance is expressed. The result is the same. If continuing good works are a co-condition with faith, then they are clearly indispensable to assurance. Even if they are only the inevitable outcome of true saving faith, they still become indispensable to assurance. That is, only the presence of good works in one's life can verify the genuineness of one's faith.

Consequently, when the Gospel is so presented that the necessity for ongoing good works is stressed, it becomes a gospel that can no longer offer true assurance of eternal life. The individual who professes faith in Christ cannot possess, at the moment of faith, a certainty about his eternal destiny. Under some forms of theology, he cannot even be sure he has really believed. But this result is nothing less than a denial of a fundamental aspect of the Biblical Gospel.

Sometimes this tragic loss of assurance is concealed by the statement, "I *believe* I am a child of God." But this trades on an ambiguity in the English word "believe." The statement may mean, "I am *truly convinced* that I am a child of God." But it may also mean, "I *think* I am a child of God." A person who only considers it *probable* that he is a true Christian does not understand the New Testament offer of eternal life.

Assurance: Part of God's Offer

A careful consideration of the offer of salvation, as Jesus Himself presented it, will show that assurance is part of that offer.

One forceful example of this is John 5:24:

> "Most assuredly, I say to you, he who hears My word and believes in Him who sent Me has everlasting life, and shall not come into judgment, but has passed from death into life."

Anyone who takes this statement at face value should be able to say, "I *know* I have everlasting life. I *know* I will not come into judgment."

But if assurance arises from a simple promise like this, it has nothing to do with works. To begin with, the statement of Jesus does not call for works. It calls only for faith. Moreover, the guarantee which He makes is relevant to the very moment of faith. "He who hears…believes…has…" On the authority of Jesus, the believer can know he has eternal life at the very moment he believes God for it.

The importance of this cannot be stressed too much. Assurance does not await the day of our death. It does not await the day when we stand before God in judgment. For in John 5:24 it is declared that, for the believer, there is *no* judgment. That is, there is no final assessment by which *his eternal destiny* hangs in balance. Already he has passed out of the sphere of spiritual death and into the realm of spiritual life.

It is precisely such a verse that confronts those who insist on works with an insoluble problem. If works are a co-condition with faith for eternal life, the Lord's failure to say so cannot be explained. But if works are a necessary outcome of saving faith, the problem is equally great. For in that case, one of two propositions must be true: (1) the believer also knows at the moment of faith that he will persevere in good works, or (2) the believer does not know whether he has in fact truly believed.

Neither proposition can be defended successfully.

(1) Does A Believer Know in Advance He Will Persevere?

Not many would wish to maintain the first proposition. Although some believe the Bible teaches that a true Christian will persevere in good works, few believe that when a man trusts Christ he can know in advance that he will persevere in these works. The countless warnings of the New Testament against failures of every kind ought to be sufficient to show that such a guarantee is not Biblical. When Paul wrote to the Christians at Rome, he used these words:

> For if you live according to the flesh you will die; but if by the Spirit you put to death the deeds of the body, you will live (Rom 8:13).

In the original Greek, the form of the conditional statements in both parts of the verse is exactly the same. The level of probability is the same for both. That two possibilities are placed before the readers is as clear as words can make this.

In reference to himself as well, Paul recognized the possibility of tragic failure. In 1 Cor 9:27 he wrote:

> But I discipline my body and bring it into subjection, lest, when I have preached to others, I myself should become disqualified.

In the face of a verse like this, it is impossible to maintain that Paul possessed a certainty about even his own spiritual victory. Obviously, this great servant of Christ took the spiritual dangers he faced as grim realities. He was motivated by these dangers to take care that he did not run a losing race.

In neither of the passages just mentioned is there any reason to find a threat to the believer's eternal security. A Christian who lives after the flesh is certainly in danger of death, but he is not in danger of hell. And to be disqualified in the Christian race, about which Paul is speaking in 1 Cor 9:24-27, is not the same as losing eternal life.

More will be said about such matters in subsequent chapters. For now it is sufficient to note that an unqualified certainty about victory in Christian experience does not exist. The New Testament cannot correctly be said to offer a certainty like this.

(2) Does A Believer Not Know Whether He Believes?

It is not surprising that most of those who hold that works must verify faith adopt the second alternative. This is not always done explicitly, but it remains the only other option.

If a believer cannot be certain at the time of conversion that he will live effectively for Christ, on the premise that he *will* do so *if* he is saved, it follows that he cannot know at the time of conversion that he is truly saved. And since eternal life is offered by faith alone, then it also follows that he cannot know whether he has truly believed.

This view of things involves a psychological absurdity. At the level of everyday experience, if a man is asked whether he believes a certain fact or trusts a certain person, he can always give a definite answer. Even an answer like, "I'm not sure I trust that man," reflects a definite psychological state. What it reflects is an attitude of *dis*trust toward the individual in question.

On the other hand, when someone says, "I trust that person," he is expressing a state of mind of which he himself is thoroughly aware.

To claim that a man may trust Christ without knowing whether or not he has trusted Christ, is to articulate an absurd idea. *Of course* a man can know whether or not he believes in the offer of salvation.

The Bible everywhere takes this fact for granted. When the Philippian jailor enquired of Paul and Silas, "Sirs, what must I do to be saved?" (Acts 16:30b), their answer clearly offered him certainty. The words, "'Believe on the Lord Jesus Christ, and you will be saved, you and your household'" (Acts 16:31), invite a specific, identifiable response. Having made it, the jailer could know he was saved. That he *did* know this is clear from verse 34: "And he rejoiced, having believed in God with all his household."

The seriousness of this issue must not be passed over. An insistence on the necessity or inevitability of perseverance in good works undermines assurance and postpones it, logically, until death. But this denial of assurance clashes directly with the clear intent of the Gospel proclamation. It flies in the face of the offer of eternal life made by the Son of God Himself.

Jesus and the Offer of Life

The lovely story of Jesus and the woman at the well of Sychar is a case in point. His opening words to her were simple and direct:

> "If you knew the gift of God, and who it is
> who says to you, 'Give Me a drink,' you would
> have asked Him, and He would have given
> you living water" (John 4:10).

This is perfectly plain. If the woman had asked, Jesus *"would have given"* her *"living water."* Obviously, she could have certainty about the result of this transaction.

It should be observed that the transaction of which our Lord speaks is a definitive and unrepeatable one. A few moments later He tells the woman:

> "Whoever drinks of this water [from the well] will thirst again, but whoever drinks of the water that I shall give him will never thirst" (John 4:13-14).

The Greek phrase translated as "will never thirst" is a highly emphatic one. It might be translated, "will by no means thirst forever."

According to Jesus, this water meets a need which can never return. This fact clearly shows the eternal security of the believer. For if a person could lose eternal life, he would obviously thirst again, but according to the Savior's words, that experience is an eternal impossibility.

It is hard not to be impressed with the magnificent simplicity of the offer Jesus makes to this sinful Samaritan woman. Its very lack of complication is part of its grandeur. It is all a matter of giving and receiving and no other conditions are attached.[4] In fact, the Greek tenses in John 4:10 would permit the following interpretation of the NKJV rendering:

> "If you [now] knew the gift of God, and who it is who says to you, 'Give Me a drink', you would [already] have asked Him, and He would [already] have given you living water."

This understanding clarifies the conclusion of the story. As I have pointed out in *Absolutely Free!* the "water of life" is the life-begetting truth that "Jesus is the Christ." The Samaritan woman asked Jesus for this (v 25) and He gave it to her (v 26). Her statement in verse 25 is clearly a functional question which implies: "Are you perhaps the Messiah?" When Jesus replied that He was, her reception of this great truth in faith, that is, her persuasion that it was true, brought salvation. Once she knew this truth by

---

[4] Zane Hodges, *Absolutely Free! A Biblical Reply to Lordship Salvation* (Dallas: Redencion Viva, 1989), 41-42.

faith (see John 20:31; 1 John 5:1), the asking and giving had already occurred.

The story is an illustration in narrative form of the truth expressed in Rev 22:17b, "Whoever desires, let him take the water of life freely." There is no effort to extract from the woman a promise to correct her immoral life. If she wants this water, she can have it. It is *free*.

If the mind of man draws back from so daring an expression of divine generosity, it draws back from the gospel itself. If it should be thought necessary to add some built-in guarantee that the woman would not continue her sexual misconduct—and, according to Jesus, she was currently engaged in adultery (John 4:18)—that guarantee would be a false addition to the words of our Lord Himself. The result could only be a false gospel.

It must be emphasized that there is no call here for surrender, submission, acknowledgement of Christ's Lordship, or anything else of this kind. A gift is being offered to one totally unworthy of God's favor. And to get it, the woman is required to make no commitment for the future whatsoever. The water of life is free. It is precisely this impressive fact that distinguishes the true gospel from all its counterfeits.

Did the woman therefore simply return to her former sinful lifestyle? The Scripture does not tell us. It is not at all the point of the story. But those who think that some promise from her, expressed or implied, would have guaranteed that she did not, have an unjustified confidence in human commitments.

Such an opinion would also reflect a lack of understanding about the strength of habitual sin. The bestowal of a superlatively valuable gift as an act of unconditional generosity was precisely the kind of action most likely to woo her from her former ways. It is more likely by far to have accomplished this result than any legalistic commitment into which she might have entered.

The woman *was* grateful. Her testimony to the men of Sychar proves that (John 4:28-29).

But her assurance did not rest on what she might later do. It rested instead upon the uncomplicated promise of the Son of God.

The Free Gift in Paul

Naturally it is not only in the Gospel of John that the experience of salvation is seen as an unmerited gift. Paul also saw things this way. He wrote:

> For by grace you have been saved through faith, and that not of yourselves; it is the gift of God, not of works, lest anyone should boast (Eph 2:8-9).

Here too assurance is plainly implied in the Apostle's words, since Paul directly declares that the readership is saved and obviously takes it for granted that they know this. Moreover, this fact is not based in any way on their works but simply on God's grace and their faith. As with the woman at the well, the reception of a gift is the basic issue. The Ephesians are clearly aware of having received that gift.

Even when Paul goes on to state the importance of good works, the appeal is founded on the fact that the readers are the product of God's saving activity:

> For we are His workmanship, created in Christ Jesus for good works, which God prepared beforehand that we should walk in them (Eph 2:10).

One point is clear here. Good works are not seen as the *evidence* that we are God's workmanship, but rather as the expected *result* of that workmanship. Whether this result will be achieved is not stated. But it is both reasonable and natural to expect it to be. Since we are new creatures in Christ that is how we should live. We should fulfill God's purposes and walk in the works He has already prepared for us to do.

Plainly then, in Eph 2:8-10, g[...] grounds of assurance at all. On [...] *the grounds for good works.*

How strange that so fund[...] widely overlooked. The firmn[...] true basis from which its proper [...] ordinary life this is so. Would the rela[...] and wife be the same if they were not certa[...] they were married? Would a son have the same [...] his father if he were unsure of his paternity?

To ask such questions is to answer them. Accordingly, those who so present the Gospel that the believer remains uncertain about his salvation actually undermine the intended effects of God's grace. This fact compounds the seriousness of their error.

Simplicity in Gospel Preaching

In proclaiming the gospel of the grace of God simplicity is at a premium. The faithful preacher or witness will strive, with the aid of the Holy Spirit, to make the terms as clear as Jesus made them, or as Paul did.

These standards are high, but the inclusion of works-related conditions into the proclamation must be firmly resisted. Not to resist this is to lay ourselves open to satanic manipulation. It is he who wishes to blind men and to prevent their salvation (2 Cor 4:3-4).

How simple the gospel really is can be seen with superb clarity in the greatest salvation passage of all. John 3:16 is perhaps more widely familiar to people than any other verse in the Bible. And justly so. But its content is prepared for by John 3:14-15, which declare:

> "And as Moses lifted up the serpent in the wilderness, even so must the Son of Man be lifted up, that whoever believes in Him should not perish but have eternal life."

...e Grace Primer: The Gospel Under Siege

...is speaking here to Nicodemus, a Jewish rabbi. ...d's reference to the Old Testament gave this man a ...image which illuminated the offer Jesus was making. ...passage was Numbers 21 with its story about the fiery ...pents by which the complaining Israelites were bitten. ...wo verses in particular are worth quoting in full:

> Then the Lord said to Moses, "Make a fiery serpent, and set it on a pole; and it shall be that everyone who is bitten, when he looks at it, shall live." So Moses made a bronze serpent, and put it on a pole; and so it was, if a serpent had bitten anyone, when he looked at the bronze serpent, he lived (Num 21:8-9).

Of special interest is the Old Testament expression "shall *live*," or, "he *lived*." It is plainly appropriate to Jesus' discussion of "life" in John 3. In the ancient narrative the bitten Israelite was asked simply to take a look at the serpent lifted up on the pole. This look alone sufficed to meet his need. "When he looked at the bronze serpent, he lived."

In the same way, Jesus means to say, He Himself will be lifted up on the cross, and the one who looks to Him in faith *will live*. Could anything be more profoundly simple than that? Eternal life for one look of faith. Here too we meet the unconditional gift which may be acquired by any who desire it: "Whoever desires, let him take the water of life freely" (Rev 22:17b).

In what must be a classic case of reading one's own ideas into a text, John MacArthur writes about the Israelites bitten by fiery serpents as follows: "In order to look at the bronze snake on the pole, *they had to drag themselves* [italics added] to where they could see it. They were in no position to glance flippantly at the pole and then proceed with lives of rebellion."[5] But this is a transparent effort to

---

[5] John F. MacArthur, *The Gospel According to Jesus: What Does Jesus Mean When He Says "Follow Me"* (Grand Rapids: Zondervan Publishing

extract (non-existent) support from the Old Testament text for MacArthur's own doctrine of Lordship Salvation. Clearly the story in Numbers glorifies God's grace by the extreme simplicity of the divine solution to the Israelites' desperate need. So too, faith is "looking to" Jesus for our salvation and is God's simple solution to man's urgent spiritual need.

It was after these words (John 3:14-15) that the Savior went on to express the most fruitful declaration ever made in the history of man:

> "For God so loved the world that He gave His only begotten Son, that whoever believes in Him should not perish but have everlasting life" (John 3:16).

The number of people who have found the assurance of salvation in these words defies all computation.

And assurance is precisely what one *should* find in them. There is no mention of works. Faith alone is the one condition upon which a man may acquire everlasting life. Moreover, this secures him from perishing.

Indeed, if anyone who ever trusted Jesus for eternal life subsequently perished, John 3:16 would be false. "Whoever believes" is as broad as it can possibly be and is wholly unqualified by any other condition.

Those who wish to qualify it, in fact deny it.[6]

Conclusion: Simple Faith Saves

There is no question in John 3 of "this kind of faith" versus "that kind of faith," or "a faith which leads to this rather than to that." Still less is there anything about *psychological* faith over *true* faith.

House, 1988), 46.
   [6] Gerstner, *Wrongly Dividing,* 124. See also Zane Hodges, "Calvinism Ex Cathedra: A Review of John H. Gerstner's *Wrongly Dividing the Word of Truth: A Critique of Dispensationalism,*" *Journal of the Grace Evangelical Society* 4 no. 2 (Autumn 1991): 66-67.

Theologians may complicate the issue of faith, but faith is a simple matter in the Bible. It is nothing more nor less than taking God at His Word, that is, receiving "the witness of God" as true (1 John 5:9-10).

Or we may say that faith is the inner conviction that what God says to us is true. It is "being *fully convinced* that what He has promised He is also able to perform" (Rom 4:20-22, emphasis added).

Calvin's own definition of faith is outstanding and justly famous. It is notably free of the complications introduced by Reformed and Lordship theologians. Calvin writes:

> Now, we shall have a complete definition of faith, if we say, that it is a steady and certain knowledge of the Divine benevolence toward us, which, being founded on the truth of the gratuitous promise in Christ, is both revealed to our minds and confirmed to our hearts, by the Holy Spirit.[7]

R. T. Kendall neatly summarizes Calvin's view of faith:

> The position which Calvin wants pre-eminently to establish (and fundamentally assumes) is that faith is *knowledge*. Calvin notes some biblical synonyms for faith, all simple nouns, such as 'recognition' (*agnitio*) and 'knowledge' (*scientia*). He describes faith as illumination (*illuminatio*), knowledge as opposed to the submission of our feeling (*cognitio, non sensus nostri submissio*), certainty (*certitudino*), a firm conviction (*solida persuasio*), assurance (*securitas*), firm assurance (*solida securitas*), and full assurance (*plena securitas*) (italics all in Kendall).[8]

Kendall proceeds:

---

[7] Calvin, *Institutes* 3.1.7, italics added.
[8] R. T. Kendall, *Calvin and English Calvinism to 1649* (Oxford: University Press, 1979), 19. For the terms Kendall attributes to Calvin,

> What stands out in these descriptions is the given, intellectual, passive, and assuring nature of faith. What is absent is a need for gathering faith, voluntarism, faith as man's act, and faith that must await experimental knowledge to verify its presence. Faith is "something merely passive, bringing nothing of ours to the recovering of God's favor but receiving from Christ that which we lack." It is but the "instrument (*instrumentum*) for receiving righteousness", a "kind of vessel" (*quasi vasi*), which transmits the knowledge of our justification: "a passive work, so to say, to which no reward can be paid."[9]

I am in firm harmony with Calvin's perspective on the nature and essence of saving faith. I believe it to be the true Biblical concept of faith. What I charge is simply this: That the doctrine of faith which is generally found in Reformed theology and in Lordship Salvation is *contrary to the Bible, counter-reformational* in nature, and *in sharp conflict with John Calvin himself.*

God promises eternal life to everyone who believes that Jesus is "the Christ, the Savior of the world" (John 4:42; see also 20:30-31; 1 John 5:1). Individuals are saved when they are convinced of that promise and thus are sure they have eternal life.

So, in John 3, the issue is faith, or confidence, in Christ for eternal life. Will a man *look* to the Crucified One for eternal life, or will he not? The man who does, *lives*. By this very simplicity, the gospel confronts and refutes all its contemporary distortions.

Yes, I really *can* be sure!

---

he notes the following references: *Institutes* 3 with these chapters and sections: 1.4; 2.2; 2.6; 2.14; 2.16 (three times); 2.22.

[9] Ibid., 19-20. Kendall's references are: *Institutes* 11.7 (twice); and for the idea of "a passive work," see Calvin, *Comm.* s.v. John 6:29.

3

James 2:
What Is Dead Faith?

"Faith without works is dead" (Jas 2:26). So spoke James in the second chapter of his epistle. His statement has been appealed to many times to support the idea that works are necessary for eternal salvation.

Sometimes the claim is made that unless faith is followed by good works, the believer loses eternal life. At other times, a more subtle approach is taken. If a professing Christian does not manifest good works, he was never a true believer to begin with. Whatever James is saying, however, it can be neither of these ideas.

Dead Faith Is Like a Corpse: It Was Once Alive

The second view, just mentioned, is so forced and artificial that if it were not maintained by obviously sincere men, it might be called dishonest. According to this view, a dead faith cannot save. Therefore, if a man lacks the crucial evidence of good works, it shows that this is all he has *ever* possessed—a dead faith.

This flies directly into the face of the text. In Jas 2:26 the writer affirms, "For as the body without the spirit is dead, so faith without works is dead also."

No one who has encountered a dead body, whose life-giving spirit has departed, would ever conclude that the body had never been alive. Quite the contrary, the presence of a corpse is the clearest proof of a *loss* of life. If we allow this illustration to speak for itself, then the presence of a dead faith shows that this faith was once alive.

Nor is there *anything at all* in the entire passage to support some other conclusion. As elsewhere in the epistle, it is Christian brothers who are addressed (Jas 2:14; cf. 1:2, 16, 19; 2:1, 5; 3:1, 10, 12; etc.). There is *absolutely nothing to suggest* James believed that if a man's faith is pronounced dead, it must therefore always have been dead. The assumption that a dead faith has always been dead cannot be extracted from James's text. It is nothing more than a theological idea read into the passage.[10] It is also a desperate expedient intended to salvage some form of harmony between James and the doctrine of Paul.

But by distorting the true meaning of the text, this idea has given rise to immense confusion. This confusion has had a harmful impact on men's comprehension of the Gospel of God's saving grace.

James Believed in the Free Gift of Life

We should carefully observe that James, like all the inspired writers, believed eternal life was the gracious gift of God. This is made plain in a splendid passage in his first chapter:

> Every good gift and every perfect gift is from above, and comes down from the Father of lights, with whom there is no variation or shadow of turning. Of His own will He brought us forth by the word of truth, that we might be a kind of firstfruits of His creatures (Jas 1:17-18).

Anyone who is familiar with the words of Jesus, as James certainly was, can surely hear an echo of our Lord in a statement like this. New birth is a sovereign act of God. It is one of His good and perfect gifts which comes down *from above*.

In fact, in the expression "from above," James employs exactly the same word that Jesus used when He told Nicodemus, "You must be born *again*" (John 3:7). The Greek

---

[10] Gerstner, *Wrongly Dividing*, 229.

adverb is *anothen* and means both "again" and "from above." No doubt our Lord deliberately selected it for His discourse with Nicodemus. The supernatural birth which He was describing is both a *rebirth* and a *birth from above*. The play on words which this involves is an effective one.

In James's statement about our rebirth there is also a strong emphasis on the sovereign will of God. "Of His own will He brought us forth..." James insists. This perspective recalls Paul's statement:

> For it is the God who commanded light to shine out of darkness who has shone in our hearts to give the light of the knowledge of the glory of God in the face of Jesus Christ (2 Cor 4:6).

Here, too, the sovereign act of God is stressed.

Neither Paul nor James intends to deny the necessity of faith. But faith, as we see it in the simple, direct statements of the Bible about salvation, is nothing more than a response to a divine initiative. It is the means by which eternal life is received.

Since this is so, it is proper that God Himself should be viewed as the sovereign Actor at the moment of conversion. It is He who wills to regenerate. It is His Word that penetrates our darkness. Salvation, we may say, occurs when the sufficiency of Christ for my eternal need dawns on my darkened heart. At this moment of believing illumination, I become a Christian.

So there is no reason to doubt that James and Paul were in harmony about the way eternal life is received. For both of them it is the gift of God, graciously and sovereignly bestowed. Only when we take this unity for granted can we really begin to understand the meaning of James's instruction about works.

Exposition of James 2:14-26

(1) Works and Grace Cannot Be Mixed

The place to start is where James starts. His famous discussion is opened with the words, "What does it profit, my brethren, if someone says he has faith but does not have works? Faith cannot save him, can it?" (Jas 2:14 [trans. from Greek]).

The translation just given is based on the original Greek and is crucial to a correct interpretation. The form of the question which James asks in the last part of the verse is one which expects a negative response. The expected answer, from James's point of view, would be: "No, faith cannot save him."

Anyone who holds that faith and works are *both* conditions for reaching heaven will find no problem with a question like this. In that case the question simply means that faith by itself is not enough. In fact, this is precisely what James says in verse 17: "Thus also faith by itself, if it does not have works, is dead."

But the problem comes when we try to harmonize this idea with the Apostle Paul's clear denial that works are a *condition* for salvation.

For Paul, the inclusion of works would be a denial of grace. He is emphatic on this point:

> And if by grace, then it is no longer of works; otherwise grace is no longer grace. But if it is of works, it is no longer grace; otherwise work is no longer work (Rom 11:6).

It is hard to quarrel with this point of view. In fact it is impossible to do so. Paul's point is that once works are made a condition for attaining some goal, that goal can no longer be said to be attained by grace.

But in James 2, James plainly makes works a condition for salvation. The failure to admit this is the chief source of the problems supposedly arising from this passage for most Evangelicals. We ought to start by admitting it. And we ought then to admit that James cannot be talking about salvation *by grace*.

But instead of admitting these points, many interpreters dodge them. This is frequently done by trying to translate the question, "Can faith save him?" (Jas 2:14), by "Can *that* [or, *such*] faith save him?" But the introduction of words like *that* or *such* as qualifiers for faith is really an evasion of the text. The Greek does not at all verify this sort of translation.

A. T. Robertson assigns to the article before *faith* in Jas 2:14 "almost the original demonstrative force."[11] But this is extremely unlikely here when it is not even true later in the passage where the article appears with faith (see below). Any student of the original language can examine James's text and see for himself that the article occurs with faith only when faith is a subject or has a possessive word qualifying it (as in v 18). Otherwise there is no article. There is no subtle significance to the article in 2:14. Quite rightly Dibelius rejects the special stress on the article:

> Here James uses the article before 'faith'...
> but this is not to be read 'this faith', as many
> interpreters from Bede to Mayor have argued.
> James is not speaking of any particular
> brand of faith...The only attributive which is
> expressed...is this: faith which 'has' no works.
> But this is still the Christian faith and not an
> 'alleged, false faith.'[12]

So much for building theology on an undetectable grammatical nuance.

---

[11] A. T. Robertson, *Studies in the Epistle of James* (Nashville: Broadman, n.d.), 94 n. 2.

[12] Martin Dibelius, *James,* rev. Heinrich Greeven, trans. Michael A. Williams, ed. Helmut Koester, Herm (Philadelphia: Fortress Press, Eng. ed. 1976). 152.

Support for the renderings "*such* faith" or "*that* faith" is usually said to be found in the presence of the Greek definite article with the word "faith." But in this very passage, the definite article also occurs with "faith" in verses 17, 18, 20, 22 and 26. (In v 22, the reference is to Abraham's faith.) In none of these places are the words *such* or *that* proposed as natural translations.

As is well known, the Greek language often employed the definite article with abstract nouns (like faith, love, hope, etc.) where English cannot do so. In such cases we leave the Greek article untranslated.

The attempt to single out Jas 2:14 for specialized treatment carries its own refutation on its face. It must be classed as a truly desperate effort to support an insupportable interpretation.

James's point is really quite plain: faith alone cannot save.[13]

(2) Salvation for the Believer's Life

But what are we left with? A contradiction between James and Paul? This is what many have candidly thought, and it is easy to see why.[14] If James and Paul are talking about the same thing, they *do* contradict each other.

But are they talking about the same thing?

In the opening chapter of the epistle, shortly after declaring his readers to be the offspring of God's regenerating activity (Jas 1:18), James wrote:

---

[13] Thorwald Lorenzen, "Faith without Works Does Not Count Before God! James 2:14-16," *Expository Times* 89 (1978): 231. Lorenzen writes: "The original Greek makes it clear...that the rhetorical question calls for a negative answer: No! Faith without works cannot save! Works are necessary for salvation."

[14] Lorenzen, p. 234, holds that Paul and James cannot be reconciled. He is not alone in this view.

> Therefore lay aside all filthiness and overflow
> of wickedness, and receive with meekness
> the implanted word, which is able to save
> your souls. But be doers of the word, and
> not hearers only, deceiving yourselves (Jas
> 1:21-22).

That this passage is analogous to Jas 2:14 is easy to see. Here, too, James is affirming the necessity of *doing* something, and he clearly means that only if his readers *do* God's Word will it be able to "save their souls."

At first glance, this seems only to repeat the problem already encountered. But in fact it offers us the solution. The reason we do not see it immediately is due to the fact that we are English speakers with a long history of theological indoctrination. To us, the expression "save your souls" can scarcely mean anything else than "to be delivered from hell."

But this is the meaning *least likely* to occur to a Greek reader of the same text. In fact the expression "to save the soul" represents a Greek phrase whose most common meaning in English would be "to save the life." In the New Testament it occurs in this sense in parallel passages Mark 3:4 and Luke 6:9 (see also Luke 9:56). Among the numerous places where it is used with this meaning in the Greek translation of the Old Testament, the following references would be especially clear to the English reader: Gen 19:17 and 32:30; 1 Sam 19:11; and Jer 48:6. Perhaps even more to the point, the phrase occurs again in Jas 5:20, and here the words "from death" are added.

By contrast, the expression is never found in any New Testament text which describes the conversion experience.

The natural sense of the Greek phrase translated as "to save your lives" fits perfectly into the larger context of James 1. Earlier, James was discussing the consequences of sin. He has said, "Then, when desire has conceived, it gives birth to sin; and sin, when it is full-grown, brings forth death" (Jas 1:15). Sin, states James, has its final outcome in physical death. But obedience to God can defer death and "save" or "preserve" the life. This truth is echoed also by Paul (see Rom 8:13).

This understanding of Jas 1:21 agrees completely with Jas 5:19-20, where James says to his fellow Christians:

> Brethren, if anyone among you wanders from the truth, and someone turns him back, let him know that he who turns a sinner from the error of his way will save a soul from death and cover a multitude of sins.

On this attractive note of mutual spiritual concern among the brethren, James closes his letter. But in doing so, he manages to emphasize once again that sin can lead to death.[15]

It has been observed that the Epistle of James is the New Testament writing which most clearly reflects the wisdom literature of the Old Testament. The theme of death as the consequence of sin is an extremely frequent one in the book of Proverbs. A few illustrative texts can be mentioned:

> The fear of the Lord prolongs days,
> But the years of the wicked will be shortened (Prov 10:27).
>
> As righteousness leads to life,
> So he who pursues evil pursues it to his own death (Prov 11:19).
>
> In the way of righteousness is life,
> And in its pathway there is no death (Prov 12:28).

---

[15] This point is also made by Ropes, who writes of Jas 5:20: "Note how here, as in Jas 1:15, death is the result of sin" (James Hardy Ropes, *A Critical and Exegetical Commentary on the Epistle of St. James,* ICC [Edinburgh: T. & T. Clark, 1916], 315).

The law of the wise is a fountain of life,
To turn one away from the snares of death
(Prov 13:14).

He who keeps the commandment keeps his
soul [i.e., his life.],
But he who is careless of his ways will die
(Prov 19:16).

It is clear that this is the Old Testament concept which furnishes the background for James's thought. A recognition of this fact clarifies a great deal. *To save the soul* (life) is to preserve the physical life from an untimely death due to sin.

(3) The Development of James's Thought in 1:21–2:26

It is best to regard Jas 1:21–2:26 as a single large section in the development of the epistle. James 1:21 sets the theme. The readers, who are born-again Christians (Jas 1:18), need to lay wickedness aside and receive the Word of God as the agent capable of saving their lives. But they must understand (Jas 1:22-25) that this will only occur if they are *doers* of the Word and not mere hearers. To be a mere hearer is to commit the folly of looking into the divine mirror of truth and forgetting what it tells us about ourselves. Only the man who is a "doer of work" (1:25, [trans. from Greek]) can expect God's blessing on his life.

There follows in Jas 1:26–2:13 some specific information about what a "doer of work" actually does. He controls his tongue, is charitable to the needy, and keeps himself pure from worldly defilement (Jas 1:26-27). Moreover, he rejects the spirit of partiality and favoritism which is so common in the world (Jas 2:1-13). That spirit is wholly inconsistent with his faith in the Lord of glory (Jas 2:1).

Instead of partiality, therefore, there should be true obedience to "the royal law according to the Scripture, 'You shall love your neighbor as yourself'" (Jas 2:8). In fact, love and its handmaiden, mercy, are standards by which the lives of believers will be assessed at the Judgment Seat of Christ (Jas 2:13). They should therefore "so speak and so do as those who will be judged by the law of liberty" (Jas 2:12).[16] The reference back to Jas 1:25 is obvious in the phrase "law of liberty."

In referring to judgment, of course, James does not contradict the declaration of John 5:24 that the believer does not come into judgment. There is *no* judgment for the regenerate person if by that term is meant a weighing of his merits in terms of heaven or hell. There is not even any charge that can be brought against the redeemed believer. He is *justified* before the bar of eternal justice, as Paul so plainly states (Rom 8:33-34). Thus there cannot be any trial at all *to determine the believer's eternal destiny*. God declares that a settled matter when He justifies.

But the New Testament *does* teach an assessment of the believer's earthly experience in connection with rewards, or the loss of these (e.g., 1 Cor 3:12-15; 2 Cor 5:10). More will be said of this in a later chapter.

James 2:14-26 is the final subsection of the larger unit, Jas 1:21–2:26. At Jas 2:14 James returns to the thought expressed in Jas 1:21 about "saving the life." Since he has insisted that "saving the life" is only possible when one is actually a "doer of work," he wishes now (Jas 2:14) to oppose the idea that faith can substitute for obedience and accomplish the same saving result he had mentioned earlier (Jas 1:21).

---

[16] Editor's note: In v 12 of chap. 2 James calls the readers both to *say* and to *do*. But in Jas 2:14 we learn of a believer who *says* but does not *do*. Believers will be judged at the *Bēma* not only for what we say we believe, but also whether we apply those beliefs or not (cf. Jas 2:15-16).

(4) "Dead" Faith Cannot Keep a Christian Alive (James 2:14-17)

Keeping in mind the concept of "saving the life by obedience," we can now look more closely at what James wrote:

> What does it profit, my brethren, if someone says he has faith but does not have works? Can faith save him? If a brother or sister is naked and destitute of daily food, and one of you says to them, "Depart in peace, be warmed and filled," but you do not give them the things which are needed for the body, what does it profit? Thus also faith by itself, if it does not have works, is dead (Jas 2:14-17).

Can the fact that a man holds correct beliefs and is orthodox "save" him from the deadly consequences of sin? Of course not! The very thought is absurd. That is like giving your best wishes to a destitute brother or sister when what they really need is food and clothing (Jas 2:15-16). It is utterly fruitless.

As a matter of fact, this kind of callous conduct on the part of one Christian toward another is precisely what James has been warning against (see Jas 1:27; 2:2-6). It superbly illustrates his point. Such idle words are as "dead" (ineffectual) as a non-working faith. So James says, "Thus also faith by itself, if it does not have works, is dead" (Jas 2:17)

It needs to be carefully considered why James chose the term "dead" to describe a faith that is not working. But the moment we relate this term to the controlling theme of "saving the life," everything becomes plain. The issue that concerns James is an issue of *life* or *death*. (He is *not* discussing salvation from hell.) The truth which he has in mind is that of Proverbs: "As righteousness leads to life, so he who pursues evil pursues it to his own death" (Prov 11:19).

Can a *dead* faith save the Christian from *death?* The question answers itself. The choice of the adjective *dead* is perfectly suited to James's argument. Just as the idle words of some ungenerous believer cannot save his brother from death in the absence of life's necessities, no more can a non-working faith save *our* lives from the deadly consequences of sin.

(5) An Objector Speaks (James 2:18-19)

In Jas 2:18-19 James introduces the words of an imagined objector. The importance of a correct view of these verses is hard to overstate. Sanguine indeed is the opinion of Jean Cantinat that, though verses 18-19 are very difficult—perhaps the most difficult in the New Testament—these difficulties do not greatly affect our comprehension of the text. The exact opposite is the case: these difficulties, if left unresolved, significantly block our understanding.[17] The entirety of these verses belong to the objector. The response of James only begins in verse 20. This is shown by the words, "But do you want to know, O foolish man..." The evident unity of verses 18-19 as constituting the words of a single speaker is strongly attested in the literature on this passage. Many of those who have accepted this unity, however, have regarded the speaker not as an objector but as a pious ally who takes James's point of view. But this explanation is rightly dismissed by Peter Davids because "no one has yet been able to find a case where this common stylistic introduction did not introduce an opposing or disagreeing voice."[18]

The literary format James uses here was familiar in ancient times from the Greek diatribe. The diatribe was

---

[17] Jean Cantinat, *Les Epitres de Saint Jacques et de Saint Jude* (Paris: J. Gabalda, 1973), 10.

[18] Peter H. Davids, *The Epistle of James: A Commentary on the Greek Text*, NIGNTC (Grand Rapids: Eerdmans, 1982), 124.

a learned and argumentative form of communication. The two phrases ("But someone will say" [v 18], and "But do you want to know, O foolish man" [v 20]) clearly show that the diatribe format is being employed. These two phrases bracket the words of the objector in verses 18-19. Elsewhere in the New Testament, this same format appears in 1 Cor 15:35-36. This same format is also employed in Rom 9:19-20: (Objector) "You will say to me then, 'Why does...?'" (Response): "But indeed, O man, who are you to reply against God? Will the thing formed...?" The use of such structural markers as "but someone will say" and sharp-toned epithets directed at a senseless or ungodly interlocutor are well-known features of the diatribe style so prevalent in James's and Paul's day.[19]

Since the statements in verse 19 about the belief of men and demons are the words of the objector, not of James, their use by commentators to make a theological point is totally misguided. But what does the objection mean? Since most Greek manuscripts read the word "by" in place of the familiar word "without" in verse 18,[20] the objector's statement may be given as follows:

> "You have faith and I have works. Show me your faith from your works, and I will show you, from my works, my faith. You believe that there is one God; you do well. The demons also believe, and tremble" (Jas 2:18-19, [trans. from Greek]).

---

[19] For references see Peter H. Davids, *The Epistle of James: A Commentary on the Greek Text*, NIGNTC (Grand Rapids: Eerdmans, 1982), 123 and 126. James Hardy Ropes, *A Critical and Exegetical Commentary on the Epistle of St. James*, ICC (Edinburgh: T.&T. Clark, 1916), 208 and 216. Joseph B. Mayor, *The Epistle of James*, 3rd ed. (London: MacMillan, 1910; reprint ed., Minneapolis: Klock and Klock, 1977), 99 and 102.

[20] See also Zane Hodges, "Light on James Two from Textual Criticism." *Bibliotheca Sacra* 120 (1963): 341-50.

The argument which these words express appears to be a *reductio ad absurdum* (a reduction to absurdity). It is heavy with irony.

"It is absurd," says the objector, "to see a close connection between faith and works. For the sake of argument, let's say *you* have faith and *I* have works. Let's start there. *You* can no more start with what you believe and show it to me in your works, than *I* can start with my works and demonstrate what it is that I believe." The objector is confident that both tasks are impossible.

The impossibility of showing one's faith from one's works is now demonstrated (so the objector thinks) by this illustration: "Men and demons both believe the same truth (that there is one God), but their faith does not produce the same response. Although this article of faith may move a man to 'do well,' it never moves the demons to 'do well.'"[21] The Greek phrase (*kalos poieis*) is taken by me to mean "do good," "do right," which seems the most appropriate sense in Matt 5:44; 12:12; Luke 6:27. It is also viable in Acts 10:33 ("you did the right thing to come") and even in Jas 2:8 ("If you keep the royal law...you are doing what's right"). Attention should be given also to the secular examples cited by Mayor. In Hellenistic Greek one would be unwise to insist pedantically on the good/well differentiation so dear to strict English grammarians. All they can do is tremble. Faith and works, therefore, have no built-in connection at all. The same creed may produce entirely different kinds of conduct. Faith cannot be made visible in works."

No doubt James and his readers had heard this argument before. It was precisely the kind of defensive approach a man might take when his orthodoxy was not supported by good deeds. "Faith and works are not really related to each other in the way you say they are, James. So don't criticize the vitality of my faith because I don't do such and such a thing."

---

[21] Mayor, *James*, 101.

James's reply (Jas 2:20) may be paraphrased: "What a senseless argument. How foolish you are to make it. I still say that without works your faith is dead. Would you like to know why?"

Verses 21-23 are James's direct rebuttal of the objection. This is made clear in the Greek text by the singular form of "do you see" in verse 22. This shows he is addressing the objector. Only with the "you see" of verse 24 does James return to the plural and to his readers as a whole.

(6) Justification by Works (James 2:20-24)

In refuting the objection he has cited, James selects the most prestigious name in Jewish history, the patriarch Abraham. He selects also his most honored act of obedience to God, the offering of his own son Isaac. Since in Christian circles it was well known that Abraham was justified by faith, James now adds a highly original touch. *He was also justified by works.*

James wrote:

> But do you want to know, O foolish man, that faith without works is dead? Was not Abraham our father justified by works when he offered Isaac his son on the altar? Do you see that faith was working together with his works, and by works faith was made perfect? And the Scripture was fulfilled which says, "Abraham believed God, and it was accounted to him for righteousness." And he was called the friend of God (Jas 2:20-23).

Earlier in this discussion I wrote that we can best understand James's point of view by recognizing his harmony with Paul. That is extremely relevant here. James does not wish to deny that Abraham, or anyone else, could be justified by faith alone. He merely wishes to insist that there is also another justification, and it is by works.

Of course there is no such thing as a single justification by faith *plus* works. Nothing James says suggests that idea. Rather, there are *two kinds* of justification.

This point is confirmed by a careful reading of the Greek text of verse 24. When he returns to his readers generally, James says, "You see then that a man is justified by works, and not only [justified] by faith." The key to this understanding is the Greek adverb "only," which does not simply qualify the word "faith" but the whole idea of the second clause. James is saying: Justification by faith is not the only kind of justification there is. There is also the kind which is by works. The word "alone," or "only," in Greek is adverbial in form and ought not to be taken as a modifier of "faith" in the sense of "by faith alone." This point is often ignored by writers. However, J. P. Lange grants that the Greek word for "alone" might be connected with the word "justified" in the sense, "'not only by faith but by works a man is justified,'" but he argues that in fact it ought to be joined "adjectively" with the word "faith." But in the New Testament, when the word *monos* ("alone") modifies a noun it normally has formal concord with the noun. The adverbial use is the only natural one here, i.e., "You see then that a man is justified by works, and not only (justified) by faith."[22]

Somewhat surprisingly, to most people, the Apostle Paul agrees with this. Writing at what was no doubt a later time than James, Paul states in Rom 4:2, "For if Abraham was justified by works, he has something of which to boast, but not before God." The form of this statement does not deny the truth of the point under consideration. The phrase, "but not before God," strongly suggests that the Apostle can conceive of a sense in which men are justified by works. But, he insists, that is not the way men are justified before God. That is, it does not establish their legal standing before

---

[22] J. P. Lange, *The Epistle General of James*, in *A Commentary on the Holy Scriptures: Critical, Doctrinal and Homiletical, with Special Reference to Ministers and Students* (New York: Charles Scribner, 1869), 87.

James 2: What Is Dead Faith? 181

Him. Some have indeed sought a reconciliation between James and Paul in terms of differing concepts of works. Some time ago R. C. Lenski expressed a distinction that has often been asserted in one form or another. He states:

> Paul and James deal with different kinds of works. Paul deals with law-works, which have nothing to do with true Gospel-faith...James deals with Gospel-works, which ever evidence the presence of Gospel-faith...[23]

But this distinction is without foundation and has been effectively criticized by Douglas J. Moo.[24]

In responding, therefore, to the kind of person who tried to divorce faith and works in Christian experience, James takes a skillful approach. "Wait a moment, you foolish man," he is saying, "you make much of justification by faith, but can't you see how Abraham was also justified by works when he offered his son Isaac to God?" (Jas 2:21). "Is it not obvious how his faith was cooperating with his works and, in fact, by works his faith was made mature?" (Jas 2:22). "In this way, too, the full significance of the Scripture about his justification by faith was brought to light. For now he could be called the friend of God" (Jas 2:23).

The content of this passage is rich indeed. It is a pity that it has been so widely misunderstood. The faith which justifies—James never denies that it *does* justify—can have an active and vital role in the life of the obedient believer. As with Abraham, it can be the dynamic for great acts of obedience. In the process, faith itself can be "perfected." The Greek word for *perfected*, suggests development and maturation. Faith is thus nourished and strengthened by works.[25]

---

[23] R. C. H. Lenski, *The Interpretation of the Epistle to the Hebrews and of the Epistle of James* (Columbus, OH: Lutheran Book Concern, 1938), 587.

[24] Douglas J. Moo "'Law,' 'Works of the Law' and Legalism in Paul," *Westminster Theological Journal* 45 (1983): 73-100.

[25] About the statement in v 22 ("by works faith was made perfect"), Adamson aptly observes: "The force of the statement seems to be that

It would hardly be possible to find a better illustration of James's point anywhere in the Bible. The faith by which Abraham was justified was basically faith in a God of resurrection. Referring to the occasion when that faith was first exercised, Paul wrote:

> And not being weak in faith, he did not consider his own body, already dead (since he was about a hundred years old), and the deadness of Sarah's womb. He did not waver at the promise of God through unbelief, but was strengthened in faith, giving glory to God, and being fully convinced that what He had promised He was also able to perform (Rom 4:19-21).

Abraham had confidence that the God he believed in could overcome the "deadness" of his own body and of Sarah's womb. But it was only through the testing with Isaac that this faith becomes a specific conviction that God could literally raise a person from the dead to fulfill His oath. Accordingly, the author of Hebrews declares:

> By faith Abraham, when he was tested, offered up his only begotten son, of whom it was said, *"In Isaac your seed shall be called,"* concluding that God was able to raise him up, even from the dead, from which he also received him in a figurative sense (Heb 11:17-19).

Thus the faith of Abraham was strengthened and matured by works. From a conviction that God could overcome a "deadness" in his own body (inability to beget children), he moved to the assurance that God could actually resurrect his son's body from literal, physical death. In

---

faith is fulfilled, strengthened, and matured by exercise" (James B. Adamson, *The Epistle of James,* NICNT [Grand Rapids: Eerdmans, 1976], 130).

the process of carrying out the divine command to sacrifice his beloved boy, his faith grew and reached new heights of confidence in God.

In this way, too, the Scripture that spoke of his original justification "was fulfilled." That statement (Gen 15:6) was not a prophecy, of course. But its implications were richly developed and exposed by the subsequent record of Abraham's obedience. Abraham's works "filled it full" of meaning, so to speak, by showing the extent to which that faith could develop and undergird a life of obedience. Simple and uncomplicated though it was at first, Abraham's justifying faith had potential ramifications which only his works, built on it, could disclose. Fenton Hort explains "the Scripture was fulfilled" (v 23) as follows:

> The Divine word spoken is conceived of as receiving a completion so to speak in acts or events which are done or come to pass in accordance with it. The idea of filling, or giving fullness to, is always contained in the Biblical use of fulfilling, though not always in the same sense.[26]

And now he could be called the "friend of God," not only by God Himself, but also by men (cf. Isa 41:8; 2 Chr 20:7). This is in fact the name by which Abraham has been known down through the centuries in many lands and by at least three religions (Christianity, Judaism, Islam). Had Abraham not obeyed God in the greatest test of his life, he would still have been justified by the faith he exercised in Gen 15:6. But by allowing that faith to be *alive* in his works, he attained an enviable title among men. In this way he was also justified by works.

---

[26] Fenton John Anthony Hort, *Expository and Exegetical Studies: Compendium of Works Formerly Published Separately: The Epistle of James* (reprint ed., Minneapolis: Klock and Klock, 1980), 64. See also the stimulating discussion of Adamson, 130-32.

When a man is justified by faith he finds an unqualified acceptance before God. As Paul puts it, such a man is one "to whom God imputes righteousness without works" (Rom 4:6). But only God can see this spiritual transaction. When, however, a man is justified by works he achieves an intimacy with God that is manifest to men. He can then be called "the friend of God," even as Jesus said, "You are My friends if you do whatever I command you" (John 15:14).

Note J. N. Darby's comment on this passage:

> James' remark never says that works justify us *before God* [italics his]: for God can see the faith without its works. He knows that life is there. It is in exercise with regard to Him, towards Him, by trust in His word, in Himself, by receiving His testimony in spite of everything within and without. This God sees and knows. But when our fellow creatures are in question, when it must be said "shew," then faith, life, shows itself in works.[27]

(7) James's Concluding Words (James 2:24-26)

Leaving the imagined objector behind, James returns in verses 24-26 to address the readership directly. Rahab furnishes him with his final Biblical example of justification by works. James said:

> You see then that a man is justified by works, and not by faith only. Likewise, was not Rahab the harlot justified by works when she received the messengers and sent them out another way? For as the body without the

---

[27] J. N. Darby, *Synopsis of the Books of the Bible: Colossians– Revelation,* new ed. rev. (reprint ed., New York: Loizeaux, 1942), 361.

James 2: What Is Dead Faith?

spirit is dead, so faith without works is dead also (Jas 2:24-26).

It should be carefully observed that he does *not* say, "Was not Rahab justified by faith *and* works." As already mentioned, such an idea is foreign to James. He is talking about exactly what he says he is talking about: justification by works.

Rahab, however, is superbly suited to tie his thoughts together. The passage had begun, as we have seen, with a reference to his theme of "saving the life" (Jas 2:14; 1:21). Not surprisingly, Rahab is selected as a striking example of a person whose physical life was "saved" precisely because she had works.

With James's words the statement of the writer of Hebrews can be profitably compared. In Heb 11:31, that author writes of her, "By faith the harlot Rahab did not perish with those who did not believe, when she had received the spies with peace."

Notice that the author of Hebrews points to her faith and lays the stress on the fact that she "received" the spies. James, on the other hand, points also to the fact that "she sent them out another way." This has considerable significance for James's argument.

Although Rahab's faith began to operate the moment she "received the messengers," she could not really be justified by works until she had "sent them out another way." The reason for this is obvious when the story in Joshua 2 is carefully considered. Up until the last moment, she could still have betrayed the spies. Had she so desired, she could have sent their pursuers after them.

That the spies had lingering doubts about her loyalty is suggested by their words in Josh 2:20, "And if you tell this business of ours, then we will be free from your oath…" But the spies' successful escape demonstrated that Rahab truly was a "friend of God" because she was also *their* friend. In this way, Rahab was justified by works.[28]

And in the process, she saved her own life and her family's. Her faith, therefore, was very much *alive* because it was an active, working faith. Though she was a harlot—and both inspired writers remind us that she was—her living faith triumphed over the natural consequences of her sin. While all the inhabitants of Jericho perished under the divine judgment which Israel executed, she *lived* because her faith *lived*.

James therefore wishes his readers to know that works are in fact the vitalizing "spirit" which keeps one's faith alive in the same way that the human spirit keeps the human body alive (Jas 2:26). Whenever a Christian ceases to act on his faith, that faith atrophies and becomes little more than a creedal corpse. "Dead orthodoxy" is a danger that has always confronted Christian people and they do well to take heed to this danger. The view that James is talking about a false, spurious faith has nothing to commend it. Even though he holds that final salvation is in view in James 2, W. Nicol is absolutely correct when he writes:

> James's point is not that faith without works is not faith: as faith he does not criticize it, but merely stresses that faith does not fulfill its purpose when it is not accompanied by works.[29]

---

[28] An indirect testimony to the depth of Rahab's vindication before men is to be found in the significant role Rahab played in Jewish legend. For specifics, see Sophie Laws, *A Commentary on the Epistle of James* HNTC (New York: Harper and Row, 1980), 137. Thanks to James, her name lives on in Christianity as a challenging role-model for every born-again believer who, though already justified by faith, also aspires to be justified by works.

[29] W. Nicol, "Faith and Works in the Letter of James," in *Essays on the General Epistles of the New Testament, Neotestamentica* 9 (Pretoria: The New Testament Society of South Africa, 1975), 16.

Alfred Plummer has also written on this topic, "But St. James nowhere throws doubt on the truth of the unprofitable believer's professions, or on the possibility of believing much and doing nothing."[30]

But the antidote is a simple one: faith remains vital and alive as long as it is being translated into real works of living obedience.

Summary

Does James contradict Paul's doctrine of free grace, or John's insistence on faith as the single condition of eternal life? Far from it. But neither does he offer support to the widespread notion that a "dead faith" cannot exist in the life of a Christian. Ironically, that is exactly what he is warning against. Thus, a misunderstanding of his words has not only promoted confusion about the terms for eternal life, but it has also deprived the Church of a much-needed warning.

Strikingly on target are the remarks of Dibelius who writes:

> But in all of the instances [in James] which have been examined thus far what is involved is the faith which the Christian has, never the faith of the sinner which first brings him to God...The faith which is mentioned in this section can be presupposed in every Christian...[James's] intention is not dogmatically oriented, but practically oriented: *he wishes to admonish the Christians to practice their faith, i.e., their Christianity, by works.*[31]

As far as it goes a better statement cannot be found in the literature on James.

---

[30] Alfred Plummer, *The General Epistles of St. James and St. Jude* (New York: A. C. Armstrong and Son, 1905), 137.

[31] Dibelius, *Epistles*, 178, italics his.

The dangers of a dead faith are real. But these dangers do not include hell.[32] Nothing James writes suggests this. Nevertheless, sin remains a deadly enemy to Christian experience which can prematurely end our physical lives. The wisdom of the Old Testament and James are agreed about this. So, if Christians are to be "saved" from that result, they will need more than faith.

They will also need works.[33]

---

[32] James 2:14-26 is also treated as unrelated to the question of eternal destiny by R. T. Kendall, *Once Saved, Always Saved* (Chicago: Moody Press, 1985), 170-172, 207-217. Although Kendall relates 2:14 to the saving of the destitute poor person described in vv 15-16, his perspective on the passage is not very dissimilar to the view I have taken.

[33] See Appendix 2.

4

Luke 14:

The Cost of Discipleship

One fact which the Lord Jesus Christ made completely clear was that discipleship involved a costly commitment. On that point His words left no doubt.

A classic expression of this truth is found in Luke 14:26-27. There the Savior declares:

> "If anyone comes to Me and does not hate his father and mother, wife and children, brothers and sisters, yes, and his own life also, he cannot be My disciple. And whoever does not bear his cross and come after Me cannot be My disciple."

Later, in the same context (Luke 14:33), He says, "So likewise, whoever of you does not forsake all that he has, he cannot be My disciple." It is part of the contemporary siege of the gospel that such words are often taken today as expressing virtual conditions for eternal salvation. The word *virtual* is deliberately chosen. It is often claimed that those who do not fulfill the terms of discipleship will not go to heaven. Yet at the same time those who say this might insist on Paul's doctrine that a man is saved by grace through faith and apart from works. The inconsistency of this is glaring.

In response to this charge, some indeed would claim that discipleship is *not* a condition for eternal life, but an *inevitable result* of possessing it. Let's put it plainly. If ongoing good works are necessary for reaching heaven, they are also a *condition* for reaching heaven. Thus, on this view, final salvation is based on faith *plus* works. But how few are the theologians who will clearly admit this. The present debate suffers from a shortage of theological honesty.

Looking at Luke 14

By no stretch of the imagination can the words of Jesus in Luke 14 be treated as portraying the "inevitable result" of regeneration. There is absolutely nothing in the passage to suggest that. On the contrary, the obvious purpose of the Lord's statements is to warn against the very real danger of failure.

The well-known image of the man and the uncompleted tower serves to highlight this aspect of the passage (Luke 14:28-30). The words with which he is mocked carry a pointed message: "This man began to build and was not able to finish." In the same way, the metaphor of the king who sues for peace carries a similar warning (Luke 14:31-32). Discipleship, Jesus warns, can end in failure.

If the claim is advanced that no real Christian is subject to such failure, that claim amounts to little more than an evasion of the warning itself. Certainly there is nothing in the Biblical text to suggest this point of view. To invoke it is to read something *into* the text that cannot be supported or verified.

The issue can be simply put: Can a man who trusts Christ for eternal life but fails to "hate" his father and mother go to heaven (Luke 14:26)? If the answer to this is "no," then it is perfectly clear that "hating" one's father and mother is a *condition* for final salvation. No amount of theological re-articulation can conceal this result. But in the process, the terms of the Biblical gospel have been radically transformed. Heaven cannot be reached except by the most strenuous self-denial and loyalty to Christ. Salvation by grace through faith alone becomes a mere fiction or a theological illusion.

How serious this is can hardly be overstated. Those who express their conception of the gospel of Christ this way must necessarily feel restless and uncomfortable in the presence of our Lord's free and unencumbered offer to the sinful woman of Sychar. Had she been told the stringent demands of Luke 14, she could scarcely have imagined that she was being offered a *gift*. For that matter, who could?

It is an interpretative mistake of the first magnitude to confuse the terms of discipleship with the offer of eternal life as a free gift. "And whoever desires, let him take the water of life freely" (Rev 22:17) is clearly an unconditional offer. By *unconditional* I mean that it is freely available. Naturally one must "take" the water (i.e., "believe" in Christ) to have it. An unconditional offer in ordinary life certainly does *not* mean that something is given whether one wants it or not. "Whoever desires..." is precisely the phrase that marks the unconditionality of this offer (Rev 22:17). The text means, "if you want it, you can have it." "If anyone comes to Me and does not...he cannot be My disciple" clearly expresses a relationship which is fully conditional. Not to recognize this simple distinction is to invite confusion and error at the most fundamental level.

Looking at John 8

The distinction between salvation and discipleship is openly recognized in the Gospel of John. In John 8:30 we are told, "As He spoke these words, many believed in Him." In the original Greek the words "believed in Him" represent a special phrase which is almost (though not quite) unique to the Fourth Gospel. This phrase involves the use of a Greek preposition (*eis*) after the verb, translated as *believe* and, so far at least, it has not been found in secular Greek. Among the instances of its use in John's Gospel may be mentioned the following: John 1:12; 2:11; 3:15, 16, 18, 36; 6:29, 35, 40, 47; 7:38, 39; 9:35, 36; 10:42; 11:25, 26, 45; and 12:44, 46.

Even a rapid examination of these texts shows that this specialized expression is John's standard way of describing the act of saving faith by which eternal life is obtained. To deny this in John 8:30 would be to go directly counter to the well-established usage of the author. Yet precisely to these individuals who had exercised saving faith, Jesus adds:

> "If you abide in My word, you are My disciples indeed. And you shall know the truth, and the truth shall make you free" (John 8:31-32).

On the authority of Jesus Himself it can be said that the believers of John 8:30 received eternal life in response to their faith. It was He who had affirmed, "Most assuredly, I say to you, he who believes in Me has everlasting life" (John 6:47). But to these who now had that life, Jesus set forth a *conditional* relationship: "*If* you abide in My word, you are My disciples indeed."

Plainly we have here, as also in Luke 14, a relationship which depends on the individual's continuing commitment to the discipleship experience. Should this commitment fail, he would become like the man who "began to build and was not able to finish." But this reality should not be confused with a man's permanent possession of the gift of eternal life. That gift, like all God's gifts, is irrevocable (Rom 11:29). The one who acquires it can never hunger or thirst for it again (John 6:35). Moreover, the Lord Jesus Christ will never lose anyone who has trusted Him for it (John 6:37-40).

Despite what has just been said, it has actually been argued that the individuals of John 8:30 exercised a faith that was not regenerating. An appeal is sometimes made to the Greek phrase in verse 31, "the Jews who believed Him." Here it is said that John uses an expression without the preposition (that is, without the *eis* found in v 30) and that this signals the inadequacy of the faith which these Jews had.

This argument is groundless. John knows nothing about a faith in Christ that is not saving. The construction found in John 8:31 appears also in John 5:24 where no one would regard it as expressing faulty belief. It is equally obvious

Luke 14: The Cost of Discipleship

that the individuals of John 8:31 are the same as those of verse 30 where John employs his specialized expression. The effort to distinguish different *kinds* of faith, both here and elsewhere, is entirely futile.

Brooke Westcott takes the faith mentioned in verse 30 as faith "in the fullest sense." Yet he contrasts this with the faith mentioned in verse 31, taking the latter to mean "the simple acceptance of a person's statements as true."[34] But this forced disjunction between the believers in the two verses is a transparent over refinement based on, at best, a grammatical subtlety and, at worst, on a non-existent distinction. The latter is the case as a comparison with John 5:24 shows. (John 2:23 and 12:42 are sometimes suggested, but on question-begging grounds. In both cases, genuine salvation occurs since John's single condition of faith is met.)[35]

It has also been claimed, however, that the believing Jews of John 8:30-31 are the speakers in verses 33, 39, and 41. It is then pointed out that in verse 44 Jesus tells them, "You are of your father the devil, and the desires of your father you want to do." Along with the whole tenor of verses 33-47 (and especially the statements of vv 39, 40, and 42) this is seen as a clear indication that the faith described in John 8:30 was not regenerating faith.

But this argument involves a misassessment of the whole context in which John 8:30-32 is placed.

John 8:13-59 is clearly a controversial section which has its setting in the Jewish Temple (John 8:20). Jesus' opponents throughout the section are His general audience in the Temple treasury. They are described as Pharisees (John

---

[34] Brooke Foss Westcott, *The Gospel According to John: The Authorised Version with Introduction and Notes* (London: James Clark, [1978 edition]), 132-33.

[35] Zane Hodges, "Problem Passages in the Gospel of John, Part 2: Untrustworthy Believers—John 2:23-25," *Bibliotheca Sacra* 135 (1978): 139-52. For an excellent treatment of the use of the verb *pisteuein* ("to believe") in John, see Richard W. Christianson, "The Soteriological Significance of *PISTEUO* in the Gospel of John," unpublished Th.M. Thesis, Grace Theological Seminary (Winona Lake, IN), 1987.

8:13), as Jews (John 8:22, 48, 52, and 57), and more simply as "they" (John 8:19, 25, 27, 33, 39, 41, 59). John does not expect us to understand the "they" of verse 33 any differently than we do the same word in verses 19, 25, and 27. He means the larger audience. Although Raymond Brown needlessly assigns verses 30 and 31 to editorial and redactional activity, he does say, "Almost certainly the words of Jesus in this section were addressed to the same type of disbelievers that we have been encountering all along."[36]

Verses 30-31a (about those who believe in Him) are a kind of "aside" to the reader to explain the background and purpose of Jesus' statement in verses 31b-32 (about continuing in His Word). In this way the reader is allowed to learn the reason why Jesus' words are misunderstood and how they serve to intensify the controversy that is already raging.

This technique is thoroughly Johannine. Throughout the Fourth Gospel, the words of Jesus are frequently misunderstood (cf. John 3:4; 4:11, 12; 6:34; 7:35; 8:22; etc.). Where necessary, John offers the readers the crucial clue to their actual meaning (cf. John 2:19-22; 11:11-13). This is what he is doing in verses 30-31a. The reader is "tipped off" about the real purpose behind the words in John 3:31b-32.

Thus there is no reason at all to suppose that when John states that "many believed in Him" (John 8:30) he means anything different than he does with nearly identical statements in John 10:42 and John 11:45. The effort to see the "believers" of 8:30-31 as belonging to some special category (like an "unregenerate believer") is without foundation and is totally misguided.

John 8:30-32 can therefore stand as a significant contribution to our understanding of the difference between the terms of discipleship and the condition for receiving eternal life. The latter here, as everywhere in the Fourth Gospel,

---

[36] Raymond E. Brown, *The Gospel According to John (I-XII)*, The Anchor Bible (Garden City, NY: Doubleday, 1966), 354.

is the result of faith. But discipleship depends upon the believer's continuance in the Word of Christ. This is plain enough and should occasion no confusion at all.

Disciples Are Pupils

Of course, the Greek word for *disciple*, meant simply a *pupil* or a *learner*. Thus a disciple was one who was "in school"—that is, he was under the guidance and instruction of a teacher.

In the Greco-Roman world of New Testament times there were many traveling teachers. Experts in such fields as philosophy or rhetoric traveled from place to place and taught their specialty. Jewish rabbis often did the same. The idea of a pupil, or disciple, leaving home to follow such a teacher around and learn from him was not a strange idea at all.

The cultural gap between ourselves and the first century has probably contributed to the modern confusion about discipleship. No doubt close attention to the Scriptures could have spared us from that. But it is important to see things like this in their historical setting.

In the first century, no one would be surprised if someone who had left home to follow a traveling teacher was tempted to "drop out" and return to his loved ones. In this light, continuing commitment to Christ and His Word, even above commitment to the family itself, is a natural condition for the kind of relationship which discipleship describes. By contrast, regeneration points to a family relationship in which God becomes the Father of the one who trusts His Son. Such relationships on earth are permanent. The divine family is no exception.

It is not surprising that in the Book of Acts the word *disciple* becomes a standard way of describing those who became a part of the visible church. The "school" in which they now received their instruction was the church itself. It was there that the doctrine of the Apostles brought them into vital contact with all that Jesus Himself had taught these original disciples.

It was in the church that the first disciples reproduced themselves by making other disciples. The steps involved in this process were twofold, as Matt 28:19-20 disclose:

> "Go therefore and make disciples of all the nations, baptizing them in the name of the Father and of the Son and of the Holy Spirit, teaching them to observe all things that I have commanded you; and lo, I am with you always, even to the end of the age."

The process of disciple-making involves an initiation (baptizing) followed by indoctrination (teaching). Both steps were begun promptly on the first day of the Church's history, immediately after the conversion of three thousand souls (Acts 2:41-42).

It should be noticed that from the beginning baptism was associated with the making of disciples. John notes that "the Pharisees had heard that Jesus made and baptized more disciples than John (though Jesus Himself did not baptize, but His disciples)" (John 4:1-2). Baptism can properly be seen as the first concrete step which a disciple takes in obedience to Christ.

A Disciple "Abides"

It is of considerable interest that the word used by our Lord in John 8:31 to describe the responsibility of a disciple is an important one in the Fourth Gospel. The word *abide* is exactly the same word that is also translated *abide* in John 15:1-7. There it is the crucial term in the metaphor about the vine and its branches.

Of course, the same word can be used of the mutually shared life of the believer and Christ (John 6:56) as well as of a purely physical dwelling ("staying," John 1:38-39). But in John 15 its role in the metaphor is evidently to describe the discipleship experience.

This observation is supported by the text. The discussion of the vine and branches is concluded in John 15:8 with the words, "By this My Father is glorified, that you bear much fruit; so *you will be My disciples.*" A recognition that this famous passage applies to discipleship dissolves the problems which have often been associated with it.

As already observed, discipleship is a conditional relationship that can be interrupted or terminated after it has begun. This obviously is also true of the vine/branch relationship described in John 15. It is the responsibility of Jesus' disciples (to whom these words are spoken) to "abide" in Him (John 15:4). When this condition is fulfilled, there is fruitfulness (John 15:5) and answered prayer (John 15:7). If the condition is *not* fulfilled, tragic consequences occur (John 15:6).

"Abiding," we may say, is based on learning and keeping the commands of our Teacher. When we live disobediently, we are not abiding (see 1 John 2:5-6).

The consequences that follow when a disciple fails to abide in Christ (John 15:6) are very meaningful in terms of the Teacher/pupil relationship. First, there is the loss of the relationship itself: "he is cast out as a branch." Next, there is the loss of the spiritual vitality associated with that relationship: "and is withered." Finally, there is chastening: "they gather them and throw them into the fire, and they are burned."

It is entirely unnecessary to associate the "fire" of John 15:6 with the literal fires of hell. After all, the entire passage involves a figure of speech. The "vine" is not a literal vine, the "branches" are not literal branches, nor the "fruit" literal fruit. There is no reason why the "fire" must be literal fire. Instead it serves as an effective metaphor for whatever trials or hardships may attend the life of a lapsed disciple. "Fire" as a figure for temporal afflictions is a commonplace in the Bible and, indeed, in all of literature (see Deut 32:22-24; Ps 78:21; Isa 9:18-19; Jer 15:14; Amos 1:4, 7, 10, 12; etc.).

Whether restoration of a branch to its former position in the vine is possible or not is a point that lies outside the scope of the metaphor. But it can be noticed that the process of withering suggests a lapse of time prior to the experience of the fire itself. What is not possible in nature, of course, is possible with God. It is unwise to push a figure of speech too far or to require it to express ideas which it is not capable of bearing. It is sufficient to learn from our Lord's words that abiding is crucial to fruitfulness and that the failure to abide can lead to spiritual disaster.

Much perplexity has been created by expositions of John 15 which identified John's ideas with Paul's concept that believers are "in Christ" (e.g., Eph 1:3). But this identification is superficial and unwarranted. The conditional character of the abiding relationship should have told us that from the beginning.

John 10:27-28 and Discipleship

It is extremely dangerous in the interpretation of Scripture to equate unthinkingly the meanings of words and expressions that are found in widely differing contexts. The equation of the "in Me" of John 15 with Paul's "in Christ" is only one case in point. Another which affects the present discussion on discipleship involves John 10:27-28.

In those verses Jesus affirms:

> "My sheep hear My voice, and I know them, and they follow Me. And I give them eternal life, and they shall never perish; neither shall anyone snatch them out of My hand."

It has been quite common to identify the term "follow" in these verses with the experience of discipleship, in which men are challenged to follow Christ. But again the identification cannot withstand examination.

Those who hold that the word "follow" in John 10:27 must mean something like "obey" have rarely stopped to ask a very relevant question. What accounts for the sequence here? Why does Jesus say, "They follow Me and I give them eternal life," rather than, "I give them eternal life and they follow Me"? It sounds as though the giving of eternal life is *the result of* His sheep following Him. As a matter of fact, this conclusion is undoubtedly correct!

A comparison of John 10:27-28 with John 5:24 will show how natural this conclusion is within the familiar context of John's thought. John 5:24 contains several distinct elements: (1) the hearing of Christ's word; (2) faith; (3) the possession of eternal life; (4) a guarantee against judgment; (5) a secure situation ("passed from death into life").

All of these elements are echoed in John 10:27-28. The only new feature is the expression, "I know them," which is contextually determined by the stress on Jesus' capacity to recognize His own sheep (John 10:14, 26). Leaving this aside, we have the following features in verses 27 and 28: (1) hearing Christ's voice; (2) following; (3) the giving of eternal life; (4) a guarantee against perishing; (5) a secure situation (in Jesus' hand).

This leads readily to the conclusion that in John 10:27 the term "follow" is simply another Johannine metaphor for saving faith. Like the metaphors about receiving (John 1:12), drinking (John 4:14), coming (John 6:35, 37), eating bread (John 6:35), eating Christ's flesh and drinking His blood (John 6:54), and others, "follow" expresses the action in response to which eternal life is bestowed. When the Shepherd calls the sheep through His Word (and He knows who they are), they respond to that call by following Him. That is to say, they commit their safety and well-being to the Shepherd who has summoned them to do so. A sheep's instinctive fear of strange voices lies in the background of this analogy (see John 10:4-5), so that the decision to follow is after all an act of *trust*. It is a mistake to understand the word "follow" in John 10:27 as though it indicates something about the nature of the believer's experience *after* he receives eternal life. In fact it has nothing to do with that at all, as its position in our Lord's statements enables us to see.

In the final analysis, John 10:27-28 merely expresses in a fresh way the truth presented in John 5:24. The *immediately preceding* verses in John 10 show that the fundamental issue in Jesus' exchange with the Jews is *faith*. Thus in verses 25 and 26 Jesus tells them:

> "I told you, and you do not believe. The works that I do in My Father's name, they bear witness of Me. But you do not believe, because you are not of My sheep, as I said to you" (John 10:25-26).

When John 10:27 is read in connection with these statements, its meaning is clear. These Jews are not His sheep because they do not *believe,* but His real sheep *follow,* i.e., they *believe*. Hence, John 10:27 and 28 have nothing to do with the subject of discipleship.[37]

Conclusion

Expositors of God's Word are under a solemn responsibility to pay close attention to the exact nature of Scriptural declarations. The failure to do this is a primary reason why the theme of discipleship has often been confused with the gospel of God's free saving grace. This confusion in turn has played into the hands of the Enemy with a resulting distortion of the terms on which man may obtain a place in heaven. It is high time for the Christian Church to renounce the theological errors that result from this and to reaffirm its commitment to the gift of God.

Only then can we be completely honest about the costs and dangers of true discipleship.

---

[37] For essentially the same view, see Rudolf Bultmann, The *Gospel of John: A Commentary,* tr. G. R. Beasley-Murray, with R. W. N. Hoare and J. K. Riches (Oxford: Blackwell: Philadelphia: Westminster. 1971), 343-44.

5
First John: Tests of Life?

The first epistle of John is the work of the same inspired writer who penned the Gospel of John. It is ironic that in the modern church it is often used in a way that is incompatible with the free offer of life found in the Fourth Gospel.

One well-known view of the purpose of 1 John maintains that the epistle offers us "tests of life."[38] That is, John confronts his readership with questions about the quality of their Christian experience from which they may draw the conclusion that they either are, or are not, true believers. Should they fail to measure up, they have no reason to think that they possess eternal life.

It would be hard to devise an approach to John's first epistle more hopelessly misguided or more completely self-defeating. If the premise on which this approach is based were true, it would be quite impossible for either the original audience of 1 John or any of its subsequent readers to possess the assurance of salvation.

Since the writer repeatedly commands the "abiding" life marked by obedience to Christ's commands, one cannot really be certain that he is saved until death, if "abiding" is a test of salvation. On the view we are discussing, if I stop "abiding" at some point in the future, I was never a Christian at all.

This view is absurd in the light of the New Testament. Basically it denies the vibrant confidence in our relationship to God which the New Testament everywhere teaches us

---

[38] This view of 1 John seems to have originated with, or at least have been brought to prominence by, Robert Law in *The Tests of Life: A Study of the First Epistle of St. John*, 3rd ed. (Edinburgh: T. & T. Clark, 1914). It is very much the controlling conception in J. R. W. Stott, *The Epistles of John*, TNTC (Grand Rapids: Eerdmans, 1964).

to have. In its place it puts a gnawing doubt that my whole "Christian experience" may prove in the end to have been an illusion.

The Readers of First John Are Saved

Few errors of contemporary Bible exposition are more blatant than the one I have mentioned. Not only does John not say that he is writing to "test" whether his readers are saved or not, he says the reverse. This is amply proved from a notable passage in the second chapter:

> I write to you, little children,
> Because *your sins are forgiven* you for His name's sake.
> I write to you, fathers,
> Because you have known Him who is from the beginning.
> I write to you, young men,
> Because you have overcome the wicked one.
> I write to you, little children,
> Because *you have known the Father.*
> I have written to you, fathers,
> Because you have known Him who is from the beginning.
> I have written to you, young men,
> Because you are strong, and the word of God abides in you,
> And you have overcome the wicked one
> (1 John 2:12-14, *emphasis added*).

So far from writing to his readers because he, or they, need to "test" the reality of their Christian experience, John writes precisely because that experience is real.

It should be carefully noted that the passage quoted above is immediately followed by a solemn warning:

> Do not love the world or the things in the world. If anyone loves the world, the love of

the Father is not in him. For all that *is* in the world—the lust of the flesh, the lust of the eyes, and the pride of life—is not of the Father but is of the world (2:15-16).

Coming as this warning does directly after the reassuring words of 1 John 2:12-14, the exhortation tells us a great deal. It reveals that from John's point of view morality can be effectively produced in people who are sure about their relationship to God. Morality is not the grounds for assurance, but the fruit of it.

Paul also believed the same thing. He can therefore exhort the Ephesian Christians "to walk worthy of the calling with which you were called" (Eph 4:1). Or he can say, "Therefore, as the elect of God, holy and beloved, put on tender mercies, kindness, humility, meekness, longsuffering" (Col 3:12). He can also add, "forgiving one another... even as Christ forgave you, so you also must do" (Col 3:13). In 1 Cor 6:15-20, he even bases his appeal to avoid immorality on what his readers should know. Their body is the Spirit's temple (v 19); they belong to God in both body and spirit (v 20). *Therefore*, they should flee sexual sin.

It is a serious misconception to think that godly living is undermined if believers know already that they belong to Christ forever. On the contrary, the joy and gratitude of an assured relationship to God are precisely the wellsprings from which holiness most naturally arises. The New Testament writers, at least, believed this strongly, even if we do not. The writer of 1 John believed it emphatically.

John's Realism about Possible Failure

The appeal which John makes (1 John 2:15-17) to avoid the enticements of the world demonstrates also his practical realism. He knows full well that the world possesses a deceptive attractiveness to which even true Christians may fall prey.

In particular, in this epistle, he is concerned with the worldly point of view put forth by the false teachers against whom he writes. These antichrists, as he fittingly calls them (1 John 2:18, 22), "are of the world. Therefore they speak as of the world, and the world hears them" (1 John 4:5). The readers need to be reminded of their true relationship to Christ so that they may effectively resist the false ideas to which they are being exposed.

One idea that the antichrists may have advanced was that the readers were not after all genuinely saved. It seems possible that the false teachers were the forerunners of the later gnostic heretics, and if so, this is very likely to have been one of their opinions. A strong streak of elitism ran through gnostic thought. The gnostics alone could look forward to eternal happiness or bliss (however they may have defined this). The antichrists may have suggested that the readers did not have eternal life at all, and that they needed to adopt the "gnosis" (knowledge), which the gnostics brought, in order to have it.

But the link between the antichrists and the gnostics, or "proto-gnostics," is by no means a firm conclusion of modern scholarship. Raymond Brown writes:

> Most scholars, including those who speak of Docetists and of Cerinthus, suspect that the adversaries of I and II John had gnostic leanings; and some are content to designate them as gnostics. Gnosticism is notoriously hard to define; the gnostics were marvelously varied; and orthodox Christians used the term *gnosis*, "knowledge," almost as freely as those whom they excluded as gnostics for proclaiming a "so called *gnosis*." The complexity of the last issue as it pertains to Johannine thought is reflected by these statements: "Eternal life consists in this: that they *know* you, the one true God, and Jesus Christ, the one whom you sent" (John 17:3); and "Now this is how we can be sure that we *know* Him" (I John 2:3). All

early Christians claimed to know God—how then did the claim of the Johannine authors differ from the claim of their adversaries?[39]

Some nineteenth-century scholars thought that the adversaries of 1 and 2 John could be identified with gnostic groups named by Irenaeus and the other writers against heresy. For instance, Pfleiderer thought of them as followers of Basilides (*ca.* 120-145), and Holtzmann referred to Satornil (Saturninus). Such associations often presupposed a very late dating for 1 John and have been abandoned today in favor of speaking of the adversaries as "proto-gnostics" who antedated the named gnostic systems of the mid-second century. (Indeed, it is possible in my judgment that the Johannine adversaries played a catalyzing role in the development of such later systems...) However, in speaking of the "proto-gnostics" one has introduced the truly indefinable. How many and which features of later gnosticism need have been present for a group to be so characterized? For instance, very important in later gnosticism were such features as a series of eons intermediary between the supreme God and human beings, an evaluation of the Old Testament creator God as evil, and the preexistence of the souls of the *pneumatikoi*, or spiritually elite...Yet no such features are apparent in the statements of the false teachers of 1 and 2 John.

That something like this was indeed part of the problem is strongly hinted at toward the end of John's first critique of the antichrists. This critique, which begins in 1 John 2:18, reaches its climax in 1 John 2:25-27.

It is in verse 25 that John reminds his readers, "And this is the promise that He has promised us—eternal life."

Having said this, he adds at once, "These things I have written to you concerning those who try to deceive you" (1 John 2:26).

---

[39] Raymond E. Brown, *The Epistles of John*, AB (Garden City, NY: Doubleday, 1982), 59-60.

The close connection of these two statements certainly makes it probable that the false teachers denied the divine promise about eternal life on which the readers were relying.

The readers, therefore, must be assured that "I have not written to you because you do not know the truth, but because you know it, and that no lie is of the truth" (1 John 2:21). Their responsibility is to "let that abide in you which you heard from the beginning" (1 John 2:24a). They are not to give way before the falsehoods they are now hearing. And if they do hold on to the Christian truth they already know, the abiding life will be their continuing experience. "If what you heard from the beginning abides in you, you also will abide in the Son and in the Father" (1 John 2:24b).

But here, as we have already seen in John 8 and John 15, the abiding life is a conditional experience. The words, "*If* what you have heard from the beginning abides in you," show this. John is perfectly sure that his readers are forgiven, know God, have experienced victory over the wicked one and know the truth, because he says so (1 John 2:12-14, 21). But he is not equally sure that the readership will not be seduced by the worldly spirit which they are now confronting.

This perspective is precisely the opposite of the view that is so frequently taken of John's first epistle. So far from commanding his readers to "abide" in order to assure themselves that they are truly saved, he in fact assures them they are saved and challenges them on that basis to abide. How do they know they are saved? They have the divine promise of eternal life (1 John 2:25).

The Purpose of 1 John: Fellowship

If all of this is kept in mind, the reader of 1 John will be able to grasp the meaning of the important statement found in 1 John 5:13. There the Apostle declares, "These things I have written to you who believe in the name of the Son of God, that you may know that you have eternal life." This statement is frequently and wrongly taken as a statement of purpose for the entire epistle. It assumes mistakenly that the expression "these things" refers to the letter as a whole.[40] But this is contrary to the writer's usage. In 1 John 2:1, the words "these things I write" clearly refer to the immediately preceding discussion of sin in 1 John 1:5-10. In 2:26, a comparable statement refers with equal clarity to the previous section about the antichrists. From these two earlier examples, we would naturally draw the conclusion that the "these things" of 1 John 5:13 is most likely to refer to the subject matter right before it.

This conclusion is fully justified by the content of 1 John 5:9-12. In fact, in these verses alone do we find in this epistle a direct discussion of faith and eternal life. The passage deserves quotation:

> If we receive the witness of men, the witness
> of God is greater; for this is the witness
> of God which He has testified of His Son.
> He who believes in the Son of God has the
> witness in himself; he who does not believe
> God has made Him a liar, because he has not
> believed the testimony that God has given of
> His Son. And this is the testimony: that God
> has given us eternal life, and this life is in
> His Son. He who has the Son has life; he who
> does not have the Son of God does not have
> life (1 John 5:9-12).

---

[40] But this opinion is far from universal. Brown, *Epistles*, 608, writes: "Many scholars (Alexander, Brooke, Klopper, Schnackenburg, Schneider) refer it ['these things'] to 5:1-12 or to the last verse of the unit." One must also note Smalley's comments arguing that 5:13 concludes a unit covering 5:5-13 and he appropriately points to an *inclusio* [a technique for rounding off a literary unit] consisting of "a repeated allusion [vv 5 and 13] to faith in the Son of God." However, Smalley does not confine the reference of v 13 to vv 5-12 alone, although he admits that "these things" "may refer to John's teaching in vv 5-12." Stephen S. Smalley, *1, 2, 3 John*, WBC (Waco, TX: Word Books, 1984), 289-90.

It is to these statements that John adds in verse 13, "These things I have written to you who believe in the name of the Son of God, *that you may know* that you have eternal life" (emphasis added).

In a passage like this we are plainly breathing once again the atmosphere of the Fourth Gospel and of verses like John 5:24. There is nothing in 1 John 5:9-12 about "obedience" or "abiding" or anything else of that sort. Everything is made to hinge on whether or not we can accept God's testimony about His Son.

Moreover, eternal life is seen as something God "has given" us in His Son, that is, as always for John, it is a divine gift. It is precisely these reaffirmations of the simple Gospel that are the grounds on which the Apostle expects his readers to *know* that they possess eternal life. To put it simply, they are to trust "the promise that He has promised" them (1 John 2:25).

There is no reason, therefore, to seek the purpose of this epistle exclusively in 1 John 5:13 anymore than it is to be sought exclusively in 1 John 2:1 or 1 John 2:26. Instead, the most natural place to look for the overarching thrust of the letter is in its prologue. *And there the purpose is defined clearly* as *"fellowship" with God.*

John introduces his epistle like this:

> That which was from the beginning, which we have heard, which we have seen with our eyes, which we have looked upon, and our hands have handled, concerning the Word of life...that which we have seen and heard we declare to you, that you also may have fellowship with us; and truly our fellowship is with the Father and with His Son Jesus Christ
> (1 John 1:1, 3).

Much confusion could have been avoided in the study of John's first epistle if this initial declaration of intent had

First John: Tests of Life?

been clearly kept in mind. Fellowship is John's primary concern and goal.[41]

The Threat to Fellowship

It should go without saying that "fellowship" is not to be defined as practically a synonym for being a Christian. With this in mind, then, 'fellowship' between the believer and his heavenly Father refers to an experience of 'sharing.' At its most basic level what is shared is 'light.' God both is, and is *in,* the light (1 John 1:5, 7). When the believer "lives" (= "walks") there, he shares with God whatever the light may reveal to him. But this requires openness and a readiness to confess sins as the light may show them to us.[42] King David was surely a regenerate man when he committed adultery and murder, but he could not be said to have been in God's fellowship at the time.

Even on a human plane, a son or daughter may lose fellowship with a parent even though they do not thereby lose the family relationship. The equation of "fellowship" with "being a Christian" (or something similar) is extremely far-fetched. Fellowship, like abiding, is a fully conditional relationship. This fact is sufficiently demonstrated by the statements found in 1 John 1:5-10.

---

[41] Commenting on v 3 and the words "that you also may have fellowship with us," Smalley (*1, 2, 3 John*, 11) correctly observes: "In the second part of this verse John moves on to declare his purpose in writing."

[42] The range of the word for "fellowship" (Greek= *koinōnia*) is well presented by Smalley (*1, 2, 3 John*, 12): "'Fellowship'...is a richly significant theological term. The Gr. Word literally means 'joint ownership', or 'partnership.' In the NT this 'mutual sharing' may refer to participation in either material goods, as when Christians in Macedonia and Achaia 'raised a common fund'...for the poor among the saints in Jerusalem (Rom 15:26); or in spiritual benefits, as when Paul speaks of 'sharing'... in the blessings of the gospel (1 Cor 9:23), or enjoying—in the words of 'the Grace'—the 'fellowship of the Spirit' (2 Cor 13:13; cf. also Rom 15:27)."

Fellowship was precisely what was threatened by the false ideas of the antichrists. Since the readers had a divine promise about eternal life, nothing these false prophets could do or say could destroy the readers' fundamental relationship to God. But should the readership begin to listen to the doctrines of these men, their experience of fellowship with the Father and the Son would be in jeopardy. Up to now, the readers had apparently resisted the false teaching successfully (1 John 4:4). The Apostle wishes this resistance to continue (1 John 2:24-27).

Ironically, the antichrists with whom John is concerned had evidently arisen right out of the apostolic circle itself. This is indicated by:

> They went out from us, but they were not of us; for if they had been of us, they would have continued with us; but they went out that they might be made manifest, that none of them were of us (1 John 2:19).

In this interesting statement, the word *us* indicates the apostolic circle to which the writer belongs. This is shown by the immediate contrast with *you* found in verse 20. This we/you contrast appears for the first time in the prologue itself (1 John 1:1-3) and again, clearly, in 1 John 4:4-6. In the latter passage the *they* (1 John 4:5) refers to the antichrists, as it also does here in 1 John 2:19.

The false prophets had therefore withdrawn from the apostolic fellowship, which probably means that they had once been a part of the Palestinian church. Jerusalem and Judea had long been the orbit of direct apostolic influence and authority. But roots like this could give their teachings an aura of respectability which might have a dangerous impact on the readership to whom they had come.

In this respect, these people had something in common with the legalists of Acts 15:1, since the legalists also came to Antioch from Judea. The Jerusalem Council denied any connection with them (Acts 15:24) just as John does here.

The statement of 1 John 2:19 cannot be taken as a general proposition about the lifestyle of the born-again believer. John is talking about heresy and defection from the faith and declaring that such defection would have been inconceivable if these individuals had truly shared the Apostles' spirit and perspective.

His words bear a striking resemblance to the observation of the Apostle Paul:

> For first of all, when you come together as a church, I hear that there are divisions among you, and in part I believe it. For there must also be factions among you, that those who are approved may be recognized among you (1 Cor 11:18-19).

Paul's comment is instructive. Heresy and division, even among genuine Christians (he does *not* suggest that any of his readers are *not* Christians), is designed by God to distinguish those who merit His approval from those who do not. Heresy does not occur in a vacuum. Rather it unmasks deep spiritual deficiencies which otherwise might go undetected.

This is essentially what John declares here as well. The withdrawal of these false teachers unmasked their fundamental disharmony with the outlook of the Apostles. In that sense "they were not of us."

Smalley's view of the text (1 John 2:19) bears considerable resemblance to my own. He writes:

> This raises the question of the initial status of the schismatics [= the antichrists]. It is certainly true that by the time of 1 John the erroneous theology, and indeed behavior, of the heretically inclined members of John's church had become apparent; and, of course, we must always be alert to the distinction between true and false claims to the faith within any Christian society...But it is possible, in this instance, that those who later allowed their heretical thought and actions to

run away with them (when it could obviously be said…"they were not of us") were in the first place believers with a genuine, if uninformed, faith in Jesus.[43]

To say more than this is to go beyond the text. No doubt the antichrists *were* unsaved. But this is not the point. Even if they *had been* genuine believers, such a withdrawing could not have taken place if—and as long as—they truly shared the apostolic spirit and commitment to the truth. To make a general expression like "of us" mean something more specific than that is not warranted in any way.

The principal source of confusion in much contemporary study of 1 John is to be found in the failure to recognize the real danger against which the writer is warning. The eternal salvation of the readership is not imperiled. It is not even in doubt as far as the author is concerned.

But seduction by the world and its anti-Christian representatives was a genuine threat which had to be faced. Along with their heretical denials of the Person of Christ (1 John 2:22-23; 4:1-3), the false teachers evidently also promoted a lifestyle that was basically worldly and unloving. If the readers went in *that* direction, they would lose fellowship both with the apostles themselves as well as with the Father and the Son (see 1 John 1:3).

Fellowship and the Knowledge of God

It is certainly not by chance that a general warning against the selfish and lustful spirit of the world (1 John 2:15-17) immediately precedes the first specific warning against the antichrists (1 John 2:18-27). Again, the second direct caution against false prophets (1 John 4:1-6) is followed by an exhortation to "love one another" (1 John 4:7) and an extended passage on love (1 John 4:7-21). If the readers should begin to doubt the reality of their personal

---

[43] Smalley, 103.

salvation and their fundamental relationship to God, they would be more easily enticed into the loveless, self-seeking lifestyle all around them.

The readers need to know, therefore, that they truly have eternal life (1 John 2:25; 5:13) and are called to experience fellowship with the Apostles themselves (1:3a) and with the Father and the Son (1 John 1:3b). To surrender such fellowship (they apparently had not done so yet) would be to surrender the privilege of truly *knowing God*.

In ordinary human life, fellowship with an individual is the essential means for gaining an intimate knowledge of that individual. Friends come to know friends, and even children come to know their parents, by means of shared time and experience, that is, through "fellowship."

The same is true also at the level of our relationship to God. While in one sense all true Christians know God (John 17:3), it is possible to think of a sense in which a true Christian may *not* know God.

This is made clear in a striking remark by the Lord Jesus Christ in John 14:7. There he declares to His disciples, "If you had known Me, you would have known My Father also; and from now on you know Him and have seen Him." The form of the conditional sentence in Greek indicates (as the English does also) that up to this moment the disciples had, in a special sense, not really known Jesus or His Father.

Modern critical editions of the Greek New Testament read another form of condition which commentators often adopt. Morris is perceptive, however, when he writes:

> The conditional construction implies that the disciples have not really known Christ and accordingly that they have not known the Father. In a sense, of course, they had known Jesus. They had known him [sic] well enough to leave their homes and friends and livelihood to follow him [sic] wherever He went. But they did not know Him in His

> full significance. Really to know Him is to know His Father. Up till now all has been preparation.[44]

In a footnote he adds: "There is another reading...This would make the words a promise: 'If (as is the case) you have come to know Me, you will know my [sic] Father also.' The attestation of this reading is inferior, and the context makes the rebuke more likely."[45] When Philip at once requests to see the Father (John 14:8), his ignorance about Christ is reaffirmed:

> Jesus said to him, "Have I been with you so long, and yet you have not known Me, Philip? He who has seen Me has seen the Father; so how can you say, 'Show us the Father'?" (John 14:9).

Despite the fact that Philip and the other disciples had believed in Jesus (John 1:40-51; 2:11) and had eternal life, the Person of their Savior remained something of a mystery to them. They had not yet realized how fully He reflected His Father (John 14:10) and, in this sense, they did not *know* Him.

Later in the same chapter Jesus offers a personal self-disclosure to His disciples which is conditioned on their obedience to His commands. His statement shows that He speaks of a future experience for them which will involve intimacy with Himself and His Father:

> "He who has My commandments and keeps them, it is he who loves Me. And he who loves Me will be loved by My Father, and I will love him and manifest Myself to him." Judas (not Iscariot) said to Him, "Lord, how is it that you will manifest Yourself to us, and not to the

---

[44] Leon Morris, *The Gospel According to John*, NIC (Grand Rapids: Eerdmans, 1971), 641-42.
[45] Ibid., 642 fn 19.

> world?" Jesus answered and said to him, "If
> anyone loves Me, he will keep My Word; and
> My Father will love him, and We will come to
> him and make Our home with him. He who
> does not love Me does not keep My words; and
> the word which you hear is not Mine but the
> Father's who sent Me" (John 14:21-24).

It is plain from this passage that "fellowship" and "the knowledge of God" are implied in the offer Jesus is making. Even the concept of the "abiding" life is suggested by the Greek word for "home" which is related to the word for "abide." But everything depends on the love that the disciples have for their Lord, which is seen as the true source of obedience to His commands.

It is precisely this kind of truth that pervades John's first epistle. "Fellowship" is its overriding theme. This means quite simply the "abiding" life marked by the self-disclosure of Christ, that is, by the knowledge of God.

But just as in John 14:21-24, such an experience can only be claimed by those who obey Jesus' commandments (1 John 2:3-6). The readers need to keep this in mind with regard to any false claims to "knowledge" which they may have heard. And they need to apply it to their own personal lives.

Particularly striking in regard to the theme of "knowing God" is:

> Beloved, let us love one another, for love is of
> God; and everyone who loves is born of God
> and knows God. He who does not love does
> not know God, for God is love (1 John 4:7-8).

It would be natural to conclude from this text that "new birth" and "knowing God" can be distinguished. If a man loves (in the Christian sense of that word), both experiences can be predicated of him. If he does *not* love, all that John states is that he does not *know* God. John does not say, however, that he is not born of God. Once again, Smalley's comments are observant:

> Love by itself cannot be the criterion for knowing God (v 7); and similarly a lack of love does not by itself prove that no relationship with God exists. But because God's nature is love...the knowledge of God *should* [italics his] lead to love for others...Anyone who enters into a real relationship with a loving God can be transformed into a loving person (see v 11).[46]

It would have been easy for the Apostle to have said this if he had believed it. But when it comes to failure in Christian experience, *including the failure to love*, John is a hardheaded realist. He is, in fact much more of a realist than are many modern theologians.

Sin in the Christian's Life

John's realism extends to his discussion about sin in the believer's life.

According to John, there is no time when a Christian may say he is sinless. Indeed, "If we say that we have no sin, we deceive ourselves, and the truth is not in us" (1 John 1:8). One indication that the truth has an effective hold on the Christian's heart is his awareness that he is a Sinful person. Of course, this must be accompanied by a willingness to confess his sin whenever he detects it (1 John 1:9). Not to do so is to hide from reality and to live in the dark (cf. 1 John 1:5-7).

There is no fellowship with God in the dark. Some have thought, however, that John contradicts his earlier insistence on the reality of sin in a Christian's life by his later words in 1 John 3:6 and 9. In those places, the Apostle writes:

---

[46] Smalley, *1, 2, 3 John*, 238.

> Whoever abides in him does not sin. Whoever sins has neither seen Him nor known Him (1 John 3:6).

> Whoever has been born of God does not sin, for His seed remains in him; and he cannot sin, because he has been born of God (1 John 3:9).

These statements are straightforward enough and ought not to be watered down or explained away. Nevertheless, they do not contradict 1 John 1:8.

In modern times a popular method for dealing with the problems of 1 John 3:6, 9 has been to appeal to the use of the Greek present tense. It is claimed that this tense requires a translation like. "Whoever has been born of God does not *go* on sinning," or, "does not *continually* sin." The conclusion to be drawn from such renderings is that, though the Christian may sin somewhat (how much is never specified), he may not sin regularly or persistently. But on all grounds, whether linguistic or exegetical, this approach is indefensible.

The appeal to the present tense has long invited suspicion. C. H. Dodd expressed his own doubts some forty-five years ago when he wrote:

> Yet it is legitimate to doubt whether the reader could be expected to grasp so subtle a doctrine simply upon the basis of a precise distinction of tenses without further guidance. Moreover, it is not clear that this distinction of tenses is carried right through with the precision which would be necessary if the whole weight of the argument rested upon it.[47]

---

[47] C. H. Dodd, *The Johannine Epistles,* MNTC (New York: Harper and Row, 1946), 79.

No other text can be cited where the Greek present tense, unaided by qualifying words, can carry this kind of significance. Indeed, when the Greek writer or speaker wished to indicate that an action was, or was not, continual, there were special words to express this.

What is called "aspect" in the Greek verb system is very poorly understood by many people who have studied (and written about) the significance of the Greek tenses. The words of Maximillian Zerwick are a caution frequently ignored. He writes:

> "NB: The aspects, as was said above, *present the action as* [italics his] a simple fact, etc.; the use of the tenses is determined not so much by the objective reality *(which commonly admits all three aspects according to what the speaker wishes to express* [italics added]) as by the speaker's needs: he will use the aorist for an action which objectively lasted a long time or was repeated, if what he wishes to express is simply the fact that the action took place; or *the present for an action which is of its nature momentary* [italics added], if what he wishes to express is the nature or kind of action as distinct from its concrete realization."[48]

The idea that the Greek present tense automatically suggests on-going or continuous action is a linguistic myth. No doubt it is believed by many (even some scholars), but it is mythical nonetheless.

But this is not all. The "tense solution" lands its proponents in enormous difficulties and inconsistencies. Thus, in 1 John 1:8, if the present tense were read in this way, we would have the following: "If we say we do not *continually* have sin, we deceive ourselves and the truth is not in us."

---

[48] Maximillian Zerwick, *Biblical Greek* (Rome: Scripta Pontificii Instituti Biblici, 1963), 78.

But if the tense explanation for 1 John 3:9 were correct, we ought to be able to say this. It should not be self-deception to make this claim if "whoever is born of God does not *continually* sin".[49]

In the same way, if the tense is given this force in 1 John 5:16, we could read. "If anyone sees his brother *continually* sinning a sin...." But how could someone see a brother *continually* sinning if one born of God does not *continually* sin?

It is apparent that the "tense solution" is an example of what in logic is called "special pleading." That is, it is selectively applied to 1 John 3:6 and 9 because they are problems, but not applied elsewhere even to the same kind of idea. Nor would those who propose this kind of approach welcome its use in other doctrinally significant places.

As an example, John 14:6 might be handled as some wish to handle 1 John 3:6, 9. Then we could read this famous text as follows: "I am the way, the truth, and the life. No one *continually* comes to the Father except through Me." But the implication of this would be that *occasionally* someone might come another way. Obviously such an approach falsifies the text.

When the passage in which John's statements occur is closely considered, it is clear that the writer intends them to be taken in an absolute sense. Immediately before verse 6, he says, "And you know that He was manifested to take away our sins, and in Him there is no sin" (1 John 3:5).

Clearly, the declaration "in Him there is no sin" is an absolute denial of sin in the Son of God. But this is followed at once by the statement, "Whoever abides in Him does not sin." The point unmistakably is: if you abide in a sinless Person, you do not sin. As Brown puts it, "The logic of the statement [in v 6a] flows from the preceding verse: there is

---

[49] This problem was pointed out years ago by Dodd, *Epistles*, 79.

no sin in Christ, and so those who abide in him should have no sin in them."⁵⁰

The same can really be said also of 1 John 3:9. The reason one who is born of God does not sin is that "His seed remains in him; and he cannot sin, because he has been born of God." In other words, the regenerate one is sinless because he is begotten by a sinless Parent. It is completely contrary to the intent of the author to water such statements down. A sinless Parent does not beget a child who only sins a little. To say this, is in fact to deny what the text intends to communicate.

But how are such claims to be harmonized with the direct statement of 1 John 1:8 that no believer can claim to be sinless? There seems to be one simple way in which this can be done. The claims of 1 John 3:6 and 3:9 pertain to the believer when he is viewed only as "abiding" or as one who is "born of God." That is, sin is never the product of our abiding experience. It is never the act of the regenerate self per se.

On the contrary, sin is the product of ignorance and blindness toward God. "Whoever sins has neither seen Him nor known Him" (1 John 3:6b). When a believer sins, he is acting out of darkness, not out of knowledge.

One must be careful in 1 John 3:6b not to make the statement mean, "Whoever sins has *never* seen Him nor known Him." The Greek perfect tense, which is used in the verbs "seen" and "known," does not suggest this. This statement is helpful:

> In essence, though not exactly in use, the Greek perfect tense corresponds to the English one, in that it is *not a past tense but a present one*, indicating *not the past action*

---

⁵⁰ Brown, *Epistles,* 403.

as such but *the present <state of affairs> resulting from the past action.*[51]

It is possible to paraphrase the statement of the verse like this: 'Whoever sins *is in a condition of failure to see and know* God." The impression left by this rendering is somewhat different than the one left by the English present perfects ("has not seen nor known"). The English verbs *can* imply "never" in the tight context, but do not necessarily do so. If someone asks, "Have you seen Joe?" and the reply is, "No, I haven't seen Joe," this will normally *not* be taken to mean, "I've *never* seen Joe." The point we must get from 1 John 3:6b is that, *in the act of sinning,* a person has neither seen nor known God. That is, sin proceeds from darkness and ignorance toward God, never from a true "seeing" or "knowing" of Him. Sin, as it were, turns our eyes from God, or blinds us to Him, so that in committing it we can only be said to operate in spiritual darkness and in a profound lack of moral understanding. We are not talking about what our intellect may know—which can be much indeed. I am talking about moral blindness and moral ignorance, which is quite another thing. He is acting as a man of flesh, not as a regenerate person.

Not surprisingly, even Paul could view sin as something fundamentally foreign to his true inner self. So, in recounting his personal struggle against sin in Romans 7, he can write:

> Now if I do what I will not to do, *it is no longer I who do it,* but sin that dwells in me. I find then a law, that evil is present with me, the one who wills to do good. For I delight in the law of God according to the inward man. But I see another law in my members, warring against the law of my mind, and bringing me into captivity to the law of sin which is in my members. O

---

[51] Zerwick, *Biblical Greek*, 96, italics added.

> wretched man that I am! Who will deliver me from this body of death? I thank God—through Jesus Christ our Lord! So then, with the mind I myself serve the law of God, but *with the flesh* the law of sin (Rom 7:20-25, emphasis added).

In this significant text, the Apostle discloses a self-perspective in which he can actually admit that he sins and yet still say that "it is no longer I who do it." His true self ("I myself," v 25) serves God's law, even while he confesses that "with the flesh" he serves the law of sin.

It is of great importance that this form of self-analysis precedes the solution to his problem which is given in Romans 8. To view sin as basically foreign to what we are as regenerate people in Christ, is to take the first step toward spiritual victory over it.

From a slightly different perspective, the same conclusion can be drawn for the statement found in Gal 2:20, "I have been crucified with Christ; it is no longer I who live, but Christ lives in me." But if only Christ truly lives, sin cannot be a part of that experience at all. If the person sins in whom Christ lives, that sin is in no way a part of that person's fundamental life, since Christ is that life.

Very close indeed to my view is the view of Plummer who states (on 1 John 3:6):

> By these apparently contradictory statements [i.e., 1:1-8; 2:27; 3:6] put forth one after another S. John expresses that internal contradiction of which everyone who is endeavoring to do right is conscious. What S. John delivers as a series of aphorisms, which mutually qualify and explain one another, S. Paul puts forth dialectically as an argument. 'If what I would not, that I do, it is no more I that do it, but sin which dwelleth in me' (Rom vii. 20). And on the other hand, 'I live;

yet not I, but Christ liveth in me' (Gal ii. 20).[52]

Plummer adds later (under 1 John 3:9):

> The strong statement is exactly parallel to *v.* 6 and is to be understood in a similar sense. It is literally true of the Divine nature imparted to the believer. That does not and cannot sin. A child of the God who is Light can have nothing to do with sin which is darkness: the two are morally incompatible."[53]

It is the final irony that the "tense solution" not only mishandles the linguistics of the text, but undermines its true force and power. By adopting an interpretation that tolerates a "moderate amount" of sin, this view destroys the author's point. *All sin* is the fruit of blindness and ignorance toward God (1 John 3:6b). It is satanic since "the devil has sinned from the beginning" (1 John 3:8). To make *any sin* less than these things, is to soften its character and to prepare the ground for tolerating it.

When everything is considered, the "tense solution" is a logical and theological quagmire. No wonder that the most recent major commentaries on 1 John abandon it. The "tense solution" is an idea whose time has come—and gone![54]

---

[52] Alfred Plummer, *The Epistles of St. John* (Cambridge: University Press, 1886; [reprint ed., Grand Rapids: Baker, 1980]), 76.

[53] Ibid., 79.

[54] The declining popularity of the "tense solution" is perhaps to be traced to the significant article by S. Kubo, "1 John 3:9: Absolute or Habitual?" *Andrews University Seminary Studies* 7 (1969): 47-56. The "tense solution" is abandoned by I. Howard Marshall, *The Epistles of John*, MC (Grand Rapids: Eerdmans, 1978), 180, 187-188. Raymond Brown, *Epistles*, writes of it (p. 414), "Alexander, Dodd and Prunet question whether the author would let such an important distinction rest on so fragile a grammatical subtlety. Would the readers perceive such a subtlety?" Brown also treats the view as contextually unsupported (p. 415). Smalley likewise rejects the "grammatical" solution and regards

It follows from what has been said, that if a regenerate man *cannot* sin *at all* as a regenerate man (but only as an expression of his sinful flesh), he can never *manifest* his true inward nature by any other means than righteousness. By contrast, a "child of the devil" manifests his nature through sin.

This is precisely what John goes on to say in 1 John 3:10a, "By this the children of God are manifest and the children of the devil" (trans. from Greek). The key word here is "manifest." A sinning Christian *conceals* his true character when he sins and *reveals* it only through holiness. On the other hand, a "child" of Satan *reveals* his true character by sin.

We should be cautious about calling all unsaved people "children of the devil." This kind of designation is rare in the New Testament and seems confined to those who are Satan's direct agents in a religious context (Matt 13:35, 38-39; Acts 13:10). For John, the expression "children of the devil" probably refers to the antichrists.[55]

Clearly, John wishes his readers to manifest their true nature by being victorious over sin. They are to shun the ideas and conduct of the Devil's children.

God's Children: Loving and Hating

The words *by this* (1 John 3:10a; NKJV="in this") appear to round off the discussion found in 1 John 3:1-9. At 1 John

---

it as "stressing artificially the continuous element in the present tense" (p. 159); and he raises the pertinent question: "If God, whose nature remains in the Christian (3:9) and keeps him safe (5:18), can be said to protect the believer from habitual sin, why can he not preserve him as well from occasional sins?" (p. 160). Thus the "tense solution" is an explanation whose serious inadequacies are now widely recognized. Its true place in the history of the interpretation of 1 John is as an exegetical curiosity.

[55] The identification of the "antichrists" with "the children of the devil" is made also by Brown, *Epistles*, who calls them "the secessionists" (p. 416), and by Smalley who calls them "the antichristian secessionists" (p. 180).

3:10b, a new thrust appears.[56] It builds, of course, on what has just been said.

If *all* sin—of whatever kind or extent—is satanic, it follows that it never finds its source in God. The one who does it, therefore, is not "of God" in the sinful thing that he does. This does not mean that such a person is unsaved. It means rather that he is acting outside of all vital contact with God. Satan, not God, is the source of his actions.

The Greek expression *einai ek* ("to be of...") is helpfully discussed by Brown, though not without some theological imprecision. Yet I can basically concur when he writes: "The main theological usage of *einai ek* is in the Johannine dualistic worldview to indicate origin from and/or adherence to one side or the other."[57] To put it plainly, we could say that verse 10b means: "Whoever does not do righteousness *is not on God's side*." But this is not the same as saying that they are unsaved. Believers can choose "the wrong side" by choosing unrighteous courses of action. This is precisely what James warns his Christian readers about in Jas 4:4, for example: "Adulterers and adulteresses! Do you not know that friendship with the world is enmity with God? Whoever therefore wants to be a friend of the world makes himself an enemy of God."

John goes on to say, "Whoever does not do righteousness is not of God, nor is he who does not love his brother" (1 John 3:10b, [trans. from Greek]). That these words are intended for Christians is obvious on their face. The words "his brother" indicate this quite plainly. An unsaved man cannot hate *his* Christian brother since a true Christian is not really *his* brother. If John was thinking of unregenerate people, he could easily have said: "nor is he who does not

---

[56] Brown, *Epistles*, 416, concurs with this analysis: "Structurally it seems to make better sense if ['in this'] refers to what precedes, while what follows (3:10bc) is seen as transitional to the next unit. The ['in this'] statement in 3:10a then becomes the conclusion of the whole apocalyptic theme that began with the mention of 'the last hour' in 2:18."

[57] Ibid., 313.

love *a* brother." The fact that he personalizes the relationship with the word *his* must not be overlooked.

Quite naturally John appeals to the commandment given to Christians to "love one another" (1 John 3:11). He warns against brotherly hatred such as Cain exhibited toward Abel and describes such hatred as Satanic (1 John 3:12a). He touches a sensitive nerve when he suggests that this hatred can arise from the superior character of our brother's righteousness (1 John 3:12b). Such hatred is also worldly, and its presence in people of the world should occasion no surprise (1 John 3:13). Only its presence in believers is abnormal.

At this point John slips into the first person plural. "*We* know that *we* have passed from death to life, because *we* love the brethren" (1 John 3:14a; emphasis added). This is followed by the warning that, *"He who does not love his brother abides in death"* (1 John 3:14b, emphasis added).

It is likely that the "we" of the first half of the verse is the familiar apostolic "we" of the epistle (cf. 1 John 1:1-5; 4:6).[58] The writer would thus be claiming that love of the brethren characterizes the apostolic circle to which he himself belongs. The apostles find their experience in the sphere of "life." Anyone who hates a brother is living in the sphere of death to which also the world belongs. Here (in 1 John 3:14b) the Greek has no word for "his" before "brother." The statement is applicable to anyone—saved or unsaved—who hates a Christian brother.

It is quite true that the expression "passed from death to life" occurs elsewhere in John 5:24. But that is the only other place in the New Testament where it does occur, outside of the present instance. So it is hardly a stereotyped or fixed expression even for John. The context here suggests

---

[58] The same threefold division in 3:13-14 ("the world," "you," and "we") is found also in 4:4-6 ("you," v 4; "they...of the world," v 5; "we," v 6). It is thus easy to see the "we" of 3:14, which is quite emphatic in the Greek, as a third group, the Apostles, who are contrasted with the loveless world, in particular the "antichrists."

that John is using it in an experiential sense and not with reference to conversion.

John means to say that he and his fellow apostles know that they are operating in a sphere which can be described as "life" because they actually love their brothers in Christ. If anyone does not love a brother he is clearly "abiding" in the sphere of death. That is to say, he is out of touch with God. (This is true whether a man is saved or unsaved.) He is not living as a disciple of Jesus Christ (cf. John 13:35).

There follows a verse that has perplexed many. In it John asserts, "Whoever hates his brother is a murderer, and you know that no murderer has eternal life abiding in him" (1 John 3:15). The idea that a Christian cannot commit murder encounters insuperable obstacles. For one thing, King David was guilty of murder in a fully literal sense. Moreover, upon confession of that sin, God forgave him (2 Sam 12:13; see Psalm 51 and 1 John 1:9). Even Peter feels it necessary to warn his Christian readers against murder (1 Pet 4:15). In the face of such facts, it is plain that a genuine believer is not immune even to this sin.

If anyone were to maintain that a Christian not only cannot commit murder, but he cannot even hate his brother, such a view would be totally lacking in Biblical realism. It is also quite contrary to actual Christian experience, as anybody who is fully honest must confess.

But John does not say that a murderer does not *have* eternal life. He says that a murderer does not have eternal life *abiding* in him. Since, for John, eternal life is nothing else than Christ Himself (cf. John 14:6; 1 John 1:2 and 5:20), this is the same as saying that "no murderer has *Christ* abiding in him."

Thus the key word in 1 John 3:14-15 is once again the word *abide*. In the sense in which this word is used in John 15 and everywhere in this epistle, this is a conditional experience dependent upon the Christian's obedience to God's commands. If a believer disobeys the command to "love one another" (1 John 3:11), he cannot claim to be "abiding" in the sphere of "life" or to have God's life "abiding" in him. Hatred breaks our *experiential contact* with the life of Christ, plunges us into spiritual darkness, and endows us with a quality of existence which can best be described as "death."

J. L. Houlden comes very close to my position when he writes on 3:14 as follows:

> V. 14 is ambiguous: but the last clause depends on the verb *know*, not on *passed*. So it does not mean that love brings about the transition from the sphere of death to that of (eternal) life (cf. i. 2; ii. 25; v. 11 ff.)—justification by works!—or even that the conviction that the transition has taken place is only held because brotherly love is observed to be present; but rather that the new life is savoured and enjoyed, and its reality assured, in the atmosphere of love which prevails. *We know*: not in the sense of intellectual demonstration but rather of experiential conviction. The love shows the genuineness of God's gift to believers, not because they are tempted to distrust it, but because they are concerned to show to those outside that this is their possession.[59]

This is a highly commendable treatment of this text.

As always, Paul also thought along these lines. When he attempted to live the Christian life under the law he discovered that "sin, taking occasion by the commandment, deceived me, and by it *killed me*" (Rom 7:11, emphasis added). In fact, speaking to Christians directly he states:

---

[59] J. L. Houlden, *A Commentary on the Johannine Epistles,* HNTC (New York: Harper and Row, 1973), 98. However, Houlden assigns v 15 to the unsaved heretics (the antichrists).

> And if Christ is in you, the body is dead
> because of sin, but the Spirit is life because of
> righteousness (Rom 8:10).

But if even the Christian's body may be called dead in a spiritual sense, what will the Christian experience if he lives according to the dictates of the body? The answer is obvious: he will have an experience that can be described as "death." Thus Paul goes on to warn: "For if you live according to the flesh *you will die*" (Rom 8:13, emphasis added).

It is clear that the Christian only *experiences* the eternal life God has freely given him when he is obedient to God. All else is an experience of *death*—at a spiritual level, first of all, but if continued in long enough, at a physical level as well (Jas 1:15; Prov 11:19; etc.).

In 1 John 3:10b-15, the Apostle's point is really quite simple. The failure to love one's brother is not a true experience of eternal life at all. It is an experience of moral murder and of death. Brown has surfaced some parallels which are pertinent to the view expressed in my text:

> This imagery appears in Jewish thought as well, e.g., Philo, *On Flight* 11 #58, "What is good and virtuous constitutes life; what is bad and wicked constitutes death." But in a general discussion on Abel, Philo, *That the Worse* 14 #48, warns of motion in the opposite direction: "The soul that has extirpated from itself the principle of the love...of virtue and the love of God has died to the life of virtue." Granted I John's reference to just/justice, the comment in the *Letter of Aristeas* is interesting: "Injustice is equivalent to the deprivation of life..." (212).[60]

The death/life motif was both fluid and flexible in ancient thought. Modern commentators who are fixated

---

[60] Brown, *Epistles*, 445-46.

on soteriology at every occurrence of the words "death" or "life" should broaden their horizons. This is putting it quite starkly, but it furnishes an effective antidote to inward tendencies which every honest believer will admit that he has.

Let us return for a moment to the statement of 1 John 4:7. If a person truly loves his fellow Christians, he shows thereby that he is both "born of God and knows God." If he does not, then he surely does not really *know* God at the level of real fellowship and intimacy with Christ.

Of course, the unsaved world does not know God either. The believer who harbors hatred toward another believer is stepping into the same sphere of spiritual darkness and death where unsaved people live and operate. This by no means calls his salvation into question, but it firmly negates every claim to intimacy with the Father and the Son. In the final analysis, it is this intimacy that the first epistle of John is all about (1 John 1:3-4).

Conclusion

In conclusion, therefore, it must be emphasized that the First Epistle of John is both internally consistent and fully harmonious with the uncomplicated offer of eternal life presented in the Fourth Gospel.

But the epistle will continue to be misunderstood by those who insist on equating "fellowship" and "abiding" with "regeneration" and "being a Christian." Once these unjustified equations are made, the message of John's letter is hopelessly obscured. The theological conclusions that arise as a result are fundamentally and irreconcilably hostile to the simple Biblical gospel. In fact, they clash with the offer of assurance of salvation based on the testimony and promise of God alone.

It is in this way that John's powerful letter about fellowship has been sadly distorted and violently thrust into service in the siege of the gospel.

6

The Christian and Apostasy

One of the most shocking questions in the Bible is recorded in Matt 11:3: "Are You the Coming One, or do we look for another?"

The reason we find this question astounding is because it came from John the Baptist himself. The man who asked it was the same one who had once announced, "Behold! The Lamb of God who takes away the sin of the world!" (John 1:29). He had also declared. "And I have seen and testified that this is the Son of God" (John 1:34). But this faith was clearly not present in the question, "Are You the Coming One?"

Of course, John was in prison at the time (Matt 11:2). No doubt his drained physical and mental condition contributed to the doubts he was experiencing. But one thing is plain. For the moment, his faith in Christ had failed.[61]

Was he now a lost man? Of course not. To the woman at the well of Sychar, to the rabbi Nicodemus, to all His hearers, Jesus had offered a gift to be appropriated by faith. It was the gift that was permanent, not necessarily the faith that laid hold of it to begin with.

Faith Is Fragile

Many present-day Christians think that the faith of a genuine believer cannot fail. But this is not an idea that can

---

[61] Editor's note: Postmodern Evangelicals now use this very incident to show that faith and doubt can coexist. However, this incident, as Zane shows, proves the opposite. When John the Baptist doubted that Jesus was the Messiah, he no longer believed that. Of course, after he heard Jesus' reply, he surely believed again. But while he doubted, he did not believe.

be supported from the New Testament. On the contrary, we learn the opposite from a statement:

> And their message will spread like cancer. Hymenaeus and Philetus are of this sort, who have strayed concerning the truth, saying that the resurrection is already past; and *they overthrow the faith* of some (2 Tim 2:17-18, emphasis added).

The Apostle Paul obviously knew of actual cases where the faith of individuals had been overthrown by false teaching. Yet, as the following verse makes clear, Paul is sure that such a calamity does not affect anyone's eternal destiny. He wrote:

> Nevertheless the solid foundation of God stands, having this seal: "The Lord knows those who are His," and, "Let everyone who names the name of Christ depart from iniquity" (2 Tim 2:19).

It is obviously true, of course, that God knows who are His. But this observation is so self-evident that it is not likely to be Paul's meaning. Instead, the Greek word for "know" can imply relationship, and the Apostle's statement is best understood in this sense. God knows intimately and personally all who stand in relationship to Him. This fact is undisturbed even when the believer's faith wavers or is overthrown.

The statement under discussion is drawn almost verbatim from the Greek (Septuagint) translation of Num 16:5, except that Paul substitutes "Lord" for "God." The Old Testament context suggests that the expression meant that God maintained His established relationship with Moses and Aaron despite the false claims of Korah and his rebels.

The budding of Aaron's rod, which followed the judgment on the rebels, showed the truth of this claim by Moses. The line of Aaron was God's elect high priestly line.[62]

Moreover, the reality just stated in no way compromises God's holiness. His demand remains unaffected: "Let everyone who names the name of Christ depart from iniquity." But these words are a *command*, while the words preceding them are a statement of fact. It is not said that the command is always heeded. The following verses (2 Tim 2:20-21) show that in God's house it is *not* always heeded. Nevertheless the demand remains.

Paul's words show clearly that human faith is fragile but that God's relationship to those who exercise that faith is permanent. To confuse the stability of a man's faith with the stability of God's purposes is to confuse two different things. Naturally, such confusion leads inevitably to doctrinal error.

It is often claimed by theologians that man has no capacity to believe and that faith, like salvation, must be given to him as a gift. But this view is contradicted by 2 Cor 4:3-4 where Paul wrote: "But even if our gospel is veiled, it is veiled to those who are perishing, whose minds the god of this age has blinded, who do not believe, lest the light of the gospel of the glory of Christ, who is the image of God, should shine on them."

From Paul's words it appears that Satan himself does not regard men as *constitutionally incapable* of faith. Instead, from his point of view, men are *in danger of*

---

[62] Martin Dibelius and Hans Conzelmann, *The Pastoral Epistles*, trans. Philip Buttolph and Adela Yarbro, ed. Helmut Koester, Herm (Philadelphia: Fortress Press, 1973), 112-13. Dibelius/Conzelmann properly connect the word "knows" in 2 Tim 2:19 with election, and they write: "The latter [the use of 'knows'] was perhaps understood by the author, not mystically, but in line with the conception of the church and election. *Odes of Sol.* 8.14f also points to the origin of the first saying in Christian poetry: 'For I do not turn away my face from them that are mine; /For I know them; /Before they came into being, /I took knowledge of them, /And on their faces I set my seal.'" The quotation from the *Odes of Solomon* is too striking, and too appropriate to Paul's context, to be ignored.

believing unless he actively blinds them. He must therefore prevent the truth from dawning on their hearts. This may be compared to an effort to keep light out of a dark room by (for example) drawing together a thick pair of curtains. The room *can* receive light but is prevented from doing so by the curtains. If someone pulls the curtains apart, light will automatically shine into the room.

God's role in bringing men to faith is therefore revelatory. (See our Lord's statement to Peter in Matt 16:17.) As Paul puts it in 2 Cor 4:6, God shines His light into our hearts. Perceiving God's Word as light (i.e., as truth) is precisely what faith does. When the truth of the sufficiency of Christ for the eternal salvation of every believer dawns on our hearts, we are *believing* the light and thus know that, in so believing, we ourselves are eternally saved. Thus faith is a capacity built into man by His Creator, just like the capacity to think or to speak. None of these capabilities are obliterated by the Fall, but man's use of them is seriously impaired by his own sinfulness. As a sinner, he prefers to believe a lie rather than the truth (see Rom 1:20-25).

Yet, despite man's darkened heart and Satan's special efforts to prevent man's illumination, God can break through all this darkness with the light of His truth and in so doing can meet a response of faith in man. So it is clear from all this that man's created capacity to believe things is awakened by the illumination God gives in the gospel. Belief in the truth is impossible for any man so long as he remains persuaded that the truth is false. Once he is persuaded of the truth of the saving message, he has believed it.

Finally, one must say that the Reformed view that man is in every sense a "corpse" without even the capacity to believe the light when it shines forth to him is a gross distortion of reality. It is a transparent effort to press a metaphor like "dead in trespasses and sins" (Eph 2:1) well beyond the legitimate parameters of that metaphor. Man is "dead in sins"[63] precisely because he is separated from God's own kind of life, as Paul states in Eph 4:18: "being alienated from the life of God, through the ignorance that is in them." But the metaphor is seriously misused when it is made the basis for denying to man any and all capacity to receive the truth of God as light. If man had no such capacity, he could not be charged with sin for his unbelief, as Jesus told the Pharisees: "If you were blind, you would have no sin" (John 9:41).

Apostasy in Hebrews 6

If this simple distinction had been kept in mind, the epistle to the Hebrews could have been taken by the Church at face value. Its solemn warnings against apostasy could have had their intended effect. Instead, that epistle has suffered much at the hands of expositors who felt, no doubt sincerely, that true Christians could not really give in to the dangers the writer of Hebrews describes.

As is well known, in Heb 6:4-5 the author describes individuals "who were once enlightened, and have tasted the heavenly gift, and have become partakers of the Holy Spirit, and have tasted the word of God and the powers of the age to come." These phrases very naturally describe real Christians. This will be obvious to all who have not already decided that the remainder of the passage cannot refer to Christians.

---

[63] Editor's note: Zane held that in Eph 2:1 Paul was *not* saying that before regeneration the Ephesians were dead *because of* trespasses and sins. Instead, as his comments here show, Zane understood Paul to mean that before regeneration people are spiritually dead and hence are slaves of sin in their experience (cf. Rom 6:18, 20-22).

It seems almost needless to refute in detail the efforts made to show that unregenerate people are in view here. All such efforts are strained and unconvincing.

However, it is worth noting that to take the word *tasted* as an inadequate appropriation (in contrast to "eating") is an idea clearly without foundation in this epistle. According to the author, "Jesus...was made a little lower than the angels...that He, by the grace of God, might taste death for everyone" (Heb 2:9). No one will maintain that the Savior's "taste" of death was anything but the most profound experience of death. The idea of "tasting" is also a recognizable Biblical figure for genuine appropriation of God's goodness (see 1 Pet 2:1-3; Ps 34:8). To take the word in another sense in Heb 6:4-5 has no valid support whatsoever.[64]

Additionally, the Greek verb for "enlightened" (Heb 6:4) is used again later in the letter to describe the readers' conversion experience ("illuminated," Heb 10:32), while the term "partakers" (Heb 6:4) also describes their relationship to their heavenly calling (Heb 3:1). On all grounds the effort to see unsaved people in this text is extremely unnatural.[65]

But those whom the writer describes in Heb 6:4-5 can "fall away." This fact is partially concealed by the familiar English translation, "if they shall fall away" (Heb 6:6). Actually there is no word for "if" in the Greek text and none is required in the English translation. The verb form which is rendered "fall way" is a Greek participle which stands

---

[64] James Moffatt, *A Critical and Exegetical Commentary on the Epistle to the Hebrews,* ICC (Edinburgh: T & T Clark, 1924), 78. As Moffatt pointed out long ago about the Greek word for "tasted" (*geusamenos*), it "recalls the partiality of Philo for this metaphor...but indeed it is common throughout contemporary Hellenistic Greek as a metaphor for experiencing."

[65] Moffatt, who rightly calls vv 4-5a a "fourfold description of believers," defines "enlightened" as "in the sense of having their eyes opened (Eph 1:18) to the Christian God" (p. 78). See also Donald Guthrie, *The Letter to the Hebrews: An Introduction and Commentary,* TNTC (Grand Rapids: Eerdmans, 1983), 144-145. His overall conclusions seem ambiguous (to me), but he is right to say: "...the words of this epistle...give no impression of incomplete enlightenment" (p. 144).

The Christian and Apostasy

last in a series of participles. The first of these participles is represented by the words "those who were once enlightened" (v 4). It ought to be translated as follows:

> For *it is* impossible, for those who were once enlightened, and have tasted the heavenly gift, and have become partakers of the Holy Spirit, and have tasted the good word of God and the powers of the age to come, and have fallen away, to renew them again to repentance...(Heb 6:4-6a).

The writer clearly talks as if he knew of such cases.

However, we should not understand "falling away" here as though it meant the loss of eternal life. This conclusion (so frequently drawn) is unwarranted. The author repeatedly urges his readers to maintain their Christian profession and confidence (cf. Heb 3:6, 12-15; 6:11-12; 10:23-25). The man who "falls away" is evidently the one who casts away his Christian confidence with its promise of "great reward" (Heb 10:35).

Here again we meet the fragile nature of human faith. Man's faith needs continual nurture and admonition. Apart from that, apostasy is possible.[66]

The author states that the man who "falls away" is impossible to "renew to repentance." This suggests a hardness of heart which resists all attempts to woo the man

---

[66] The "falling away" described in Hebrews 6 is taken to refer to *Christians who apostatize* by Moffatt (pp. 76-78); Jean Hering, *The Epistle to the Hebrews,* trans. A. W. Heathcote and P. J. Allcock (London: Epworth Press, 1970). 45-48; Hugh Montefiore, *A Commentary on the Epistle to the Hebrews* BNTC (London: Adam and Charles Black, 1964), 107-108; and William L. Lane, *Call to Commitment: Responding to the Message of Hebrews* (Nashville, TN: Thomas Nelson, 1985). 91-94. Lane, who believes (as do the other writers cited here) that the apostate will be lost, is as emphatic as anyone about the apostate being a Christian. He writes (p. 94): "The sin that the preacher warns his friends to avoid is commonly called 'apostasy.' It is a sin only a Christian can commit. *Apostasy consists in a deliberate, planned, intelligent decision to renounce publicly association with Jesus Christ*" (italics his).

back to faith. But the writer probably thinks only of the normal efforts which other Christians may make to do this. This impossibility can hardly apply to God. In fact, in the metaphor which follows (Heb 6:7-8), the author plainly implies the possibility of restoration after punishment has been experienced.

The image which he uses is of a field which partakes of the rain of heaven and brings forth fitting fruits (Heb 6:7). In that case, the field enjoys divine blessing. On the other hand, "if it bears thorns and briers, it is rejected and near to being cursed, whose end is to be burned" (Heb 6:8).[67]

The burning of fields was a practice known in antiquity and would doubtless be a familiar idea to the readers of the epistle. But this practice was not designed to destroy the field, but to destroy the unacceptable growth which made it unfruitful. By using such an illustration the author clearly signals the ultimate purpose of God's judgment on the apostate Christian. That purpose is restoration to fruitfulness.[68]

This in no way makes the anticipation of judgment a pleasant one. On the contrary, it is a fearful expectation (see Heb 10:26-27). The guilt of the apostate is enormous since his renunciation of the faith is like a personal re-crucifixion of God's Son in which his Savior is openly shamed once again (Heb 6:6b). His life as an apostate meets with divine rejection and falls under a curse which is realized in the retribution to which he is now exposed (Heb 6:8). One might recall in this connection the "curses" which fell on God's Old Testament people as a result of their disobedience to the covenant of their God (see Deut 27:9-26).

Apostasy in Hebrews 10

Hebrews 10:26-39 must be understood in essentially the same way. This famous passage follows a call to "hold fast the confession of our hope without wavering" (Heb

---

[67] Jean Hering, *Hebrews*, 48.
[68] Ibid. Moffatt, *Hebrews*, 80.

10:23) and a warning against "forsaking the assembling of ourselves together, as is the manner of some" (Heb 10:25). The *willful* sinning of Heb 10:26 is thus to be understood specifically of this kind of sin, namely, abandonment of the Christian faith and of the church. And this is said to be "after we have received the knowledge of the truth."

In other words, the writer again addresses the problem of apostasy.[69]

The author warns that to abandon Christianity is to abandon the only sacrifice (the death of Christ) which affords real protection and that apart from this "there no longer remains a sacrifice for sins" (Heb 10:26b). To take so fateful a step is to stand exposed to God's "fiery indignation." It is to range oneself with "the adversaries" of the Christian faith and to share in their calamities (Heb 10:27). But nothing in verses 26 and 27 ought to be taken as a reference to hell.

The punishment which the author predicts for the apostate will be a "worse punishment" than the summary execution which offenders against the Mosaic law experienced (Heb 10:28-29a). Of course, there are many forms of retribution which are "worse" than swift death. The writer of Lamentations gives eloquent expression to this reality (Lam 4:6, 9). One thinks readily of the distressing spirit that afflicted King Saul in the period of his declining years (1 Sam 19:9). Lingering illness, loss of loved ones, and many other experiences might be mentioned. The writer, however, is not concerned with being specific. He is only concerned with warning about the severity of the retribution which an apostate has in store for him. But it is precisely because the apostate is a Christian that his crime is so great. This point is forcefully driven home by the words of Heb 10:29:

---

[69] Moffatt, *Hebrews*, 149; Hering, *Hebrews*, 94; Lane, *Hebrews*, 141; Guthrie, *Hebrews*, 217; F. F. Bruce, *The Epistle to the Hebrews,* NIC (Grand Rapids: Eerdmans, 1964), 259; Philip Edgcumbe Hughes, *A Commentary on the Epistle to the Hebrews* (Grand Rapids: Eerdmans, 1977), 418-19.

> Of how much worse punishment, do you
> suppose, will he be thought worthy who has
> trampled the Son of God underfoot, counted
> the blood of the covenant *by which he was
> sanctified* a common thing, and insulted the
> Spirit of grace (emphasis added).

In the words "by which he was sanctified" the writer makes it inescapable that he is speaking of Christians.

The author has already spoken about sanctification in the immediately preceding context of Hebrews 10. His statements show clearly what he means by this idea:

> By that will we have been sanctified through
> the offering of the body of Jesus Christ once
> for all (Heb 10:10).

> For by one offering He has perfected forever
> those who are sanctified (Heb 10:14).

It follows that in describing the apostate as one who has "counted the blood of the covenant by which he was sanctified a common thing," the writer is describing one who has been "perfected forever."[70] Precisely for this reason, his apostasy is an enormous offense against divine grace. It fully merits the "worse punishment" which the author predicts.

All attempts to deny that a real Christian is in view here can only be described as a refusal to face the author's true meaning. The explanation that the "he" in the expression "by which he was sanctified" refers to Christ has absolutely

---

[70] Thomas Hewitt, *The Epistle to the Hebrews*, TNTC (Grand Rapids: Eerdmans, 1960), 71. The concept of "sanctification" in Hebrews is well-stated by Hewitt: "The sanctified are those who have been made free from guilt through cleansing from sin and who have access into God's presence (x. 10, 14, xiii. 12). *Hagiazein*, 'to sanctify', has almost the same meaning as *dikaioun*, 'to justify', so frequently used by Paul. Denney [*The Death of Christ*, p. 126] draws attention to this similarity and then goes on to say: 'The sanctification of the one writer is the justification of the other...'"

nothing to commend it. No impartial reader could so understand the text. Furthermore, in Hebrews, Christ is not described as sanctified, but as the Sanctifier (Heb 2:11).[71] The writer of Hebrews obviously believes that a true Christian can apostatize.[72]

The remainder of the passage (Heb 10:30-36) reinforces this point. Vengeance and judgment await the apostate (vv 30-31). But the readers can be strengthened against such failure by the recollection of their former fidelity in time of trial (vv 32-34). This past confidence is to be maintained now: "Therefore do not cast away your confidence, which has great reward" (v 35). What they need is "endurance" so that they may accomplish God's will and receive the reward He has promised (v 36). The coming of Christ draws near (v 37) and this should give them courage to hold on.

Of particular interest is the statement of verse 38, "Now the just shall live by faith; but if he draws back, my soul has no pleasure in him" (trans. from Greek). The words are drawn from Hab 2:3-4 and include the famous Pauline proof-text about justification by faith.

But the writer does not introduce this quotation with a formula of citation like "the Scripture says, etc." There is a good reason why he does not. What he has done is to alter the form of the Old Testament reference in a way that fits

---

[71] For this view see, for example, Roger Nicole, "Some Comments on Hebrews 6:4-6 and the Doctrine of the Perseverance of the Saints," *Current Issues in Biblical and Patristic Interpretation,* ed. Gerald F. Hawthorne (Grand Rapids: Eerdmans, 1975), 356.

[72] Among commentators who agree that the phrase "by which he was sanctified" refers to an actual sanctification of the Christian/apostate, we should likely include: Moffatt, *Hebrews,* 151; Hering, *Hebrews,* 92, 94; Montefiore, *Hebrews,* 179; Guthrie, *Hebrews,* 219; Lane, *Hebrews,* 142. The sanctification is treated as simply claimed and not experienced by Hughes, *Hebrews,* 423; Hewitt, *Hebrews,* 362; R. Nicole, *Hebrews,* 362. Bruce, *Hebrews,* 259 seems ambiguous. But the text declares the person's sanctification as a basis for the severe retribution. The text says nothing of a "claimed" sanctification, which would be less serious. The greatness of the benefit to the apostate is precisely the point of the phrase. This would be obvious if it were not for the theological presuppositions that have been brought to the passage.

the context of his thought. In that sense the statement of verse 38 is more strictly an Old Testament allusion than an Old Testament quotation.

In this altered form it is plain that it is the just one who may draw back.[73] If so, of course, God will not be pleased with him. The words "my soul has no pleasure in him" are a figure of speech called *litotes*. In litotes a positive idea is expressed by negating its opposite. As the larger context makes plain, the meaning is, "God will be severely angered" (see v 27).[74]

Hebrews 10:39 is misleading in its present English form. The Greek word for *perdition* is not (as is sometimes claimed) a technical term for "hell." Instead it may be used of simple waste (Matt 26:8; Mark 14:4) or of execution (Acts 25:16). In secular Greek its fundamental meanings were "destruction," "ruin," and similar ideas. Likewise, the particular Greek expression rendered "the saving of the soul," *psychē*, does not occur elsewhere in Biblical Greek. It is not the same Greek phrase which we met in Jas 1:21. But the precise phrase used here is found in classical Greek with the meaning "to save the life."[75] The verse might be more appropriately translated:

> But we for our part [the Greek pronoun is emphatic] are not of those who draw back to ruin, but of those who have faith for the saving of our life.

---

[73] As Moffatt, *Hebrews*, 158 states: "The aim of the change [from the Old Testament text] was to make it clear, as it was not clear in the LXX, that the subject of ['draw back'] was ['the just one'], and also to make the warning against apostasy the climax."

[74] Montefiore, *Hebrews*, 185 notes: "To *take no pleasure in* someone is tantamount to condemnation (cf. x. 6)."

[75] Moffatt, *Hebrews*, 158 observes: "[*Peripoiesis*] occurs three times in the LXX [2 Chr 14:13, Hag 2:9, Mal 3:17] and several times in the NT, but never with [*psuches*], though the exact phrase was known to classical Greek as an equivalent for *saving one's own life*" (emphasis added). For references, see Hering, *Hebrews*, 97 n.28.

In this sense the verse fits perfectly with the larger context. The apostate faces disaster and ruin. His punishment may not be swift execution as under Moses' law (cf. Heb 10:28), but the judgment he experiences could easily end in death as other sin also does (Jas 1:15; 5:20; Prov 10:27; 11:19; etc.). But faith is the means by which the "just one" lives and is therefore indispensable to the preservation of his life (cf. Heb 10:38).

From Heb 10:32-36 the author has used the second person plural *you* to address his readers. The swift change to an emphatic *we* in verse 39 appears to be a reference to himself. The literary *we* is the author's regular way of indicating himself (see Heb 2:5; 5:11; 6:9, 11; 8:1; 13:18). The writer seems to be stating his own intention to hold on to his Christian profession and hope. He means something like: "But we ourselves (I myself) do not belong among the number who draw back, but among those who preserve their lives by a continuing faith."

G. H. Lang sees this text as I do. He writes:

> Obviously this [Luke 17:33] agrees exactly with the warnings already considered that believers may be cut short by premature death and thus lose their life. It will therefore harmonize with the Lord's words should our passage [Heb 10:39] be rendered, "we are of them who have faith unto the *keeping safe of life*."[76]

Hebrews 10:39 is a fitting conclusion to a passage on the "willful" sin of apostasy. The sin of apostasy (i.e., turning away from Christianity) can only be committed deliberately. The refusal to commit it is equally deliberate. The author has definitely decided not to commit apostasy. He trusts that his readers will refuse to do so as well.

---

[76] See G. H. Lang, *The Epistle to the Hebrews* (London: Paternoster Press, 1951; [reprint ed., Miami Springs: Conley and Schoettle, 1985]), 193 (italics his).

Apostasy in Hebrews 3

The Epistle to the Hebrews is fundamentally concerned with the problem of those who draw back from their Christian commitment and conviction. Those who do so, of course, abandon the church (cf. Heb 10:25). It is therefore the *visible household of faith* from which they withdraw. They cannot withdraw from the family of God, however. Precisely for this reason they are subject to God's discipline.

If the epistle is read in this way, it offers no fundamental problems at all. It clashes in no way with the basic truths of the Gospel. Christians in the local church are in active partnership with the Apostle and High Priest of their Christian profession. They must take care to hold on to this partnership.

In Heb 3:1, the word *partakers* is used to describe this relationship. The Greek word can refer to business partners and this is its actual meaning in its only New Testament occurrence outside of Hebrews (Luke 5:7). It is common in the Greek in this sense.[77] But "partnership" with Christ is a priestly occupation in which there is a spiritual altar that offers spiritual food (Heb 13:10) and in which there are spiritual sacrifices to be made (Heb 13:15-16). One must hold on to this role.

If the Christian withdraws from the visible, functioning, priestly household, that is, from the church itself, he ceases to be a "partner of Christ." This is the meaning of the statement in Heb 3:14 where the word for "partaker" is the same word as the one used in Heb 3:1:

---

[77] Moulton and Milligan state of *metochos*: "This adj. in the sense of 'sharer', 'partner', as in Luke 5:7 (cf. Heb 3:14) is common in the papyri..." James Hope Moulton and George Milligan, *The Vocabulary of the Greek Testament Illustrated from the Papyri and Other Non-Literary Sources* (Grand Rapids: Eerdmans, 1960), 406.

> For we have become partakers [partners] of Christ if we hold the beginning of our confidence steadfast to the end (Heb 3:14).[78]

The same truth is also stated in Heb 3:6:

> ...whose house we are if we hold fast the confidence and the rejoicing of the hope firm to the end.

Thus we participate in the visible household of faith, in partnership with Christ, only so long as we hold fast to our Christian confidence and hope. If we cast away this confidence and withdraw from the house, we cast away the privileges that belong to the house. This is like a son in an earthly household who leaves home and ceases to be an active partner in that home, even though he does not thereby cease to be a son.[79]

No doubt the warnings of Hebrews against abandonment of the faith are sharp and forceful. But this is no reason to deny that they apply to us. Indeed, this kind of denial robs them of the impact they were intended to have. When the exhortations of the epistle are redirected toward supposed "false professors of faith," they are in reality distorted.

The author of Hebrews shows not the slightest trace of a belief that his audience might contain unsaved people. Instead, he persistently addresses them as brethren (Heb 3:1, 12; 10:19; 13:22) who share the heavenly calling (Heb

---

[78] Robert Govett, *Govett on Hebrews* (London, 1884; [reprint ed., Miami Springs: Conley and Schoettle, 1981]), 87-88. Govett rightly links 3:14 with 1:9 where the Greek word for "partners" (="fellows" or "companions") is used.

[79] G. H. Lang, who believed strongly in free grace, held that the term *house* in Heb 3:6 referred to the indwelling of God in believers or in the local church. He believed also that God's indwelling could be withdrawn, although those from whom it was withdrawn remained secure in Christ. I cannot agree that the Spirit's indwelling can be withdrawn from a believer (see Eph 1:12-14; Rom 8:9). Yet Lang's approach to Heb 3:1 is essentially like my own. See Lang, *Hebrews*, 68-71.

3:1) and who have a High Priest through whom they can approach the throne of grace (Heb 4:14-16). The suggestion that he nevertheless thinks some of his audience are unregenerate is not founded on anything at all in the text.

Conclusion

No doubt the conclusions reached in this chapter will be stoutly resisted by those who cannot believe that a Christian could abandon his faith. But I insist that refusing to admit this possibility is an obvious begging of the question. The view that a Christian cannot apostatize is at bottom an arbitrary theological conviction. Since it is not supported by the Bible, it ought to be given up.

When this is done, many passages can be read in their normal sense and the warnings they contain can be directly faced. Moreover, we can then also hear a note of hope for those whose faith has suffered shipwreck. It is such a note that sounds in the solemn statements Paul makes:

> ...having faith and a good conscience, which some having rejected, concerning the faith have suffered shipwreck, of whom are Hymenaeus and Alexander, whom I have delivered to Satan that they may learn not to blaspheme (1 Tim 1:19-20).

What is striking here is that the Greek word, translated *learn* literally means "to be trained," "to be educated." It is a normal Greek word for the education of a child who is a minor. Its only other uses by Paul are all in reference to Christians (1 Cor 11:32; 2 Cor 6:9; 2 Tim 2:25; Titus 2:12). First Timothy 1:20 is no exception to this.

Clearly the most natural understanding here is that Paul regarded Hymenaeus and Alexander as Christians whose false doctrine amounted to blasphemy. They are now under divine discipline for which Satan is the instrument (One might compare with this Paul's similar concept in 1 Cor 5:4-5). Paul hopes that the outcome of this spiritual education will be that these men will renounce their false doctrine.[80]

It is quite natural to suspect that this Hymenaeus is the same as the one mentioned in 2 Tim 2:17 and who taught that the resurrection was already past. Whether in the end the discipline had a positive effect on either Hymenaeus or Alexander is a matter on which the Scripture is silent. But the element of hope remains, just as it did also in the metaphor of the burnt field in Heb 6:7-8.

Nevertheless, the tragic dangers of doctrinal shipwreck remain a grim reality in the history of the Church and in its contemporary experience. A disservice is done to the cause of Christ when it is claimed that such dangers do not exist for real Christians.

"Therefore let him who thinks he stands take heed lest he fall" (1 Cor 10:12).

---

[80] As Dibelius and Conzelmann, *Epistles*, 34 observe: "The purpose here is 'education through punishment'...which wants to prevent blasphemy (whether such blasphemy is seen as false teaching or, possibly, in the mere fact of opposition)."

7
Problem Passages in Paul

Certain passages in the Pauline letters have been taken to prove that perseverance in good works is an inevitable outcome of genuine saving faith. As has already been pointed out, this kind of idea destroys the believer's ground of assurance. A man who must wait for works to verify his faith cannot know until life's end whether or not his faith was real. This leads to the absurd conclusion that a man can believe in Christ without knowing whether he has believed in Christ.

Naturally the Pauline texts in question are all consistent with his fundamental doctrine of justification by faith apart from works. When the Apostle writes that God saved us "not by works of righteousness which we have done, but according to His mercy" (Titus 3:5), his true conviction comes through clearly. Paul could never have so expressed himself if he had regarded works as the real means by which we can know we are saved. To the contrary, he directs our focus away from the works *we* have done to the mercy of *God*. How can anyone read Paul and still believe that we can only be sure of God's mercy by our works?

Similarly, Paul also wrote, "But to him who *does not work* but believes on Him who justifies the ungodly, his faith is accounted for righteousness" (Rom 4:5, emphasis added). Can anyone imagine that Paul would then go on to add, "But you need to work or you will not know whether you have been justified or not"? Such a proposition is a monstrous distortion of Pauline truth. Any articulation of the Gospel which can affirm such a thing ought to be forcefully rejected by the Christian Church.

In the next few pages some Pauline statements will be examined which are claimed to lead to the result we have just criticized. A few others will be considered in chapter 9 in connection with the subject of heirship. The first text that claims attention here is Gal 6:8.

Galatians 6:8

Paul wrote as follows:

> Do not be deceived, God is not mocked; for whatever a man sows, that he will also reap. For he who sows to his flesh will of the flesh reap corruption, but he who sows to the Spirit will of the Spirit reap everlasting life. And let us not grow weary while doing good, for in due season we shall reap if we do not lose heart (Gal 6:7-9).

It is important to see exactly what this text says. Everlasting life, Paul states, will be the direct consequence of sowing to the Spirit, of doing good. Corruption is what you reap if you do evil. It is all part of the law of the harvest. A man gets what he deserves to get.

It goes almost without saying that there is nothing said here about the "inevitable" results of saving faith. Indeed, the hortatory thrust of the passage shows the opposite. The Galatians must be careful about how they sow. They must never suppose that they can *mock* God or avoid the inexorable law of the harvest. The final reaping is not a foregone conclusion, but rather it is contingent on not *growing weary* while doing good.

But equally there is nothing here about justification by faith or the concept of a free gift. Nothing is plainer than that the *everlasting life* of which Paul speaks is not free, but based on the moral merits of those who reap it. To deny this is to deny the most obvious aspect of the text.

All becomes clear if we simply remember that the Apostle is addressing believers (see, for example, Gal 3:2-5) who have already been justified by faith and who possess everlasting life as a free gift. Naturally Paul knew that eternal life was freely given (Rom 6:23; see also Rom

5:15-18), just as the Apostle John knew this. But Paul is not speaking about what the Galatians *already had*, but about what they may *yet receive*. Herein lies the key to this text.

(1) The Nature of Eternal Life

It must not be forgotten that eternal life is nothing less than the very life of God Himself. As such it cannot be thought of as a mere fixed and static entity. Rather, its potentialities are rich beyond the power of the mind to conceive them. Thus we find Jesus declaring, "I have come that they may have life, and that they may have it *more abundantly*" (John 10:10b, emphasis added). From this we learn that eternal life can be experienced in more than one measure or degree.

But it cannot be experienced at all unless first received as a free gift. Not surprisingly, the Creator of the universe has illustrated this with every human life that is born into the world.

No man or woman possesses physical life at all except by his parents imparting it to him. Even physical life, therefore, is a free gift. But when a child is born into this present world, the capacities of human life (all present at birth) must be developed by him under the guidance of his parents and subsequent teachers. How *abundantly* he will experience human life is determined by his response to instruction and to experience itself.

So it is in the spiritual realm too. In order to have life *more abundantly*, one must meet the conditions for this. One must respond properly to his heavenly Parent.

Here it should be stated clearly that in the New Testament eternal life is presented both as a free gift and as a reward merited by those who earn it. But one important distinction always holds true. Wherever eternal life is viewed as a reward, it is obtained in the future. But wherever eternal life is presented as a gift, it is obtained in the present.

Naturally, it goes without saying that no one can ever receive eternal life as a reward who does not first accept it as a free gift. This is the same as saying that a person must first *have* life before he can experience it richly.

(2) Harvesting Eternal Life

If Gal 6:8 is understood as speaking only of a man's final salvation from hell, then it teaches clearly that this final salvation is by works. Not to admit this is not to be candid. But no one excludes works from his doctrine of salvation more vigorously than Paul does, and he insists that to mix works and grace is to alter the character of both (see Rom 11:6).

Galatians 6:8 is irreconcilable with fundamental Pauline truth so long as one holds the view that final salvation is under discussion.

But why hold this view? It is easy to understand how the measure and extent of one's experience of God's life must depend on the measure of his response to God. From that perspective the image of a harvest is exactly right. The nature and quantity of the seed we sow determines the nature and quantity of the harvest.

It is obviously wise for a Christian to be reminded that every act he performs is like a seed sown in a field. Its harvest will be either corruption or eternal life.[81] And is there a Christian alive who has not sown much more often to his flesh than he ought to have done? Clearly the Church needs this reminder about the law of life. To make the issue here a man's final destiny in heaven or hell is to lose the whole point of the exhortation.

If the matters just discussed are kept in mind, other passages which offer eternal life as a future experience based on works can be understood in their proper bearing. One might think especially of Matt 19:29 with its parallels

---

[81] See Appendix 3.

in Mark 10:30 and Luke 18:30. The eschatological "harvest" is in view in these places. Obedient men reap an experience of eternal life precisely because they are obedient.[82] But this in no way conflicts with the reality that such obedience must be preceded by, and motivated through, a gift of life given freely and without any condition but faith alone.

Colossians 1:21-23

Colossians 1:21-23 has sometimes been taken to teach that perseverance in the faith is a condition for final salvation. The passage reads as follow:

> And you, who once were alienated and
> enemies in your mind by wicked works, yet
> now He has reconciled in the body of His
> flesh through death, to present you holy, and
> blameless, and above reproach in His sight—
> if indeed you continue in the faith, grounded
> and steadfast, and are not moved away from
> the hope of the gospel which you have heard…
> (Col 1:21-23a).

It is clear that *condition* is the only appropriate word here. There is nothing to support the view that perseverance in the faith is an *inevitable* outcome of true salvation. On the contrary, the text reads like a warning. Naturally, in the context of the Colossian heresy (Col 2:8, 16-23) that is exactly what it is.

---

[82] F. F. Bruce, *The Epistle to the Galatians*, NIGNTC (Grand Rapids: Eerdmans, 1982), 265. Bruce stresses the eschatological bearing of Gal 6:8. He writes: "The eternal life is the resurrection life of Christ, mediated to believers by 'the Spirit of him who raised Jesus from the dead' (Rom 8:11)…But its future aspect, with their appearance before the tribunal of Christ, to 'receive good or evil, according to the deeds done in the body' (2 Cor 5:10), is specially implied here. Anyone who did not seriously believe in such a coming assessment, or thought that the law of sowing and reaping could be safely ignored, would indeed be treating God with contempt."

Concerning the conditional clause in Col 1:23, J. B. Lightfoot remarks that the Greek particles (*ei ge*) "express a pure hypothesis in themselves, but the indicative mood following converts the hypothesis into a hope."[83]

But once again the mistake is made of referring the statement of the text to a man's final salvation. Words like *holy, blameless,* and *above reproach* do not require the sense of *sinless* or *absolutely perfect*. Men can be described in all these ways who are not completely sinless. The word translated as a*bove reproach* is actually found in the Pauline list of qualifications for deacons and elders in the sense of *blameless* (1 Tim 3:10; Titus 1:6-7).

A comparison of Col 1:22 with 1:28 is also helpful. In Col 1:28 Paul wrote:

> Him we preach, warning every man and teaching every man in all wisdom, that we may present every man perfect in Christ Jesus.

This statement is connected with Col 1:22 by the presence of the special word *present*. But here Paul employs the word *perfect* which is the normal Greek word for *mature* (and is so used in 1 Cor 2:6; 14:20; Heb 5:14). Obviously this word also does not have to suggest sinless perfection.

It is natural to see Col 1:22 and 1:28 as slightly different forms of the same idea. The aim of Christ's reconciling work at the cross is the aim Paul serves by his teaching ministry. He seeks to bring men to that matured experience of

---

[83] J . B. Lightfoot, *Saint Paul's Epistles to the Colossians and to Philemon* (London: MacMillan, 1979; [reprint ed., Grand Rapids: Zondervan, 1959]), 163. Lightfoot's words are as far as the grammar can lead us and those who read more into the clause are misunderstanding the text. Equally plain is the statement of A. Lukyn Williams that, in the phrase *ei ge*, "the addition of [*ge*] lays emphasis on the importance of observing the condition, but determines nothing as to whether or not they will do so." See A. Lukyn Williams, *The Epistles of Paul the Apostle to the Colossians and to Philemon,* CGNT (Cambridge: University Press, 1907), 60.

holiness which will enable them to be presented acceptably to God. When they stand on review before Him their lives ought to meet with His approval (see also Rom 14:10-12; 2 Cor 5:10).

But this approval can only be achieved, he cautions his readers, if they hold firmly to their faith in the gospel and do not allow new ideas and doctrines to move them away from fundamental truths (Col 1:23).

Alexander MacLaren's treatment of Col 1:22-23 is edifying. He writes:

> No matter how mighty be the renewing powers of the Gospel wielded by the Divine Spirit, they can only work on the nature that is brought into contact with and continues in contact with them by faith. The measure in which we trust Jesus Christ will be the measure in which He helps us. "He could do no mighty works because of their unbelief." He cannot do what He can do, if we thwart Him by our want of faith. God will present us holy before Him *if* [italics his] we continue in the faith.[84]

Later, connecting verses 28 and 29 with 22 and 23 (as I also do), MacLaren has this to say:

> We found this same word "present" in verse 22. The remarks made there will apply here. There the Divine purpose of Christ's great work, and here Paul's purpose in his, are expressed alike. God's aim is Paul's aim too. The Apostle's thoughts travel on to the great coming day, when we shall all be manifested at the judgment seat of Christ, and preacher and hearer, Apostle and convert, shall be gathered there. That solemn period will test

---

[84] Alexander MacLaren, *The Epistles of St. Paul to the Colossians and Philemon* (New York: A. C. Armstrong and Son, 1897), 107.

> the teacher's work, and should ever be in view
> as he works. There is a real and indissoluble
> connection between the teacher and his
> hearers, so that in some sense he is to blame
> if they do not stand perfect then, and he in
> some sense has to present them as in his
> work—the gold, silver, and precious stones
> which he has built on the foundation.[85]

As we have seen already, Paul knew perfectly well that Christians were not immune to the influences of heresy (1 Tim 1:18-20; 2 Tim 2:17-19). He is saying, then, that the Colossians will never reach maturity in holiness if they listen to the wrong voices. In that event, they could not be presented to God in a spiritual state which truly fulfilled the aims of the cross. Their lives would be open to His censure. They are, therefore, to hold firmly to the faith they had heard from the beginning.

But about perseverance in the faith as a condition for final salvation from hell, Paul here says nothing at all.

First Corinthians 15:2[86]

It might be thought, however, that such an idea *does* find expression in 1 Cor 15:1-2. There Paul wrote:

> Moreover, brethren, I declare to you the
> gospel which I preached to you, which also
> you received and in which you stand, by
> which also you are saved, if you hold fast that
> word which I preached to you—unless you
> believed in vain.

The problem in correctly understanding this verse is caused by the English translation. A very flexible Greek verb (*katechō*) is translated "hold fast" in the NKJV (the

---

[85] Ibid., 144.
[86] Editor's note: see Appendix 5 for a different Free Grace understanding of 1 Cor 15:2.

AV has "keep in memory"). But the verb could equally be rendered "take hold of" or "take possession of." In that case it would refer to the act of appropriating the truth of the gospel by faith.[87]

Commentators long ago noticed a word-order problem in 1 Cor 15:2, when the verse is taken in the sense of "if you hold fast to the word which I preached to you." The problem is that, in Greek, the phrase "(to) the word which I preached to you" *precedes* "if you hold fast." (A minor problem is the sense of the Greek word *tini* which precedes *word* and is rendered as *that* by the NKJV and not at all by the NIV.)

One solution offered has been to connect the phrase "the word which I preached to you" with the expression "I declare to you the gospel" in verse 1. This yields the sense: "I declare (or, 'make known') to you the gospel...with what (*tini*) word which I preached to you." But this connection requires a long leap backward in the text and is quite improbable.

The usual solution has been to make the phrase "with what (that) word which I preached to you" the object of "if you hold fast" which follows it. This is not impossible by any means, but neither is it entirely natural.

It would be preferable to connect the phrase "with what word which I preached to you" with something immediately preceding it. In fact this can easily be done with the interpretation we offer in our text. The troublesome *tini* might be taken as an ellipsis for "what word it was which I preached to you" and may be shortened to, "the very word which I preached to you."

Thus the text can be read: "...the gospel...by which also you are saved, by the very word which I preached to you, if you take hold of (it)—unless you believed in vain." This is a clean-cut treatment of the Greek grammar and lexicography which avoids the puzzling word-order inversion required by the standard renderings of this passage. But obviously such

---

[87] Meanings like "to take," "to take into possession," are found in Matt 21:38 (NKJV), Luke 14:9, and in secular sources.

an interpretation eliminates any reference to perseverance In 1 Cor 15:2.[88] From this it appears that Paul is thinking of the saving effect of the preached word when it is duly appropriated, unless in fact that appropriation (by faith) has been in vain.

What he means by believing "in vain" is made clear in verses 14 and 17:

> And if Christ is not risen, then our preaching is empty and your faith is also empty [the AV has "vain" for "empty"].

> And if Christ is not risen, your faith is futile; you are still in your sins [the AV has "vain" for "futile"].[89]

First Corinthians 15:2 must be read in the light of the subsequent discussion about resurrection. Paul is simply saying, in verse 2, that the gospel he has preached to them is a saving gospel when it is appropriated by faith, unless, after all, the resurrection is false. In that case, no salvation has occurred at all and the faith his readers had exercised was futile. But naturally Paul absolutely insists on the reality of the resurrection of Christ. He therefore does not think that the Corinthians have believed "in vain."

But neither here nor anywhere else in the Pauline letters can the Apostle be correctly understood as teaching that perseverance in the faith is a condition of, or an indispensable sign of, "final salvation" from hell.

---

[88] For discussions of the problem, see: Heinrich August Wilhelm Meyer, *Critical and Exegetical Handbook to the Epistles to the Corinthians*, trans. D. Douglas Bannerman, translation rev. and ed. William P. Dickson (New York: Funk and Wagnalls, 1884), pp. 341-42; and G. G. Findlay, "St. Paul's First Epistle to the Corinthians," in vol. 2 of *The Expositors Greek Testament*, gen. ed. W. Robertson Nicoll (reprint ed., Grand Rapids: Eerdmans, 1970), 918-19.

[89] The Greek words are different in each verse (15:2, *eike*; 15:14, *kene*; 15:17, *mataia*) but they are all functionally synonymous here.

1 Corinthians 1:8

In the opening chapter of his first letter to the Corinthian church, Paul speaks positively and hopefully about the church's spiritual prospects. The context shows clearly that he is speaking of the church corporately:

> I thank my God always concerning you for the grace of God which was given to you by Christ Jesus, that you were enriched in everything by Him in all utterance and all knowledge, even as the testimony of Christ was confirmed in you, so that you come short in no gift, eagerly waiting for the revelation of our Lord Jesus Christ, who will also confirm you to the end, that you may be blameless in the day of our Lord Jesus Christ. God is faithful, by whom you were called into the fellowship of His Son, Jesus Christ our Lord (1 Cor 1:4-9).

Here the Corinthian church is praised because it is so richly endowed with spiritual gifts, because the testimony of Christ has received confirmation in the church's life and experience, and because it waits eagerly for the coming of Christ. Paul fully expects God to bring the church to the place where it is blameless before Him (the letter shows the church has a long way to go), and he bases this expectation on God's faithfulness. Paul is sure that the many problems at Corinth, which he is about to discuss, can be worked out.

It would be a mistake to read more into the text than that. There is not to be found here a guarantee that each and every Christian individual will necessarily be brought to the place where his Christian life is "blameless" before God. (The word *blameless* is the same one we have met as *above reproach* in Col 1:22.) In Paul's mind no such guarantee existed.[90]

---

[90] Interestingly, Barrett refers 1 Cor 1:8 to the doctrine of justification by faith. The term *irreproachable* (*blameless*, NKJV) is referred to the

(1) Paul's View in 1 Corinthians 3

This is made perfectly plain in this very letter. In chap. 3 the Apostle describes the evaluation of the Christian's life and work which will someday take place at the Judgment Seat of Christ (see again, Rom 14:10-12; 2 Cor 5:10). His words are these:

> For no other foundation can anyone lay than that which is laid, which is Jesus Christ. Now if anyone builds on this foundation with gold, silver, precious stones, wood, hay, straw, each one's work will become clear; for the Day will declare it, because it will be revealed by fire; and the fire will test each one's work, of what sort it is. If anyone's work which he has built on it endures, he will receive a reward. If anyone's work is burned, he will suffer loss; but he himself will be saved, yet so as through fire (1 Cor 3:11-15).

It is clear from this text that Paul entertained the possibility that in the Day of divine evaluation, a Christian's work might be "burned up." The Greek verb employed in verse 15 (rendered, "burned") is in fact an intensive word like our own verb "burned down." Should a Christian's works suffer such a fate, Paul insists that his eternal destiny nevertheless will not be affected. "But he himself will be saved, yet so as through fire."[91]

---

imputed "righteousness of Christ himself." Paul is thus "stating the doctrine of justification by faith without the use of the technical words he employs elsewhere". See C. K. Barrett, *A Commentary on the First Epistle to the Corinthians*, HNTC (New York: Harper and Row, 1968), 39-40.

[91] Very appropriately does Barrett translate "he will suffer loss" as "he will be mulcted of his pay." He subsequently remarks: "The servant of God who uses improper or unworthy materials, though himself saved, will miss the reward he might have had. We have thus already noted the next words, which are clear enough and need little comment: **he himself will be saved** (it is underlined that salvation is to be distinguished

This declaration is so straightforward that it is absolutely amazing how widely it has been ignored. Obviously, if a believer's works are "burned down" he will not stand "blameless" before God. So 1 Cor 1:8 does not claim that a "blameless" state will be true of every Christian at the Judgment Seat of Christ. Paul was speaking primarily about the spiritual status which he expected the Corinthian church to achieve corporately.

(2) A Further Caution

But even here caution must be exercised not to make the words of 1 Cor 1:8 say more than they actually do.

If a counselor says to a troubled counselee, "God will strengthen you and see you through," this claim ought not to be taken as a flat and unconditional prediction. Instead it is an expression of the counselor's conviction that God can be relied upon by the troubled individual who needs Him. Naturally he expects the counselee to appropriate God's help in the proper ways.

In 1 Cor 1:4-9 Paul begins his epistle on a positive note. He commends in the Corinthian church what there is to commend (there was a great deal to criticize), and he expresses the expectation that "God will confirm you [that is, 'give you strength'] to the end, that you may be blameless in the day of our Lord Jesus Christ." But it is implied in such a declaration that the Corinthians must *want* that strength and must appropriate it properly.

Paul's main point is that God will furnish the needed help, because He is faithful (1 Cor 1:9). Those who have elevated the statement of 1 Cor 1:8 to the level of a theological claim about Christian perseverance have misunderstood Paul's meaning.[92] They have also created false theology.

---

from reward, or pay; It cannot be earned)." One could hardly improve on this. See Barrett, 89.

[92] E. D. Hirsch, *The Aims of Interpretation* (Chicago: University of Chicago Press, 1976), 25-26. The hermeneutical issue here is about the

Philippians 1:6

It has often been said that the epistle to the Philippians is a thank you note. The Philippians have sent a monetary gift to Paul for which he is deeply grateful (Phil 4:10-19). Naturally at the very beginning of the epistle he refers to their material generosity. In Phil 1:3-6 he wrote:

> I thank my God upon every remembrance of you, always in every prayer of mine making request for you all with joy, for your fellowship in the gospel from the first day until now, being confident of this very thing, that He who has begun a good work in you will complete it until the day of Jesus Christ.

It is natural to understand this passage in special reference to the Philippians' recent generosity. This is implied rather plainly by the Greek word *fellowship*. This word very often refers to material *sharing* and can sometimes even mean *contribution* (see Rom 15:26). Paul is assuring the Philippians that their *good work of sharing in the spread of the gospel* will be carried to full fruitfulness by God. Its total effects (for example, in the winning of souls) will only be manifest in the day of Jesus Christ, the Judgement Seat of Christ.

In fact, this very epistle can be seen as part of the fruit which that *good work* produced, since the Philippians' gift occasioned the letter. Whatever spiritual impact Paul's

---

"illocutionary force" of Paul's words. The significance of "illocutionary force" is aptly summarized by Hirsch: "Such an attempt at compromise [between intuitionists and positivists] can be discovered in the recent discussions of speech-act theory, based on the posthumous writings of J. L. Austin, who introduced into verbal meaning the concept of illocutionary force...Austin discusses how the very same word-sequence can have a different meaning by virtue of having a different illocutionary force. Thus, 'You are going to London,' could have the illocutionary force of an assertion, a command, a request, a question, a complaint, or an ironic comment on the fact that you are headed towards Bristol." Interpreters ignore this issue at their peril.

letter has had on the Church down through the centuries (who can calculate it?) is therefore part of the *interest* which has accumulated on this simple material investment in the cause of Christ.[93]

It may also be suggested that every good work which we do has a potential for usefulness that lies far beyond its original intent. God alone can *perfect* our good works and give them their full impact; often far beyond the lifetime of the one "in" whom the good work begins. Only the day of Jesus Christ (i.e., the Judgment Seat of Christ) will disclose all that God does with what we do for Him.

Philippians 1:6 is a lovely and thought-provoking utterance by an appreciative Apostle. But about the issue of Christian perseverance it has nothing to say at all.

Philippians 2:12-13

Philippians 2:12-13 are more relevant to the issues under discussion. In these verses Paul wrote:

> Therefore, my beloved, as you have always obeyed, not as in my presence only, but now much more in my absence, work out your own salvation with fear and trembling; for it is God who works in you both to will and to do for His good pleasure (Phil 2:12-13).

It is clear that if the *salvation* Paul speaks of here refers to escape from hell, then obedient works are a *condition* for that. Once again it would be unwarranted to read into the passage the idea that such obedience is merely the evidence of true faith. That idea has nothing whatsoever to support it in the text. It can only amount to an evasion of the plain declaration that this *salvation* must be *worked out*.

---

[93] Editor's Note: For an excellent extended discussion of the good work in Phil 1:6 see John F. Hart, "Does Philippians 1:6 Guarantee Progressive Sanctification, Parts 1 and 2," *Journal of the Grace Evangelical Society* 9 (Spring and Autumn 1996): 37-58 (Part 1) and 33-60 (Part 2). Both articles are available online at faithalone.org.

Whatever is involved here, it is manifestly salvation by works.

It follows that Paul must be talking about something quite different from the salvation he speaks of in Eph 2:8-9 and Titus 3:4-7. As a matter of fact he is.

(1) Salvation Equals "Deliverance"

In only two other places in the epistle does Paul use the term *salvation*. One of these is in Phil 1:19-20 where he wrote:

> For I know that this will turn out for my deliverance [AV, salvation] through your prayer and the supply of the Spirit of Jesus Christ, according to my earnest expectation and hope that in nothing I shall be ashamed, but with all boldness, as always, so now also Christ will be magnified in my body, whether by life or by death.

The first century reader was not likely to have any problem understanding this. The Greek word for *salvation* (*sōtēria*) simply meant *deliverance*, as the NKJV now translates it here. Like the English word *deliverance* it could have wide application and was particularly applicable to life-threatening situations. Paul now confronts a life-threatening situation in which the outcome of his impending trial cannot be predicted with absolute certainty.

His readers knew this, of course. When Paul writes, "I know that this will turn out for my deliverance," their first impression would be that he anticipated release from his imprisonment. But the remainder of his words show them that this is not what he has in mind. "For me," says Paul, "real 'deliverance' (or, *salvation*) will consist of magnifying Christ whether I live or die. For this, I need your prayers and the help of God's Spirit."

In a very courageous way Paul elevates his natural human concern with *deliverance* (or *salvation*) from trouble to the level of a spiritual concern that he will be *delivered* (or *saved*) from failing to honor God in whatever befalls him. In saying this, of course, he hopes to motivate his readers to a similar objective.

(2) The Parallel in Philippians 1:27-30

In fact, that is exactly what he tries to do directly a little later in this chapter. In Phil 1:27-30 he wrote:

> Only let your conduct be worthy of the gospel of Christ, so that whether I come and see you or am absent, I may hear of your affairs, that you stand fast in one spirit, with one mind striving together for the faith of the gospel, and not in any way terrified by your adversaries, which is to them a proof of perdition [or, ruin, as it could be translated] but to you of salvation [or, deliverance], and that from God. For to you it has been granted on behalf of Christ, not only to believe in Him, but also to suffer for His sake, having the same conflict which you saw in me and now hear is in me.

In this exhortation, the Apostle applies to the readers the idea he had earlier expressed concerning himself.

The Philippians also have sufferings just as he does. But they too can aspire to a *deliverance* (or *salvation*) in which Christ is magnified in them as well. If they will stand unitedly for the gospel and are not terrified by their adversaries, that will be proof that this *deliverance* (or *salvation*) is being realized in their lives.

By contrast, their courage and fidelity foretell the ruin of their enemies, whether temporally or eternally.

Paul and his readers are aware that there is a *deliverance* (or *salvation*) from hell which they have already obtained by faith in Christ. But the *deliverance* (or *salvation*) he offers them here is over and above that which they already have. It is one that issues from sufferings.

Therefore, Paul can say, "For to you it has been granted… not only to believe in Him, but also to suffer for His sake." In other words, just as there is a salvation through faith, so there is one through suffering. That too is being granted to the Philippians.

But *this salvation* (or *deliverance*) must be *worked out*. It is the product of obedience even under the most trying of circumstances. When Phil 2:12-13 is properly referred back to the Apostle's earlier references to s*alvation*, then its bearing becomes clear. Since this *salvation* consists essentially in honoring Christ by life or by death, it is necessarily inseparable from a life of obedience.

In the words that follow immediately in Phil 2:14-16, the nature of this life is once more described. The Philippians are encouraged to be "children of God without fault in the midst of a crooked and perverse generation, among whom you shine as lights in the world" (Phil 2:15). Clearly, such a result would be a magnificent triumph, a kind of spiritual *deliverance* or *salvation*, in the midst of a hostile and dangerous earthly situation.[94]

Interlude: Biblical Salvation

What we have just seen in Philippians is important for the Bible as a whole. The exact meaning of the term "salvation" must never be taken for granted.

---

[94] For other presentations of this view see Gregory Sapaugh, s.v. "Philippians" in *The Grace New Testament Commentary* (Denton, TX: Grace Evangelical Society, 2010), 900-901; Ralph Martin, *Philippians*, Tyndale Series (Grand Rapids, MI: William B. Eerdmans Publishing Co., 1959, 1987), 114-15.

(1) The Word for Salvation in the Greek Bible

When the Greek translation of the Old Testament is considered along with the Greek New Testament, it can safely be said that the most common meaning of the word *salvation* (*sōtēria*) in the Greek Bible is the one which refers to God's deliverance of His people from their trials and hardships. This meaning is widespread in Psalms especially. Among the references which can be cited are Pss 3:8; 18:3, 35, 46, 50; 35:3; 37:39; 38:22; 44:4; etc. In all these places, and many more besides, the LXX uses the word *sōtēria* (*salvation*).

First century Christians, therefore, were every bit as likely to understand a reference to *salvation* in this sense as they were to understand it in the sense of *escaping from hell*.

New Testament interpreters forget this fact *very* frequently. In place of careful consideration about the sense which the term *salvation* has in any given context, there is a kind of interpretive *reflex action* that automatically equates the word with final salvation from hell. This uncritical treatment of many New Testament passages has led to almost boundless confusion at both the expository and doctrinal levels.

Serious interpreters of the New Testament must carefully avoid this kind of automatic response. They should seek to determine from the context the kind of *deliverance* in question. It may well be deliverance from death to life or from hell to heaven. But equally it may be a deliverance from trial, danger, suffering or temptation. The context—sometimes the larger context of the book itself (as in Romans and Hebrews)—must determine the exact meaning.

(2) "Saving the Life" in the Bible

Furthermore, in the teaching of Jesus a distinctive note is sounded which is not really found in the Old Testament passages about *salvation*. Although the Old Covenant saint thought instinctively of the preservation of his physical life, the New Covenant person is taught to go beyond this consideration.

According to Jesus, a man can *"save his life"* even when he *"loses"* it (see Matt 16:25 and parallels). This paradox suggests that even death itself cannot destroy the value and worth of a life lived in discipleship to Christ. Such a life survives every calamity and results in eternal reward and glory.[95]

Paul is not far from such a thought in Philippians. To be truly *delivered* in suffering is not necessarily to survive it physically, but to glorify Christ through it.

The same idea is present in the Apostle Peter's famous passage on suffering found in 1 Pet 1:6-9. The expression in verse 9 which is translated "the salvation of your souls" would be much better translated according to its normal Greek sense: "the salvation of your lives." Peter is describing the messianic experience in which the believer partakes of Christ's sufferings first, in order that he might subsequently share the glory to which those sufferings lead (1 Pet 1:10-11). In this way the *life* is saved, even when paradoxically it is lost, because it results in "praise, honor, and glory at the revelation of Jesus Christ" (1 Pet 1:7).

One might wonder exactly what Hort means in his discussion of "salvation of souls" (1 Pet 1:9), but it's possible to think Hort's ship might be *listing* in the direction of Free Grace when he writes:

> Here, again, as I had occasion to say on *v*. 5, we have to be on our guard against interpreting the language of Scripture by the sharp limitations of modern usage. Salvation is

---

[95] For a fuller exposition of this kind of teaching found in the words of our Lord, see chap. 4 in my book, *Grace in Eclipse: A Study on Eternal Rewards*. For a definition of saving the life which follows the lines we are suggesting, see R. E. Neighbour, *If They Shall Fall Away* (reprint ed., Miami Springs, FL: Conley and Schoettle, 1984), 29-30.

> deliverance from dangers and enemies and above all from death and destruction. The soul is not a particular element or faculty of our nature, but its very life (cf. Westcott on John xii. 25). The bodily life or soul is an image of the diviner life or soul which equally needs to be saved, and the salvation of which is compatible with the death and seeming destruction of the bodily life and soul. Here St. Peter means to say that, when the true mature faith possible to a Christian has done its work, a salvation of soul is found to have been thereby brought to pass, the passage from death into life has been accomplished.[96]

In fact, it can be said that there is not a single place in the New Testament where the expression "to save the soul" ever means final salvation from hell. It cannot be shown that any native Greek speaker would have understood this expression in any other than the idiomatic way. That is, he would understand it as signifying "to save the life."

In modern use, of course, "to save the soul" is almost universally understood as a reference to eternal salvation. But this fixity in its meaning is not relevant to its New Testament use. In the New Testament we should always understand it as equal to our expression: "to save the life."

In Philippians Paul never uses the word *salvation* to refer to the question of heaven or hell. After all, both he and his readers *knew* where they were going. Their names were in the Book of Life (Phil 4:3).

Romans 2:7, 10, 13

It is a tragic feature of the modern debate over salvation, that certain statements made by Paul in his great epistle to

---

[96] F. J. A. Hort, *The First Epistle of St. Peter. 1.1–2.17: The Greek Text with Introductory Lecture, Commentary, and Additional Notes* (London: MacMillan, 1898), 48.

the church at Rome have been turned upside down. These statements are found in Romans 2 and are intended by the Apostle to underline man's hopeless state before the bar of God's judgment. Instead, some modern theologians take them as proof-texts that good works, as the fruit of faith, will be the final test of a person's salvation.[97]

Let us look at the Pauline statements in question:

> ...who "will render to each one according to his deeds": eternal life to those who by patient continuance in doing good seek for glory, honor, and immortality...(Rom 2:6-7).
>
> ...but glory, honor, and peace to everyone who works what is good, to the Jew first and also to the Greek (Rom 2:10).
>
> ...for not the hearers of the law are just in the sight of God, but the doers of the law will be justified...(Rom 2:13).

It is certainly astounding that these words could be taken in such a way as to nullify the doctrine Paul goes on to teach in this epistle when he writes emphatically, "Therefore by the deeds of the law no flesh will be justified in His sight, for by the law is the knowledge of sin" (Rom 3:20). This tragic confusion could have been easily avoided. In Romans 2 Paul is discussing how God will deal with men in the final judgment (Rom 2:5). One should remember that

---

[97] Cranfield, for example, prefers the view that the phrase "doing good" (literally, *good work*) in Rom 2:7 refers to "goodness of life, not however as meriting God's favour but as the expression of faith." But this is wholly gratuitous. The text says nothing at all about faith, much less about works as the *expression* of faith. The context in no way supports this view, and Cranfield is guilty of reading his own theology (which is *not* Paul's) into the passage. See C. E. B. Cranfield, *A Critical and Exegetical Commentary on the Epistle to the Romans*, Vol. I: *Introduction and Commentary on Romans I-VIII*, ICC (Edinburgh: T. & T. Clark, 1975), 147.

born-again believers do not come into that judgment (John 5:24).

Correctly, Charles Hodge writes:

> When Paul says *the doers of the law* shall be justified, he is of course not to be understood as teaching, contrary to his own repeated declarations and arguments, that men are actually to be justified by obedience to the law. This is the very thing which he is labouring to prove impossible. The context renders his meaning plain. He is speaking not of the method of justification available for sinners, but of the principles on which all who are *out of Christ* are to be judged. They shall be judged impartially, according to their works, and agreeably to their knowledge of duty. On these principles no flesh living can be justified in the sight of God. The only way, as he afterwards teaches, to escape their application, is to confide in Christ, in virtue of whose death God can be just and yet justify the ungodly who believe in him (italics his).[98]

This is precisely the view I take of this text. But I also extend it to verses 7 and 10 as Hodge (inconsistently) does not (pp. 46-48). For Paul, eternal life—no less than justification—is God's free gift (Rom 5:18; Eph 2:8-9). One can no more earn eternal life by "patient continuance" (that is, *perseverance*) in doing good works than one can be justified by keeping the law. The reason? Because "there is none who does good, no, not one" (Rom 3:12). At the Great White Throne Judgment, the day of grace will be past and men will stand before their Judge for His final assessment of their lives (see Rev 20:12). His judgment will be impartial and based on their works. Those who have persevered in

---

[98] Charles Hodge, *A Commentary on the Epistle to the Romans*, 19th ed. (Philadelphia: James S. Claxton, 1836), 49.

doing good may expect eternal life. Those who have not only heard, but kept, God's law, will receive God's justification.

But who are these? There are none. Romans 3:20 says so plainly. So does Rom 3:9-19—very emphatically.

The Catholic writer Karl Kertelge is on the right track when he writes on Rom 3:9:

> Here in verse 9 Paul is dealing in the first place simply with the general guilt of both Jews and Greeks. He now draws the conclusions of his previous argument: Jews as well as Greeks are guilty. In the preceding discussion, in 1:18–3:10, Paul has accused all, which means that all are under sin. This statement is the conclusion of Paul's whole exposition of human wickedness. That mankind as a whole is under sin, which men have helped to power by their own actions, is a final and conclusive argument for their need of salvation.[99]

Those who interpret Rom 2:7, 10, and 13 as somehow validating the need for good works for "final salvation" have left the stream of Pauline thought entirely and are shipwrecked on the shoals of a modern scholasticism.

The standpoint in Romans 2 is analogous to a judge who has a line of defendants ranged before his tribunal. Speaking in the non-prejudicial language of the law-courts he might say to them: "In this courtroom *everyone* will get exactly what he deserves. The innocent will be cleared, but the guilty will be condemned to punishment." Does this statement imply that some of the defendants *are* innocent and *will* be cleared? Of course not. The judge is simply stating the principles which will obtain in his court. Justice and equity will be the hallmarks of this judicial proceeding.

Romans 2:7, 10, and 13 are not spoken as a *prediction*, as though there actually *will* be people whose works entitle

---

[99] Karl Kertelge, *The Epistle to the Romans* (New York: Herder and Herder, 1972), 44.

them to eternal life and justification. Instead, these verses state the *principles* on which judgment will be based in God's final assessment of lost men. Each person will get what he deserves. But Paul's doctrine was that no one would gain eternal salvation on the basis of principles like these. In the very next chapter of this epistle (Romans 3), Paul will demonstrate that very point.

Because men fail to persevere in good works or truly to do God's law, they are utterly shut up to "the righteousness of God which is through faith in Jesus Christ" (Rom 3:21-26).

John Calvin himself took Rom 2:13 as I have taken it. He writes:

> The sense of this verse, therefore, is that if righteousness is sought by the law, the law must be fulfilled, for the righteousness of the law consists in the perfection of works. Those who misinterpret this passage for the purpose of building up justification by works deserve universal contempt. It is, therefore, improper and irrelevant to introduce here lengthy discussions on justification to solve so futile an argument. The apostle urges here on the Jews only the judgement of the law which he had mentioned, which is that they cannot be justified by the law unless they fulfill it, and that if they transgress it, a curse is instantly pronounced upon them. We do not deny that absolute righteousness is prescribed in the law, but since all men are convicted of offense, we assert the necessity for seeking another righteousness.[100]

---

[100] John Calvin, *Commentary on Romans*, s.v. Rom 2:13. To argue otherwise in Romans 2 is to seek to reverse the Reformation.

Other Pauline Texts

Within the limited scope of this book it is not possible to touch every single passage which at one time or another has been used to prove that Paul treated good works as an inevitable outcome of true regeneration. Paul simply did not hold such a view of works, though no writer insists more strongly than he that Christians ought to do them.

Unfortunately, Paul has not always been credited with being truly consistent with his fundamental insistence that works have nothing to do with determining a Christian's basic relationship to God. That relationship, in Pauline thought, is founded on pure grace and nothing else.

Often Paul's statements are treated in a very one-dimensional way. Even though every epistle he wrote is addressed to those who have already come to saving faith, his teachings are frequently taken as though he was constantly concerned about the eternal destiny of his readers. But there was no reason why he should have been. His many direct declarations that his audiences have experienced God's grace show that he was not concerned about this.

John MacArthur criticizes me for making these statements. He writes:

> As a pastor, I take issue with Hodges' assertion that Paul was unconcerned about the destiny of members of the flocks he pastored.[101]

But MacArthur's phraseology employs a rhetorical "trick" by making it sound as if I had painted Paul as a detached and "unconcerned" pastor. On the contrary, my point is that Paul had "no reason" for such a concern.

MacArthur appears to be reading the modern church situation back into the first century. First, we must remember that none of the Pauline churches were mega-churches

---

[101] MacArthur, *The Gospel According to Jesus,* 190.

on the order of MacArthur's own. In such churches the elders undoubtedly knew each individual and could easily ascertain whether he or she believed in Christ or not, based not on their conduct, but what they professed to believe.

But, secondly, Paul preached a gospel in which assurance of salvation was of the essence of saving faith. As I point out previously, Paul everywhere takes for granted that his readers are Christians and know it. Since MacArthur does not preach a gospel that offers real assurance at the moment of faith, it is understandable that he should be constantly concerned about the eternal destiny of his membership. With such a theology, both pastors and their flocks must always be beset by uncertainty on this crucial matter.

Such declarations abound in the Pauline letters, and Ephesians 2 and Titus 3 are merely two of the most notable. Simple statements like, "For you were bought at a price: therefore glorify God in your body and in your spirit, which are God's" (1 Cor 6:20), show exactly what he thought about his readers' relationship to God. There is not even a single place in the Pauline letters where he clearly expresses doubt that his audience is composed of true Christians.

(1) Romans 8:14

So when Paul writes, "For as many as are led by the Spirit of God, these are the sons of God" (Rom 8:14), he is not offering a "test" by which his readers may decide if they are saved or not. His readers possess a faith which "is spoken of throughout the whole world" (Rom 1:8). They enjoy "peace with God through our Lord Jesus Christ" as well as "access by faith into this grace in which we stand" (Rom 5:1-2: note the repeated use of "we"). That they could conceivably be unregenerate is the farthest thought from the Apostle's mind.

But for Paul the concept of being a "son of God" involved more than simply being regenerate. As he makes clear in Gal 4:1-7, a *son* is one who has been granted *adult* status, in contrast to the *child* who is under *guardians and stewards* (Gal 4:1-2). This, of course, means that the Christian, as a *son*, is free from the law. Thus the statement of Rom 8:14 is identical in force to that of Gal 5:18: "But if you are led by the Spirit, you are not under the law." The identity between the statements is confirmed also by the reference to "the spirit of bondage" in Rom 8:15.

Consequently, both in Rom 8:14 and Gal 5:18, Paul is talking about the way in which our freedom from the law is experientially realized. When the Spirit leads the life, there is no more legal bondage. The believer enters into the freedom of real s*onship* to God and that sonship becomes a reality in his day-by-day experience.

Romans 8:14 is best read against the background of 8:12-13. I have not found a better discussion of Rom 8:12-13 than the one presented by Anders Nygren who writes:

> The Christian has escaped from that ruler, death. But the intention is that he is actually to *live*. If death has been deposed, we are to let it be deposed in our lives, and no longer shape our lives according to its demand.[102]

I here call to mind again the dualism in the Christian life, to which Paul has referred again and again in the foregoing. In the sixth chapter of Romans, for example, he declared that the Christian is "free from sin"; and from that he immediately drew the conclusion that the Christian must battle against sin and all that would bind us to it. Out of the indicative, Paul educes an imperative. Through Christ we are free from sin; and *for that very reason* we are to fight against it...The same dualism emerges here, where Paul speaks of the Christian's freedom form death. Through Christ the Christian has actually been freed from death; but that does not mean that there is no longer any possibility for death to threaten him...The life of the Christian is

---

[102] Anders Nygren, *Commentary on Romans* (Philadelphia: Fortress Press, 1949), 325-26.

still lived all the time in the scope of the first creation. He still lives "in the flesh," and there death has its chance to lay hold, when it strives to regain its power over him. Out of the flesh come all sorts of claims on him; and if he were to follow these, the result would be that he would be carried straight back along the way to bondage under death. It is therefore imperative to resist these claims and reject them as unjustified. Just as, in chapter 6, Paul was concerned to show that the Christian is truly free from sin, so that it can no longer come with any warranted claim on him...so he is now concerned to show that, in like manner, the Christian's freedom from death means that the flesh can no longer come with any justifiable claim.

> So then, brethren, we are debtors, not to the flesh, to live according to the flesh—for if you live according to the flesh you will die, but if by the Spirit you put to death the deeds of the body you will live (Rom 8:12-13).

So there are two different ways to live. Man can "live according to the flesh" or "live according to the Spirit." As to the former manner of life, it must be said that it is not really life. On the contrary, in its basic nature it is quite the opposite. Therefore Paul says, "If you live according to the flesh you will *die*." In that case one does not speak of what is properly life. When we hear Paul speaking here about a life that is really death, our thoughts turn automatically to the famous words of Augustine: "Such was my life—was that life?" Obviously, this splendid exposition enables us to understand what it means truly to *live* as God's adult *sons*, who are led in this experience by God's Spirit. Christians who live at the level of the flesh and of death, are operating experientially far below their standing in Christ.

(2) Titus 1:16

Nor should a "test" of regeneration be detected in a verse like Titus 1:16: "They profess to know God, but in works they deny Him, being abominable, disobedient, and disqualified for every good work." It is superficial to take the word *deny* as though it meant nothing more than "in works they reveal they are not believers."

A little reflection will show that there are various ways in which a believer may *deny* God. He may do it *verbally*, as Peter did on the night of our Lord's arrest. But he may also do it *morally* by a lifestyle that contradicts the implications of the truth he professes. How easily this can be done even by a single act that clashes with our Christian profession, every honest Christian ought to be able to know out of his own experience.

Besides, the people Paul has in mind in Titus 1:16 are evidently the same as those of whom he says in verse 13: "Therefore rebuke them sharply, that they may be sound in the faith."

The Greek word for *sound* means to be healthy. Hence, the persons he thinks of are not individuals who are completely outside the Christian faith. Rather, they are people whom he regards as spiritually *sick* and who need a rebuke designed to restore them to good health. So far from showing that Christians cannot drift disastrously from the path of good works, Titus 1:16 shows exactly that!

(3) Romans 1:5 and 16:26

Finally, an expression like "obedience to the faith" (Rom 1:5; 16:26) has nothing to do with the works that follow salvation. The fact that it does not is widely recognized since the Greek expression is more literally rendered "the obedience of faith." In harmony with one well-known Greek usage of such expressions, the *obedience* in question is *faith itself*.[103]

Naturally, God demands that men place faith in His Son and is angry with them when they do not (John 3:36). Faith is an obedient response to the summons of the gospel. But the man who exercises faith is reaching out for the unconditional grace of God.

(4) Conclusion

The Apostle Paul remains the apostle of divine grace. No doubt there were those who could twist his teachings into *antinomian* formulations (see Rom 3:8).

Ironically, the charge of *antinomianism* has frequently been hurled at the book you are now reading. But this theological swear word is totally inapplicable here, just as was such a charge in Paul's case.

Paul never allowed such accusations to keep him from teaching the freeness of God's salvation nor did he neglect to call for a lifestyle that was truly responsive to this divine generosity. But the Apostle was also a realist and a pastor who knew only too well the failures to which Christians are prone. Yet he does not for that reason modify his concept of God's saving grace. He simply redoubles his efforts to stir up his fellow Christians to live so that they will honor their true calling (Eph 4:1).

It may safely be said that no man in Christian history—with the exception of our Lord Himself—ever motivated

---

[103] Cranfield, *Romans*, 66-67; and John Murray, *The Epistle to the Romans*, 2 vols. in one (Grand Rapids: Eerdmans, 1959, 1965 [one vol. ed., 1968]), 13-14. Despite other grammatical possibilities, the view I have given in the text is precisely the view of the phrase taken by both Cranfield and Murray ("The obedience which consists in faith"). Yet both writers proceed to read their theology into the expression so as to extract from it a call to works. But in doing this, they are no longer exegeting the text at all. The phrase means no more than what it says: "the obedience which is faith." When one believes the gospel, he has obeyed the gospel, since the gospel calls for a response of faith.

believers more or threatened them less than did this great servant of Christ. Those who feel unable to inspire lives of obedience apart from questioning the salvation of those whom they seek to exhort have much to learn from Paul.

Postscript: 2 Corinthians 13:5

In the first edition of this book there was no discussion of 2 Cor 13:5. This proved to be a significant oversight. Critics of the book sometimes spoke as though the oversight was due to a reluctance on my part to confront this text.

John MacArthur wrote of 2 Cor 13:5 that this "admonition is largely ignored—and often explained away in the contemporary church."[104] He attached a footnote after that comment in which he responded to a statement I made on p. 95 of the first edition of this book. In his comment MacArthur notes: "Hodges does not mention 2 Corinthians 13:5 or *attempt to explain* [italics added] what possible second dimension it might have."[105] But this is fair enough. My silence *might* raise the suspicion that the text was too difficult for me to address. But the fact is, I simply underrated its importance to the discussion. I repair this error by considering the verse in this edition.

In 2 Corinthians 13, the Apostle Paul is announcing his intention to visit the Corinthian church once more. He writes:

> I have told you before, and foretell as if I were present the second time, and now being absent I write to those who have sinned before, and to all the rest, that if I come again I will not spare—since you seek a proof of Christ speaking in me, who is not weak toward you, but mighty in you. For though He was crucified in weakness, yet He lives by the power of God. For we also are weak in

---

[104] MacArthur, *The Gospel According to Jesus*, 190.
[105] Ibid., p. 190 fn 3.

Him, but we shall live with Him by the power
of God toward you. Examine yourselves as to
whether you are in the faith. Test yourselves.
Do you not know yourselves, that Jesus
Christ is in you?—unless indeed you are
disqualified. But I trust that you will know
that we are not *disqualified* (2 Cor 13:2-6,
emphasis added).

Just as with most of the verses already discussed in this chapter, 2 Cor 13:5 is often ripped out of its context. Failure to consider the context is almost always a formula for misunderstanding and doctrinal confusion.

(1) The Situation at Corinth

The situation at Corinth was somewhat different from that which existed earlier when 1 Corinthians was written. Although the church as a whole still had warm regard for Paul (2 Cor 7:6-16), Paul now had critics and enemies in Corinth. The believers there had listened to these people more than they should have (2 Cor 10:7-12; 11:12-15).

Apparently some of Paul's own converts wondered whether Paul could furnish "proof of Christ speaking" in him (2 Cor 13:3). Paul is now insisting that he will indeed revisit Corinth (see 2 Cor 13:1), though a previously planned trip had been canceled (see 2 Cor 1:15–2:2). Furthermore, he insists that when he comes his conduct toward them will be marked by the "power of God" (v 4).

The tone of 2 Cor 13:2-4 is both humble and confident. Paul promises not to s*pare* those Christians among them who had sinned and had remained unrepentant (see 2 Cor 13:4 and 12:20-21). This implies that Paul will either lead the church to discipline these people or that he himself, through prayer, will deliver them to Satan who will be an instrument for their chastisement. As we saw in the previous chapter, this is what Paul did at a later time with Hymenaeus and Alexander (1 Tim 1:20).

Paul knows, of course, his own weakness (2 Cor 13:4), yet he has total confidence that his actions at Corinth will be effective because God's power will work through him. The sinning believers will be dealt with in such a way that the Corinthians will get "a proof of Christ speaking in me" (v 2). In short, Paul says, "we will live with Him [Christ] by the power of God *toward you*" (v 4, emphasis added).

(2) Paul's Challenge to the Corinthians

Yet Paul is not so arrogant as to suggest that such confidence was a special privilege belonging to him alone. True, he knew perfectly well that Christ lived dynamically in him and used him. But could not the Corinthians have the same confidence about themselves?

Of course they could. Provided, of course, that their lives did not stand under God's disapproving censure.

So he wrote:

> Examine *yourselves* as to whether you are in the faith. Test *yourselves*. Do you not know *yourselves*, that Jesus Christ is in you?—unless indeed you are disqualified (2 Cor 13:5, emphasis added).

Unfortunately these forceful words are often read as though they challenged the Corinthians to find out whether or not they were *saved*.

This is unthinkable and absurd. After twelve chapters in which the Apostle takes his readers' Christianity for granted, can he *only now* be telling them to make sure they are born again? The question answers itself.

It is impossible to read the first twelve chapters of 2 Corinthians carefully without seeing how frequently the Apostle expresses confidence that his readership is truly Christian. Let me list a few places where this is true:

Paul...to the church of God which is at
Corinth, with all the saints who are in all
Achaia (2 Cor 1:1-2).

Now I trust you will understand to the end...
that we are your boast as *you also are ours
in the day of Jesus Christ* (2 Cor 1:13-14,
emphasis added).

Now He who establishes us *with you* in
Christ...(2 Cor 1:21, emphasis added).

You are our epistle written in our hearts,
known and read by all men; *clearly you are an
epistle of Christ*, ministered by us, written not
with ink but *by the Spirit of the living God*,
not on tablets of stone but *on tablets of flesh*,
that is, *of the heart* (2 Cor 3:2-3, emphasis
added).

Do not be unequally yoked together with
unbelievers [the Corinthians are believers].
For what fellowship has *righteousness* with
lawlessness? And what communion has *light*
with darkness?...Or what part has a *believer*
with an unbeliever? And what agreement
has *the temple of God* with idols? *For you are
the temple of the living God* (2 Cor 6:14-16,
emphasis added).

But as you abound in everything—*in faith*, in
speech, in knowledge, in all diligence, and in
your love for us—see that you abound in this
grace also (2 Cor 8:7, emphasis added).

It is needless to extend this list further. How can anyone read 2 Corinthians and conclude that Paul thought his readership needed to find out whether they were really saved or not?[106] To draw this conclusion from 2 Cor 13:5 is to impose on that verse an alien theology, about which Paul knew nothing at all.

Paul is *not* saying, "Examine yourselves to see whether you are born again, or justified." But he *is* saying, "Examine yourselves to see if you are *in the faith.*" And this is a different matter.

(3) The Meaning of "in the Faith"

It is tragic how often a text like this can be read with preconceived notions about the meanings of certain words or phrases. Why should anyone assume that the expression "in the faith" equals "to be a Christian"? On what grounds is such an assumption based?

What about the same phrase in 1 Cor 16:13? There we read, "Watch, stand fast *in the faith,* be brave, be strong." Or equally, what about this phrase in Titus 1:13? "Therefore rebuke them sharply, that they may be sound [healthy] *in the faith*" [see also Titus 2:2].

There are other passages where an equivalent expression appears. These, too, are helpful, "[Barnabus and Paul] returned...strengthening the souls of the disciples, exhorting them to continue *in the faith*" (Acts 14:22). Paul commanded the believers in Rome: "Receive one who is weak *in the faith*" (Rom 14:1).

> As you therefore have received Christ Jesus the Lord, so walk in Him, rooted and built up

---

[106] Although Ironside's view of the text is not quite my own, in its essentials it is extremely similar. Thus he can write: "In replying again to the suggestion that Paul was not a real apostle, he says, 'If you seek a proof of Christ living in me, examine yourselves.' Now if you take this fifth verse out of its connection you lose the meaning of it. Many people take it, as though he meant that we are to examine ourselves to see if we are real Christians, but this is not what Paul is saying." For his full view of the verse, see H. A. Ironside, *Addresses on the Second Epistle to the Corinthians* (Neptune, NJ: Loizeaux Brothers, 1939), 282-83.

in Him, and established *in the faith* (Col 2:6-7, emphasis added).

Be sober, be vigilant; for your adversary the devil walks about like a roaring lion, seeking whom he may devour. Resist him, steadfast *in the faith* (1 Pet 5:8-9, emphasis added).

In all of the passages I have mentioned, the phrase *in the faith* relates in some way to our Christian walk or warfare. The meaning *to be a Christian* is not relevant in any New Testament passage at all that uses the expression *in the faith*.

We must conclude that the expression *in the faith* refers instead to the proper sphere of our spiritual activity. It is the sphere in which we are to "remain," "stand fast," "stand," "resist the devil," and "be spiritually healthy." It is this type of meaning alone that fits the context of 2 Cor 13:5.

Paul is quite sure that he himself is "in the faith" in the sense that he is dynamically related to Christ. Christ speaks in him; God's power works through him. He is confident this will be evident when he returns to Corinth.

But the Corinthians can see this in themselves, too, if they will but examine their experience. They can see Jesus Christ living dynamically in themselves as well.

Thus the statement, "Do you not know yourselves, that Jesus Christ is in you?" has no more to do with the question of salvation than do the words "in the faith." What Paul has described of his own experience shows that he is thinking of Jesus Christ being in himself, or in the Corinthians, in a dynamic, active and vital sense.

In the language of the Apostle John this could be expressed in terms of the abiding life, where the disciple is in Christ, and Christ is in the disciple, in a *dynamic*, fruit-bearing relationship (see John 15:1-8; 14:19-24).

William Baird's treatment of 2 Cor 13:5 closely approximates my own when he writes:

> In the intense light of the cross, the Corinthians ought to examine themselves (v 5; *see* 1 Cor 11:28). They have been putting Paul to the test when they ought to be testing themselves. The crucial question is, Are you 'in the faith'; is Jesus Christ 'in you'? (NASB). Faith is the original response to the Christian message (Rom 1:16; 3:22), and the believer continues to stand in faith (1:24; 1 Cor 16:13) and to 'walk by faith' (5:7). This *life of faith is characterized as life in Christ or Christ in you*—a life conditioned by the redemptive power of God (see Rom 8:9-11; Gal 2:20). Though the Corinthians may fail the test, they ought to be able to recognize that Paul has passed; the credentials of his service (11:23-29) are the suffering marks of Christ (italics added).[107]

So Paul is saying, "Take a look at yourselves: test yourselves. Can you not see Jesus Christ actively living in you, just as I can see Him in me? Of course you can—unless, however, you are 'disqualified.'"

(4) The Meaning of "Disqualified"

The word *disqualified* is a significant one for Paul. He used it in his first letter to the Corinthian church when he wrote:

> But I discipline my body and bring it into subjection lest when I have preached to others, I myself should become *disqualified* (1 Cor 9:27, emphasis added).

In this passage, the Apostle has been talking about the Christian life as a race. He is careful to pursue God's

---

[107] William Baird, *1 Corinthians 2 Corinthians* (Knox Preaching Guides), ed. John H. Hayes (Atlanta: John Knox Press, 1980), 109.

approval in that race so that he will not be "disqualified" from winning the proper reward.

But the Greek word translated "disqualified" basically means "disapproved." In 2 Cor 13:5 Paul is telling his Christian readers that as long as they have God's approval on their lives (that is, as long as they are obedient to Him) they will be able to see in their own experience the dynamic reality of Christ living in them.

This could be observable in terms of answered prayer, spiritual blessing, and fruitfulness in the lives of others. Obedient Christians experience such things. Disobedient Christians do not. Obedient believers are living their lives "in the faith." Disobedient believers are cut off from this kind of vital fellowship with Christ. They may be described as living "according to the flesh" (Rom 8:13) or as "walking in darkness" (1 John 1:7).

(5) *Paul's Concluding Comment*

Paul knows he is in fellowship with Christ. "I intend to prove that when I come to Corinth," he says. "But such confidence is not mine alone. It's for you Corinthians too. You can see its reality in yourselves, if you take the trouble to look—unless, after all, God disapproves of your way of life" (paraphrase).

Then he adds: "But I trust that you will know that *we* [the Greek pronoun is emphatic] are not disqualified" (2 Cor 13:6).

"When I come to Corinth," says Paul, "I hope to convince you that God's approval rests on me. You can know this about yourselves, and I expect you to know it about me as well" (paraphrase).

Such then was the confident spirit with which the Apostle prepared to go back to Corinth. No doubt he would be horrified to hear his words to his brethren twisted into a call to test their justification by examining their own good works.

It should be a major embarrassment to Reformed theologians to discover that their treatment of 2 Cor 13:5 was completely unknown to Calvin himself. As I have pointed out, Calvin did not believe in testing the reality of our salvation by examining our works. Moreover, he regarded such an idea as a dangerous dogma [*Institutes* 3.2.38]. Naturally he did not find this "dangerous dogma" in 2 Cor 13:5. Let us hear Calvin's own words:

> *Try yourselves.* He confirms, what he had stated previously—that Christ's power showed itself openly in his ministry. For he makes them the judges of this matter, provided they descend, as it were, into themselves, and acknowledge what they had received from him. In the first place, as there is but one Christ, it must be of necessity, that the same Christ must dwell alike in minister and people. Now, dwelling in the people, how will he deny himself in the minister. Farther, he had shown his power in Paul's preaching, in such a manner that it could be no longer doubtful or obscure to the Corinthians, if they were not altogether stupid. For, whence had they faith? whence had they Christ? whence, in fine, had they every thing? It is with good reason, therefore, that they are called to look into themselves, that they may discover there, what they despise as a thing unknown. Then only has a minister a true and well grounded assurance for the approbation of his doctrine, when he can appeal to the consciences of those whom he has taught, that, if they have any thing of Christ, and of sincere piety, they may be constrained to acknowledge his fidelity. We are now in posession of Paul's object.
>
> This passage, however, is deserving of particular observation on two accounts. For, in

the first place, it shows the relation, which
subsists between the faith of the people, and
the preaching of the minister—that the one
is the mother, that produces and brings forth,
and the other is the daughter, that ought
not forget her origin. In the second place, *it
serves to prove the assurance of faith*, as to
which the Sorbonnic sophists have made us
stagger, nay more, have altogether rooted
out from the minds of men. They charge with
rashness all that are persuaded that they are
members of Christ, and have Him remaining
in them, for they bid us be satisfied with a
"moral conjecture," as they call it—that is,
with a mere opinion, so that our consciences
remain constantly in suspense, and in a state
of perplexity.[108]

It would be hard for Calvin to make any clearer his fundamental theological stance that *assurance is of the essence of saving faith*. The distortion of Paul's text into an appeal to confirm one's faith because true faith cannot be verified apart from works, makes a mockery of one of Calvin's most settled convictions. The Reformed treatment of 2 Cor 13:5 subverts Biblical assurance no less than did the sophists of the Sorbonne against whom Calvin so vigorously protested.

Conclusion

Nothing highlights the tragedy of today's evangelical church like the degree to which Paul's teachings are distorted into anti-Pauline thought. After all, it was Paul who wrote:

> But to him *who does not work* but believes
> on Him who justifies the ungodly, his faith

---

[108] Calvin, *Commentary on 2 Corinthians*, s.v. 2 Cor 13:5, italics added.

is accounted for righteousness (Rom 4:5, emphasis added).

But today, many theologians respond to this with a "yes, but…" "Yes, but if you don't do works you are not justified at all."[109] In this way, the Pauline declaration is annulled in favor of a faith/works synthesis which is contrary to both the Scriptures and to the doctrine of faith expounded in the Reformation by Calvin and Luther.

What I allege here is to be carefully noted. The faith/works synthesis which makes *works* an inherent or implicit part of *faith* so that *works* are indeed a *condition* for salvation does *not* represent the Reformers' view of faith and works. Even when the Reformers insisted on good works as an outgrowth of faith, they did not make *works* a part of faith or a "condition" for salvation. It might indeed be argued that the Reformers left a measure of tension between their doctrines of faith and works. But Reformed theology's solution to this tension is neither Biblical nor reformational. The Reformers themselves would have been horrified by the resulting theology. For them, good works were never the test of true faith, but rather, good works flowed out of *the assurance of salvation* which was inseparable from true saving faith.

This is precisely the position of this book. A strong case can be made that Reformed soteriology and "Lordship Salvation" are nothing more than a return to the Medieval Roman Catholic concept of "formed faith" (*fides formata*), in which faith is not effective for justification apart from works.[110]

---

[109] W. Nicol "Faith and Works in the Letter of James," in *Essays in the General Epistles of the New Testament, Neotestamentica* 9 (Pretoria: The New Testament Society of South Africa, c1975), 22. Nicol's statements are commendable for their frankness, if not for their theology, when he writes: "Logically, then, good works must be a condition of justification…" and, "From this it is clear that Paul might say: you must do good works, otherwise in the end God will not justify you."

[110] Paul Holloway, "A Return to Rome: Lordship Salvation's Doctrine of Faith," *Journal of the Grace Evangelical Society* vol. 4 no. 2 (Autumn

It is nothing less than a retreat into the theological darkness that made the Reformation necessary in the first place. Although those who advocate such doctrine describe it as "orthodox" and "reformational," in reality it is neither.

The evangelical church will have no message for the world if it allows this false doctrine to prevail.

8

Faith and Water Baptism

The relationship of water baptism to the question of eternal salvation has often been discussed. It is well known that there are many churches where the rite of water baptism is regarded as an indispensable step in Christian conversion. A great deal of commentary literature on the New Testament has been authored by writers who are associated with such churches. It seems necessary to give at least brief consideration to this question here.

John 3:5

In the Gospel of John water baptism is never associated with the offer of eternal life. Yet many have thought that baptism *is* referred to in John 3:5. There Jesus says:, "Most assuredly, I say to you, unless one is born of water and the Spirit, he cannot enter the kingdom of God." The conclusion that the word "water" in this verse refers to "baptism" is not well-founded. If John really had believed that baptism was essential to obtaining eternal life, it is both astounding and inexplicable that he never says so directly. John 3:5 can be adequately interpreted without making the equation "water" = "baptism."

Since the Greek word for "spirit" also meant "wind," it is likely that the expression was originally intended to be understood as "born of water and wind" (see v 8). In that case, "water" and "wind" are a dual metaphor intended to symbolize the life-giving ministry of God's Spirit. Nicodemus should have been familiar with Old Testament texts which used these images of the Spirit's work. See Isa 44:3-5, where the Spirit is compared to life-giving waters poured out from above; and Ezek 37:5-10, where He is a life-imparting wind or breath.

Raymond Brown holds open the questions about (1) whether John 3 represents an historical scene, and (2) whether the words "of water" belong to the original text. Yet he has some helpful comments:

> A second argument against the originality of the phrase 'of water' is theological. The objection that Nicodemus could not have understood the phrase and that therefore it was not part of the original tradition is weak. We have shown above that many of the Old Testament passages which mention the outpouring of the spirit also mention water; thus water and spirit do go together. Moreover, several other passages in the Johannine works join water and spirit (John 7:38-39; 1 John 5:8), and so John 3:5 is not an isolated instance. If the phrase 'of water' were part of the original form of the discourse, then it would have been understood by Nicodemus against the Old Testament background rather than in terms of Christian Baptism.[111]

Calvin likewise dismisses the baptismal interpretation in favor of the view that "water and spirit" both refer to the same idea. He wrote:

> Accordingly He used the words *Spirit* and *water* to mean the same thing, and this ought not to be regarded as harsh or forced...It is as if Christ had said that no one is a son of God until he has been renewed by water and that this water is the Spirit who cleanses us anew and who, by His power poured upon

---

[111] Brown, *Gospel*, 1:142-143. Additionally, the kind of view I present in the text is recognized as definitely viable by Robinson, who writes: "It is clearly possible to take 'water and spirit' as a hendiadys, two terms for a single idea." See D. W. B. Robinson, "Born of Water and Spirit: Does Jo. 3,5 Refer to Baptism?" *Reformed Theological Review* vol. 25 (1966): 15-23; quote is from 19.

us, imparts to us the energy of heavenly life
when by nature we are utterly barren.[112]

I defend this view in some detail in an article, "Water and Spirit—John 3:5."[113] It is sufficient to say here that there is no adequate reason to take Jesus' words as a reference to baptism. The silence of the Fourth Gospel about the spiritual significance of this rite is deafening.[114]

First Corinthians 1:17

When we turn to the Apostle Paul, he clearly did not view baptism as indispensable to his ministry in the gospel. In fact, he actually writes, "For Christ did not send me to baptize, but to preach the gospel" (1 Cor 1:17). It was apparently not Paul's practice even to baptize his own converts (1 Cor 1:13-16). At the very least, this does not sound like he thought no one could be eternally saved unless they were baptized.

Outside of 1 Corinthians 1 (and 15:29) all the other references to Christian baptism in Paul can be understood as references to baptism by the Holy Spirit. It was *this*

---

[112] *Comm.* John 3:5.

[113] Zane Hodges, "Water and Spirit—John 3:5," *Bibliotheca Sacra* vol. 135, no. 539, (1978): 206-20.

[114] The view that "of water" in John 3:5 refers to physical procreation is often suggested. Leon Morris (p. 218), who holds this view, writes that the "allusion [to physical birth] would be natural to him [Nicodemus]." But would it? Can it really be shown that this was a comprehensible concept for Nicodemus? Such extra-biblical evidence as has been advanced seems to fall seriously short of demonstrating that the suggested meaning is viable. But see the discussion in Morris, *Gospel*, 215-19. For some of the proposed sources, see Hugo Odeberg, *The Fourth Gospel interpreted in its relations to Contemporaneous Religious Currents in Palestine and the Hellenistic-Oriental World* (Uppsala: Almquist and Wiksells Boktryckeri-A.-B., 1929), 48-71.

The view that "of water" refers to physical birth apparently has no convincing parallel in Jewish sources. Thus it seems forced and artificially clinical. The view of Brown, that the OT would be the natural background for Nicodemus to understand the reference to water, is clearly a more likely position.

baptism which was so vital to Pauline thought. It furnished the grounds on which the believer could be said to be *in* the Body of Christ (see 1 Cor 12:13).

We should keep in mind that the key word in John's doctrine of eternal salvation is "life," specifically "eternal life." For Paul, the key word is "justification." Neither writer ever associates his basic idea with anything other than faith. For John, baptism plays no role in obtaining *life*. For Paul, it plays no role in *justification*. In fact, there is no New Testament writer who associates baptism with either of these issues. The importance of this observation cannot be overstated.

Even the famous passage about baptism found in 1 Peter 3:21 is no exception. (In the text of this chapter I consider this verse briefly a bit further on.) But here I must note that Peter mentions neither "eternal life" nor "justification" anywhere in that paragraph (3:17-22).

Acts 2:38

If all this is kept in mind, a new light is cast on the kind of statement found in Acts 2:38. In that place, Luke reports the Apostle Peter as having said:

> "Repent, and let everyone of you be baptized in the name of Jesus Christ for the remission of sins; and you shall receive the gift of the Holy Spirit" (Acts 2:38).

This text seems clearly to say that the hearers must be baptized to get their sins forgiven and then, but only then, will they be given the gift of the Holy Spirit. An effort is sometimes made to avoid this conclusion by rendering the word "for" (Greek, *eis*) as "because of," but this procedure lacks any adequate linguistic basis. The effort to show that *eis* can mean "because of" has been a failure.[115]

---

[115] In the standard Greek lexicon in use today (BDAG, 2001), the so-called "causal *eis*" does not even have an entry of its own. The lexicon

What the text does *not* say is how the hearers were *regenerated* and *justified*. But the answers of John and Paul to this question are the only Biblical ones that can be given: they were justified and regenerated by faith. There is nothing in Acts 2:38 to contradict this.

On the contrary, Peter concludes his address with the declaration that "God has made this Jesus, whom you have crucified, both Lord and Christ" (Acts 2:36). His hearers then reply, "Men and brethren, what shall we do?" (Acts 2:37). But such a reaction presumes their acceptance of Peter's claim that they have crucified the One who is Lord and Christ. If this is what they now believed, then they were already regenerate on John's terms, since John wrote: "Whoever believes that Jesus is the Christ is born of God" (1 John 5:1; see John 20:31).

(1) Justification and Forgiveness

It seems plain that in Peter's audience there were many who accepted the claims of Christ which Peter has presented. These people are enormously convicted of their guilt in the crucifixion and ask what they need to do now. Acts 2:38 is the answer.[116] This verse could never have become a problem to interpreters as long as fundamental Pauline and Johannine truths were kept in mind. Even the reference to the forgiveness of sins is not hard to understand when it is properly considered.

Justification by faith establishes a man's legal standing before his Judge. Forgiveness enables him to have communion with his God.

Even on the level of everyday experience, forgiveness has nothing to do with the courts. A judge does not *forgive* anyone; he finds a man either guilty or innocent.

---

merely mentions the claims made for it by J. R. Mantey in his articles and the rebuttal material by R. Marcus and J. Davis. For the references, see BDAG, 291c, under 10.a.

[116] See Appendix 4.

Forgiveness relates instead to personal relationships. Men exclude from their fellowship those whom they refuse to forgive and in turn are excluded by those who will not forgive them.

It may be said then that when a man is *justified* he is given a righteousness which comes from God (Rom 3:21-26). When he is *regenerated,* he is given the very life of God (John 1:12-13). But *forgiveness* introduces him to fellowship with the One whose life and righteousness he has been granted through faith.

Not surprisingly, therefore, even those who are both justified and regenerated are taught to seek forgiveness on a regular basis (Luke 11:4; 1 John 1:9). Justification and new birth are irrevocable free gifts (Rom 5:15-18; 11:29). Fellowship is a conditional privilege (1 John 1:7).

(2) The Special Situation in Acts 2

The situation in Acts 2 is apparently exceptional. It is not repeated in the experience of Gentile converts (Acts 10:43-48). It is probably related to the special guilt of those who had been implicated in the crucifixion. But there is no actual conflict with fundamental Pauline and Johannine truth.

In this special transitional situation, fellowship with God is withheld from these converts until they have been baptized. Following this, the gift of the Spirit is bestowed. But his latter gift was a new one, not given before Pentecost (John 7:39). It is not to be confused with the experience of regeneration which has always been the fundamental requirement for entrance into God's kingdom (John 3:3). At Pentecost, God gave the Spirit only to those who had entered into fellowship with Him.[117]

---

[117] For a full and very valuable discussion of Acts 2:38, see Lanny Thomas Tanton, "The Gospel and Water Baptism: A Study of Acts 2:38," *Journal of the Grace Evangelical Society* vol. 3 no. 1 (Spring 1990): 27-52.

Acts 22:16

The experience just described was Paul's own as well. Clearly Paul came to faith in the Lord Jesus Christ on the road to Damascus (Acts 9:3-5; 22:6-8; 26:12-15). The blazing light in which he met his Savior is probably behind the imagery found in 2 Cor 4:6, about the light of the knowledge of Christ shining into our hearts.

If anyone thinks that Paul was not really converted on the Damascus road, this idea would be far-fetched in the extreme. Obviously, from that occasion onward, he was a believer in Jesus, whom he now calls Lord (Acts 22:10).

But he was forgiven three days later. This is plainly indicated by the words of Ananias in Acts 22:16 when he tells Saul, "Arise and be baptized, and wash away your sins, calling on the name of the Lord." Since his faith on the Damascus road had already brought him eternal life and justification, this additional step must have introduced him into the dynamic experience of Spirit-led fellowship with God (see Acts 9:17-20). After three days of fasting and prayer (Acts 9:9, 11), he had found the answer to his question, "What shall I do, Lord?" (Acts 22:10). That answer, his Lord had told him, would be given to him in Damascus (Acts 9:6: 22:10).

It is obvious that this type of experience is completely parallel to the situation in Acts 2:38—even down to the question, "What shall we do?" It is an experience in which baptism plays an important, but highly exceptional, role. Its terms are never repeated in the book of Acts anywhere on the Gentile mission fields. Neither are such terms presented anywhere else in the epistles of the New Testament.

These terms for fellowship evidently belong to the historic record of God's dealings with the generation of Palestinians who had been exposed to, and had rejected, the ministries of both John the Baptist and Jesus Himself. (See the reference to "this perverse generation" in Acts 2:40.) In both the ministries of John and our Lord, baptism played a significant part (cf. John 4:1-2). It was suitable for people in this unique historical situation to be required to enter fellowship with God through baptism.[118]

Acts 19:1-7

It is along these lines that we can understand Acts 19:1-7. There we read:

> And it happened…that Paul…came to Ephesus. And finding some disciples he said to them, "Did you receive the Holy Spirit when you believed?" So they said to him, "We have not so much as heard whether there is a Holy Spirit." And he said to them, "Into what then were you baptized?" So they said, "Into John's baptism." Then Paul said, "John indeed baptized with a baptism of repentance, saying to the people that they should believe on Him who would come after him, that is, on Christ Jesus." When they heard this, they were baptized in the name of the Lord Jesus. And when Paul laid hands on them, the Holy Spirit came upon them, and they spoke with tongues and prophesied. Now the men were about twelve in all.

The disciples in this passage, whom Paul met, were already believers. Paul's question to them makes this plain: "Did you receive the Holy Spirit when you believed?" (Acts 19:2), But they were also probably Palestinians, since they had experienced John's baptism (Acts 19:3). In harmony with the conditions of Acts 2:38, Paul baptizes them and subsequently imparts to them the Holy Spirit (Acts 19:5-6).

---

[118] For Acts 22:16, see the follow-up study to the one mentioned in the previous footnote: Lanny Thomas Tanton, "The Gospel and Water Baptism: A Study of Acts 22:16." *Journal of the Grace Evangelical Society* vol. 4 no. 1 (Spring 1991): 23-40. In both studies, Tanton critiques alternative views with skill.

Non-Palestinians, who had no contact with John's baptism, are never said in the New Testament to have had any such experience as this. Of course, the Samaritans of Acts 8:12-17 were Palestinians.

This is plainly not normative Christian experience. Normative Christian experience takes the form set forth in the crucial story of the conversion of Cornelius in Acts 10. There forgiveness and the reception of the Spirit take place at the moment of faith (Acts 10:43-44). Water baptism *follows* and in no way conditions these blessings (Acts 10:47-48).

The situations described in Acts 2, 8, and 19, as well as Paul's own in 22, are a matter of instructive Biblical record. But by the time Paul wrote the Epistle to the Romans, it could be said that all Christians possessed the Spirit of God (Rom 8:9; see 1 Cor 12:13). The transitional features of the Christian message, which Luke faithfully reports, are not pertinent today. In fact, they never were pertinent (even in Acts) on the Gentile mission fields.

Salvation in Luke, Paul, and John

This leads to a further important observation. In Luke's writings, and also in Paul's, the term "salvation." Or "saved" (in reference to converts to Christianity) is reserved for those who have received *not only* eternal life and justification, *but also* the gift of the Holy Spirit.

Thus the word *saved* is used of Cornelius's experience in direct connection with the gift of the Spirit (Acts 11:14-18). It is applied to the first converts in Acts only when they have been baptized and incorporated into the Church through the bestowal of the Spirit (Acts 2:41, 47). It is the baptism of the Spirit, not new birth alone, that introduces men into the Body of Christ (1 Cor 12:13). Neither Luke nor Paul ever used the term *saved* of those not yet baptized with the Holy Spirit. In Titus 3:4-7, the outpouring of the Holy Spirit is a prominent part of Paul's description of how God "saved" us.

By contrast, John apparently can refer the term *saved* to those who have simply received eternal life. His use of the expression *saved* is rare, but the examples seem sufficient to prove the point just stated (John 3:17; 5:34; 10:9). It must be kept in mind that those who believed in Jesus during the course of His earthly life received only eternal life. The gift of the Spirit awaited the post-ascension situation (John 7:39).

It follows from this that, in the Johannine sense, the converts of Acts 2 were *saved before* they were baptized. That is, they received eternal life the moment they believed in Jesus Christ. But in the Pauline and Lucan sense, they were not *saved* until *after* they were baptized, since only then did they receive the gift of the Spirit.

Even in Paul and Luke's sense of the word, however, all but the first century Palestinians received this *salvation* on the basis of faith alone, But everyone, in all times and places, has received eternal life (and been *saved* in John's sense of the word) by faith and faith alone.

Mark 16:16

If these distinctions are kept in mind, the significance of Mark 16:16 can be properly analyzed. (The grounds for rejecting Mark 16:9-20 as not an authentic part of the original Gospel of Mark are exceedingly insufficient.)[119] In Mark 16:16 Jesus states, "He who believes and is baptized will be saved; but he who does not believe will be condemned." Here the Lord Jesus anticipates Luke and Paul's use of the term *saved*. The bestowal of the Spirit, with His accompanying gifts, is clearly in His mind as is proved by verses 17-18.

---

[119] The two most valuable defenses of the textual authenticity of Mark 16:9-20 are: (1) John W. Burgon, *The Last Twelve Verses of the Gospel According to S. Mark* (London, 1871; [reprint edition, Ann Arbor, MI: The Sovereign Grace Book Club, 1959]); and (2) William R. Farmer, *The Last Twelve Verses of Mark* (Cambridge: University Press, 1974). Though Farmer's conclusions are very tentative, his material is of considerable value.

Thus our Lord speaks here of a "salvation" that involves *not only* eternal life, *but also* the gift of the Spirit.

Naturally His statement is a summary statement. It is designed to cover *all* the post-Pentecostal cases of *salvation*. And as exceptional as the situations of Acts 2, 8, and 19 are, they need to be covered by His declaration. So He announces that *everyone* who takes the two steps specified (faith and baptism) will experience the *salvation* He is speaking of.

Yet it has often been noticed that the condemnation in Mark 16:16 rests simply on the failure to believe. This is what we would expect. Eternal life is granted by faith alone (John 3:16; 5:24; etc.), and anyone who has it can never go to hell, whether they are baptized or not. But today, of course, the Holy Spirit is given to every believer, *before* baptism, at the moment of faith in Christ.

First Peter 3:21

It is not possible here to fully analyze the famous passage in 1 Pet 3:18-22 in which there is a statement that baptism "now saves us" (1 Pet 3:21). It is enough to say that the emphasis in the context on the Spirit and "spirits" (1 Pet 3:18-19) points strongly to the conclusion that the Apostle has "Spirit baptism" (not water baptism) in mind. For the purposes of this discussion about the rite of baptism with water, 1 Pet 3:21 may be understood as similar to the Pauline and Lucan use of the word *save*.

As noted earlier, in 1 Pet 3:21 Peter mentions neither "eternal life" nor "justification." The sense of the word "saves" is not to be taken for granted either. Furthermore, "baptism" need not be understood as referring to *water* baptism. The contextual stress on "Spirit" and "spirits" (3:18-19) suggests that the analogy is with "Spirit baptism" and that Noah's entrance into the ark is seen as a visual image of our incorporation into the body of Christ (the Church). We are thus preserved (saved) from the eschatological woes of the Tribulation, since the Church will be delivered from these by the Rapture (1 Thess 1:10; 5:1-11). 'The days of Noah" are a well-known example in our Lord's teaching of the end-time events (see Matt 24:37-38; Luke 17:26-27). Although Luther understood "baptism" here as water baptism, he certainly lays the foundation for our view when he writes:

> But we take ship in the ark, which represents the Lord Christ, or the Christian Church, or the Gospel which Christ preaches, or the body of Christ to which we cling through faith; and we are saved just as Noah was saved in the ark.[120]

How easy it seems now, centuries later, to bring 1 Cor 12:13 to bear on Luther's comments and to find in 1 Pet 3:21 no necessary reference to the sacrament at all. "Water baptism" lies behind this passage only in the sense that the physical ritual is a visualization of the spiritual reality embodied in baptism by the Holy Spirit. In treating the flood as a type of Christian deliverance from God's coming wrath, Peter can move directly to the true antitype for that, which is not water baptism but Spirit baptism.[121]

Forgiveness "in Christ"

Finally, we must say that whenever an individual is baptized by the Holy Spirit and placed "in Christ," he receives

---

[120] *Luther's Works*, vol. 30: *The Catholic Epistles*, ed. Jaroslav Pelikan and Walter A. Hansen, (St. Louis: Concordia Publishing House, 1967), 115.

[121] However, no one can deny the truth expressed by J. W. Dalton, who has written a major monograph on 1 Pet 3:18–4:6 when he states: "3:21 is an extremely difficult verse, and we cannot hope to solve all its problems adequately in this essay." See William Joseph Dalton, *Christ's Proclamation to the Spirits: A Study of 1 Peter 3:18–4:6* (Rome: Pontifical Biblical Institute, 1965), 210. See his material on 210-37.

at that moment a kind of "positional" forgiveness. This is described in Eph 1:7:

> *In Him* we have redemption through His blood, the forgiveness of sins, according to the riches of His grace (emphasis added).

Naturally, like all else that pertains to our *position* in Christ, this forgiveness is perfect and permanent. But this in no way contradicts the fact that we also experience forgiveness continually at the level of our day-to-day experience.

An unconverted sinner brings years of unforgiven sin to the moment of his conversion. Experientially, he obtains the forgiveness of all those past sins and begins to have fellowship with God. But whenever he commits further sins, he must acknowledge them and seek God's forgiveness (Luke 11:4; 1 John 1:9).

Nevertheless, as a man in Christ he has a position that is not altered by his daily experience of failure. In fact, he is seated "in the heavenly places in Christ Jesus" (Eph 2:6). This superlative relationship to God is never changed by any earthly interruption in his communion with the Father.

The failure to distinguish our permanent experience of forgiveness in Christ from our daily experience of cleansing has led to doctrinal confusion. It has actually led some to deny that a believer should ask for forgiveness for his sins, even though Christians are plainly told to do so. After all, the Lord's prayer was given to *disciples,* not to unconverted sinners, and its petitions are to be made *daily* (Luke 11:1-4).

The thought that a believer need never ask God's forgiveness for his sins is an aberration rightly rejected by the Church as a whole. But because a believer possesses eternal life, and is also in Christ, his sins jeopardize only his fellowship with God day by day. They do not jeopardize his final salvation from hell.

At the level of everyday experience, repentance for our sins is as fitting for us as it was for the converts on the day of Pentecost (Acts 2:38). Only in our case, confession alone (apart from baptism) secures the forgiveness we need (1 John 1:9).

Conclusion

When the New Testament passages on water baptism are studied closely, they in no way conflict with the grace of God. Eternal life is now, and always has been, a gift conditioned by nothing else but faith alone in Christ alone.

9
Who Are the Heirs?

Christian heirship is a great New Testament theme.[122] On this subject, the Apostle Paul has made a vital and instructive comment. His statement is found in Rom 8:16-17, where he wrote:

> The Spirit Himself bears witness with our spirit that we are children of God, and if children, then heirs—heirs of God and joint heirs with Christ, if indeed we suffer with Him, that we may also be glorified together.

This declaration is often read as if only one heirship were in view. However, with only a slight alteration of the English punctuation (which is equally permissible in the original Greek), Paul's words may be read as follows:

---

[122] It is particularly in reference to my discussion of heirship that some critics have thought that my ideas were without precedent in Christian literature. But in thinking so, they are seriously mistaken. Most of my suggestions on this theme were anticipated before the turn of the twentieth century by George N. H. Peters (1825-1909), who was born in Berlin, PA, graduated from Wittenberg College, and who pastored a number of Lutheran churches in Ohio. His magisterial three-volume magnum opus, *The Theocratic Kingdom of our Lord Jesus, The Christ, as Covenanted in The Old Testament and Presented in The New Testament*, was first published in 1884 by Funk and Wagnalls, New York. I have used the 1972 reprint edition by Kregel Publications, Grand Rapids, MI, for the citation below.

Another significant volume which anticipates the contents of this chapter to a considerable degree, is G. H. Lang, *Firstborn Sons: Their Rights & Risks*, first published by Samuel Roberts Publishers, London, England, in 1936. I have used the reprint edition of Conley and Schoettle, Miami Springs, FL, 1984. I cite it below as Lang, *Firstborn Sons*, to distinguish it from his volume on Hebrews.

Although Lang held the view that unfaithful Christians, even though eternally saved, would miss the Millennium altogether, his analysis of the Biblical teaching on Christian accountability is hard to surpass.

>...and if children, then heirs—heirs of God, and joint heirs with Christ if indeed we suffer with Him, that we may also be glorified together (author's translation).

Under this reading of the text, there are two forms of heirship. One of these is based on being children of God. The other is based on suffering with Christ. This distinction is crucial for understanding the New Testament teaching on this subject.

Double Heirship

The concept of two kinds of heirship is very natural indeed in the light of Old Testament custom. As is well-known, in a Jewish family all the sons shared equally in their father's inheritance, except for the oldest, or firstborn, son who received a double portion. That is, he inherited twice as much as the other sons.

Against this background, Paul can be understood as saying that *all* of God's children are heirs, simply because they are children. But those who suffer with Christ have a special "joint heirship" with Christ. It is of great significance that later in this chapter Christ is actually described as "the *firstborn* among many brethren" (Rom 8:29).

Naturally, all believers are God's heirs. In the eternal future they will most assuredly inherit all of the blessings which are unconditionally promised to them. Among these is an eternal glory (Rom 8:30) which is inherent in the resurrection itself. Hence Paul can say, "The body is sown in dishonor, it is raised in glory. It is sown in weakness, it is raised in power" (1 Cor 15:42-43). Elsewhere he writes that "we also eagerly wait for the Savior, the Lord Jesus Christ, who will transform our lowly body that it may be conformed to His glorious body" (Phil 3:20-21).

Of course, participation in the resurrection is unconditionally guaranteed to every believer in Christ. Jesus' own declaration on this point is definitive:

> "For I have come down from heaven, not to
> do My own will, but the will of Him who sent
> Me. This is the will of the Father who sent
> Me, that of all He has given Me I should lose
> nothing, but should raise it up at the last
> day. And this is the will of Him who sent Me,
> that everyone who sees the Son and believes
> in Him may have everlasting life; and I will
> raise him up at the last day" (John 6:38-40).

This passage is emphatic concerning the eternal security of the believer in Christ. The Lord Jesus Christ has never lost, nor will he ever lose, anyone who has belonged to Him through faith. But equally, though the word *inheritance* is not used here, such words seal the heirship of every Christian. A share in the glorious immortality of the future world is assured to the believer, because Jesus has promised to "raise him up at the last day."

But in Rom 8:17, Paul speaks also of a *co-heirship* that results in *co-glory*. This contrast is a bit easier to see in Greek than it is in English.

In the Greek text, Paul juxtaposes two words for *heir*, one of which is the simple word for this, and the other a compound word roughly equal to the word *co-heir*. Likewise, two other compound words in Paul's text express the thought of *co-suffering* and *co-glorification*. As Paul's words make clear, such an heirship is dependent on something more than saving faith. This heirship is contingent on our experience of suffering with Christ. Romans 8:17 thus confronts us with a double heirship. One of these is for all believers. The other is for believers who suffer in fellowship with Christ.

Co-Reigning with Christ: 2 Timothy 2:12

A similar thought occurs in 2 Tim 2:12. There the Apostle writes, "If we endure, we shall also reign with Him." Here again we meet the thought of suffering. The Greek verb *endure* refers primarily to the endurance of hardships and trials. Moreover, the verb translated "reign with Him" is another compound word like those we met in Rom 8:17. The idea is: "If we endure [suffering], we shall co-reign" (the words "with Him" are implied by the compound verb).

Putting Rom 8:17 together with 2 Tim 2:12, it is natural to conclude that to be *co-glorified* with Christ involves *co-reigning* with Him. In other words, the glory of co-heirship is more than merely participating in the glorious future world. It is to share the portion of the Firstborn Son of God and to *reign* in His kingdom.

Lang wrote most aptly:

> Joseph, David, Daniel, Esther became more than subjects under their respective sovereigns. Each attained to rulership and glory. It is for such supreme honour that God is now training the co-heirs of His Son (Rom 8:17, 2 Tim 2:10-12).[123]

With so glorious a prospect in view, no wonder Paul aspired to know Christ in "the fellowship of His sufferings" (Phil 3:10).

Service and Co-Reigning: Luke 19:11-27

The connection between fidelity to Christ and the privilege of sharing the authority of His kingdom appears already in the teaching of Jesus Himself. Its most striking expression is found in the famous parable of the minas in Luke 19:11-27.

The parable begins with a reference to the inter-advent period in which we live today as we wait for the kingdom of God. Jesus introduces the story with these words:

---

[123] G. H. Lang, *Hebrews*, 56. Following the quoted statement, Lang also writes: "A royal father may have a large family, but of these only a few may prove competent to rule in the kingdom and share its glory" (p. 57).

> "A certain nobleman went into a far country to receive for himself a kingdom and to return. So he called ten of his servants, delivered to them ten minas, and said to them, 'Do business till I come.'" (Luke 19:12-13).

It is easy to see how this relates to contemporary Christian experience. The minas (a mina was a unit of money) represent the potential for useful service to Christ with which every believer is entrusted. His marching orders are: "Do business till I come."

According to the story which Jesus told, when the nobleman returned he called each of his servants to account. This clearly suggests the Judgment Seat of Christ (Rom 14:10-12; 2 Cor 5:9, 11; 1 Cor 3:11-15; 4:5). The outcome of this review, as the parable unfolds it, is varying degrees of authority in the kingdom. The degree of authority is based on the measure of each servant's faithfulness and productivity. Thus one servant receives authority over ten cities (Luke 19:17), another over five (Luke 19:19).

Both servants are sharply distinguished from the unproductive servant, who is given no cities to rule and is even deprived of his mina (Luke 19:22-24). He thus bears an unmistakable resemblance to a Christian whose works are "burned up" and who "will be saved, yet so as through fire" (1 Cor 3:15). He had a job to do but he failed to do it. Therefore he is stripped of further responsibility. His mina is taken away.

It would be hard to improve on G. H. Lang's succinct statement of the central point of this parable. He wrote:

> Upon the return of the nobleman he richly rewarded those servants who had been diligent and successful during his absence. And the special reward indicated is that *'authority over cities'* was given in proportion to their fidelity; that is, they were appointed to high places in the kingdom of their lord. And thus both the governmental authority and personal

> glory of our Lord He will most graciously and royally share with such as are accounted worthy of these dignities. And the degree of our faithfulness now will be the measure of our worthiness then (italics his).[124]

As emphasized in the previous chapters, it is an illusion to think that every Christian will necessarily persevere in holiness until the end of his life. Such a view finds no support in the New Testament. This is not to say that there *must* be believers who are *totally* without any good word or work whatsoever. The Scriptures do not teach *that* either. Even in 1 Cor 3:15 Paul only says, "*if* anyone's work is burned [up]..."

So great is the miracle of regeneration that it is virtually unthinkable that it could have no effect at all on what a person says or does over an extended period of time. But God alone may see these effects and the absence of visible works in no way signals that a person is unsaved. However, those who teach that a lifelong perseverance in holiness *must be* the result of true conversion should read their New Testaments again, this time with their eyes open.

Michael Green definitely had his eyes open when, commenting on 2 Pet 1:11, he wrote:

> This passage agrees with several in the Gospels and Epistles in suggesting that while heaven is entirely a gift of grace, it admits of degrees of felicity, and that these are dependent upon how faithfully we have built a structure of character and service upon the foundation of Christ. Bengel likens the unholy Christian in the judgment to a sailor who just manages to make shore after shipwreck, or to a man who barely escapes with his life from a

---

[124] Lang, *Firstborn Sons*, 58-59.

burning house, while all his possessions are lost.[125]

The *wicked servant* in Jesus' parable failed to engage in his lord's *business* with the mina he had been given. He was not involved in *serving* his master. Whether or not he did other commendable things is not the point of the parable. At least he did not *labor* for his lord. As a result, he does not co-reign with his master over even a single city.

That he also went to hell would be an absurd and unfounded deduction from this parable.[126]

All Christians, then, are heirs of God. But they are not heirs to an equal degree. Their fidelity to the service of Christ, with all its attendant hardships and sufferings, will be the gauge by which that heirship will be measured out to them. Not to teach this simple truth is to deprive believers of one of the most powerful motivations to endurance which the Scriptures contain.

Inheriting the Kingdom: 1 Corinthians 6:9-10

It is not surprising that those who do not recognize the truths being discussed are impoverished in their ability to motivate both themselves and other believers. Tragically, they often fall back on the technique of questioning the salvation of those whose lives do not meet Biblical standards. But in the process, they undermine the grounds for a believer's assurance and take part (however unwittingly) in the siege of the gospel.

---

[125] Michael Green, *The Second Epistle General of Peter and the General Epistle of Jude: An Introduction and Commentary* TNTC (Grand Rapids: Eerdmans, 1968), 76-77.

[126] Editor's note: When I heard Zane teach on this passage, he gave several proofs of the regenerate status of the wicked servant: 1) He is a servant of Christ, 2) He was given a stewardship, 3) He is judged at the Judgment Seat of Christ with other believers, and 4) He is not "slain," like Jesus' enemies in v 27.

Paul did not do this, even though he has sometimes been read as if he did. In writing to the Corinthian church he is exasperated that they engage in lawsuits against one another. Of course, he does not question the salvation of those who do this. Instead he says, "But brother goes to law against brother, and that before unbelievers!"(1 Cor 6:6). The enormous disgrace of this, from Paul's point of view, is that Christians carry Christians to court where unsaved people preside. He denounces this emphatically.

His criticism of such conduct continues:

> Now therefore, it is already an utter failure for you that you go to law against one another. Why do you not rather accept wrong? Why do you not rather let yourselves be cheated? No, you yourselves do wrong and cheat, and you do these things to your brethren! (1 Cor 6:7-8).

It is precisely at this point that the Apostle turns to the theme of heirship:

> Do you not know that the unrighteous will not inherit the kingdom of God? Do not be deceived. Neither fornicators, nor idolators, nor adulterers, nor homosexuals, nor sodomites, nor thieves, nor covetous, nor drunkards, nor revilers, nor extortioners will inherit the kingdom of God (1 Cor 6:9-10).

It is as plain as possible that Paul intends these words as a warning against the kind of conduct he has been describing in the Corinthian Christians. This is made doubly obvious by the opening statement that "the *unrighteous* will not inherit the kingdom of God." Paul has just charged them with being unrighteous ("you yourselves do wrong"). The connection is clearer in Greek than in English. The word translated "you do wrong" in verse 8 is the Greek verb *adikeite*, and the word for "unrighteous" in verse 9 is a related word, *adikoi*.

What Paul is saying is that the Corinthians are engaged in conduct that can make it impossible to inherit the kingdom of God. Persistence in this type of behavior will obviously disqualify them from this kind of heirship. No other deduction about Paul's meaning can possibly be fair to the text.

(1) Paul Knows His Readers Are Saved

But does he thereby call their salvation into question? That is precisely what he does *not* do. Instead he wrote:

> And such were some of you. But you were washed, but you were sanctified, but you were justified in the name of the Lord Jesus and by the Spirit of our God (1 Cor 6:11).

Paul is so far from suggesting to them that perhaps they are not Christians at all, that he even appeals to the fact that they *are!*

Obviously, Paul's catalogue of sins (vv 9-10) lays heavy stress on immorality. This was also a major problem with the conduct of the Corinthian Christians (see 1 Cor 5:1-13; 6:12-20). But always he appeals to the certainty that they are Christians, not to any possibility that they are not. So he can say:

> Do you not know that your bodies are members of Christ? Shall I then take the members of Christ and make them members of a harlot? Certainly not! (1 Cor 6:15).

And he ends the chapter with this appeal:

> Or do you not know that your body is the temple of the Holy Spirit who is in you, whom you have from God, and you are not your own? For you were bought at a price; therefore glorify God in your body and in your spirit, which are God's (1 Cor 6:19-20).

Paul's whole argument for moral behavior by his readers is based on the fact that they are truly God's temple and members of the Body of Christ. They ought to act like what they are.

The widespread idea that Paul actually doubted (or, could doubt) the salvation of his readers on the basis of their behavior is so far from his real perspective that it is incomprehensible how that conclusion could ever be drawn. Such an approach to his statements here about heirship is so hopelessly confused that it manages to miss his point entirely. It draws from these statements an outlook that was totally foreign to Paul's mind.

In speaking of heirship in 1 Cor 6:9-10, Paul did not threaten his readers with the loss of eternal salvation. He did not even raise a question about their salvation. But he warned them plainly that, if they did not correct their unrighteous behavior, they confronted a serious consequence. They would not inherit the kingdom of God.

(2) To Inherit the Kingdom

Many have assumed that to *inherit* the kingdom must be the same as *entering* it. But why should such an equation be made?

Even in everyday speech there is a difference between saying, for example, "you will *live* in that house" and "you will *inherit* it." If a wealthy man tells me that I will inherit his house, has he told me nothing more than that I shall reside in it someday? Obviously, he has told me more than that. He has told me that I will *own* that house.

It is extremely careless not to give deeper thought to a significant concept like "inheriting" the kingdom of God.

In fact, a survey of the Biblical use of the word "to inherit" shows that it is most frequently a synonym for "to possess" or "to own." Equally, the word "inheritance" usually indicates "property" of some sort which a person *owns*. One can find numerous passages where this is true (for example, Gen 15:7-8; Exod 34:9; Lev 20:24; 25:46; Num 16:14; 18:21; 26:52-55; Deut 12:12; Josh 17:14; Judg 2:6; Ruth 4:5; 1 Kgs 21:2-3; Job 42:15; Mark 12:7; Acts 7:5; and many more).

If we keep the idea of *ownership* in mind, obviously the kingdom is not *owned* by those who are only citizens there. Citizens are *subjects* of a kingdom, not its *owners*. Instead, it is the king to whom a kingdom really *belongs*.

It is not surprising, then, to find the future kingdom of God described as an *inheritance* and as a *possession* of God's Son. So the Psalmist writes:

> "Yet I have set My King
> On My holy hill of Zion."
>
> "I will declare the decree:
> The Lord has said to Me,
> 'You are My Son.
> Today I have begotten You.
> Ask of Me, and I will give You
> The nations for Your inheritance,
> And the ends of the earth for Your possession.
> You shall break them with a rod of iron;
> You shall dash them in pieces like a potter's vessel'" (Ps 2:6-9).

If the future kingdom of God is seen as the *inheritance* of the King, God's Son, one thing surely follows. Those who also *inherit* that kingdom must be those who co-reign with the King.

But for this privilege, perseverance in holiness is an indispensable condition. That point is plainly stated in Rev 2:26-27:

> "And he who overcomes and keeps My works
> until the end, to him I will give power over
> the nations—'he shall rule them with a rod
> of iron; they shall be dashed to pieces like the
> potter's vessels'—as I also received from My
> Father."

Note that the faithful believer gets precisely what God promised in Psalm 2 as an *inheritance* for His Son. This is co-heirship.

A similar promise is found in Rev 3:21:

> "To him who overcomes I will grant to sit with Me on My throne, as I also overcame and sat down with My Father on His throne."

It is clear that spiritual victory, *and keeping Christ's works until the end*, are essential if one wishes to sit with Him on His throne. But could there be any greater challenge to such victory than so splendid an outcome?

In 1 Cor 6:9-11, Paul's point is simple and direct. Unrighteous people of the type he describes can never be co-heirs with Jesus Christ. They can never inherit the kingdom of God. And that is exactly what some of the Corinthians *formerly were*. But now the slate has been wiped clean by the grace of God. They were washed...sanctified...justified. So Paul is saying, don't become that kind of person again. Don't forfeit the inheritance that otherwise can be yours.

In the light of verse 11 it is even astounding that anyone has found a "test" of salvation in this passage. Paul is addressing these who are justified, set apart, and cleansed.

How could he have said it more plainly?

Rewards: A Biblical Motivation

The Pauline passage found in Gal 5:19-21 is similar to 1 Cor 6:9-11. It can be interpreted in exactly the same way. In Galatians, also, the statement about *inheriting* the kingdom of God occurs in the heart of an exhortation that warns believers against fulfilling "the lust of the flesh" (Gal 5:16-26). Evidently Paul used this truth about the kingdom as a powerful motivational technique for his Christian brethren. And so should we.

The intensely motivational character of this truth shines through in Lang's skilled articulation of it as he comments on Heb 2:5 ("For He has not put the world to come...in subjection to angels"):

> In the purpose of God the *oikoumene* [world] of the future has not been put under the control of angels, but of men. This is a key thought, the resolving of many obscurities and perplexities which hinder believers from grasping the exact significance of the plans of God and the final and highest outcome of redemption. It is the key to some present enigmas also. At present God is not saving the human race entire and its affairs corporate, but is selecting from it the company that are to rule the universe, superseding the existing government. He is preparing for a complete reorganization of His entire empire, and is giving to these future rulers the severe training which is indispensable to fitting them for such responsible duties and high dignities. The Gospel has *not failed*, but is fulfilling the purpose God plainly announced, though not the end that many preachers have mistakenly proposed, namely, the conversion of the whole race. That general and most desirable betterment of this sin-cursed earth is in the plans of God, but falls for accomplishment in the *next* period of the divine programme, not in this age. There is manifest wisdom in a great Leader first training a body of efficient subordinates before seeking to reorganize society at large.[127]

In fact, the Scriptures open up to the faithful believer a marvelous and highly motivating vision of the future. The promises to the "overcomers" in Revelation 2 and 3 are a significant part of this vision.

---

[127] Lang, *Hebrews*, 52-53.

For example, it is in Revelation 2 that we meet the mysterious tree of life, "To him who overcomes I will give to eat from the tree of life, which is in the midst of the Paradise of God" (Rev 2:7). Clearly this is a *reward* for the "overcomer." A person who has Christ within him will not need a physical tree, however wonderful, to sustain his spiritual life. Yet obviously such a tree could offer some kind of superlative enrichment of one's experience in the kingdom of God. But whatever the tree of life has to impart to those who are granted the right to partake of it, this must be truly worth striving for.

It seems evident that in exploring the territory set before us in these promises to the *overcomers,* we come close to realities impossible to describe precisely to men still in their earthbound flesh. Paul had once been exposed to "inexpressible words" which he was not allowed to repeat (2 Cor 12:4). The vagueness surrounding the promise of the tree of life is an example of the deliberate indefiniteness of the rewards mentioned in Revelation 2 and 3. Almost all of the other promises to *overcomers* have something of the same undefined, but spiritual, character.

Yet this very vagueness makes the rewards more tantalizing and alluring. Motivation through rewards is found frequently in the New Testament.

Postscript: Revelation 2:11 and 3:5

However, there are two promises to *overcomers* which are often taken as a threat to the security of the believer. These are:

> He who overcomes shall not be hurt by the second death (Rev 2:11).

> He who overcomes shall be clothed in white garments, and *I will not blot out his name from the Book of Life*; but I will confess his

name before My Father and before His angels (Rev 3:5, emphasis added).

Both promises are best understood as examples of "litotes." "Litotes" is the name for a figure of speech in which a positive idea is stated by negating its opposite. We use it all the time in everyday speech.

Some examples may help: "that test was no snap" (meaning, "the test was hard"); "this suit sure isn't a bargain" ("this suit's expensive"); "he couldn't solve it to save his life" (he's completely stumped"); "you aren't the first to make that mistake" ("lots of people have made the mistake"); Heb 6:9—"God is not unjust to forget your work…" (in context "God will remember and stand by you").

One frequent feature of litotes is that the negative statement is so obviously true ("God is not unjust") or so clearly exaggerated ("you are not the first") that the positive idea easily suggests itself ("God is fair" or "many others preceded you"). Such is the case in Rev 2:11 and 3:5.

The first century hearer or reader of Revelation, who knew John's doctrine, *knew* that no Christian was in danger of the second death or of having his name erased from the Book of Life (see John 4:13-14; 5:24; 6:37-40; etc.). Thus it was self-evident that a Christian would "not be hurt by the second death" or that Christ would "not blot out his name from the Book of Life." Litotes is thus suggested. A positive idea is implied.

What is the positive idea implied in Rev 2:11? Verse 10 gives us some direction: "Be faithful until death, and I will give you *the crown of life*" (emphasis added). The overcomer will have a superlative, *crowning* experience of life in the age to come. So much so, in fact, that to say he is not "hurt by the second death" is an enormous understatement. Life *far beyond* the reach of the second death is implied. To say it another way (using litotes), the overcomer is certainly *not* among those who are "saved…through fire" (1 Cor 3:15).

Frederick Tatford wrote about the promise of Rev 2:11 as follows: "True life lay beyond. In no wise should he be touched by the second death and the very form of the expression but emphasizes the certainty of that truer and fuller life."[128]

What is the positive idea implied in Rev 3:5? This time direction is offered by the closing words of the verse: "but I will confess his name before My Father and before His angels." The overcomer will possess a glorious name which is highly honored before God and the angels. To say that the Lord will "not blot out his name from the Book of Life" is an enormous understatement. A name *far above* such disgrace as that is implied. To say it another way (again using litotes), God will certainly *not* "blot out the remembrance" of the overcomer "from under heaven" (cf. Exod 17:14).

Again Tatford interpreted through litotes when he wrote this about Rev 3:5:

> Practically every city of that day kept a roll or register of its citizens…one who had performed some great exploit deserving of special distinction, was honoured by having his name inscribed in golden letters in the citizen's roll. Our Lord's emphatic statement, therefore, implies not merely that the name of the overcomer shall not be expunged, but *per contra* that it shall be inscribed in golden letters in the heavenly roll.[129]

Finally, let it be observed that the litotes in Rev 2:11 and 3:5 fit the indefinite and spiritual character of all the promises to "overcomers." In each of these promises we catch only a glimpse of the reward that is offered. Each reward is deeply attractive. The inspired text deliberately leaves us wanting to know more.

---

[128] Frederick A. Tatford, *Prophecy's Last Word* (London: Pickering and Inglis, 1947), 46.
[129] Ibid., 63.

Conclusion

One further point needs to be made. First John 5:4-5 cannot be used to define the term "overcomer" in Revelation 2 and 3. The content and thrust of each context are widely different. First John 5:4-5 declare that faith in Christ is itself a victory over the world which lies under Satanic delusion (1 John 5:18: compare 2 Cor 4:3-6). In that sense all believers are *overcomers*. But Revelation 2 and 3 are talking about the struggles and snares faced by the Christians in the various churches of Asia. It is by no means declared that all of them will *overcome*. A careful reading of the seven letters will show that the opposite is suggested.

As one writer has correctly pointed out in connection with the promises to the *overcomers*: "A command that everyone keeps is superfluous, and a reward that everyone receives for a virtue everyone has is nonsense."[130] Fuller continues:

> Surely the burden of proof is on the shoulders of those who would argue that the warnings are not genuinely addressed to true believers as they seem to be and that the promises are genuinely addressed to all believers (as they seem not to be). Hence the 'overcomer' is the individual Christian who enjoys special benefits in eternity for refusing to give up his faith in spite of persecution during life on earth.[131]

Of course, this general view of the *overcomers* has a long and respectable history.[132]

---

[130] J. William Fuller, "'I Will Not Erase His Name from the Book of Life' (Revelation 3:5)," *Journal of the Evangelical Theological Society* 26 (1983): 299.

[131] Ibid.

[132] See, for example, J. N. Darby, *Synopsis of the Books of the Bible*, 5: *Colossians – The Revelation* (Kingston-On-Thames: Stow Hill Bible and Tract Depot, 1949 printing), 380; William Kelly, *Lectures on the Book of Revelation*, new ed. (London: G. Morrish, n.d.), 36; Walter Scott,

It is utterly unbiblical to claim that fidelity, even to the point of martyrdom (Rev 2:10), and dedication to resist the spiritual corruption and decline all around us (Rev 2:5, 15, 16: 3:3, 4: etc.) are *inevitable* results of simply being a true Christian. Those who claim this are looking at life from an ivory tower that is totally divorced from the down-to-earth realism of the New Testament writers. If we refuse to face the possibility of failure, we in fact prepare the way for failure.

> Therefore let him who thinks he stands take heed lest he fall (1 Cor 10:12).

The price of spiritual victory is high. Let no one be under any delusion about that. But the price is well worth paying. Every sacrifice will be more than amply rewarded. And at the end of the path lies co-heirship with the King of kings.[133]

Exposition of the Revelation of Jesus Christ, 4th ed. (London: Pickering and Inglis, n.d.), 64-65.

[133] Lang succinctly capsulizes what is central to this chapter when he writes: "Salvation from perdition is definitely without works (Rom 4:1-8), and to teach otherwise is to falsify the gospel: but equally definitely ruling with Christ depends on works, as Rev 2:26 states, and to teach otherwise is to falsify our hope, by putting it on a false basis" (Lang, *Hebrews,* 71).

10

Grace Triumphant

Perhaps it would be well to restate the thesis of *The Gospel Under Siege* as clearly as possible.

Basically I insist that *the New Testament gospel offers the assurance of eternal life to all who believe in Christ for that life. The assurance of the believer rests squarely on the biblical promises in which this offer is made, and on nothing else.*

I emphatically reject the claim that a believer must find his assurance in his works. This idea is a grave and fundamental theological error. It is an error that goes right to the heart of the nature of the Gospel proclamation. It seriously distorts that proclamation and creates in its place a new kind of message that would have been unrecognizable to the New Testament writers.

In taking this stance, I also agree with John Calvin's insistence that assurance is part and parcel of what it means to believe in Christ.[134] I fully approve of this statement by him:

> In short, no man is truly a believer, unless he be firmly persuaded, that God is a propitious and benevolent Father to him…unless he depend on the promises of the Divine benevolence to him, and feel an undoubted expectation of salvation.[135]

Modern teachers and theologians who separate faith and assurance have abolished the Biblical concept of faith and denied the Biblical grounds for assurance. Their concept of saving faith is neither orthodox nor reformational. The

---

[134] See Appendix 6.
[135] John Calvin, *Institutes* 3.2.16.

"gospel" that results from such theology cannot avoid the anathema of Gal 1:8-9. This is a serious charge. But it is made thoughtfully and with much grief that it is necessary to make it at all.

Preachers and theologians cannot have it both ways. Either a man can be perfectly sure that he is born again and going to heaven at the moment he believes in Christ, or he cannot. If works must verify a man's faith, then he cannot. It can even be argued that he can *never* be sure until he meets God. But this is not what the New Testament teaches. It is therefore a falsehood and subversive of Biblical truth.

Let it be said clearly: the point of this book is *not* to argue that Christians should not take sin seriously. Of course they should. In fact, they should cast themselves on the strength and power of God to avoid it. And spiritual victory, along with rich fellowship with the Father and the Son, is marvelously available to all who do.

So this book is not written to justify the sin and failure that so often occur in the Christian Church. This book is an attempt to face that failure honestly, just as the New Testament writers did. But there is no attempt to excuse it.

This book is about the gospel. And it is also about a satanic siege of the gospel in which the simplicity, clarity, and freeness of the gospel message have come under assault. It is an effort to focus the Church on the issues which are at stake in this attack. It is the prayer of the writer that many will be aroused to stand firmly for the true grace of God.

Grim as the battle is, however, its outcome is not in doubt. Grace will be triumphant. No matter how much confusion the Enemy of souls is able to inject into professing Christendom, there will always be those who understand and proclaim God's free gift of eternal life. The Bible is clear about this gift and God's message has never lacked messengers.

But grace will be triumphant in another way as well. Someday the failures now so painfully evident among those who trust Christ will be forever gone. Everyone who has ever accepted God's gracious salvation will one day be conformed to the image of His Son (Rom 8:29) and will enter the eternal world totally free from the least trace of sin. No doubt not all of them will have attained to *co-heirship* with Jesus Christ. But all of them will be among those in the kingdom.

It is one measure of the triumph of God's grace that the Apostle John can describe the eternal state with these words:

> But the cowardly, unbelieving, abominable, murderers, sexually immoral, sorcerers, idolaters, and all liars shall have their part in the lake which burns with fire and brimstone, which is the second death (Rev 21:8).

This is not, of course, salvation by works after all. It is rather a declaration that in the new heavens and the new earth (see Rev 21:1), there are no more cowards, no more idolaters, no more liars—except those who have been consigned to the lake of fire.

But what about born-again people who have done these things? To be specific, what about wise Solomon who ended his life in spiritual departure from his God and with idolatry (1 Kgs 11:1-10)? The answer is that all born-again people will be in the presence of God as citizens of the eternal world. And whatever their failures on earth may have been, these are gone. If they had been liars, they are liars no more. If idolaters, they are idolaters no more. Now they are immortal and sinless. They are conformed to the image of God's Son.

How did they come to this place? By the grace of God. For even when God's people fail Him, He does not fail them. He always keeps His Word. In that sense, too, grace will be triumphant.

No wonder that it is with direct reference to God's faithfulness that the great Apostle of grace declares, "Indeed, let God be true but every man a liar" (Rom 3:4). And again, in 2 Tim 2:13, he wrote, "If we are faithless, He remains faithful; He cannot deny Himself."

Postscript:
The Sufficiency of the Cross

False doctrine in today's church often begins like this: "If he is *really* saved, he will…"

The ways of completing this statement are extremely numerous:

> "…he will be baptized."
> "…he will never deny the faith."
> "…he will persevere in good works."
> "…he will never commit murder."

And so on. The list could be lengthened greatly.

What is wrong with all these statements?

First, they are *man's* statements, not *God's*. And no matter how often they are repeated, they are unsupported by the Bible. One of the aims of this book has been to show that there are no Scriptural proofs for such claims.

But second, these statements are an insult to the cross of Christ. As tests of our salvation, what they basically imply is this, "You cannot find peace or assurance by looking to Christ and His cross alone."

Without exception these claims focus a person's heart on what *he* does, or does not, do. By so much they tell us that it is dangerous—even wrong—to trust completely in what Christ *has done for* us in dying for all our sins (1 John 2:2; John 1:29). Such claims tell us that unless *we* do something, we are not saved.

No doubt the statements we are criticizing are often made sincerely. Both theologians and lay people often think that these *provisos* are needed to protect God's reputation from dishonor and disgrace. They think that God is defamed if He is identified with people who fail in these ways.

But they should read their Bibles more carefully. God's name is forever associated with the nation of Israel, whose failures and rebellion are recorded in Scripture with total frankness. Moreover, Israel's greatest king, David, committed adultery and murder, and her wisest king, Solomon, compromised with idolatry. But while such failures in His people give God's enemies a chance to blaspheme Him, they do not in any real way diminish His holiness and His glory. The cross of Christ remains the ultimate vindication of the holiness and glory of God the Father, who "sent His Son to be the propitiation for our sins" (1 John 4:10).

We must stop trying to defend God. He does this far better than we can. And in our feeble efforts to maintain His reputation for holiness, we can wind up slandering the cross on which His Son died for our sins.

Either a man can look to the cross and find peace by believing, or he cannot. If he must watch his subsequent performance, then he cannot.

There is no escape from this conclusion. If I cannot trust *completely* in Christ and what He *did* on the cross, then the cross can give no peace about my eternal destiny.[136] I must trust, at least partly, in what *I do* for Him.

The truth that the believer must focus on Christ and His sacrifice is the most profound insight of the Reformation. Yet this insight has been lost by many Protestant churches in the world today as their theology sinks backward towards the old Roman Catholic formulation that faith cannot save apart from works of love. We need to hear again the words of Luther, writing in his famous commentary on Galatians—words which are as relevant today as when they were first penned:

---

[136] Editor's note: Zane is not saying here, as some have suggested, that all who believe that Jesus died on the cross for their sins have everlasting life. A careful reading of this statement and the context shows that Zane has eternal destiny in mind. His point here is that the cross of Christ should lead people to believe in Him *for everlasting life.*

Postscript: The Sufficiency of the Cross

Now the truth of the Gospel is, that our righteousness cometh by faith alone, without the works of the law. The corruption or falsehood of the Gospel is, that we are justified by faith, but not without the works of the law. With this condition annexed, the false apostles preached the Gospel. Even so do our sophisters and Papists at this day. For they say that we must believe in Christ, and that faith is the foundation of our salvation: but it justifieth not, except it be furnished with charity [love]. This is not the truth of the Gospel, but falsehood and dissimulation. But the true Gospel indeed is, that works of charity [love] are not the ornament or perfection of faith: but that faith of itself is God's gift and God's work in our hearts, which therefore justifieth us, because it apprehendeth Christ our redeemer. Man's reason hath the law for his object, thus thinking with itself: This I have done, this I have not done. But faith being in her own proper office, hath no other object but Jesus Christ the Son of God, delivered to death for the sins of the whole world. It looketh not to charity [love]; it saith not: What have I done? What have I offended? What have I deserved? But [it saith]: What hath Christ done? What hath he deserved? Here the truth of the Gospel answereth thee: He hath redeemed thee from sin, from the devil, and from eternal death. Faith therefore acknowledgeth that in this one person, Jesus Christ, it hath forgiveness of sins and eternal life. *He that turneth his eyes away from this object, hath no true faith*, but a phantasy and a vain opinion, and turneth his eyes from the promise to the law, which terrifieth and driveth to desperation (italics added).[137]

And that, gracious reader, is what this book has been all about. So what about you? Where do you look for peace and assurance of salvation? Are you asking, "Have I done enough to prove I am saved?" Or is the question instead, "Has Christ done enough on the cross to save me, whatever my faults and failures are or may become?" Does your entire hope for heaven rest on what *He has done* and *not at all* on what you can, have, or will, do? If your answer to this last question is yes, then—clearly!—you have believed the gospel and you already know that your eternal destiny is secure.

Let it be said plainly: any system of doctrine that forbids us to find complete peace by simply looking to God's Son, who was lifted up for us on the cross, can by no means claim to be the true gospel. But if it is not, then it must be a false gospel and must stand under the anathema Paul pronounced in Galatians 1.

Yet despite the widespread denial of the Bible's simple message of faith, the truth of God stands firm. The words of Jesus remain dependable in all their wondrous simplicity:

> And as Moses lifted up the serpent in the wilderness, even so must the Son of Man be lifted up, that whoever believes in Him should not perish but have eternal life (John 3:14-15).

Needless to say, so superb a message has left its unmistakable imprint on Christian hymnology:

---

[137] Martin Luther, *A Commentary on St. Paul's Epistle to the Galatians, Based on Lectures Delivered by Martin Luther at the University of Wittenberg in the Year 1531 and First Published in 1535*, a rev. and completed trans. based on the 'Middleton' edition of the English version of 1575 (London: James Clarke, 1953), 98.

Postscript: The Sufficiency of the Cross

Nothing in my hand I bring,
    Simply to Thy cross I cling,
Naked come to Thee for dress;
    Helpless look to Thee for grace;
Foul, I to the fountain fly,
    Wash me, Savior, or I die![138]

* * *

Just as I am, without one plea,
    But that Thy blood was shed for me,
And that Thou bidd'st me come to Thee,
    O Lamb of God, I come! I come!

Just as I am, Thou wilt receive,
    Wilt welcome, pardon, cleanse, relieve;
Because Thy promise I believe,
    O Lamb of God, I come! I come![139]

* * *

My faith has found a resting place,
    Not in device nor creed,
I trust the Everliving One,
    His wounds for me shall plead.

My heart is leaning on the Word,
    The written Word of God,
Salvation by my Savior's name,
    Salvation through His blood.

I need no other argument,
    I need no other plea,
It is enough that Jesus died,
    And that He died for me.[140]

---

[138] *Rock of Ages*, by A. M. Toplady and Thomas Hastings.
[139] *Just As I Am*, by Charlotte Elliott and William B. Bradbury.
[140] *No Other Plea*, by Lidie H. Edmunds and William J. Kirkpatrick.

May the Lord Jesus revive His church again to exalt His marvelous grace.

"Thanks be unto God for His unspeakable gift!" (2 Cor 9:15, KJV).

Appendix 1

John Gerstner's Contention That Saving Faith Includes Good Works

At the start of *The Gospel Under Siege*, I characterized Reformed theology as saying "unless you persevere in good works, you cannot be saved" and "unless you yield your life to the Lordship of Christ, you cannot be saved." Gerstner admits the accuracy of those statements about Reformed thought: "We will grant that is an accurate statement of our contention."[141] But he goes on to argue that I really do not understand what Reformed theology is saying, since he claims I think that "works are some sort of addendum, something beyond faith itself" in Reformed teaching.[142] But Gerstner did not read the page from which he quotes carefully enough. In some forms of theology, works are an addendum to faith, but immediately after I point this out (see p. 146 above), I have Reformed doctrine in mind when I write:

> Often, a distinction is drawn between the kind of faith which saves and the kind which does not. But the kind of faith which *does* save is always seen to be the kind that results in some form of overt obedience...'Saving' faith has thus been subtly redefined in terms of its fruit.

My charge against Reformed theology is that its insistence on the doctrine of perseverance requires it to redefine "saving faith" in a way that abandons the Biblical and

---

[141] John H. Gerstner, *Wrongly Dividing the Word of Truth: A Critique of Dispensationalism* (Brentwood, TN: Wolgemuth and Hyatt, 1991), 225.
[142] Ibid., 226.

reformational teaching about faith and assurance. Is this not precisely what Gerstner in effect admits when he writes: "Lordship teaching does not 'add works,' as if faith were not sufficient. *The 'works' are part of the definition of faith*" (italics added).[143] Neither the Bible nor the great Reformers (Calvin, Luther, Melanchthon) know anything of a definition of faith like this.

The results of this redefinition of saving faith are a theological disaster. So Gerstner can say this: "The question is not whether good works are necessary. As the inevitable outworking of saving faith, they are necessary for salvation."[144] On the same page, two sentences earlier he had written, "Thus good works may be said to be *a condition for obtaining salvation* in that they inevitably accompany genuine faith" (italics added).[145] Calvin would surely have recoiled at such statements. Let us hear Calvin's own words:

> The sophists who amuse and delight themselves with perversion of Scripture and vain cavils, think they have found a most excellent subterfuge, when they explain *works* in these passages, to mean those which men yet unregenerate perform without the grace of Christ, merely through the unassisted efforts of their own free-will; and deny that they relate to spiritual works. Thus, according to them, a man is justified both by faith and by works, only the works are not properly his own, but the gifts of Christ and the fruits of regeneration. For they say that Paul spoke in this manner, only that the Jews, who relied on their own strength, might be convinced of their folly in arrogating righteousness to themselves, whereas it is conferred on us solely by the Spirit of Christ,

---

[143] Ibid., 257.
[144] Ibid., 210.
[145] Ibid.

not by any exertion properly our own. But they do not observe, that in the contrast of legal and evangelical righteousness, which Paul introduces in another place, all works are excluded, by what title soever they may be distinguished. For he teaches that this is the righteousness of the law, that he who has fulfilled the command of the law shall obtain salvation; but that the righteousness of faith consists in believing that Christ has died and is risen again. Besides, we shall see, as we proceed, in its proper place, that sanctification and righteousness are *separate blessings of Christ* (italics added). Whence it follows, that even spiritual works are not taken into the account, when the power of justifying is attributed to faith. And the assertion of Paul, in the place just cited, that Abraham has not whereof to glory before God, since he was not justified by works, ought not to be restricted to any literal appearance or external display of virtue, or to any efforts of free-will; but though the life of the patriarch was spiritual, and almost angelic, yet his works did not possess sufficient merit to justify him before God.[146]

It is clear that the theology of Gerstner is light-years removed from that of John Calvin. For Calvin, in no sense are "works" (either before or after justification) a "condition for salvation." At its essential core, Gerstner's soteriology is not reformational, but Roman Catholic.

---

[146] Calvin, *Institutes* III.XI.14

* * * * *

John Gerstner on John 3:16

Gerstner rejects the universal scope of John 3:16 due to his doctrine of limited atonement. His statements about it are both bald and horrifying. He writes that this verse

> ...is supposed to teach that God so loved everyone in the world that He gave His only Son to provide them an opportunity to be saved by faith. What is wrong with this interpretation? First, such a love on God's part, so far from being love, would be *a refinement of cruelty* [italics added]. As we have seen, offering a gift of life to a spiritual corpse, a brilliant sunset to a blind man, and a reward to a legless cripple if only he will come and get it, are *horrible mockeries* (italics added).[147]

As I pointed out in my review of Gerstner's book in the GES Journal,[148] we might more readily say that *Gerstner's view* is "a refinement of cruelty." In his view God made no saving provision for most of humanity. The idea that most people are born with absolutely no possibility that they could escape eternal condemnation sounds very much like a "horrible mockery."

---

[147] Gerstner, *Wrongly Dividing*, 124.
[148] Zane Hodges, "Calvinism Ex Cathedra: A Review of John H. Gerstner's *Wrongly Dividing the Word of Truth*," *Journal of the Grace Evangelical Society* Vol. 4 no. 2 (Autumn 1991): 59-70.

John Gerstner on James 2:26

Gerstner seeks to counter my suggestion that "There is *absolutely nothing* to suggest that James believed that if a man's faith is pronounced dead, it must therefore always have been dead" when he writes:

> James 2:26 makes the point of the passage perfectly clear. All that James says is that, just as you cannot have a man without a body and spirit together, so you cannot have a Christian without works and faith together.[149]

But what impartial reader would ever get *this* idea out of James's text? In no way does James say that one does not "have a man" simply because his spirit has left his body. What we have in fact is a *dead* man—which is exactly James's point. A dead man is produced by the departure of his spirit from his physical body. Just so, a person's faith dies (becomes like a 'dead man') when it ceases to be invigorated by good works.

Surely Gerstner would admit that if a physical body is dead, it was clearly once alive. But he wishes not to draw any theological comparison with faith at this point because that would contradict his theological premises. My point still stands: The idea that a dead faith can never have been alive cannot be extracted from the text of Jas 2:26 or of Jas 2:14-26 as a whole. It is pure and simple theology, unsupported by evidence. In view of Jas 2:26, the text *might indeed* be read just as I read it.

---

[149] Gerstner, *Wrongly Dividing*, 229.

Appendix 2

John Calvin's Understanding of James 2:14-26

A word should be said about John Calvin's own treatment of Jas 2:14-26. To the surprise of some, perhaps, we do not find in Calvin anything that reflects the theological tangle into which Reformed theology has fallen. In two critical points, Calvin agrees with the present writer *against* Reformed theology. The two points are these: (1) justification by works does not refer to our justification before God, but rather before men; (2) our good works are not the basis of our assurance of salvation.

Calvin says these things plainly:

> So when the sophists set James against Paul, they are deceived by the double meaning of the term 'justification'. When Paul says we are justified by faith, he means precisely that we have won a verdict of righteousness in the sight of God. James has quite another intention, that the man who professes himself to be faithful *should demonstrate the truth of his fidelity by works.* James did not mean to teach us *where the confidence of our salvation should rest*—which is the very point on which Paul does insist. So let us avoid the false reasoning which has trapped the sophists, by taking note of the double meaning: To Paul, the word denotes our free imputation of righteousness before the judgment seat of God, to James, *the demonstration of righteousness from its effects, before men*; which we may deduce from the preceding words, *Shew me thy faith, etc.* [italics in the text]. In the latter

sense, we may admit without controversy that man is justified by works, just as you might say a man is enriched by the purchase of a large and costly estate, since his wealth, which beforehand he kept out of sight in a strongbox, has become well-known (italics added except in the case specified).[150]

Neither does Calvin fall into the hopeless quagmire of talking about a "spurious" faith which simulates the real thing so that true faith can only be recognized by works (as many modern Calvinists assert). Calvin will not give the name of faith to those whom he considers James to be attacking. He writes, for example:

> He [James] is speaking of false profession, and his words make this certain. He does not start, 'If a man has faith', but 'If a man says he has faith…' Plainly he implies that there are hypocrites who make an *empty boast* of the word, when they have no real claim on it.[151]

A few sentences later, he says, "Just remember, he is not speaking out of his own understanding of the word when he calls it 'faith,' but is disputing with those who *pretend insincerely* to faith, but are entirely without it" (italics added).[152]

Although I might quarrel with Calvin's exegesis here, at least he is consistent with the fundamental premises of his own theology. Since, for Calvin, assurance was of the essence of saving faith, he does not ascribe this "false profession" to any who have found that assurance, but describes those without works as *insincere* pretenders who make a *false* claim to faith. Thus he will also ascribe to such people only "an indifferent and formal understanding

---

[150] John Calvin, *Commentary on James*, s.v. Jas 2:21.
[151] Ibid., s.v. Jas 2:14.
[152] Ibid.

of God"[153] or "a certain uninformed opinion of God"[154] or "a bare and empty awareness of God."[155] This is a far cry from his own definition of faith as "a steady and certain knowledge of the divine benevolence toward us [which is] founded on the truth of the gratuitous promise in Christ."[156] Calvin does *not* hold that faith must be subjectively verified to *ourselves* by works, but objectively verified *before men*.

To be sure, Calvin expected good works to be produced in the life of the justified; but so do I.

---

[153] Ibid.
[154] Ibid., s.v. Jas 2:19.
[155] Ibid., s.v. Jas 2:23.
[156] *Institutes* III.II.7.

Appendix 3

John Calvin's Interpretation of Galatians 6:8

I share John Calvin's view that Gal 6:8 deals with the subject of *rewards* and does not provide any kind of "test" of salvation. Let us hear Calvin on this verse, as he comments on the phrase, *But he that soweth unto the spirit*:

> By 'the spirit' I understand the spiritual life, to which they are said to sow who look to heaven rather than to earth and who so direct their lives as to aspire to the kingdom of God. *Therefore they will reap in heaven the incorruptible fruit of their endeavours.* He calls them spiritual endeavours on account of their end, although in some cases they are external and relate to the body. This is so here, where he is dealing with the support of pastors. If the Papists try, in their usual way, to build on these words the righteousness of works, we have shown elsewhere how easily their absurdities can be refuted. Although eternal life is a *reward*, it does not follow that we are justified by works or that works merit salvation. The fact that God so honours the works which He grants us freely as to promise them an *undeserved reward* is itself of grace.
>
> If a more complete solution is required, then first I deny that in us there are any good works which God *rewards* except those which we have from His grace. Secondly, I say that the good works which we perform by the guidance and direction of the Holy Spirit are the freely granted fruits of adoption. Third, I say

> that they are not only unworthy of the smallest and meanest reward but deserve to be wholly condemned, because they are always spattered and stained with many blemishes; and what agreement have pollutions with the presence of God? Fourthly, I say that even if reward had been promised to works a thousand time, it is due only to the perfect fulfillment of the whole law. And we are all far from that perfection. Now let the Papists go and try to break their way into heaven by the merit of works! We gladly agree with Paul and the whole of Scripture in acknowledging that we can do nothing but by the free gift of God, *and yet the requital made to our works receives the name of reward.*[157]

Clearly Calvin's comments are evangelical to the core. I find nothing here of the Reformed doctrine that works test the genuineness of our faith. Indeed, Calvin was insistent that assurance *should not be sought* in our post-conversion works.

Bell nicely summarizes this facet of Calvin's theology:

> As a general principle, Calvin emphatically warns against looking to ourselves, that is, to our works or the fruit of the Spirit, for certainty of our salvation. We must turn from ourselves to rest solely on the mercy of God [*Institutes* 3.19.2]. The Scholastics taught that the Christian should look to works and to the virtues of righteousness as proof of salvation [as does Reformed theology today]. However, Calvin rejects this exhortation to self-examination as a dangerous dogma [*Institutes* 3.2.38], and argues that we can never rely on such a subjective basis for assurance, for our sinfulness insures that we shall not find

---

[157] John Calvin, *Commentary on Galatians*, s.v. Gal 6:8 (italics added).

Appendix 3: Calvin on Galatians 6:8

peace in this way. Forgetting the judgment of God, we may think ourselves safe, when, in fact, we are not [*Comm.* Rom 5:1]. By placing our trust in works, rather than in God's freely given grace, we detract from his salvific work in Jesus Christ [*Institutes* 3.14.21; cf. 3.11.11]. If we look to ourselves, we encounter doubt, which leads to despair, and finally our faith is battered down and blotted out [*Institutes* 3.13.3]. Arguing that our assurance rests in our union with Christ, Calvin stresses that contemplation of Christ brings assurance of salvation, but self-contemplation is 'sure damnation.' For this reason, then, our safest course is to look to Christ and distrust ourselves [*Institutes* 3.2.23-4].[158]

Every one of these complaints drawn from Calvin can be laid at the door of Reformed theology today, which in so many ways is the modern counterpart to the scholasticism which Calvin vigorously rejected.

---

[158] M. Charles Bell, *Calvin and Scottish Theology: The Doctrine of Assurance* (Edinburgh: The Handsel Press, 1985), 28. The bracketed references are those of Bell's endnotes (p. 38). For more information see: Zane Hodges, "Review of *Calvin and Scottish Theology: The Doctrine of Assurance* by Charles M. Bell," *Journal of the Grace Evangelical Society* Vol. 1 no. 1 (Autumn 1988): 72-74.

Appendix 4

H. A. Ironside's Understanding of Acts 2:38

The view of Acts 2:38 which I give in the text (see pp. 296-298) was anticipated in its fundamentals by H. A. Ironside, who wrote as follows:

> The Apostle Peter had just preached his wonderful sermon setting forth the life, the death, and the resurrection of the Lord Jesus Christ. He had particularly emphasized the fact that the Lord Jesus came to the nation of Israel in accordance with Old Testament prophecy as their Messiah, the One they had been looking for down through the centuries, but they failed to recognize Him when He came. They rejected Him and delivered Him over to the Gentiles to be crucified; but Peter concludes with this triumphant word, "Therefore let all the house of Israel know assuredly, that God hath made that same Jesus, whom ye have crucified, both Lord and Christ."
>
> We need to remember that the word "Christ" means "The Anointed" and is the equivalent of the Hebrew term *Mashiach* or Messiah. Our Lord Jesus is God's anointed King. Men said, His own people said, "We will not have this Man to reign over us" (Luke 19:14). But God has raised up from the dead the One whom the nation rejected and He has confirmed His Messiahship to Him in

resurrection. He has declared Him to be Lord and Messiah.[159]

* * *

Now the effect of Peter's message was tremendous. We are told "there were dwelling at Jerusalem Jews, devout men." He was addressing himself not to the ribald crowd that had been in front of Pilate's judgment hall who cried, "Crucify Him, crucify Him"; but addressing primarily the devout Jews who were awaiting the coming of the Messiah, also a number of proselytes from the nations who had the same sincere expectations. And when these honest men heard Peter's proclamation, we read, "They were pricked to the heart." This was the work of the Holy Ghost. He so carried the message home to their hearts that they were deeply stirred.[160]

* * *

There was no attempt to deny what Peter said. On the contrary, they accepted the message. Let us be very clear about that. Having accepted the message we can be very sure of this—they were *already born of God* [italics added]. The Apostle Peter tells us in the first chapter of his first Epistle, "Being born again, not of corruptible seed, but of incorruptible, by the Word of God, which liveth and abideth for ever...And this is the Word which by the gospel is preached unto you." These people had heard the gospel. They

---

[159] H. A. Ironside, *Lectures on the Book of Acts* (Neptune, NJ: Loizeaux Brothers, 1943), 64-65.
[160] Ibid., 67-68.

> were pricked to the heart, they were deeply exercised; they believed the message, and that implies necessarily they had received divine light and were regenerated. They turned to Peter and the rest of the apostles and cried out in sore distress, "Men and brethren, what shall we do?"[161]

I have quoted Ironside extensively here because it is hard not to admire the clear and methodical way this gifted servant of God builds his case for this view of the text. In the paragraphs that follow the quoted material, Ironside goes on to expound the force of the question, "Men and brethren, what shall we do?"

Essentially, Ironside holds that this was fundamentally a question about what they and their nation should do in the light of their horrible mistake. For Ironside, Peter's answer tells them: "Repent. Right about face. Instead of going on as a part of the nation that rejected Him, change your mind, and separate from the apostate group by taking your stand for Christ."

On the question of the forgiveness of sins in Acts 2:38, Ironside writes:

> You see, as part of the nation they were responsible for the rejection of Christ and now Peter says, Change your attitude toward the Lord Jesus Christ and give this outward witness—be baptized in the name of the One you have rejected, and God will look at you standing there and you will no longer be under condemnation as those who rejected Christ, but you will be under His grace because your sins are forgiven. It was not baptism, but change of attitude toward Christ, that gave them forgiveness. The

---

[161] Ibid., 69.

baptism was the outward manifestation of their hearts' new attitude.[162]

Since I was exposed to Dr. Ironside's writings many, many years ago, as a young man, I think it is probable that my own views developed out of the thoughts Ironside had expressed on Acts 2:38. Though Ironside himself cannot be blamed for any refinements I have made, I gratefully acknowledge my heavy debt to this thought-provoking discussion.

The reader will be rewarded by reading Ironside's entire treatment of this passage.

---

[162] Ibid.

Appendix 5

Another Free Grace Understanding of 1 Corinthians 15:2

This appendix is being written not by Zane, but by the editor, Bob Wilkin. I am expressing my own view here.[163]

For years when asked about 1 Cor 15:2, I would explain Zane's view. But I would always say something like:

> This is the best view I've yet heard. It is quite possibly the correct one. However, I find it hard to explain and I'm open to the fact that there may be some other understanding. What we know for sure is that Zane is right that Paul isn't saying that the readers were born again if they continued to hold fast to his gospel. Paul never taught that. Paul taught that the moment anyone believed in Jesus, he was saved once and for all, apart from perseverance.

Around 2000 I came to what I considered a better understanding of 1 Cor 15:2. I noticed that there is a huge difference between 1 Cor 15:2 and Eph 2:8-9. In the latter passage, when Paul refers to the salvation of his readers, he says "you have been saved" (*este sesōsmenoi*). Paul uses the perfect tense here, referring to something which occurred in the past and which has an abiding result. In addition, previously, in Eph 2:5, he used the same expression to explain what "He made us alive together with Christ" meant. Thus for Paul in Eph 2:8 the expression "you have been saved" clearly means "you have been born again."

---

[163] See above on pp. 256-258 for Zane's explanation of 1 Cor 15:2.

However, in 1 Cor 15:2 Paul uses not the perfect tense, but a present tense (*sōzesthe*). The NKJV translates this "you are saved." It could even be translated "you are [spiritually] healthy," as we shall see.

Whatever our interpretation, we need to consider why Paul chose a present tense here and not a perfect? And why does Paul use the word *if* (*ei* in Greek) rather than *when* (*hote* in Greek, as in Acts 8:12; Rom 13:11) when he says, "if you hold fast" or, in Zane's view, "if you grasped." If Zane's view were correct, we would expect Paul to have said, "You have been saved [not *you are being saved*] by the word which I preached to you, when [not *if*] you took it—unless you believed in vain."

If we look at the use of the word *save* (*sōzō*) elsewhere in 1 Corinthians, we find several places in which it refers to being *spiritually healthy*. Indeed, it was Zane himself who explained to me that in 1 Cor 5:5 *sōzō* means *spiritually healthy*. He suggested this translation of 1 Cor 5:5 to me: "Deliver such a one to Satan for the destruction of his flesh [i.e., sinful inclinations], that his spirit may be healthy in the day of the Lord Jesus [i.e., the Judgment Seat of Christ]." It makes good sense in the context of 1 Cor 15:1-11 that *sōzō* refers to being spiritually healthy in 1 Cor 15:2 as well.

Another difficulty I have with Zane's view is that the object of this "saving" faith in 1 Cor 15:2 is not the message of life, but the gospel, which Paul identifies as Jesus' death, burial, resurrection, and post-resurrection appearances. There is no mention here of everlasting life and the promise of life to all who simply believe—or of justification by faith alone—unlike in Ephesians 2, for example. Zane seems to assume that the word *gospel* here refers to the message of life, but there is no hint of that.

Finally, I find it significant that there isn't a single place in the New Testament where Paul or anyone else uses the verb *katechō* to refer to believing. If that is what Paul means here, this is the only place, which is possible, but not highly probable. Even in the examples Zane cites where *katechō* means *to seize* or *to take* (Matt 21:38; Luke 14:9), it clearly does not refer to faith. While I agree that *katechō might* refer to faith, I don't see any evidence that it did anywhere else and the evidence that it refers to faith here is not strong.

Here is what I think Paul is saying: The gospel, which includes not only Jesus' substitutionary death and burial, but also His bodily resurrection and appearances, is foundational to successful Christian living. In order to remain spiritually healthy, believers must hold fast to Paul's gospel. Believers need to have their minds continually set on Jesus' death and resurrection and soon return. Indeed, 1 Corinthians 15 ends with reference to the doctrine of eternal rewards and the fact that our labor in the Lord is not in vain (1 Cor 15:58).

Some of the believers in the church of Corinth—"some among you"—were saying, "There is no resurrection of the dead" (1 Cor 15:12). This led Paul to say, "But if there is no resurrection of the dead, then Christ is not risen...and your faith is also empty...[and] your faith is futile" (1 Cor 15:13, 14b, 17).

The fact that some of the believers in Corinth were not holding fast to Paul's gospel teaching on the resurrection fits well with the idea that in 1 Cor 15:2 Paul was warning about the need to hold fast to the great gospel truth of the resurrection (and appearances) of Christ, as well as, of course, Jesus' death (and burial). If the believers in Corinth stopped holding fast to the gospel, then they would cease being spiritually healthy. What we believe matters greatly in terms of our spiritual health.

I offer this understanding of 1 Cor 15:2 as another Free Grace understanding, one that fits with Zane's explanation of Col 1:21-23, another famous problem text in Paul.

Appendix 6

We Believe In:
Assurance of Salvation[164]

by Zane C. Hodges

I. Introduction

It is a privilege to write about the subject of assurance of salvation. In today's Evangelical world the doctrine of assurance is the subject of vigorous debate. Naturally, those who hold that a person can lose his salvation teach that assurance must be qualified by the fact that a true believer could be eternally lost. But, equally, those who hold to Lordship Salvation must qualify assurance as well.

Many advocates of Lordship Salvation believe in eternal security, yet lack personal assurance about *their own* eternal destiny. The reason is that, according to Lordship thought, all born-again Christians will live generally holy lives and will persevere to the end in godly conduct. A person is not a Christian at all if these things are not true of him. But this view just means that one cannot tell for sure that he is saved until he has persisted in holiness to the conclusion of his life. Some Lordship teachers are not very candid in telling people that they cannot actually have assurance until shortly before death—if, in fact, it is even possible then.

In sharp contrast with both Arminian and Lordship thought stands the Biblical doctrine of assurance. In his First Epistle, the Apostle John states, "These things I have written to you who believe in the name of the Son of God,

---

[164] This article appeared in the Autumn 1990 issue of the *Journal of the Grace Evangelical Society*, making it the first journal article *JOTGES* published by Zane Hodges.

that you may know that you have eternal life...(1 John 5:13a, italics added)."

Clearly the inspired author believed that assurance was possible. His readers could *know* that they had eternal life.

Let us consider this great Biblical truth. For convenience we may do this under three headings. Each heading represents a fundamental facet of, or affirmation about, the New Testament doctrine of assurance.

Our three affirmations are these: (1) Assurance is based on the promises in God's Word; (2) Assurance must not be based on our works; and (3) Assurance is an inseparable part of saving faith.

II. Assurance Is Based on the Promises in God's Word

The well-known text quoted above—1 John 5:13—teaches us that assurance of salvation is based on the *testimony of God*. That is to say, assurance is founded on *God's Word*.

Regrettably this obvious fact is often overlooked. A very large number of commentators regard the words "these things I have written to you" as a statement about the purpose of the entire epistle.[165] They then often go on to take ideas like "abiding in him" (1 John 2:6, 24, etc.) and "keeping His commandments" (1 John 2:3, 7-10, etc.) as intended to be "tests" to determine whether we are saved or not.[166]

---

[165] Many but by no means all. Indeed, Raymond E. Brown (*The Epistles of John*, The Anchor Bible [Garden City, NY: Doubleday, 1982], 608) writes: "What is the reference for...'these things'? Many scholars (Alexander, Brooke, Klöpper, Schnackenburg, Schneider) refer it to 5:1-12 or to the last verse of that unit." Brown himself takes the reference to be to the whole epistle, but obviously there is no consensus view among technical commentators.

[166] This approach to the epistle seems traceable to the work by Robert Law entitled, *The Tests of Life: A Study of the First Epistle of St. John* (Edinburgh: Clark, 1909). At least, Law's work popularized this conception of 1 John.

Appendix 6: Assurance

This view is a serious misreading of John's letter. It is also a dead end street. If "keeping His commandments," is the way we can know we have eternal life, how long must this obedience continue before we are sure? Clearly, the logic of this view requires the answer to be: "to the end of life." No matter how well I may be doing right now, if I stopped "keeping His commandments" at some point in the future, I would prove myself to be without eternal life. In that case, one might say either that I had lost eternal life or that I never really had it at all.

Of course, the Arminian theologian is free to say that we do *know* that we have eternal life *as long as* we are "keeping His commandments." When we stop doing this we *lose* eternal life. Thus an Arminian can hold to *present* assurance but must reject any assurance about our final destiny in heaven or hell. The objection to this view is based on the plain fact that the author of 1 John simply did not believe eternal life could be lost. In his Gospel he makes this unmistakably clear (John 4:13-14; 6:35-40, 50-51; 10:27-30; 11:25-26). Thus, the Arminian reading of 1 John 5:13 clashes directly with the Apostle's basic theology.

But if it is claimed that the true believer is eternally secure—yet must base his assurance on his obedience to God's commands—in that case 1 John 5:13 becomes a highly misleading statement. For even if I am living obediently right now, the possibility exists (as we have said) that I may cease to do so in the future. And if I did cease to do so, that would prove that I am not *now* a Christian despite my obedient lifestyle. Thus my present obedience does *not* prove my Christianity and thus, too, I cannot *know* at any time before the end of my earthly career that I possess eternal life. So if John had meant we must test our Christianity by our current or ongoing obedience, he could not have honestly said that we can *know* we have eternal life. But that is precisely what he does say.

The mistake made here is simple. It is wrong to read 1 John 5:13 as a statement of purpose for the entire epistle.

The purpose for the epistle is given precisely where we would expect it to be—in the Prologue (1:1-4). There the inspired writer makes plain that his purpose for writing is "fellowship" between the apostolic circle and the readers (1:3a) and, beyond that, "fellowship...with the Father and with His Son Jesus Christ" (1:3b). There is not a word about "assurance"—however basic that may be to true fellowship with God.

But in 1 John 5:13 the phrase "these things I write to you" ought to be taken as a reference to the material immediately preceding it. This, in fact, is how this phrase is used elsewhere in the epistle (see 2:1 referring to 1:5-10; and 2:26 referring to 2:18-25). Here, in chapter five, the relevant passage is found in verses 9-12. In the NKJV the verses read as follows:

> If we receive the witness of men, the witness of God is greater; for this is the witness of God which He has testified of His Son. He who believes in the Son of God has the witness in himself; he who does not believe God has made Him a liar, because he has not believed the testimony that God has given of His Son. And this is the testimony: that God has given us eternal life, and this life is in His Son. He who has the Son has life; he who does not have the Son of God does not have life (1 John 5:9-12).

From these words it is clear that John is insisting on the believability of the "witness (= testimony) of God." This "testimony," he asserts, can be either accepted or rejected. If we accept it, we have internalized that testimony so that the believer has that testimony "in himself"—in his heart (v 10a). To reject this testimony is to make God out to be a liar (v 10b). Obviously the issue here is the truth or falsity of what God declares.

And what does God declare? What is His testimony about His Son? Simply this: that eternal life is God's gift to us in Christ (v 11a). And since this kind of life is in God's Son, there is no other qualification for possessing it than to possess God's Son (vv 11b, 12). The believer in the Son may therefore know that he has eternal life (v 13a).

Upon reflection, the assumption which underlies the Apostle's flow of thought is clearly this: To believe in God's Son as the Appointed Giver of eternal life (1 John 5:11) is to possess the Son and the life He gives (vv 12-13). Thus the one who believes God's testimony about His Son possesses within himself or herself the testimony, the Son, and eternal life all at once. Or, as James would say, "Of His own will He brought us forth *by the word of truth*" (Jas 1:18; italics added).

All of this is extremely simple. There is absolutely no effort on the apostle's part to add additional "checks," "tests," or "verifications." The believer's assurance that he possesses eternal life is directed totally and unambiguously toward the truth of what God says about His Son. In that truth he is invited to rest.

Notably absent from all this is the agonizing search which introspective believers often make in an effort to be sure that they have *really* believed. Such a search is misdirected. We are not called upon to "have faith in our faith." We are called upon to have faith in what God says about His Son. All efforts to find assurance somewhere else than in the testimony of God are doomed ahead of time to dismal failure.

Thus, also, in such a simple salvation verse as John 5:24 we meet again the message of assurance:

> Most assuredly, I say to you, he who hears
> My word and believes in Him who sent Me
> has everlasting life, and shall not come into
> judgment, but has passed from death into life.

My own father found personal assurance of salvation through this verse. And why should he not? Its declarations are not in the least complex. If we hear Christ's Word and believe the One who sent Him (the Greek has no word here for "in")—that is, if we accept what God has to say through Christ!—*then* we possess eternal life, are safe from judgment, and have moved out of the sphere of spiritual death into the sphere of spiritual life. If anyone can read this verse and yet *not realize* that eternal life is his, he has either rejected the truth of the verse or has failed to understand it.

Even more simple (if that is possible) is John 6:47, "Most assuredly, I say to you, he who believes in Me has everlasting life."

One notices here the solemn affirmation, "Most assuredly, I say to you." We might paraphrase these words like this: "You can certainly count on what I now say to you." And what does He now say? This: "He who believes in Me has everlasting life." If I take His word for that, then I will know that in the very act of believing His word I am guaranteed eternal life.

If a person cannot find assurance from so straightforward a declaration as this, then he is clearly looking for assurance in the wrong places. For here, beyond doubt, Jesus offers a guarantee to every believer in Him. "Take My Word for it!" He declares. "When you believe, you *have* eternal life."

One is tempted to marvel that in the face of such direct, uncomplicated declarations, so many Evangelicals continue to struggle with doubts and lack of assurance. But wherever this is the case, the struggling soul is looking for something *in his own experience*—even in his own experience of "believing"—rather than looking to Christ and the sufficiency of His cross. To put it another way, such a person is not looking at God's testimony about His Son, or to our Lord's own words of promise to the believer. If he were, he would be sure.

III. Assurance Must Not Be Based on Our Works

The reader of John's Gospel will note how often it is mentioned that the one who believes in Jesus has eternal life. Not once, however, does the inspired writer suggest that this guarantee can be disallowed if there are no good works in a believer's life.

Of course, there is every reason to believe that there *will* be good works in the life of each believer in Christ. The idea that one may believe in Him and live for years totally unaffected by the amazing miracle of regeneration, or by the instruction and/or discipline of God his heavenly Father, is a fantastic notion—even bizarre. *I reject it categorically.*

But this is not at all the point. The issue here is assurance. And with this, works can play no decisive role whatsoever.

We should have known this fact all along. After all, did not the Apostle Paul write, "But to him *who does not work* (italics added) but believes on Him who justifies the ungodly, his faith is accounted for righteousness..." (Rom 4:5)?

In the face of this assertion, how can anyone suppose that "works" must nevertheless be the real grounds on which I am assured of my salvation? That is, how can good works be indispensable to my certainty that I am justified *without works?*

What nonsense. It is as though God had said, "My justification is for the person who does *not* work, but *assurance* of my justification is only for someone who *does.*" Any form of theology that reduces to that stands self-condemned.

In the same way, the Apostle Paul declares that salvation is God's free gift and that it is "not of works, lest anyone should boast" (Eph 2:8-9). But according to many teachers today—both of the Arminian and Lordship persuasions—*assurance is* "of works." It is not surprising that such theology reinvigorates man's latent desire to boast. For, on this view, my "good works" become the badge of my acceptance before God and they are the basis on which I can judge others as "unworthy" of the name of Christian. Let there be no mistake, where such views are held they are often accompanied by spiritual pride and by a harsh, judgmental spirit toward those who do not "measure up."

Furthermore, Paul also wrote, "Now to him who works, the wages are not counted as grace *but as debt.*" (Rom 4:4, italics added). And later he said:,

> And if by grace, then it is no longer of works; *otherwise grace is no longer grace.* But if it is of works, it is no longer grace; *otherwise work is no longer work* (Rom 11:6, italics added).

"Grace and works," says the Apostle, "are mutually antithetical. Works are rewardable endeavors, the pay they gain is a matter of obligation. Thus to say that a thing is by grace is to exclude works—or it is to so change the nature of grace that it is no longer grace at all."[167]

But despite these clear distinctions, many forms of theology hopelessly mix grace and works. This is precisely what is being done by Lordship thought. Salvation is by grace but

---

[167] Commenting on Rom 4:4-5, Anders Nygren has written refreshingly: "With that [the statement of 4:3] Paul has reached a point which is of utmost importance in his interpretation. Here he can tolerate no mistiness. He must insist on clear and precise characterization. He tolerates no indecision between faith and works. He sets forth a clear either/or. Either it depends on works—and then boasting can continue, since it is not by grace but by his own merit that man is judged righteous. Or it depends on faith—and then all else is excluded, works, merit, wages, boasting; and then it is indeed the justification of the sinner. In other words, it is no longer a matter of our works, but of God's. Faith always has the action of God as its correlative. Faith is what it is because of its dependence on God. When Paul speaks of faith, he never means, so to say, a mere psychological operation; for faith is always determined by it object. Thus he speaks, in this connection, of faith as 'faith in him who justifies the ungodly.' Only in this way, that God acts and we allow Him to act, can the righteousness of God come to us. Thus, by the nature of the case, the righteousness of God cannot be other than the righteousness of faith. Scripture testifies for Paul, in the passage cited, 'Abraham believed God, and it was reckoned to him as righteousness.'" See Anders Nygren, *Commentary on Romans* (Philadelphia: Fortress Press, 1949), 169-70.

Appendix 6: Assurance

assurance is impossible apart from works.[168] Thus I can be sure that God has been gracious to me only if I work hard for Him. God's *goodness* to me in Christ thus is held hostage to my *performance* for Him. In the process grace ceases to be grace, as Paul said.

It is pure sophistry to argue that what is meant in such theology is only that works are produced by grace and are simply its necessary results. On the contrary, if I cannot get to heaven apart from the regular performance of good works, those works become as much a condition for heaven as faith itself. Many theologians who hold to the kind of synthesis we are discussing, honestly admit that good works are a condition for heaven.[169] But in so saying, they run their ship aground against Rom 4:4 and 11:6, and indeed against the whole biblical doctrine of grace.

I said earlier that I believe that all born-again Christians will do good works. I believe it, however, because it appears to be the only rational inference from the scriptural data. But, let it also be said clearly, it is an inference. No text of Scripture (certainly not Jas 2:14-26) declares that all believers will perform good works, much less that they cannot be sure of heaven unless they do.[170] *No text says that.*

When the New Testament writers speak of eternal salvation they always use the language of John and Paul.

---

[168] Cf. John F. MacArthur, Jr., *The Gospel According to Jesus* (Grand Rapids: Zondervan Publishing House, 1989), 23: "Genuine assurance comes from seeing the Holy Spirit's transforming work in one's life..." MacArthur means, of course, that assurance comes by seeing "good works" in our lives. Attributing such works to the Spirit does not change the fact that he is still talking about our "works"—i.e., what we do, rather than what Christ has done on the cross.

[169] See, for example, Samuel T. Logan, Jr., "The Doctrine of Justification in the Theology of Jonathan Edwards," *Westminster Theological Journal* 46 (1984): 26-52. Note the statement, on p. 43, that "evangelical obedience is an absolute necessity, a 'condition' in man's justification." Thus Logan bids farewell to Pauline theology.

[170] For an extended and documented discussion of Jas 2:14-26, see the author's commentary on James: *The Epistle of James: Proven Character Through Testing* (Irving, TX: Grace Evangelical Society, 1994), 58-72.

That kind of language should be allowed to sink into our hearts most deeply: The *believer* has eternal life; the one who does *not* work but *believes* is justified; salvation is by *grace* through *faith* and is *not* of works; it is *not* by works of righteousness which *we* have done—the reader can add many texts of his own. It is inconceivable, in light of this scriptural teaching and terminology, that an experience so utterly divorced from our performance *must be verified* by our performance.

Indeed the only way to maintain such a position—apart from an unscriptural Arminianism—is to radically rewrite the biblical doctrine of saving faith. In the process, the whole concept of faith is shrouded in obscurity so that the introspective person is swallowed up into an abyss of fruitless self-examination. At the end there can be no assurance based on our works—only despair.

But there can be self-delusion based on our works. And anybody who believes he has verified the reality of his justification by his own good deeds has experienced that delusion fully. In fact he has forgotten the searing words of our Lord to a self-righteous young ruler, "So Jesus said to him, 'Why do you call Me good? No one is good but One, that is, God'" (Luke 18:19).

If the Lord's words are true—and they are—how can my *lack of goodness* ever verify God's gracious justification by faith? The idea reduces to nonsense or to a pointless assertion that I am *better* than I was, or that I am *better* than most other people are. But does anyone really suppose that a man who must say of himself, "I am *not* good," can ever find verification of his personal salvation in his "good" works?

The bottom line is simple. If I seek assurance through examining my good deeds, one of two things must necessarily result: (1) I will minimize the depth of my own sinfulness and the extent to which—even as a Christian—I fall short of the glory of God, or (2) I will see my deep sinfulness as hopelessly contrary to any conviction that I am saved.

Those who travel the first route are traveling the highway of self-righteousness. They are utterly blind to the reality that they are evil people whose lives are still infinitely remote from the perfect holiness of God. The claim they make that their lives are "good enough" to verify their salvation clashes blatantly with our Lord's assertion: "No one is good but One, that is, God." Such claims are the very essence of Pharisaism and are perfectly exemplified by the Pharisee who prayed, "The Pharisee stood and prayed thus with himself, 'God, I thank You that I am not like other men—extortioners, unjust, adulterers, or even as this tax collector'" (Luke 18:11).

But he *was* like other men. He was *not* good.

Those who follow the second route and decide that they are too sinful to claim to be saved are traveling a highway that leads to frustration and despair. In many such individuals the road also ends in depression.

No. Good works can never be a fundamental ground of assurance. It is logically and theologically absurd to claim that a salvation which is *apart from* works, is not recognizable *except by* works. God's Word teaches no such thing.

IV. Assurance Is an Inseparable Part of Saving Faith

The problem which modern Evangelicals have with assurance is often a problem of focus. If a person focuses on himself—his own experiences, character, or good deeds—he will discover how shifting and uncertain are the matters he is examining. Indeed, all of us are in the process of change in the present and are subject to unanticipated change in the future. Even our own understanding of ourselves is notoriously fickle and subject to alteration. The self and its experiences can furnish no solid focus for assurance at all.

But Christ and His Cross can. And God's Word about these things can. It is only as we look beyond ourselves to God's unchanging truth that we can find firm ground for our personal assurance. Indeed, Christ Himself is the same at all times (Heb 13:8), the Cross is God's definitive and final solution to the problem of man's sin, and God's Word is the unchanging bedrock on which assurance may be grounded.

Thus, in the light of all I have said so far, it is the Word of God alone that can adequately meet man's need for certainty about his eternal destiny. But now I must add this: This need for certainty is met by the very offer of the Gospel itself so that assurance is necessarily a part of believing that Gospel.

Quite appropriately John Calvin stated this truth in his *Institutes*:

> In short, no man is truly a believer unless he be firmly persuaded that God is a propitious and benevolent Father to him,...unless he depend on the promises of the Divine benevolence to him and feel an undoubted expectation of salvation (*Institutes* 111.11.16).

For Calvin assurance was of the very essence of saving faith. That is to say, assurance that I am saved is part and parcel of believing the Gospel message.

In so writing Calvin gave expression to a Biblical truth. As we have already seen, anyone who believes verses like John 5:24 and 6:47 (to name only two) also believes that he has eternal life. If one does not believe that he has eternal life he does not believe these verses. "He who believes in Me has eternal life" necessitates the conclusion that I have eternal life at the moment of my faith.

But someone may ask: Is it not possible to believe in Christ and not find out until later that I have eternal life? The answer to this question is "no" if by "believe in Me" we mean the same thing as John meant by these words.

What did John mean by them? The answer is clearly given in the Evangelist's theme statement in John 20:

> And truly Jesus did many other signs in the presence of His disciples, which are not

Appendix 6: Assurance

> written in this book; but these are written
> that you may believe that Jesus is the Christ,
> the Son of God, and that believing you may
> have life in His name (John 20:30-31).

From this crucial declaration we may conclude that to "believe in Me" means to "believe that Jesus is the Christ."

But what does that involve? Jesus' words to Martha are instructive here:

> Jesus said to her, "I am the resurrection and
> the life. He who believes in Me, though he may
> die, he shall live. And whoever lives and believes
> in Me shall never die. Do you believe this?" (John
> 11:25-26).

The challenge of Jesus, "Do you believe this?" is met by Martha as follows,

> She said to Him, "Yes, Lord, I believe that
> You are the Christ, the Son of God, who is to
> come into the world" (John 11:27).

What is striking in all this is that our Lord's claim to be the Guarantor of resurrection and eternal life to every believer is met by Martha's affirmation that Jesus is the "Christ." Thus Martha's declaration of faith is couched in precisely the terms used in the thematic statement of John 20:30-31. To believe that "Jesus is the Christ" is what it means to "believe in Me."

But the words of our Lord also help us to comprehend what is intended by the term *Christ*. The term *Christ* is not, as so often in popular usage today, a mere additional name for Jesus. Instead, as John 11:25-26 make plain, the "Christ" is the very One who assures the believer that he will rise from the dead (if he dies) and that he possesses a life that can never be terminated by death—that is, he possesses eternal life. When Martha affirmed Jesus to be the "Christ," she was affirming Him to be precisely such a Person as He had just described Himself to be.

But Martha could not have believed this truth without realizing that she herself had eternal life. *If the "Christ" guaranteed resurrection and eternal life to the person who believed Him to be the "Christ," then by believing this Martha knew that she had what He guaranteed.* In other words, to believe in Him was to accept His guarantee of eternal salvation. To doubt the guarantee (for any reason whatever) was to doubt that Jesus was the "Christ."

The bottom line is exactly what John states in his first epistle, "*Whoever* believes that Jesus is the Christ is born of God, and everyone who loves Him who begot also loves him who is begotten of Him (1 John 5:1, italics added)." There are *no* exceptions to this. "Whoever" is the pivotal word here. Belief that Jesus is the Christ—the One who assures the believer of future resurrection and of eternal life—is *saving* belief. A faith which has as its content "Jesus is the Christ" (in the Johannine sense) is *saving* faith. But to believe this is to *know* that I am saved. Assurance is inseparable from—and part of the essence of—saving faith.[171]

Consequently, the individual believer who knows that Jesus *is* the Christ, knows also that he himself *is* "born of God" (1 John 5:1). It's as simple as that.

How then did so many Evangelicals become so badly confused? There is more than a single answer to this question, but one answer is this: When we begin to test our faith by our works, we actually begin to alter the very nature of faith. And we alter it radically and without biblical warrant.

---

[171] I do not mean to imply that a person who has found assurance through faith in Christ can then never lose that assurance. I simply affirm that *at the moment of saving faith* assurance is a part of that faith. Yet Satan knows well how to attack a believer's faith and how to create doubts. But Satan cannot undo the regenerating work of God in the one who has already believed. For a discussion of this significant issue, see Charles Stanley's excellent chapter, "For Those Who Stop Believing," in *Eternal Security: Can You Be Sure?* (Nashville: Oliver Nelson, 1990), 73-83. See also Zane C. Hodges, *AbsolutelyFree! A Biblical Reply to Lordship Salvation* (Dallas and Grand Rapids: Redención Viva and Zondervan, 1989), 103-113.

In fact, once we have become preoccupied with what we imagine ought to be the "effects" of faith, we have destroyed the true focus of faith. We have withdrawn its gaze from the external and unchanging "testimony" of God and focused instead on the shifting "testimony" of our own hearts and lives.

Having done this, we try hard to turn faith into something "productive" and "effective." Faith, we decide, cannot be merely "receiving the witness of God." It cannot be merely "standing on the promises" of His Word. Surely it is not simply "resting" in who Jesus is and in what He guarantees.

But then what is it? Many of the contemporary Evangelical answers are filled with confusion and permeated by error. When faith ceases to be merely taking God's Word for things, it becomes something mysterious, imprecise, vague, and numinous. It can then be said to include such unrelated concepts as repentance, surrender, willingness to obey, devotion, a worshipful spirit, etc.—the list goes on and on. And the list is entirely unbiblical and without a shred of scriptural support.

When Jesus asked Martha, "Do you believe this?" (John 11:25), His words mean exactly what they appear to mean. "I have just stated certain claims about My own Person," our Lord is saying, "Do you accept these claims?"

Martha did, and because she did she had assurance of eternal life.

V. Dabney's Rejection of Calvin's View of Assurance

Long before the contemporary debate over the terms of salvation and over the grounds of assurance, a 19th century Reformed theologian, Robert L. Dabney, had strenuously objected to Calvin's view that assurance is of the essence of saving faith. He even went so far as to charge Calvin (and Luther) with overreacting to Roman Catholic dogma. Thus, in a treatise written against Plymouth Brethren theology, Dabney asserted:

> The source of this error [of the Plymouth Brethren] is no doubt that doctrine concerning faith which the first Reformers, as Luther and Calvin, were led to adopt from their opposition to the hateful and tyrannical teachings of Rome. This mother of abominations denies to Christians all true assurance of hope, teaching that it is neither edifying nor attainable. Her purpose is clear: the soul justified by free grace, and assured of its union to Christ, would no longer be a practicable subject for priestcraft and spiritual despotism. These noble Reformers, seeing the bondage and misery imposed by this teaching upon sincere souls, flew to the opposite extreme, and (to use the language of theology) asserted that the assurance of hope is of the essence of saving faith. Thus says Calvin in his Commentary on Romans: 'My faith is a divine and spiritual belief that God has pardoned and accepted *me*.' According to these divines, it is not enough for a penitent soul to embrace with all its powers the gracious truth, 'Whosoever believeth shall be saved,' while yet its consciousness of exercising a full faith is confused, and remaining anxieties about its own salvation mar its peace. Such an act of soul is not admitted by them to be even a true yet weak faith; they hold that until the believer is assured that *Christ has saved* HIM, there is no exercise of saving faith at all. This old error is evidently the source of Dr. [César] Malan's view of faith, which, as visitors to Geneva twenty years ago remember, he was so sure to obtrude upon all comers. Now our Plymouth Brethren and their sympathizers have a contempt

Appendix 6: Assurance

and mistrust for great ecclesiastical names and church authorities, which prevents their employing the recognized nomenclature of historical theology on this and many other subjects. Hence they prefer to express their peculiarities in terms of their own, less discriminating than the old. We do not find them indeed deciding that 'the assurance of hope is of the essence of a true saving faith;' but we find them in substance reviving *this extravagance of the first Reformers* [italics added here only], and pressing its corollaries.[172]

Subsequent to the treatise from which I have just quoted, in a letter to the editor of the *South-Western Presbyterian*, Dabney vigorously defended his claim that both Luther and Calvin taught that assurance was of the essence of saving faith. His words (to an individual identified as M.N.) deserve somewhat extended quotation:

Now, I assert that Calvin...was incautious enough to fall into the erroneous statement, that no faith was a living faith which did not include essentially both the assurance of faith and the assurance of hope. He is not satisfied that even the weak, new believer shall say, 'I believe, with head and heart both, that Christ saves *all who truly come to him,* and I accordingly try to trust him alone for my salvation, and so far as I have any hope, rest it on him alone.' He requires every one to say, in substance, I believe fully that Christ *has saved* me. Amidst all Calvin's verbal variations, this is always his meaning; for he is consistent

---

[172] "Theology of the Plymouth Brethren," in *Discussions by Robert L. Dabney, D.D., LL.D., Professor of Moral Philosophy in the University of Texas, and for Many Years Professor of Theology in Union Theological Seminary in Virginia*, ed. C. R. Vaughan, vol.1: *Theological and Evangelical* (Richmond, VA.: Presbyterian Committee of Publication, 1890), 173.

in his error. What else is the meaning of that definition of which M. N. himself quotes from the *Institutes*: 'Our steady and certain knowledge of the divine benevolence *toward us.*' But I will show, beyond all dispute, that the theological 'Homer nodded,' not once, but all the time, on this point. See then *Institutes,* Book III., Chap. II., Sec. 16. 'In short, no man is truly a believer, unless he be firmly persuaded that God is a propitious and benevolent Father *to him,*…and feel an undoubted expectation of salvation.' *Commentary,* on Rom. viii. 16: 'The opinion consequently stands, that no one can be called a son of God *who does not know himself to be such.*' On Romans viii. 34: 'Because our faith is naught *unless we certainly persuade ourselves that Christ is ours,* and that the Father is propitious to Us in him.' On I Cor. ii. 12: 'Let us know, therefore, that this is the nature of faith, that the conscience has from the Holy Spirit a certain testimony of the divine benevolence towards itself.' On 2 Cor. xiii. 5: 'Paul here testifies, *that whoever doubt whether they possess Christ, are reprobate.*' Is MN. satisfied? *Heidelberg Catechism* (not written by Calvin, but by two of his pupils): 'What is faith?' (Qu. 21)…'A certain trust,' 'by which I acquiesce in God, certainly concluding that remission of sins, and eternal righteousness and life, *have been bestowed,* not on others only, but *on me also,*' etc. *Genevan Catechism* (written by Calvin himself): It is 'a certain and stable knowledge of God's paternal benevolence *towards us.*'

When I represented Calvin's view of faith, as substantially set forth in his *Commentary on Romans,* as amounting to this: 'My faith

Appendix 6: Assurance

is a divine and spiritual belief that God has pardoned and accepted me,' M. N. said that if it were so (which he disputes), 'Homer must have been nodding when it slipped in.' Have I not showed that it is there, and everywhere in Calvin, and that it did not 'slip in,' but is his deliberate opinion? M. N. has *confessed that it is untenable.* Why then should there be any more difference between us, except that while I cherish a great, I do not feel *an indiscriminate* admiration for this Reformer?

I will complete this part of my proof as to Luther also, who shared Calvin's error. The *Augsburg Confession,* written by Melanchthon, but under Luther's eye, says, Art. IV., the Lutherans also teach that men are 'justified gratuitously on account of Christ by faith, *when they believe themselves* to be received into grace, and their sins to be pardoned on account of Christ.'" See (for the first quotation) "Theology of the Plymouth Brethren," in *Discussions by Robert L. Dabney, D.D., LL.D., Professor of Moral Philosophy in the University of Texas, and for Many Years Professor of Theology in Union Theological Seminary in Virginia,* ed. C. R. Vaughan, vol.1: *Theological and Evangelical* (Richmond, Va.: Presbyterian Committee of Publication, 1890), 173, as well as 216-17 (for the second quotation, contained in a section also entitled "Theology of the Plymouth Brethren").[173]

Obviously, by charging Calvin and Luther with "extravagance" in reacting to Roman Catholic teaching, Dabney is confessing that his own theology is closer, by so much, to

---

[173] Ibid., 216-17.

Catholicism than the theology of the Reformers. His candor on this subject is refreshing compared to the "fudging" done by some contemporary theologians.

What could be more candid than this assertion:

> 1. That Calvin and Dr. Malan, and the Plymouth Brethren, hold a definition of the nature or essence of saving faith which is, in one respect, contrary to the Westminster Confession and to the Scriptures, as well as to the great body of the confessions of the Presbyterian Churches, and of their divines since Calvin's day. I said, by way of apology for the earliest Reformers, and most notably, Luther and Calvin, that they were betrayed into this partial error by a praiseworthy zeal against the opposite and mischievous error of Rome, who seeks to hold believers always in doubt of their salvation...M. N. will not have it so; then he will needs have his admired leader discredited, for as sure as truth is in history, Luther and Calvin did fall into this error, which the Reformed churches, led by the Westminster Confession, have since corrected."[174]

Thus Dabney *insists* on the gap that separates his theology from that of the Reformers.

VI. Conclusion

Many excellent members of the Grace Evangelical Society like to define faith in terms of trust. There is no problem with this so long as we are careful about how we say it.

We must be careful not to make faith and trust somehow essentially different. Faith *is* trust, and trust *is* faith. When

---

[174] Ibid., 215.

Appendix 6: Assurance

I believe that any particular message is true (even a human one), I am trusting that message. I am also trusting the Person who gives me the message—I am accepting that person's veracity and reliability.

The Scriptural message (from John's point of view) is very simple and direct: *Jesus is the Christ.* If I "receive the testimony of God" about this, then I am trusting this message. And I am also trusting the God who gives me that message.

Evangelicals must resist the seductive temptation to attach riders and provisos to our message about faith alone in Christ alone. We must resist the specious allurement of telling people that *saving* faith is a certain kind—or a special kind—of faith.

It is not. The faith that saves is not qualitatively distinct from faith exercised in other situations. What is distinctive about *saving* faith is that it has a particular message to believe. And that message *is* distinctive—it is even radical, unique, and life-begetting (Jas 1:18; 1 Pet 1:23-25). And the radical message may be stated like this: *The one who believes that Jesus is the Christ possesses divine, unending life.*

No one can believe this message without being saved (1 John 5:1). And no one can believe this message without being *sure* that he is saved![175] The message is God's true, reliable, and unchanging witness to us.

It is "the testimony that God has given of His Son" (1 John 5:10). And by itself—altogether apart from the help of good works—*God's testimony* furnishes a totally sufficient basis for our personal assurance of salvation. Furthermore,

---

[175] Editor's Note: As Zane asserted above (see footnote on p. 370), he is not saying that one who is currently not sure of his eternal destiny is necessarily unregenerate. His point is that *at the moment of faith*, one is sure. But since assurance can be lost—that is, since a believer might cease believing the promise of life—a born-again person might presently lack assurance.

this testimony is permanently recorded for us in His holy Word. It is always there to be relied on.

So after all, if I have God's Word for something, what else do I need?

Grace in Eclipse

Prologue

Jim has been a Christian for only a short time. Last night, in a group Bible study, he was introduced to the subject of eternal rewards. This morning he is excited by the thought of running a victorious race for God.

On his break at work, Jim shares some of his new-found insights with a fellow Christian named Frank.

"Rewards, huh?" says Frank. "Isn't that just a little selfish?"

"What do you mean?" replies Jim. It hadn't sounded selfish last night.

"Well, what I mean is this," Frank begins, with a slight tone of condescension. "We really ought to serve God because we love Him and are grateful for what He's done for us. We don't need rewards to motivate our Christian life."

"Oh!" says Jim. He can feel the air going out of his balloon.

"Besides," Frank continues, "you don't really think some Christians are going to be a lot better off in heaven than other Christians, do you?"

"Well, I hadn't quite thought about it that way," Jim admits with a trace of dejection in his voice.

"Look, Jim," Frank pursues his theme, "good works are what every Christian does just as a natural result of believing in Christ. That's part of what it means to be a Christian in the first place."

"But we're not *saved* by works," Jim objects.

"No, of course not! But the Bible says a tree is known by its fruit, so if you're really saved, the Christian life will be as natural to you as fruit-bearing is to an apple tree."

"What does that have to do with it?" Jim wants to know.

"It's simple, Jim." Frank moves in for the kill. "If Christian living is part of being a Christian, why should God reward us for it?"

"You mean there are no rewards *at all?*"

"No, I don't mean that exactly," Frank responds. "But all Christians are overcomers and all of them will wear crowns someday. This stuff about Christians failing and being defeated is a bunch of nonsense!"

"Don't we all fail sometimes, Frank?" Jim is a bit put off by the whole discussion.

"Of course we do!" Frank's tone is edged with exasperation. "But good works are our Christian duty, and if you're not doing them at all you ought to examine whether you were ever saved to begin with."

"So you're telling me there are no real losers in the Christian race, is that it?" Jim is very skeptical about *that* idea.

"That's right, Jim!" Frank is emphatic. "The only reason people talk about rewards a lot is because they really don't understand what the Christian life is all about. Hey! Wasn't that the whistle to get back to work?"

"Yes, I guess break time is over," Jim agrees.

Actually, Jim was glad to get back to work. There had been something depressing about that whole conversation. It was just as if some kind of shadow had been cast across a path that a few moments before had seemed so bright and thrilling.

A shadow *had* crossed his path! In fact, that shadow was very much a part of the evangelical scene within which Jim now moved. Its darkening effects were in evidence everywhere.

To put it plainly, grace was in eclipse.

1
Grace In Eclipse

"But I discipline my body and bring it into subjection, lest, when I have preached to others, I myself should become disqualified" (1 Cor 9:27). With these words, the Apostle Paul expresses a thought that is shocking to many modern Christians. Taken at face value, his words reveal that he seriously entertained the possibility of ending his Christian life as a failure. In fact this failure, says Paul, could come after years of preaching. So to avoid it, he dealt very strictly with his own body and its impulses to do evil.

Many have thought that Paul's reference to disqualification meant that he was in danger of losing his salvation. This idea was encouraged by the familiar King James translation, "lest...I myself should be a castaway." But Paul firmly believed that God would ultimately bring those He called and justified to glory (Rom 8:30). He was convinced that nothing could separate him from God's love in Christ (Rom 8:38-39). He was positive that the gift of the Holy Spirit was a guarantee of final redemption (Eph 1:13-14).

In short, Paul knew the comforting truth expressed by the Lord Jesus Himself that "of all [the Father] has given Me I should lose nothing, but should raise it up at the last day" (John 6:39). So Paul was not talking about losing his salvation. On the contrary, as the context makes clear, he was talking about a race which could either be run victoriously or in which he might be "disqualified" from receiving a crown.

But could an apostle lose his crown and stand disapproved before his heavenly Judge? Yes, he could. Yet such a concept is barely appreciated today in some evangelical circles and is, on principle, rejected outright in others. "All Christians," we are told, "are overcomers." Disastrous Christian failure, resulting in significant loss of future reward, is an alien idea to much of contemporary theology. Rather, in these circles, catastrophic failure is thought to indicate an unregenerate condition.

But the New Testament is permeated by the concept that loss of victory is not inconsistent with true salvation. And the failure to recognize this fact has impoverished the church and clouded its perception of grace.

To put it simply, many of the New Testament warnings against failure and loss of reward are seen by many as warnings about the loss of salvation, or else they are taken as warnings against false professions of faith. In either case, the richness of God's saving grace is seriously minimized. At the same time lofty Biblical motives for godly living are lost from sight.

Faith and Works

Modern Christianity continues to wrestle with the issue of the relation between faith and works in Christian experience.[1] Many articulations of this relationship call into question the freeness of God's saving grace. The problems involved in understanding the New Testament doctrine of rewards are inseparably intertwined with the faith-versus-works controversy.

In a recent statement resulting from extensive Roman Catholic and Lutheran dialogue, it was agreed that while salvation takes place solely as an act of divine grace, the works that follow are also "necessary."[2] But logically this

---

[1] For helpful discussions in this area, see Robert D. Preus, "Perennial Problems in the Doctrine of Justification," *Concordia Theological Quarterly* 45 (1981):163-184; and A. N. S. Lane, "Calvin's Doctrine of Assurance," *Vox Evangelica* 11 (1979): 32-54.

[2] For highly critical reviews of the statement (issued Sept. 30, 1983, by the Lutheran-Roman Catholic Dialogue Group) see W. Robert Godfrey, "Reversing the Reformation," *Eternity* 35 (Sept. 1984): 26-28; and C. M. Gullerod, "U.S. Lutheran-Roman Catholic Dialogue on Justification by Faith: An Examination," *Journal of Theology* 24 (1984): 19-24. For the statement itself consult, *Justification by Faith: Lutherans and Catholics in Dialogue*, 7 (published Spring/Summer, 1985, by the U.S.A.

means that final salvation from hell depends on both faith *and* works. Accordingly, works are elevated to the level of a *condition* for salvation even if they are not seen as the *immediate cause* of salvation. This position is commonly admitted by classic Reformed theologians as well.[3]

At their core, all such systems of thought are "legalistic" in the broad sense of that term. They insist, in some way, on obedience to the "Christian law" as an essential element in the final escape from damnation. There is little room for a doctrine of rewards in such a system, since eternal felicity itself is a kind of "reward" which all Christians acquire. If a professing Christian fails significantly, he fails to attain the bliss of heaven itself.

It is foreign to such modes of thought to conceive of a God who unconditionally accepts the sinner without regard, not only to his past conduct, but also to his future conduct as well. And those who *do* conceive of God in these terms are stigmatized as "antinomian" (lawless).[4] It is as though

---

National Committee of the Lutheran World Federation and the Bishops' Committee for Ecumenical and Interreligious Affairs).

[3] For a recent example, see Samuel T. Logan, Jr., "The Doctrine of Justification in the Theology of Jonathan Edwards," *Westminster Theological Journal* 46 (1984): 26-52. Note especially pp. 42-48. At least the approach represented here is candid in its admission that "evangelical obedience is an absolute necessity, a 'condition' in man's justification" (p. 43). But nothing can conceal that this is, in principle, a return to the Roman Catholic view that both faith and works are essential to final salvation. Though Logan would no doubt reject the charge, the position he maintains (following Edwards) reduces the great soteriological issues of the Protestant Reformation to little more than a problem in theological articulation. From the much superior perspective of John Calvin, Logan's view might be described as a *"de facto* justification by works" (see the article by Lane in note 1, especially pp. 35 and 40). The same could be said of the view advanced by Daniel P. Fuller in *Gospel and Law: Contrast or Continuum?* (Grand Rapids: Eerdmans, 1980), pp. 65-120. Very serious questions have been raised recently concerning the extent to which Calvinism has departed from Calvin's own doctrine of faith and assurance. In addition to the article by Lane, see R.T. Kendall, *Calvin and English Calvinism to 1649* (Oxford: University Press, 1979).

[4] Note the harsh judgment of John H. Gerstner in *A Primer on Dispensationalism* (Phillipsburg, N.J.: Presbyterian and Reformed

the father of the Prodigal Son had been unwilling to receive that son back again without some guarantee from him that his future behavior would be better. But though the Prodigal had originally thought of asking to serve the father (Luke 15:18-19), he does not actually make the offer when he comes back (15:21). Nor does the father ask for it.

But many evangelists ask for it. They do this either by demanding repentance on the part of the sinner (in the sense of a decision to change his life),[5] or by insisting that saving faith carries with it an appropriate recognition of Christ's Lordship over the life, or in a variety of other ways. But all of these techniques are mere devices designed to extract from the sinner some kind of "commitment" to become a better person. Preachers who articulate the message in this way are blind to the unconditional grace of God. They are also regrettably imbued with that spirit which lies at the core of all legalistic modes of thought: that my fundamental acceptance before God must somehow be related to my conduct, that is, to my works.

That a man could be (as Paul was) concerned that he might forfeit significant future reward, while remaining sure that God's love would be his forever, is a conception that defies the comprehension of many evangelicals today.

Faith Subtly Redefined

The result of the lack of perception just described has been an effort, on the part of many, subtly to redefine the nature of saving faith. This has often seemed a necessity, no doubt, because of the many texts which predicate eternal life on nothing more than faith. For example, we read: "Most assuredly, I say to you, he who believes in Me has

---

Publishing Co., 1982), 29.

[5] Repentance is not a condition for eternal salvation and can either precede or follow new birth. For a study of the doctrine of repentance in scripture, see Zane C. Hodges, *Harmony with God: A Fresh Look at Repentance* (Dallas, TX: Redencion Viva, 2001).

everlasting life" (John 6:47). How does one extract from this the concept of repentance, or submission to Christ's Lordship, or anything else other than simple belief? The answer is, of course, that this can only be done by rearticulating the notion of saving faith in such a way as to embrace more than simple belief.

The methods for doing this are many and varied. Thus we may hear of the distinction between "head" and "heart" belief. Or between "dead" and "living" faith (based on a faulty understanding of James 2). Or we may be told that Biblical faith implies "commitment" or "a personal relationship" or something else. But in the end the result is that the simple Biblical concept of faith has become cluttered with all sorts of connotations that are foreign to the original New Testament word. No wonder many Christians struggle with the problem: "Do I have the right kind of faith?"

All efforts to import special content into the Biblical words for faith are fundamentally unsound. They often involve a language error, which is increasingly well-recognized, called "illegitimate totality transfer."[6] This is a procedure whereby implications drawn from a context, or a number of contexts, are wrongly made to become part of the meaning of a word.

The fact is that the Greek expressions for "believe in" or "believe that" are not significantly different from their English equivalents. No one supposes that the English words "believe in" denote a "personal relationship," much less "submission to," or anything of that sort. Much pseudo-scholarship has been expended in an attempt to make the Biblical concept of faith carry the freight of a preconceived theology. The time has long since passed for this to stop.

Equally invalid is the well-known treatment of Acts 16:31. The words, "Believe on the Lord Jesus Christ," are

---

[6] See Moises Silva, *Biblical Words and Their Meanings* (Grand Rapids: Zondervan, 1983), 25-26; but especially, James Barr, *The Semantics of Biblical Language* (Oxford: University Press, 1961), 217-19. Barr called this kind of error "illegitimate identity transfer."

often treated by those teaching a form of "Lordship salvation" as a call for submissive acknowledgment of Christ's Lordship as a condition for eternal life. But this is a glaring semantic fallacy.

If one says, "Put your faith in the President," it is not at all the same thing as saying, "Submit to the authority of the President." In the first instance the title "President" simply presents the President as an authoritative figure who can probably follow through more effectively on his guarantees than can "private-citizen" Smith. In the same way, the title, Lord, used of Jesus presents the Savior as a divinely authoritative Person who can be believed in very easily. To make more of it than that is to read one's own ideas into the text.

The attentive reader of John's Gospel will note that the expressions "believe in" (or, "believe on") are interchanged with "believe that." Thus we may read:

> "He who *believes* in the Son has everlasting life" (John 3:36, emphasis added).

But we also read:

> ...but these are written that you may *believe that* Jesus is the Christ, the Son of God; and that *believing* you may have life in His name (John 20:31, emphasis added).

Thus it is clear that to "believe in," "believe that," and "believe" can all refer to the same act of saving faith.

From this it follows that to "believe in" Jesus is to believe something about Him, namely, that He is the Christ.[7] What exactly this entails for John is made clear from a famous passage in the eleventh chapter of his Gospel. Here we find Jesus declaring to Martha:

---

[7] See *Theological Dictionary of the New Testament*, ed. by Gerhard Friedrich, trans. and ed. by Geoffrey W. Bromiley (Grand Rapids: Eerdmans, 1968), 6:203.

> "I am the resurrection and the life. He who *believes in* Me, though he may die, he shall live. And whoever lives and *believes in* Me shall never die" (John 11:25-26, emphasis added).

This self-declaration is followed by a simple, "Do you believe this?" (John 11:26).

In response, John quotes Martha as uttering a statement of faith strikingly like his own thematic statement in John 20:30-31. Martha replies,

> "Yes, Lord, I *believe that* You are the Christ, the Son of God, who is to come into the world" (John 11:27, emphasis added).

This tells us much about John's thought. For John, the "Christ" was the One who could make the claim of John 11:25-26 in which He guarantees the eternal destiny of the individual who believes in Him. To *believe that* He was the "Christ" was, in fact, to believe Him to be such a Person as that. It was to *believe in* Him as the Guarantor of one's eternal felicity and well-being. It was the "Christ" who guaranteed resurrection and unending life to the believer.

There is no room here for the subtle reshapings which some theologians have commonly given to the simple word "believe."[8] I either believe that Jesus is the Christ in the Johannine sense of the term, or I do not. But, by John's own statement, when such belief occurs, eternal life is thereby possessed. What could be simpler than,

> Whoever *believes that* Jesus is the Christ is born of God (1 John 5:1, emphasis added).

---

[8] By far the most important recent discussion of saving faith (which this writer has seen) is the little volume by Gordon H. Clark entitled, *Faith and Saving Faith* (Jefferson, Md.: The Trinity Foundation, 1983). Clark vigorously rejects the many confused, and confusing, definitions of saving faith which are current today. See also, footnote 10 on p. 391

It is precisely the loss of this pristine simplicity about the Biblical notion of saving faith that has created enormous confusion. When the word *belief* is subtly redefined, so as to ensure the sinner's commitment to good works, the result is an eclipse of the Scriptural doctrine of grace. In the half-light—or sheer darkness—that ensues, there is little room for a viable doctrine of rewards.

2
False Professors

The question may be raised how a doctrine of salvation through simple faith in Christ affects our conception of who is a Christian and who is not. Is it then no longer permissible to speak of false professions of faith, or of false professors? Is everyone a Christian who claims to be?

To ask that question is to answer it. Paul himself apparently believed that the Jerusalem church harbored people who were not genuine Christians. He thought of them as infiltrators of the Christian movement carrying on a "spying operation" in the interests of legalistic Judaism (Gal 2:4-5).[9] But by so describing them— especially in the context of Galatians—he makes it plain that he regarded them as hostile to his own proclamation of the grace of God. If they were not Christians, it was because they had in fact rejected the offer of divine grace.

Here, then, is one clear category of false professors. Those who claim the name Christian, but have never believed the simple gospel of salvation by grace, have no right to that name. And by the same token those who think themselves Christians, but have never understood the gospel offer, must also be considered false professors, however sincere they may be in their error. A person cannot believe what he does not know or understand.[10]

---

[9] See F. F. Bruce, *The Epistle to the Galatians* (Grand Rapids: Eerdmans, 1982), 112.

[10] Faith has often been analyzed by theologians as consisting of three components, *notitia* (understanding), *assensus* (assent), and *fiducia* (trust). In his book, *Faith and Saving Faith* (pp. 52, 118), Gordon Clark has rightly pointed out that the last of these (*fiducia*) involves a tautology, since it is like saying that faith includes faith. Clark's definitions of faith in general, and saving faith in particular, are noteworthy: "Faith, by definition, is assent to understood propositions. Not all cases of assent, even assent to Biblical propositions, are saving faith; but

Indeed, experience suggests that among the multitudes who go forward in mass evangelistic campaigns are many who are merely moved by the message, rather than actually converted by it. Conversations with such people often disclose how little they have comprehended the real nature of God's offer of eternal life. And far too frequently it is the evangelist himself who has clouded the issue.

It was not for nothing that the Lord Jesus Christ said to the woman at Sychar's well,

> "If you *knew* the gift of God, and who it is who says to you, "Give me a drink," you would have asked Him, and He would have given you living water" (John 4:10, emphasis added).

Saving faith is not some blind leap amid the darkness of human ignorance. It is the intelligent appropriation of a divine gift by faith in Christ. Faith has been aptly described as the hand of the beggar reaching out for the divine benefit.[11] And the claim to being a Christian, without actually receiving that gift, constitutes a false profession.

But those who speak of false professors often mean more than that. Indeed, what is often meant are people who have apparently understood, and responded to, the terms of the gospel but are thought to have an inadequate faith due to the lack of fruit in their lives. This conception is

---

all saving faith is assent to one or more Biblical propositions" (p. 118). It only needs to be added that, for John, the saving proposition to be believed is the one stated in John 20:30-31. It may be pointed out also that faith in a person is no different than belief in some proposition about that person (cf. Clark, *Faith and Saving Faith*, 106-107). For example, we might say, "Mr. Jones can be believed when he says he will do this."

[11] Preus rightly rejects the opinion that justifying faith can be considered a good work (a Roman Catholic perspective shared by many Protestants). Instead, he affirms the Lutheran view "that faith's role in justification is purely instrumental, that faith is an *organum leptikon*, like the empty hand of a beggar receiving a gift, that it alone (*sola fide*) is the appropriate vehicle to receive reconciliation, forgiveness, Christ and His merits" (Preus, "Perennial Problems," 172).

totally inappropriate and is subversive of the simple gospel of God's saving grace. It is a conception that leads directly to the misguided efforts to redefine saving faith that were described in the previous chapter.

The result is that many Christians are plagued by the question, "Is my faith real saving faith, or am I a false professor?" The turmoil which such a question can arouse can hardly be appreciated by those who have never encountered it in the Lord's people. Those Christian teachers whose doctrines have been influential in creating it will have much to answer for at the Judgment Seat of Christ. And obviously, when a believer's appreciation of grace suffers so fearful an eclipse, it will be difficult, if not impossible, for him to build a life worthy of eternal reward when every rewardable effort is viewed as somehow a necessary evidence of true faith. It is only in the full blaze of God's unconditional favor and grace that the Christian will be able to focus, unhindered, on activities that will enrich his experience of the eternal future.

In short, the doctrine of eternal rewards is a clear stream only when it finds its source in the simplicity and magnificent freeness of the gospel offer. Sourced anywhere else, it is muddy, shallow, and ultimately ends in a dry bed.

The Narrow Gate

Ironically, perhaps the greatest utterance on the subject of false profession was made by our Lord in the midst of a passage which has been frequently, and at many points, misunderstood. The conclusion to the Sermon on the Mount (Matt 7:13-27) contains more than one well-known piece of imagery and is often quoted. The solemn words of verses 21-23 are directly concerned with false professors, but they are best appreciated in the larger context of the conclusion as a whole.

Following a summary of the morality on which His Sermon insists (Matt 7:12), Jesus begins its conclusion with the familiar saying about the wide and narrow gates:

> "Enter by the narrow gate; for wide is the gate and broad is the way that leads to destruction, and there are many who go in by it. Because narrow is the gate and difficult [lit., 'compressed'] is the way which leads to life, and there are few who find it" (Matt 7:13-14).

Many expositors read a text like this without reference to the larger teaching of the New Testament as a whole. But this is a mistake and an open invitation to read into it ideas which appeal to the interpreter but are foreign to its true meaning.

There is no good reason for thinking that these verses mean something radically different from our Lord's words in John 10:9, where He declares:

> "I am the door. If anyone enters by Me, he will be saved, and will go in and out and find pasture."

It would be pointless to ignore the transparent similarity between the statements of John and Matthew. Especially so since both come from the lips of Jesus. In Christianity as taught by Christ, access to eternal life is available only on very restrictive terms. One only enters into this life *by faith—and* by nothing else—by faith in Christ and in no one else. No gate could be more narrow than that.

From the viewpoint of an ancient traveler approaching a Middle-Eastern city, the gate was a point of entrance. It is natural that Jesus should employ this parable to encourage His hearers to find the right starting point for their spiritual activities. They need to be sure that they have found the entrance that leads to life. And that means finding the narrow gate and traversing the road ("way") which runs through it. Here, too, in the word *way* we hear another echo of Johannine thought (cf. John 14:6), for the Son of God is both the "gate" and the "road" that lead to life.

In contrast to this is the wide gate through which runs a broad road ("way"). Here man's liberal conceptions about the many ways by which God can be approached hold sway. This gate is thronged and crowded. It is the popular gate, a veritable marketplace of religious ideas (even first-century Judaism was multifaceted and rent by sectarian divisions). Precisely for this reason Jesus must now caution about false prophets.

By Their Fruits

Few passages of the New Testament have been so grotesquely twisted as our Lord's warning about false prophecy. Misapprehension begins with its very first verse:

> "Beware of false prophets, who come to you in sheep's clothing, but inwardly are ravenous wolves" (Matt 7:15).

From this it should be transparent that false prophets do not give themselves away by their external behavior. In fact, they "dress" like sheep. That is, viewed from the outside they *seem like Christians*. They do not behave like the wolves they inwardly are.

But there is one key to their detection: "You will know them by their fruits" (Matt 7:16). This famous verse has been woefully misread. As the previous verse should have warned us, it has nothing to do with the "life-style" of the false prophets. On the contrary, it has to do with their *words*.

This becomes unmistakable when Matt 7:16-20 is compared with Matt 12:33-35:

> "Either make the tree good and its fruit good, or else make the tree bad and its fruit bad; for the tree is known by its fruit. Brood of vipers! How can you, being evil, *speak* good

things? For out of the abundance of the heart the mouth *speaks*. A good man out of the good treasure of his heart brings forth good things, and an evil man out of the evil treasure brings forth evil things" (emphasis added).

Clearly both passages employ identical imagery, and Matthew 12 makes explicit a meaning which is required also in Matthew 7. A false prophet must be tested by his message. If he is inwardly corrupt and ravenous this will stand revealed by the character and quality of his communications. Men ought not to be deceived by his gentility, urbanity, or sophistication. They must reject such sheep's clothing when the spoken words expose the growl of a wolf.

It goes without saying that this text has nothing at all to do with the alleged necessity of testing a man's faith by means of his works. It would be hard to imagine a text less suitable for that purpose than this one.

False Prophets/Professors

It seems clear that false prophets are still in mind when Jesus utters the words that follow. But now these men stand as a stark warning to any who might follow in their steps. Our Savior therefore declares:

> "Not everyone who says to Me 'Lord, Lord,' shall enter the kingdom of heaven, but he who does the will of My Father in heaven. Many will say to Me in that day, 'Lord, Lord, have we not prophesied in Your name, cast out demons in Your name, and done many wonders in Your name?' And then I will declare to them, 'I never knew you; depart from Me, you who practice lawlessness!'" (Matt 7:21-23).

This is an arresting text, but it does not say what some have made it say. To begin with, it does not affirm salvation by works. Ironically, it is works that the false professors lay claim to. They have engaged in prophecy, exorcisms, and miracle-working in Jesus' name and yet are denied access to God's kingdom.

It must be remembered that this is a scene set in a future day of judgment. These are not conscious charlatans trying to deceive their Judge with bogus claims to miraculous activity. On the contrary, they are all too desperately sincere. Nor are their claims denied.

What is denied is that they have a valid connection with their Judge, or He with them. "I never knew you" are His stinging words. And in this regard, as well, Johannine conceptions are relevant. Thus in John 17:3 Jesus declares:

> "And this is eternal life, that they may know
> You, the only true God, and Jesus Christ
> whom you have sent."

Elsewhere He affirms: "I am the good shepherd; and I know My sheep, and am known by My own" (John 10:14). These men are not His sheep even if they did dress in sheep's clothing. They do not possess eternal life, otherwise He would know them and they would know Him.

They had not done "the will of My Father in heaven." But what was that? What did God want them to do in order to gain entrance to His kingdom? Only one thing (the gate is narrow). He wanted them to trust His Son for eternal life. They had not done so. Whatever else they had done was irrelevant to their claims. And worse, it was wickedness (NJKV, "lawlessness") since it was done outside of a living relationship with Christ.

Matthew and John

But someone will object to this that I am reading John's theology back into Matthew. But why should I not? Were their theologies diverse? Let this diversity be demonstrated by those who think so.

On the contrary, the Fourth Gospel is written with the avowed purpose of making eternal salvation clear and accessible (John 20:30-31). Matthew makes no such claim. Indeed, the absence of explicit statements of the type which we meet everywhere in the Gospel of John (1:12; 3:15-16, 36; etc.) argues powerfully that Matthew writes for a Christian audience for whom the basic issues relating to faith and eternal life are settled and plain.[12] He can then presume that his readers will read such texts as this (Matt 7:13-23) in the clear light of their knowledge of God's saving grace.

Regrettably, he could not have made the same assumption if he had been writing in our day. In fact, so clouded is the conception many Christians have of the gospel itself that if a text *can be* understood somehow as demanding obedience for final salvation, it *will be* understood that way. This lamentable situation—this eclipse of grace—has sadly distorted many of the passages in the New Testament which teach the doctrine of eternal rewards. It is precisely such passages that need to be recovered in all their edifying power.

---

[12] It is essentially correct to say with Beare that, "The Gospel according to Matthew may be described as a manual of instruction in the Christian way of life, which the author sees as the fulfillment in Jesus Christ of the revelation of God given to Israel and preserved in the sacred scriptures" (Francis Wright Beare, *The Gospel according to Matthew* [Oxford: Basil Blackwell, 1981], 5). It does not follow, however, as Beare thinks, that "the promises made to Israel are now inherited by the church of Christ's foundation" or that Matthew teaches salvation by means of works-righteousness (p. 6). But it is a useful conception to describe Matthew's Gospel as a "manual of instruction in the Christian way of life."

3

The Sermon on the Mount

The Gospel of Matthew stands in impressive contrast with the Gospel of John in that Matthew reports an extended ethical discourse by Jesus rather early in His public ministry. In John, the even earlier discourses are private ones which deal with the issue of personal salvation. The two Gospels complement each other remarkably.

Both the conversation with Nicodemus (John 3:1-21) and the one with the woman at the well (John 4:1-26) took place before the Sermon on the Mount. We know this from the references in John 3:24 and 4:1 which show that John the Baptist was still active. In Matthew, in Mark, and apparently in Luke, our Lord's public ministry commences after the Baptist is imprisoned (Matt 4:12-17; Mark 1:14-15; Luke 3:20). This is of considerable importance.

What it means quite simply is this: that before Jesus undertook to become a public preacher, He had already indoctrinated His disciples in the basic truths of eternal salvation. In John's Gospel we see that the disciples of Jesus have already become believers before the public ministry begins (John 1:35-51; 2:11). They are with Him as He evangelizes Sychar (4:27-42). There is no reason why they should have construed the Sermon on the Mount—when they heard it—as furnishing an ethical formula for reaching heaven. That would have been to forget the simple gospel which they already knew quite well.

Yet modern expositors often forget that gospel when they read this Sermon. Indeed, they forget a great deal of the New Testament when they read it. This is true when they read these words of Jesus,

> "For I say to you, that unless your righteousness exceeds the righteousness of the scribes

and Pharisees, you will by no means enter the kingdom of heaven" (Matt 5:20).

Most interpreters of this statement overlook the Book of Romans. *Of course* one cannot enter God's kingdom apart from a righteousness superior to that of the religious models of that day (Jesus had not yet begun to denounce them publicly). But what kind of righteousness is that? There is only one Biblical answer to this question—the Pauline answer.[13] No righteousness of any kind is sufficient except the very righteousness of God which is imputed to men on the basis of faith alone (Rom 3:21-26).

The words of Jesus are pre-Pauline.

Jesus and Paul

Once again the objection may be raised that it is inappropriate to read the words of Jesus through Pauline spectacles. But why? Paul himself claimed to have received his gospel directly from Jesus Christ (Gal 1:11-12). Are we to assume that Jesus never in His public ministry spoke about justification by faith alone? Hardly (see Luke 18:9-14).

In fact, though it is hardly ever noticed, in the Sermon on the Mount as a whole, Jesus is doing something that is distinctly Pauline in nature. He is using the law as a means of convicting men of the fact that they are sinful.

The Sermon on the Mount had a double audience. On the one hand it was ostensibly preached to Jesus' disciples who were gathered before Him (Matt 5:1). Technically, Jesus was instructing them (5:2). From their perspective, the Sermon on the Mount can be understood as laying down the

---

[13] It has been suggested that the thought of an imputed divine righteousness may be anticipated in Matthew by the Suffering Servant's own dedication to "fulfill all righteousness" (Matt 3:15). See S. Craig Glickman, *The Temptation Account in Matthew and Luke* (unpublished Th.D. dissertation, University of Basel, 1982), 37-44; esp., 42-44. The Old Testament background for this idea is most clearly seen in Isa 53:10-12.

The Sermon on the Mount 401

standards of conduct appropriate to a disciple of Jesus as he lives in anticipation of the coming kingdom of God.[14] Viewed from this perspective, the Sermon contributes significantly to the doctrine of rewards.

But the Sermon had another audience as well. This was composed of the multitudes who followed our Lord (Matt 4:25; 5:1). And Jesus never forgets their presence, even while He is prescribing a code of behavior for His own disciples. In fact, the Sermon on the Mount can be seen as a masterful interweaving of Christian ethics with pre-evangelistic activity.

To be sure, the Sermon contains no obvious text about eternal salvation, such as John 3:16. We cannot be certain, however, that in its uncondensed form it did not. As all would agree, Matthew 5–7 takes only a few minutes to read, and the actual sermon must have been much longer. Matthew's condensation is what serves the purpose of his Gospel, and there is no good reason for thinking that Matthew's Gospel was not written with a Christian audience in view. Evangelism, then, was not one of his aims.

But perhaps the Sermon did not, even in its fullest form, get more specific about the terms of salvation than the portion which we actually have. If it did not, then what remains can be suitably called *pre-evangelism*. This is to say that the Sermon is neatly crafted to arouse in an unsaved hearer not only curiosity about the narrow gate to life, but also an urgent need to find that gate.

Jesus begins the Sermon on the Mount by describing the qualities of character which His disciples must cultivate (the beatitudes, Matt 5:3-12) and by specifying the disciples' special role in the world (Matt 5:13-16). The two sections

---

[14] It is correct to observe that some commentators on the Sermon on the Mount "tend to forget that the Great Instruction in Matthew was directed to the inner circle of the disciples, and not to the whole people." Albright and Mann, *Matthew*, 49. It is also true to say: "Nor is this salvation by Law or by works, as puzzled commentators on Matthew have been known to suggest" (Albright and Mann, *Matthew*, 51-52).

together constitute an introduction to the entire Sermon. By itself this introduction would be potentially convicting to an unregenerate man who could easily perceive how contrary his inner impulses were to such lofty ideals.

The body of the Sermon (Matt 5:17–7:12) might very well be described as "kingdom living." The standards of conduct which are here laid out are viewed from the perspective of the standards that will be enforced when the kingdom actually comes. But these standards are nothing more nor less than the righteous demands of "the law and the prophets" raised to the highest power (cf. Matt 5:17-18 and 7:12).

Thus, when the kingdom appears, anyone within it who disobeys even its smallest demand and teaches others to do likewise, will have the lowest possible status therein (Matt 5:19). Here it should be remembered that disobedience to the King will not be unknown during the kingdom's first one thousand years, that is, during the Millennium (cf. Zech 14:16-19). In fact, this initial thousand years will be climaxed by a Satanically inspired rebellion (Rev 20:7-10).

So strictly will human relationships be governed in the kingdom of God that a man can go on trial for unjustified anger with his brother or for calling him a numbskull (Matt 5:22). When harsher language than that is used, the offender may be liable to immediate banishment into Gehenna (Matt 5:22). Unregenerate inhabitants of the kingdom will be very numerous, as the final rebellion proves. At any time, during the thousand years, the King may send any of them away to this abode of torment to await the judgment of the Great White Throne (Rev 20:11-15).

Clearly, in every respect, the rod with which King Jesus will rule His realm will be a rod of iron (see Rev 12:5; 19:15). The rebellious spirit of the nations will be shattered by that rod, and repressed, until that spirit rises one last time under the guidance of Satan himself. This time, however, mankind's obstinate will is broken for good and forever.

This portrait of kingdom righteousness is daunting even to the believer in Christ. So how much more daunting must it be to anyone who thinks in terms of entering that realm on the basis of merit? And this was precisely how the typical Jew viewed that issue. Like Paul prior to his conversion, a religious Jew sought final acceptance before God through the righteousness which was in the law (cf. Rom 10:1-4). What was such a Jew to think after hearing our Lord's exposition of how lofty the standards of kingdom righteousness really were (Matt 5:21-48)?

Conviction of sin and unworthiness was the only natural result. The kingdom was a place where every jot and tittle of the law would be required (Matt 5:17-18). Indeed, the passing away of heaven and earth, to which Jesus refers, will occur only after the first thousand years are over (see Rev 21:1). In that millennial era disobedience to the law's least demands, and the teaching of such disobedience, would result in the lowliest status which the kingdom could confer (Matt 5:19). How easily a hearer might think, "What about disobedience to *many* of the law's demands *right here and now?*"

Obviously, entrance into the kingdom of God demanded a righteousness that was excellent indeed. In fact, said Jesus, it must be greater than that possessed by the scribes and Pharisees (Matt 5:20). But who could ever attain to a righteousness like that?

No one, Paul (the former Pharisee) was later to tell us. For if a man did not acquire righteousness as a free gift, he could never be justified before God at all. But the law was designed to prepare men for this realization. Like a stern and demanding tutor it was intended to lead men to Christ (Gal 3:19-24). By the law came—not justification—but the knowledge of sin (Rom 3:20).

And no one ever used the law to that end more effectively than Jesus did in His Sermon on the Mount. For if the exact nature of the righteousness required to enter God's kingdom is left unspecified, at least the unsaved hearer is compelled to ask some searching questions about it. He is driven also to think carefully about the narrow gate and the need to seek it diligently. Indeed, Paul's concept of the tutorial role of the law of Moses is superbly demonstrated in this Sermon by Jesus, man's Tutor *par excellence*.

The Sermon and Rewards

The divine Tutor's skill is not exhausted by this facet of His message. In fact, nowhere is the suitability of the Sermon on the Mount to its two sets of hearers more impressive than in its final paragraph (Matt 7:24-27). In this conclusion to His conclusion (the larger unit is 7:13-27), the Lord Jesus Christ presents His memorable simile about the wise and foolish builders. The warning which He gives serves well as a solemn admonition to both saved and unsaved hearer alike.

The "life" which a man constructs—his "house"—needs an enduring foundation. But only the words of Jesus offer such a foundation. All else is unstable and shifting sand. In the great crises of life the floods and the winds of adversity test the stability of one's "house" and, if it is well-founded, the "house" survives. If not, it collapses in ruins.

The words come very forcefully to any unregenerate man in that vast audience. If his righteousness was not acceptable to God, if he had missed the narrow gate, then calamity lay ahead. If the convicting arrows had reached the target of his heart, he must inevitably sense that he was building on sand. The search for stable ground must begin at once.

But for the disciple there was an equally sobering thought. Though he had found the narrow gate and, by faith, passed through it on the restricted way, the question remained about how and where he should now construct his life's experience. And to this there could be but one answer for him also. He must build on the words of Jesus, for if he did not, calamity awaited him as well—not the calamity of eternal hell, to be sure, but calamity just the same.

Death is the ultimate storm. The survival of one's life experience, one's "house," is a pressing issue for all men, whether regenerate or not. The soul that must pass into eternity without Christ leaves behind a wreckage that is pitiful indeed. But so may a real Christian leave behind such wreckage. A life not lived on the firm foundation of divine truth invites disaster, no matter who lives it.

No wonder that Paul strove to run a winning race and to avoid disqualification by his Judge (1 Cor 9:27). No wonder he entertained the thought that the life's work of a man might be consumed by the flames of the Judgment Seat of Christ (1 Cor 3:11-15). It is quite true that Paul taught justification apart from works. But he did not teach Christian living apart from works. Nor did he affirm that those works flowed inevitably from justifying faith. Instead, Paul instructed Titus:

> This is a faithful saying, and these things I want you to affirm constantly, that those who have believed in God should be careful to maintain good works. These things are good and profitable to men (Titus 3:8).

Here too, as we might expect, we meet the harmony between Jesus and Paul. The maintenance of good works is an effort—not an effort unassisted by God—but an effort nonetheless. It is the labor of building a life that is securely founded on the rock of divine truth. It is good and profitable to construct a life like that. It is calamitous not to do so.

Thus the closing words of our Lord's first recorded public sermon are rich with implications about the life of a disciple. He must choose how and where to raise the edifice of his earthly experience. Built on the sand, that edifice will someday be rudely swept away. Founded on the rock it will outlast every storm, including death itself.

By inference this last kind of "house" is eternal. And a life that can be so described is clearly rewardable.

4
The Indestructible Life

Our Lord's crucial concept about building an enduring life resonates throughout the New Testament. In addition to its role at the end of the Sermon on the Mount, this concept echoes clearly in Jesus' own later public ministry, as well as in the teaching of His closest disciples. But despite the significant role this theme plays in the pages of the New Testament, it is rarely appreciated in the modern church,

This is due to the eclipse of grace. Passages which ought to have powerfully inspiring effects on Christian readers are reduced to statements about final salvation which square awkwardly (if at all) with the simple gospel of God's saving grace. The confusion created thereby is devastating and deplorable.

In the language of contemporary Christianity, the expression "to save the soul" has one meaning and one meaning only. It conveys to its hearers the concept of deliverance from hell. It is surprising to discover that such a meaning has not the slightest scriptural warrant. To state it differently, the New Testament never speaks of the "salvation of the soul" in the sense of escape from eternal damnation.

As a matter of fact, in the Greek Bible as a whole (which includes the Greek translation of the Old Testament) the expression "to save one's soul" had chiefly the same significance which it had in ordinary secular Greek. It meant "to preserve the life."[15] But in the teaching of Jesus, this everyday Greek expression is raised to a new level of meaning which is pregnant with significant implications.

---

[15] For examples, see the Septuagint rendering of the following texts (English references are given here): Genesis 19:17; 32:30; 1 Sam 19:11; Job 33:28; Ps 31:7; 72:13; 109:31; Jer 48:6; etc.

Saving and Losing the Life

In a memorable saying which is reported in all three of the Synoptic Gospels, and even reflected in John, the Lord Jesus issued a stirring challenge that was paradoxical in form. His words recorded by Mark were these:

> "Whoever desires to come after Me, let him deny himself, and take up his cross, and follow Me. For whoever desires to save his life will lose it, but whoever loses his life for My sake and the gospel's will save it" (Mark 8:34-35; cf. Matt 16:24-25; Luke 9:23-24; and see John 12:25).

It is worth noting here that the Greek word rendered "life" is the same one which in similar expressions elsewhere is rendered "soul."

How such a declaration must have struck Jesus' contemporaries is not hard to imagine. Its hearers are variously described as "His disciples" (Matthew), "the people...with His disciples" (Mark), and "all" (Luke). Like the Sermon on the Mount this statement had a point for everyone, but must initially have seemed hopelessly perplexing. How could one preserve one's life and at the same time lose it? How could he lose it and at the same time save it? Can one die and live at the same time?

Of course our Lord was dealing in metaphor. One cannot *literally* both lose and save the life. But on a spiritual level things are different. On that level eternal realities come into play. From that vantage point one can speak of a life that is lost when viewed from an earthly perspective, but preserved when viewed from a heavenly one.

Conversely, one may speak of a life preserved from the standpoint of temporal experience, but lost from the standpoint of eternity.

Thus a martyr for the cause of Christ has certainly lost his life in a temporal sense. But the life laid down for God is not *really* lost. Indeed, such a life achieves a kind of immortality. Its value and impact are unending, as is also the glory it gains for the Christian who has made such a sacrifice.

On the other hand, to shrink from the pathway of obedient suffering may be temporarily self-preserving. But the life thus selfishly held back is lost in terms of enduring eternal worth.

It would be a mistake to think here of heaven or hell. The call which precedes this challenging conception is a call to self-denial and bearing one's cross. It is a call to follow Jesus, that is, a call to discipleship.

Of course there are many who equate such a call with conversion, but by so doing they either explicitly or implicitly deny the freeness of the gospel. By no stretch of the imagination is the demand for self-denial and self-sacrifice an invitation to receive a free gift. The attempt to harmonize these polarities always ends either in hopeless absurdity or in theological sophistry.

In this respect the man on the street is often more perceptive than the theologian. If someone were to offer him a gift in return for self-denying obedience, he would readily recognize that offer as grotesquely misrepresented.

The Son of God never engaged in such contradictions. What was free, He represented as free. What was costly, He presented as costly. The experience here described is costly.

But it is also splendid. It is the construction of a life—a house— which can survive anything, even when it appears not to survive at all.

Of this fact our Lord's own experience is the superlative illustration. At the height of His ministry and public popularity He is betrayed by a professed disciple and put to death by the Jewish and Roman authorities. It was a life apparently lost, a ministry apparently prematurely cut off. But as every Christian understands, it was the death of Jesus that gave to His life permanent and eternal worth. To have turned aside from the cross would have made that wonderful life spiritually valueless to all mankind. To have avoided this suffering would have frustrated God's purposes for that life.

The same truth, in principle, applies to the committed disciple. Indeed, in John, Jesus' way of saying this is instructive:

> "Most assuredly, I say to you, unless a grain of wheat falls into the ground and dies, it remains alone; but if it dies, it produces much grain [lit., fruit]. He who loves his life will lose it, and he who hates his life in this world will keep it for eternal life. If anyone serves Me, let him follow Me; and where I am, there My servant will be also. If anyone serves Me, him My Father will honor" (John 12:24-26).

There is much to be learned from this way of putting it.

Losing one's life for God is like the death of a seed of some type of grain. The life is "planted" and becomes fruitful precisely because it is a life of service to Christ. The self-denial which this entails is now expressed in terms of "hating" our lives *in this world*. Instead of "loving" our lives—instead of guarding them selfishly for our own use—we abandon them to God's will. But in doing this we actually fuse our earthly experience into a continuum that stretches on into an unending future. We "keep it for eternal life."

Or, to put it another way, the "house" we have built survives our physical death. It becomes an integral part of our experience of eternal life in the world-to-come.

But the "house" which collapses in ruins is another thing altogether. In that case we encounter the *radical discontinuity* between the kind of living that is essentially temporal and that which is fundamentally eternal.

The Financial Statement

It follows from this that no amount of temporal gain can possibly compensate for the loss of one's life. It is, therefore, no exaggeration for Jesus to inquire,

> "For what will it profit a man if he gains the whole world, and loses his own soul [= life]? Or what will a man give in exchange for his soul [= life]?" (Mark 8:36-37).

It is unfortunate that the familiar English rendering of these questions employs the word "soul." The continued use of "life" (found in vv 34 and 35) was much to be desired. The Greek word in all four verses is the same.

What Jesus is doing is computing the financial statement of human experience. Suppose that in the column headed "assets" one could list "the whole world." And suppose in the column labeled "liabilities" one must write "my life." What, in that case, is the bottom line? Jesus' answer is stark and arresting. The financial statement shows a net loss. The life is more valuable than anything that might be offered for it in exchange.

It is precisely this truth that is so tellingly expressed in the parable of the rich fool. After refusing to arbitrate between two brothers who were quarreling over an inheritance, Jesus says to the crowd around Him:

> "Take heed and beware of covetousness, for one's life does not consist in the abundance of the things he possesses" (Luke 12:15).

Then He adds:

> "The ground of a certain rich man yielded plentifully. And he thought within himself, saying, 'What shall I do, since I have no room to store my crops?' So he said, 'I will do this: I will pull down my barns and build greater, and there I will store all my crops and my goods. And I will say to my soul, "Soul, you

> have many goods laid up for many years; take your ease: eat, drink, and be merry."' But God said to him, 'You fool! This night your soul [= life] will be required of you; then whose will those things be which you have provided?' So is he who lays up treasure for himself, and is not rich toward God" (Luke 12:16-21).[16]

Here, if anywhere, we encounter the collapse of an apparently splendid "house."

We are not told whether the rich man of this parable was saved or unsaved. Nor does it matter. The lesson which our Lord's story is designed to communicate would be true in either case. This man's life experience vanished the moment it was overtaken by physical death. The goods he was planning to hoard for his personal enjoyment over the years to come were totally lost to him. He left this world utterly impoverished.

Not surprisingly, Jesus follows this memorable narrative with an extended admonition to His disciples against an undue concern for the physical necessities of life (Luke 12:22-31). This warning is climaxed by urging them to give priority to the kingdom of God (v 31), and He adds:

> "Do not fear, little flock, for it is your Father's good pleasure to give you the kingdom. Sell what you have and give alms; provide yourselves money bags which do not grow old, a treasure in the heavens that does not fail, where no thief approaches nor moth destroys. For where your treasure is, there your heart will be also" (Luke 12:32-34; cf. Matt 6:19-21).

---

[16] The flexibility of the Greek word *psychē* is evident in Luke 12:19-20. In verse 19, it refers to the personal self whom the rich man addresses reflexively. In verse 20, it refers to the life he is about to lose. The *paronomasia* (word play) would appeal to the Greek ear, but it must be sacrificed in a fully accurate translation.

And that was exactly the rich man's problem. His treasures were on earth and his heart was there as well. When he died, he left those treasures behind. He was not rich in his relationship to God.

But the disciples are urged to look at things differently. It was possible for them, Jesus declares, to store up heavenly treasure. It was possible for them to be "rich toward God."

Nevertheless, such wealth was not theirs automatically. On the contrary, it was something they were to *provide* for themselves (v 33). Or, as the Savior had put it in His Sermon on the Mount, they were to *lay it up* for themselves (Matt 6:20). This is what the rich man had conspicuously failed to do. The disciples must not follow his example.

It is evident that the Lord Jesus Christ engages in a different form of accounting than men usually do. It was well for His unsaved hearers to know this truth about earthly wealth, just as it was urgent that His disciples should know it.

In the case of the unsaved, this truth could provoke them to reexamine their own values and begin to seek God's. And in the sincere pursuit of those things which counted with God, it was inevitable that they should ultimately find the narrow gate to life. In fact, in addressing doubters about His own Person, Jesus had once said, "If anyone wants to do His will, he shall know concerning the doctrine, whether it is from God or whether I speak on My own authority" (John 7:17). Indeed, it is always true that God is "a rewarder of those who diligently seek Him" (Heb 11:6).

But it was every bit as worthwhile for his disciples to hear this teaching, too. Moreover, as believers in Him, they could begin to act on it at once. They could begin at once to construct their "house" on the solid rock of their Teacher's words. They could commence immediately to lay up heavenly treasures for themselves. In short, they could cast their life into the soil of obedience to God—like a mere seed of grain—and could look forward to a bountiful harvest. They could save their lives by losing them.

That was what earthly life was really all about anyway. No wonder that in Matthew's form of our Lord's saying there was a fresh and delicate shade of meaning: "For whoever loses his life for My sake will find it" (Matt 16:25; cf. 10:39). One's life was not really *found* until it was discovered in self-denying service to Christ. And those who seemed to find it somewhere else—like the rich fool—had not found it at all. They had lost it![17]

This was solemn truth. And though it did not at all address the terms on which a man might be delivered from hell, it was still profoundly important. It was a warning that one's earthly life could be wasted, and heavenly reward could be forfeited, by misguided living.

And that was something everyone needed to hear.

---

[17] For a succinct statement of the interpretation of "saving the life," as given in this chapter, see R. E. Neighbour, *If They Shall Fall Away*, reprint edition (Miami Springs, FL: Conley & Schoettle, 1984), 29-30.

5
The Rich Young Ruler

Rich fools do not appear only in parables. They also appear in real life. On one notable occasion Jesus met one. He was a wealthy young man, and his interview with our Lord is both familiar and classic. It was an interview that plainly disclosed the Savior's striking capacity to probe beneath the issues men raise—in order that He might reach the issues they *should* have raised.

The disciples, as usual, were with Him, and they stood to profit immensely from the exchange, which they are allowed to overhear. Indeed, Jesus makes sure that they do profit by dealing directly with the problems which the encounter raised for them. In the process He achieves—as He so often did—a double result.

On the one hand, He softens the ground in the young man's heart in order to prepare it for the seed of the simple gospel of His saving grace. On the other hand, He drives home to the disciples important truths about heavenly treasure.

The Young Man's Question

According to the account given in the Gospel of Mark, the interview began when the ruler reached Jesus on the run. Though he is only called "young" by Matthew (19:22), the eagerness of youth is apparent in his hasty form of approach. Perhaps there was a breathless quality to his words when he said, "Good Teacher, what shall I do that I may inherit eternal life?" (Mark 10:17).

The question plainly reflects the typical Jewish perspective. According to the common Jewish theology of that time, eternal life was a privilege that belonged to the age to come. Morever, it could be acquired only by those whom

God deemed worthy to have it. The man's choice of the word "inherit" simply underscored this perception of things. That was a word which the rabbis often used to describe the meritorious acquisition of bliss in the future world.[18]

No wonder that the young man thought he must *do* something to get eternal life. In fact, in Matthew's account the adjective "good" is part of the question: "What *good* thing must I do...?" (Matt 19:16).

The Jewish outlook was both right and wrong. It was quite true that when eternal life was perceived as *an acquisition in the age to come* it could only be meritoriously obtained. In that respect Jewish thought was not misguided. But that was only half the story.

There remained a severe problem. Man was a sinner. He stood under divine condemnation. If he could acquire eternal life only at some future day—and only on the basis of his merits—then his situation was hopeless. He could, in fact, never acquire it at all.

But the coming of Jesus Christ into the world shed light on this issue in a fresh way. As Paul was later to say, He "brought life and immortality *to light* through the gospel" (2 Tim 1:10). What was always latent in the Old Covenant revelation—what was there in shadowy form—was now brilliantly illuminated by the incarnation of the Son of God and by the gospel message which He proclaimed. According to Jesus, a person could acquire the life of the age to come *immediately.* And not on the basis of merit at all, but as a free gift!

What else, indeed, did the Son of God mean when He declared,

> "Most assuredly, I say to you, he who hears
> My word and believes in Him who sent Me
> *has* everlasting life, and shall not come into

---

[18] For a discussion of the rabbinic perspective, see William E. Brown, *The New Testament Concept of the Believer's Inheritance* (unpublished Th.D. dissertation, Dallas Theological Seminary, 1984), 34-40.

judgment, but *has passed* from death into life" (John 5:24, emphasis added)?

Or again, when He went on to state,

> "Most assuredly, I say to you, the hour is coming, and *now is*, when the dead will hear the voice of the Son of God; and those who hear will live" (John 5:25, emphasis added)?

Staggering revelation. Resurrection, spiritually, at once. The life of the age to come possessed right here and now—by faith and nothing more.

But of this the rich young ruler knew nothing. His was not a wrong question to ask—it just wasn't the primary one. The primary question was one which he could not even guess.

No One Is Good but God

How then could he be moved in the right direction? What could deflect him from his preoccupation with merit? The response of Jesus could do that, if the young man would rightly hear it.

That response must have sounded initially as if it had no connection whatever with the rich man's inquiry. No doubt he was even taken aback when Jesus replied:

> "Why do you call Me good? No one is good but One, that is, God" (Mark 10:18).

But nothing could have been more to the point. It was precisely the issue on which this man needed to focus.

He had addressed Jesus as "Good Teacher." No doubt it was glibly said no matter how respectfully it was intended. But was He *really* good? In the definitive sense of that word, He could not be "good" if He was a mere mortal man. The Old Testament bore witness to that fact (and Paul appealed to it) when it affirmed, "There is none who does good, no, not one" (Ps 14:3; cf. Rom 3:12).

Only God was good and that could mean only one thing. Jesus could not be good unless He was also God. The young man perceived Him to be a teacher, and such He was. But He was very much more than that. And until the rich young ruler could hear His voice as the voice of the Son of God, eternal life—whether here or hereafter—lay beyond his reach.

But there was more. The young man himself was *not* good. Only God was good. But this perception also had not truly dawned on him, as his response to the Savior's next statement painfully shows.

His concept of "good" was therefore precisely his problem. That concept clouded his perception of Jesus, and it clouded his perception of himself. Until these perceptions were corrected, he was very far from God's kingdom indeed.

You Know the Law

How could such correction take place? Ideally, it ought to have taken place by means of the law. Here, again, was the divinely appointed schoolmaster whose role was to lead men to Christ. By the law one could normally acquire the knowledge of his sin.[19]

---

[19] Very appropriately it has been said, "in the greatly misunderstood incident of the rich young ruler, it is striking that every commandment quoted by our Lord is from the Second Table of the Law; not because in the observance of these social laws men could earn eternal life, but in order that the young man might be tested by his own claims of moral perfection and come to see himself as a sinner whose only hope is in what God can do (Matt 19:19-26)." Alva J. McClain, *The Greatness of the Kingdom* (Grand Rapids: Zondervan, 1959), 290. Ray Summers also observes that, "In his response, Jesus led the young ruler to see that not even a sincere effort at obedience to the law could give life. All the law could do was point him to his need and reflect his inability to keep it. The young man's downfall was in relation to the tenth command, 'You shall not covet.'" Ray Summers, *Commentary on Luke* (Waco, TX: Word Books, 1972), 214.

Jesus says, therefore:

> "You know the commandments: 'Do not commit adultery,' 'Do not murder,' 'Do not steal,' 'Do not bear false witness,' 'Do not defraud,' 'Honor your father and your mother'" (Mark 10:19).

To this list Matthew reports that Jesus even added, "You shall love your neighbor as yourself" (Matt 19:19).

It ought to have been convicting. But it wasn't. Indeed, it actually elicits one of the most sanguine replies in all of religious history. The young man says, "Teacher, all these things I have kept from my youth" (Mark 10:20). Had he? Of course not. What son is there who has always honored his father and mother? Where is the man who loves his neighbor as himself from his youth and upward?[20] Even if he had avoided the grosser sins on the list, he had certainly not avoided them all.

He was not good of course. But he *was* self-righteous. And like all self-righteous people he had lowered the standard of good to the level of his own imagined attainments. His darkness seems impenetrable.

One Thing You Lack

Yet there follows one of the loveliest statements of Scripture: "Then Jesus, looking at him, loved him..." (Mark 10:21).

How or why Jesus loved him is beyond our ability to fathom. But so is His love for all men and for us. That love is mysterious, it is marvelous. It is not called forth by our deluded claims to goodness, nor is it deflected by our arrogant self-righteousness.

---

[20] The phrase "from my youth" may be a reference to his twelfth year, at which time Jewish youths assumed responsibility for obedience to the law's commands. See William L. Lane, *The Gospel According to Mark* (Grand Rapids: Eerdmans, 1974), 366. Lane cites the Mishnah (*Berachoth II.* 2) and Luke 2:42.

But it *is* our ultimate resource, "for God so loved the world that He gave…" It is Jesus' love for this blind young inquirer which motivates our Lord's next words: "One thing you lack" (Mark 10:21).

What was that? The answer should be obvious to every Christian with a New Testament in his hands. The one thing he lacked was faith—saving faith.[21]

But does this interpretation accord with the words of Jesus which follow immediately? Yes, in fact it does accord with those words, *properly considered*. But not in the explicit one-to-one form which some readers inappropriately expect.

Here, too, the eclipse of grace casts its shadow over the interpretation of Scripture. Can anyone suppose that selling all and giving to the poor are really conditions for going to heaven? Were they even really conditions for this particular man? And if they are, or were, how can that conception of things be harmonized with the simple offer of a free gift of life to needy men?

"Whoever desires, let him take the water of life freely" (Rev 22:17) is far from being identical with "sell whatever you have and give to the poor." Such declarations are manifestly not saying the same thing. Casuistry alone can reduce them to some form of equivalence.

No, this man lacked saving faith, just as does every unsaved man. He lacked the simple spirit of trust so characteristic of the little children Jesus had just received (see Mark 10:13-15). But the young man was not prepared just now to have his deficiency explicitly stated. He was much too self-righteous to feel the need for a Savior. After all, had he not said, "What must I do"?

---

[21] Summers, *Luke*, 215, thinks that the one thing which the young man lacked was love. This, too, would emphasize his failure and sinfulness. But since the young man's need for eternal life could not be met by any conceivable expression of love, it is more likely that our Lord is pointing to his most basic deficiency—faith.

Jesus did not believe in pouring water down a clogged hole. This man must be *prepared* to comprehend the thing he really needed. Shock treatment was clearly in order.

That is why Jesus' challenge takes the form it does:

> "Go your way, sell whatever you have and
> give to the poor, and you will have treasure
> in heaven; and come, take up the cross, and
> follow Me" (Mark 10:21).

Clearly, this is a call to discipleship. It is an invitation to complete self-denial in the form of unstinting generosity.[22] Its outcome, Jesus declares, will be heavenly treasure.[23]

Was the young man prepared for this? Naturally not. In fact he goes away saddened since his wealth was considerable. But why did he go away? Above all, he went away because he had more faith in his money than he had in Jesus.

In fact, our Lord subsequently points this out to His disciples when He tells them:

---

[22] Naturally, some have tried to put Jesus' interview with the rich young man into the service of a doctrine of Lordship salvation. This is explicitly done by Walter J. Chantry, *Today's Gospel: Authentic or Synthetic?* (Edinburgh: Banner of Truth Trust, 1970). For a critique of the doctrine of Lordship Salvation, see Zane C. Hodges, *Absolutely Free! A Biblical Reply to Lordship Salvation* (Dallas, TX: Redencion Viva, 1989).

[23] Lane is *not* correct to observe that, "The assurance of 'treasure in heaven' reflects an idiom that was current in Judaism, which allowed Jesus to enter the thought-world of his contemporaries. Here, however, it *is* stripped *of* its customary associations of merit (as if selling one's property and giving the money received to the poor will earn a significant reward), since the promised treasure signifies the gift of eternal life or salvation at the revelation of the kingdom of God" (Lane, *Mark*, 367). It *is* entirely gratuitous to read into Jesus' words the concept of "the gift of eternal life." Rather, our Lord stands fully within the contemporary Jewish "thought-world" in associating "treasure in heaven" with meritorious behavior.

"Children, how hard it is for those who *trust in riches* to enter the kingdom of God!" (Mark 10:24, emphasis added).[24]

Let there be no mistake about it. The man lacked faith in the proper object. He had faith in his money, not in Jesus. No doubt when he asked what he might do to inherit eternal life, he suspected that his wealth might be tapped for some act or acts of benevolence. But it had not entered his mind that Jesus might ask him to surrender everything. That he was unprepared to do, for then he would be surrendering the very thing in which he trusted: his money.

Clearly he was not ready to give up all that he had just on the *bare word* of this Teacher. To do that would require an enormous step of faith he was not prepared to take. And so he went sorrowfully away.

Life and Treasure

And that was a mistake. But it was a mistake Jesus knew he would make and which conditioned the form of His challenge.

This man was confused about who was good. He himself was not good and his response to Jesus proved it. He was selfish, as are all sinners. For, if he truly loved his neighbor as himself (as he had claimed to do from his youth), it would not have mattered to him whether he himself had his money or his neighbor. But it did matter. The rich young ruler was *not* good.

---

[24] The statement quoted from Mark 10:24 is not found in two famous ancient manuscripts: the Codex Vaticanus (B) and Codex Sinaiticus (Aleph). A few other witnesses also support the omission. But the longer text is overwhelmingly attested in the vast majority of the surviving Greek manuscripts of Mark. The accidental omission of a "colon" (sense-line) in a common ancestor of Aleph and B is perhaps the source of the omission. The adoption of the omission as the original reading by many modern editors and translators reflects an inappropriately high regard for the two manuscripts in question. But even so, the truth affirmed by Mark 10:24 is self-evident when the story is reflected on properly.

But Jesus *was* good, since He was God. If he were not God, His demand to give up all for Him was both fantastic and egotistical. How could a mere man offer eternal treasure to his followers on no other authority than his own? Could a mere human teacher talk like that and still be sane? Would it not be foolish to trust a man who said such things?

Ordinarily it would be. But not where Jesus was concerned. Such a leap of faith would require the rich young ruler to adopt a much higher view of this rabbi than he currently held. Indeed, it would require him to reach the conclusion that Jesus was exactly who He had hinted He was—a divine Person. And that would mean that He was the Christ, the Son of God. But to reach *that* conclusion would result in his being born again, as the Gospel of John so plainly declares (John 20:30-31).

Did the rich young ruler ever reach it? He probably did, because Jesus "loved him" and had designed His words to meet this man at the very point where his spiritual progress was blocked. All the implications were there. He now had reason to suspect that his own goodness was far less than he thought. And he had received unmistakable clues about the dignity of the Person to whom he had come.

If he drew the proper conclusions, all that remained was to believe in Jesus. That would have brought him the free gift of eternal life. Then he could take up the Lord's challenge to become a disciple. And *that* would have brought him treasure in heaven.[25]

Aftermath and Surprise

The ruler was gone now, thwarted and dismayed by Jesus' words. Now it is the disciples' turn to be startled. Jesus says to them:

---

[25] Summers so comments, "Jesus believed that heaven will be richer for one who has used earthly riches in good stewardship to God and compassion for needy men" (Summers, *Luke*, 215).

> "How hard it is for those who have riches to enter the kingdom of God!" (Mark 10:23).

And, to the disciples' amazement, He adds:

> "It is easier for a camel to go through the eye of a needle than for a rich man to enter the kingdom of God" (Mark 10:25).

The disciples are dumbfounded by these words, and they reply, "Who then can be saved?" (Mark 10:26).

Naturally, the disciples shared the common Jewish view that God enriched and prospered the righteous. There were many Old Testament examples of this: Abraham, Solomon, and Job, to name only three. If salvation was hard for people like that, must it not be nearly impossible for those less signally blessed?

For a few moments the disciples themselves were tempted to lose their grip on the gospel of divine grace. (They were certainly not the last to be swayed in this way.) But there were no grounds for their perplexity if they considered Jesus' words with care.

Salvation was hard for the rich man precisely because he trusted in his own riches. He found it difficult to feel totally dependent on Another, particularly on Jesus. The exchange with the rich young ruler had certainly demonstrated that.

It followed that a rich man was very much like an ungainly camel. He was too big, too self-sufficient, to pass through the minuscule entrance—the needle's eye—into the realm of eternal bliss. That was the narrow gate all over again. Only this time the image had undergone impressive miniaturization.

But the disciples need not worry, Jesus assured them. Salvation was always a miracle of God in any case. That which man could never bring to pass in the humblest of sinners, God could accomplish even in a rich man:

"With men it is impossible, but not with God; for with God all things are possible" (Mark 10:27).

It was an important point. If we were to judge from the attitude of that wealthy young man, we might easily have said: "That man will never get saved!" From all appearances he was much too big a camel— much too proud a man—to ever become "small" enough to pass through the needle's eye by a childlike act of faith.

But it would be wise not to write him off entirely. Nor, for that matter, any other man of wealth. For what was truly impossible for human means to accomplish, God could do. Indeed, the masterly skill with which Jesus had handled the young ruler had no doubt set this miraculous process in motion. The camel had gone away smaller— less self-assured—than when he arrived. There was hope!

Life More Abundant

That ought to have set the disciples' minds at rest. Perhaps it did. In any case the focus of the conversation changes swiftly. Peter is the catalyst:

> Then Peter began to say to Him, "See, we have left all and followed you" (Mark 10:28).

Matthew tells us that Peter also added:

> "Therefore what shall we have?" (Matt 19:27).

It was an appropriate question. After all, Jesus had offered the rich young ruler *treasure in heaven* if *he* left all. Was this promise applicable to the disciples as well?

No doubt there is a temptation to censure Peter for greed. But why? Already the disciples had been specifically taught to store up eternal wealth (Matt 6:19-21; Luke 12:32-34). It is not selfish to take an interest in matters Jesus Himself has told us to be concerned about. It is not wrong to seek what He tells us to seek.

It is wrong not to seek. It is, in fact, a sin to refuse to lay up heavenly treasure when we are explicitly commanded to do so. Moreover, the effects on our hearts of *not* doing it will be calamitous. For where our treasures are, there our hearts will be also.

The rich young ruler's heart was on earth. The thought of losing his earthly treasures saddened him. But Peter and the other disciples had abandoned everything for Jesus. It was only natural that they should be curious about their heavenly reward.

Our Lord's answer to this query is memorable:

> "Assuredly, I say to you, there is no one who has left house or brothers or sisters or father or mother or wife or children or lands, for My sake and the gospel's, who shall not receive a hundredfold now in this time—houses and brothers and sisters and mothers and children and lands, with persecutions—and in the age to come, eternal life" (Mark 10:29-30).

The answer was rich, exciting, and sobering. There were compensations to be experienced in the present age—along with its troubles—and there was compensation in the age to come as well.

With regard to the present age, the reward was to come in the form of rich personal relationships. And how often the servants of Christ have proved the truth of that guarantee. Leaving behind their earthly families, traveling often to the remote quarters of the globe, they have discovered *new* relationships created by the shared gospel of Jesus Christ. In those souls whom they have won to Christ, in those to whom they have ministered the truth, they have found new brothers and sisters, new mothers and children. Homes have been opened to them and lands laid at their service as though they owned them. And the depths of the spiritual communion established in this way with men have often seemed to be indeed a hundredfold more rich than those ties which Christ's servants have left behind. No doubt it was in the spirit of these very words of Jesus that Paul greets "Rufus...and his mother *and mine*" (Rom 16:13).

But if obedience to Jesus enriched a man's temporal lot, it equally enriched his eternal one. And here the reward was..."eternal life."

Yes, a reward. Plainly presented as such. But a reward belonging to the future age, not to the present one.

And thus Jewish theology was right—in part. Eternal life would be awarded meritoriously in a future day. What that theology failed to perceive was that, for such a reward to be within man's reach, eternal life must first be received as a gift.

Eternal life is no static entity, no mere fixed and unchanging object. Eternal life is the very life of God, and as such its potentials are without limit. Had not Jesus affirmed:

> "I have come that they may have life, and that they may have it *more abundantly*" (John 10:10, emphasis added).

No doubt Jesus was speaking in this verse about life in the resurrection experience. That experience would indeed be *more abundant* simply because resurrection life is necessarily fuller than any present experience. Therefore the Gospel of John emphasizes the connection between life *now* and the *coming* resurrection (John 6:39-40; 11:25-26).

The possibilities of such a future life are as infinite as the life itself. But to receive enrichment in that future life *as a reward*, one must first obtain it *as a gift* by faith in Jesus.

The rich young ruler had put the cart before the horse. He had asked how to *earn life* before *receiving it*. He had inquired about God's rewards, before seeking His gift. Jesus had sought to push him back to the proper starting point, but one thing remained true. Leaving all for Christ *did* lead to heavenly treasure after all.

The rich young ruler was by no means ready to do that yet. The disciples had already done it. It was well for them to hear about it. It was needful for them to discover that both present and future experience would be enriched and enhanced by their loyalty and commitment to Christ.

There was no need to envy the rich young ruler at all. Perhaps he seemed to be far ahead of them in all respects. But the sober evaluation in the light of eternity could reverse that appraisal.

Therefore, as His final comment on His encounter with the rich young ruler, Jesus tells His disciples, "But many who are first will be last, and the last first" (Mark 10:31).

6
Judged According to Works

One of the men who received instruction from our Lord's exchange with the rich young ruler was the Apostle John. A special intimacy existed between him and the Savior, so that in the Fourth Gospel he describes himself simply as "the disciple whom Jesus loved" (John 13:23; 19:26; 21:7, 20). It was he who leaned on Jesus' bosom at the Last Supper (13:23).

There is something lovely about the fact that a man so personally close to the Son of God should be selected to pen the Gospel which above all others discloses the free and unconditional love of God for sinful man. Indeed, in the Gospel of John we encounter the irreducible core of the saving message of grace, and in that message we hear the heartbeat of God Himself.

So the One who had lain *on* the Father's bosom (John 1:18) shared these sublime truths with the man who lay *in* His. No one among men has ever understood these truths better, nor communicated them more clearly and simply, than the Apostle John. In fact, it is this apostle, and no other, who reports to us a statement by Jesus that is breathtaking in its scope and impact. According to John, Jesus once said:

> "Most assuredly, I say to you, he who hears My word and believes in Him who sent Me has everlasting life, and *shall not come into judgment*, but has passed from death into life" (John 5:24, emphasis added).

This is certainly a splendid promise. It offers to the one who believes a most solemn guarantee that not only does he possess eternal life, but also that he need have no fear of judgment. Why? Because that experience is not for him: he "shall not come into judgment."

Yet, strangely, in the last book of the New Testament this same inspired writer reports another declaration of his Master which must seem to stand in tension with the earlier one. Here Jesus says:

> "And behold, I am coming quickly, and My reward is with Me, to give to every one according to his work" (Rev 22:12).

It is true that the word *judgment* is not actually used here, but it is obviously implied. It is also explicitly stated in other texts of Scripture. In his first epistle, the same author writes:

> Love has been perfected among us in this: that we may have boldness in the *day of judgment*; because as He is, so are we in this world (1 John 4:17, emphasis added).

And James, our Lord's natural half-brother, wrote:

> So speak and so do as those who *will be judged* by the law of liberty. For *judgment* is without mercy to the one who has shown no mercy. Mercy triumphs over *judgment* (Jas 2:12-13, emphasis added).

Naturally also, the Apostle Paul spoke of this event:

> For to this end Christ died and rose and lived again, that He might be Lord of both the dead and the living. ...For we shall all stand before *the judgment seat of Christ*. For it is written: "As I live, says the Lord, every knee shall bow to Me, and every tongue shall confess to God." So then each of us shall give account of himself to God (Rom 14:9-12, emphasis added; cf. 2 Cor 5:10).

What then is this? On the one hand there is the solemnity of Jesus' promise that the believer does not come into judgment, and on the other hand the repeated apostolic declarations that he does. It goes without saying that the failure to sift this question through to an appropriate resolution has been the source of considerable theological confusion and error.

Scylla and Charybdis

According to Greek mythology the navigational skills of ancient seamen were severely tested whenever they were required to sail the narrow passage of water between Scylla and Charybdis. Not a few ships, so we are told, were broken on the rock Scylla or sucked down into the whirlpool of Charybdis.

Nor have the vessels of contemporary theologians fared much better when called upon to steer a course through the scriptural channels which deal with judgment. On the one hand lies the danger of ignoring our Lord's guarantee that the believer is judgment-free. On the other hand the danger of minimizing the reality that he is not.

All of the Biblical statements in question can be taken at face value. When Jesus declared the believer would not come into judgment, He was speaking in the context of eternal salvation. The believer has eternal life *already*. He has thus passed from death to life *already*. On that score, there is nothing left to decide, nothing left to judge.

There can therefore be no such thing as a judgment to determine whether a believer goes to heaven or hell. God has already handed down a definitive legal decision. Paul called that decision *justification*. The righteousness of God has been imputed to the Christian on the sole basis of faith alone.

That has nothing to do with our works, as Paul affirmed when he wrote:

> Now to him who works, the wages are not counted as grace but as debt. But to him who does not work but believes on Him who justifies the ungodly, his faith is accounted for righteousness (Rom 4:4-5).

It follows that those who believe in a final judgment where the believer's works will be brought to bear on the issue of his final salvation—and many do believe in that—are believing a doctrine which clashes fiercely with Pauline thought. To introduce the issue of works is, for Paul, to introduce the question of merit and debt.

But since God gives salvation freely to anyone who receives it by faith, the case is closed before it can be opened. Nor will it ever be opened, or reviewed. The eternal destiny of everyone who has passed out of death into life is settled forever. *In that sense* there is no judgment for a Christian.[26]

But on the other hand, many who have perceived this magnificent truth have been reluctant to face the other texts of Scripture on this theme as directly and candidly as they should. There is no way to elude the reality that the believer does face a judgment where his works—and hence the issue of "debt" and "pay"—must be examined.

This is exactly what Jesus means when He declares, "My *reward* is with Me, to give to everyone according to his work" (Rev 22:12, emphasis added). The Greek word translated here as "reward" was one which basically meant "pay" or "wages." Our Lord's meaning is transparent: "What a man has earned he will get."

There is no more lovely doctrine in Scripture than the doctrine of God's matchless grace. But in some quarters of Christendom that superlative theme has been stretched almost beyond recognition. It is perfectly true that grace will play a significant role at the judgment of believers.

---

[26] This truth is very effectively presented by Alexander Patterson, *The Greater Life and Work of Christ* (New York: Revell, 1896), 314-16.

Who has ever accomplished anything apart from its enablement? But the Judgment Seat of Christ is a place where the Christian's *performance* comes into view. And therefore the question of merit comes into view as well.

Not to maintain this balance with regard to the Biblical doctrine of judgment is to invite—yes, to assure—the distortion of much Scripture.

Accountability

There is urgent need for a renewed recognition of Christian accountability. Not the kind of pseudo-accountability which is so frequently hawked in the religious marketplace today.

The Christian is *not* in danger of losing his eternal salvation. Every believer in Christ not only has eternal life but will still belong to Christ when he is raised up at the last day (John 6:37-40). No one who has ever drunk of the water of life will ever be thirsty for that water again (John 4:13-14).

Neither is the Christian's accountability to be held hostage to a distorted presentation of the gospel or to some subtle reshaping of the concept of saving faith.

A Christian's accountability is just that. He is saved freely and forever by the grace of God. But once he has been saved he is profoundly responsible for what he does with the rest of his life.[27]

He can build his "house" on sand if he so chooses. But the "house" will collapse in ruins around him, and he will

---

[27] On this theme, G. Campbell Morgan writes: "'We must all be made manifest'; for God does not dissociate our work from ourselves. Outward efforts count for nothing unless I am a Christ-soul; and then my life is my work. The question of each one should be, Of what sort is my life? If it is self-centered and unwatchful, so also is my work—'wood, hay, stubble' (1 Cor iii. 12). But if my life is surrendered to the King, if I am loyal to Him and absolutely under His control, mine is King's work—'gold, silver, precious stones'" (G. Campbell Morgan, *God's Methods With Man* [New York: Fleming H. Revell, 1898], 90-91).

have to give an account of his folly before God. He can "save" his life if he chooses by self-interested living, but his life will actually be lost if he does. And he will have to give an account for this before God. He can hoard his material assets if he so decides, but to the degree that he does he will impoverish himself in the world-to come. And he will have to acknowledge his greed before God.

Scripture is plain: "As I live, says the Lord, every knee shall bow to Me, and every tongue shall confess to God" (Rom 14:11). That's accountability!

It is sometimes argued that the believer's sins cannot come under consideration at Christ's Judgment Seat since they are all forgiven. But this confuses the two kinds of judgment. The Christian's eternal destiny is not an issue in the judgment of believers, hence "sin" as a barrier to his entrance into God's eternal kingdom is not an issue either.

But it must be kept in mind that to review and assess a life, the Judge must consider the life in its entirety. And that obviously includes the bad with the good. Indeed, Paul tells us this quite plainly when he writes:

> For we must all appear before the judgment seat of Christ, that each one may receive the things done in the body, according to what he has done, *whether good or bad* (2 Cor 5:10, emphasis added).[28]

That the thought was as solemn to Paul as it is to us is clear from his next words: "Knowing, therefore, the terror of the Lord, we persuade men" (2 Cor 5:11).

Getting Ready to Meet the Judge

The Christian ought to give the day of accounting some serious thought. It is an illusion cherished by many that

---

[28] On this text, see the helpful little article by John A. Sproul, "'Judgment Seat' or 'Awards Podium,'" *Spire* (published by Grace Theological Seminary, Winona Lake, IN) 13 (1984):3-5.

unsavory secrets will always be just that—secrets between themselves and God. The Scriptures do not support this view of things.

Eternity has no secrets. Jesus Himself said so. In fact, while warning His disciples against the pretense so common among the religious leaders of His day, He said this:

> "Beware of the leaven of the Pharisees, which is hypocrisy. For there is nothing covered that will not be revealed, nor hidden that will not be known. Therefore whatever you have spoken in the dark will be heard in the light, and what you have spoken in the ear in inner rooms will be proclaimed on the housetops" (Luke 12:1-3).

The Apostle Paul carried this a step further:

> Therefore judge nothing before the time, until the Lord comes, who will both bring to light the hidden things of darkness and *reveal the counsels of the hearts*. Then each one's praise will come from God (1 Cor 4:5, emphasis added).

It is too early, says Paul, to judge anything properly. To do that, one would need to know not only the dark secrets of men, but their *motives* as well. So wait until the Lord comes. Everything will be clear then. And when that happens, men will get whatever praise they truly deserve.

Therefore, since no human secret can remain a secret permanently, the Christian might well desire that the day of judgment should reveal more than "the hidden things of darkness." Why should it not also disclose secrets that are worthy of praise? It will. And Jesus told us so in His Sermon on the Mount.

In fact, one of His most motivating suggestions was this:

> "But when you do a charitable deed, do not let your left hand know what your right hand is doing, that your charitable deed may be

in secret; and your Father who sees in secret will Himself *reward you openly*" (Matt 6:3-4, emphasis added).

Shortly after, He also said this:

"But you, when you pray, go into your room, and when you have shut your door, pray to your Father who is in the secret place; and your Father who sees in secret will *reward you openly*" (Matt 6:6, emphasis added).

And a little later He added:

But you, when you fast, anoint your head and wash your face, so that you do not appear to men to be fasting, but to your Father who is in the secret place; and your Father who sees in secret will *reward you openly* (Matt 6:17-18, emphasis added).

What delightful secrets for a man to have—secret charities, secret prayers, secret fastings. Here surely are activities to be stored up in great quantity for the Judgment Seat of Christ.[29] And the reward for them—the "pay"—will be a recompense made in public.

That is one way for a Christian to get ready to meet his Judge. But there are other ways. In particular, as the

---

[29] It is worth mentioning that in Rom 2:6-10 Paul refers to the principle that God will repay men according to their works. The Apostle has the final judgment primarily in view. If a man stands in that judgment (the saved do not: John 5:24), he will get what he deserves when his works are reviewed there (Rev 20:12). Since no one qualifies for eternal life "by patient continuance in doing good" (Rom 2:7)—that is, since all are sinners—no one will obtain eternal life that way. Only "the doers of the law will be justified" at the final judgment (Rom 2:13), but, as Paul states clearly, there are none (Rom 3:19-20). He also said "as many as *have sinned* in the law will be judged by the law" (Rom 2:12, emphasis added). That covers everybody, since "all have sinned" (Rom 3:23). There is no acquittal, justification, or eternal salvation for *anybody* who stands in the final judgment. James's words should be kept in mind: "for whoever shall keep the whole law, and yet stumble in one point, he is guilty of all" (Jas 2:10).

thought of charitable deeds already suggests, one needs especially to be merciful. This was what James had in mind when he wrote, "For judgment is without mercy to the one who has shown no mercy" (Jas 2:13).

In saying this James was speaking to Christians who were to be judged by Christian standards, all suitably summed up as "the law of liberty" (Jas 2:12). He had been addressing them as people who held "the faith of our Lord Jesus Christ, the Lord of glory," but who tended to mix this with an inappropriate partiality toward the rich (2:1). This led to harsh, thoughtless, unmerciful behavior toward the poor (2:2-3), and was a serious infraction of the royal law of Scripture, "You shall love your neighbor as yourself" (2:8-9).

"All right then," James says, "just remember this. If you are an unmerciful person in your dealings with others, you must face a judgment that is not tempered by mercy!"

This is an arresting thought. For what Christian is there who can survey his earthly experience without sensing that, when called to account, he would wish to be treated with mercy? It is not a question of fearing the loss of salvation. That does not even enter the picture. But it is rather a question of being held strictly to the standards of God's Word and having our recompense measured out in those demanding terms alone. No honest believer wants a judgment exactly like that.

But many Christians are rigid and uncompromising in their demands on others. In addition, they can be thoughtless, unforgiving, unkind, and even cruel. And if this has been their manner on earth— if mercy has not marked their dealings with others—mercy will not mark their own judgment either. So to get ready to meet their Judge, the Christian should specialize in mercy. After all, says James, "Mercy triumphs over judgment" (2:13).

But—and it is close to being the same thing—the Christian should also specialize in love. Mercy was James' word. Love is John's.

We should expect that love would be John's word. This was "the disciple whom Jesus loved." He had leaned on Jesus' bosom and felt there the heartbeat of God. He is preeminently the apostle of love.

John believed firmly in the unconditional love of God, lavishly expressed in the giving of His Son that men might have eternal life. Naturally, there is no judgment ahead to test whether that love is still the believer's possession or not. A judgment like that is unthinkable.

But there *is* a judgment ahead to test the believer's works. "Behold, I am coming quickly, and My reward is with Me, to give to everyone according to his work," are words recorded by the apostle of love himself. John believed very deeply in that sort of judgment.

And he also believed that such judgment could be fearful. Like Paul he knew "the terror of the Lord" (2 Cor 5:11). But though this *can* be fearful, it need *not* be. And the way to avoid the fear which that day could bring, is…*to love*.

This, in fact, is the burden of his exhortation in the fourth chapter of his first letter. And its climax is reached in the apostle's reference to the day of judgment as potentially free from fear:

> Love has been perfected among us in this: that we may have boldness in the day of judgment; because as He is, so are we in this world. There is no fear in love, but perfect love casts out fear, because fear involves torment. But he who fears has not been made perfect in love (1 John 4:17-18).

So that is it. As Christians enter a mature, perfected experience of loving each other, they no longer need to anticipate the day of accounting with trepidation. Why? Because they become like their Judge. "As He is" so we also may become in this world by love. Mature love expels fear when moral likeness exists between the Judge and the one who is to be judged.

There is torment in all fear, of course. Fear carries its own punishment with it. Though the believer can know himself to be eternally secure, this fact does not automatically eliminate the "torment" involved in anticipating the day of accounting. To stand before so majestic a Person (even John once fell at His feet as though dead: Rev 1:17), to consider the standards by which our life must be assessed, to realize that much of it may meet with His censure and reproof—in all of that, and more, there are ample grounds for fearful anticipation.

But it need not be so, said John. Love can become the hallmark of our temporal experience, just as it is the key to our eternal one. There is an irresistible logic to this correlation, and John stated it plainly:

> In this is love, not that we loved God, but that He loved us and sent His Son to be the propitiation for our sins. Beloved, if God so loved us, we also ought to love one another (1 John 4:10-11).

The saving, propitiatory work of Jesus Christ was an outflow of the unconditional love of God to men. By it, every believer is delivered from all judgment that would decide his eternal destiny in heaven or hell.

But that love is now a model for our love to one another. And when we really live that model we are then prepared to be judged without fear—according to our works.

7
Ten Cities

The distinctively "Christian judgment," to which the New Testament writers refer so often, is a theme whose roots are found in the teachings of Jesus. And that is precisely what we should expect. In fact, it is doubtful whether any major truth expounded in the Epistles is entirely absent from the recorded words of our Lord.

It was the Lord Jesus Christ who first taught His disciples the reality of Christian accountability. Indeed, when the pages of the Synoptic Gospels are carefully searched, it is even surprising how extensively He dwelt on this subject. This fact goes unrecognized only because the first three Gospels are usually read today in the half-light of the eclipse of grace.

It is precisely the theme of accountability that underlies our Lord's teaching about saving or losing one's life. The loss of one's life, said Jesus, was a forfeiture for which there could be no adequate compensation: "Or what will a man give in exchange for his soul [= life]?" (Mark 8:37). It is not surprising to find these words immediately followed by a solemn reference to the future:

> "For whoever is ashamed of Me and My words
> in this adulterous and sinful generation, of
> him the Son of Man also will be ashamed
> when He comes in the glory of His Father
> with the holy angels" (Mark 8:38).

There is nothing here about the loss of eternal life. On the contrary, what is suggested plainly is the loss of honor and recognition in the glorious presence of Jesus Himself when He returns to reign. For what could be more honorable than to gain His approval in that day? And what could be more shattering to a child of God than to become the object of his Lord's embarrassment and shame?

Naturally, if *He* is ashamed of us, *we* will be ashamed of ourselves. And this possibility was pointedly expressed by the Apostle John when he wrote:

> And now, little children, abide in Him, that when He appears, we may have confidence and *not be ashamed* before Him at His coming (1 John 2:28, emphasis added).

It is often overlooked that the experience of shame described in this text belongs to a *transformed believer.* John says quite clearly, in the next chapter, that "when He is revealed, we shall be like Him, for we shall see Him as He is" (1 John 3:2). But the possibility of shame is not eliminated by the fact that the sight of our Lord will be transforming. Instead, that transforming sight increases this possibility.

Shame, when it has a valid basis in our behavior, is always experienced in direct proportion to our sensitivity to sin. But so long as we are in our mortal bodies, deep shame over spiritual failure is greatly inhibited by the sinful side of our nature. But not so in the bodies we are destined to have at the Second Coming.

In those bodies, transformed so that they are like the Savior's own glorious body (Phil 3:20-21), we will be able to see things as they really are. In them we shall know even as we are known (1 Cor 13:12). At that moment the capacity to feel holy shame over a badly wasted life will for the first time be unhindered by our excuses and rationalizations. No doubt such shame will be more intense than any similar feelings experienced on earth.

It will be the Son of God and His redeemed child face to face at last, and if *He* feels shame toward us, those feelings will be mirrored by our own.

But if shame in the presence of Jesus were our only concern about the day of accounting, it would probably not be adequate to motivate our stubborn hearts. Naturally, we ought to zealously seek to avoid both His shame and our own. But there is more to be avoided than that.

For this reason, the Lord Jesus told several vivid parables designed to bring the day of Christian judgment graphically before our minds. Each of them is rich with instruction and worthy of attention. But one of the clearest and most compelling is the parable of the ten minas. It is to this parable that we must turn our attention first of all.

The Prospect of Power

The parable of the minas was evidently told in the household of Zacchaeus (see Luke 19:11). This notorious publican had just been saved, and in the first flush of salvation joy had announced his intention to engage in lavish charity and acts of restitution (Luke 19:8). The parable is designed to encourage him in this course of action.

It should be pointed out that Zacchaeus' willingness to dispose of large sums of money was no more a means to his salvation than it was for the rich young ruler. Nor does Jesus even refer to it when He proclaims the advent of salvation in that household. Instead He says:

> "Today salvation has come to this house, because he also is a son of Abraham; for the Son of Man has come to seek and to save that which was lost" (Luke 19:9-10).

The earliest Christian readers for whom Luke was writing no doubt understood Jesus' words quite well. If, as seems likely, they were Pauline Christians, they would detect at once the rich connotation of the expression "son of Abraham."[30] After all, it was Paul who wrote:

---

[30] The opinion is now widely held that Luke-Acts was written with a Christian audience in view. See, for example, Robert Maddox, *The Purpose of Luke Acts* (Edinburgh: T & T Clark, 1982). If the author is

> Therefore know that *only* those who are of faith are sons of Abraham (Gal 3:7; the translators have supplied "only").

What our Lord meant was that salvation had come to Zacchaeus precisely because he was now truly a son of Abraham by faith. Jesus' irony would be unmistakable in Jericho where Zacchaeus must have seemed less than a real Jew. Zacchaeus had been a tax-gatherer for the hated Roman overlords. But Zacchaeus had simply been lost, and because Jesus had sought him, he was now found. Like anyone else, he had been saved by the kind of justifying faith of which Abraham was the great prototype.

Yet Jesus knew that Zacchaeus needed new incentives for his fledgling Christian life. In Jericho this man, who was short in stature, stood tall in terms of personal power. He was not only a tax-gatherer, he was the *chief* tax-gatherer in that city (Luke 19:2). And he was rich. There was probably no one else in Jericho who could rival him in his capacity to exercise influence and authority.

But now his stature in the city was about to be diminished by an extensive redistribution of his personal wealth. Might he not someday regret this resolution? Might he not someday see it as a rash decision made in the midst of an immature enthusiasm?

Jesus wanted to make sure he did not. Zacchaeus's public pledge to his new Master was the most prudent financial investment he had ever contemplated. Perhaps it would diminish his influence in Jericho, but that did not matter. Jericho was only one relatively small Palestinian city—Zacchaeus should now aim for *ten* cities.

Thus the desire for power that evidently motivated Zacchaeus in his unsaved days could now be channeled in a new—and holy—direction. It should not be forgotten that

---

seen as Luke, the companion of Paul, the Christian community to which Theophilus belonged is likely to have had connections with Paul.

man was actually created for the exercise of power. This is plain from the very first chapter of Genesis:

> Then God said, "Let Us make man in Our image, according to Our likeness; let him have dominion over the fish of the sea, over the birds of the air, and over the cattle, over all the earth and over every creeping thing that creeps on the earth" (Gen 1:26).

It was undoubtedly this text that the psalmist was thinking about as he declared:

> What is man that You are mindful of him, and the son of man, that You visit him? For You have made him a little lower than the angels, and You have crowned him with glory and honor. You have made him to have dominion over the works of Your hands; You have put all things under his feet, all sheep and oxen—even the beasts of the field, the birds of the air, and the fish of the sea that pass through the paths of the seas (Ps 8:4-8).

Man was created in the image of God. But the God in whose image he was created is a God of might and dominion. He is the King of glory to whom belong the earth and "all its fullness" (Psalm 24). Thus, as a true reflection of his Maker, man was designed to exercise dominion over the creation.

But he lost this dominion by his fall. And his former position can only be recovered in and through our Lord Jesus Christ Himself. For this reason the writer of Hebrews applies Psalm 8 to "the world to come" (Heb 2:5), to the destiny of Jesus (2:8-9) and to the destiny of the "many sons" (2:10).

Consequently, there is nothing wrong with man's urge to possess power, insofar as this drive is properly focused on God's purposes in creation. But power, like all legitimate human aspirations, is subject to the corrupting impact of man's fallen state. Zacchaeus had previously sought power in a way that reflected his sinful condition. Now he must learn to seek it as a high and holy ambition which was focused on the world to come.

A Time for Investment

There was another reason for the parable told by Jesus in the house of Zacchaeus. He was close to Jerusalem, and many of those who followed Him were anticipating that God's kingdom would immediately appear (Luke 19:11).

This was a mistake. A period of time would elapse before the advent of God's reign on earth. The future King—our Lord Himself—would soon depart and go back to heaven, and only thereafter would He return to rule. Of Him it could be said:

> "A certain nobleman went into a far country
> to receive for himself a kingdom and to
> return" (Luke 19:12).

The procedure was familiar to His hearers. A man of noble birth might go to Rome, the center of imperial power, and seek the Emperor's approval of some claim to client kingship in a distant province. Indeed, it was by a process much like this that Herod the Great had secured recognition as king of Judea. He later asserted that claim by force of arms.[31]

But Jesus would carry His case to a throne that was higher than Caesar's. And in accordance with a Psalm that prophesied His unqualified acceptance before the Ruler of the Universe, God would say to Him:

---

[31] Mark Antony was Herod's patron, and it was the Roman Senate that conferred on Herod the title of king. He was also equipped with an army which he used to conquer Judea. One can scarcely miss the analogy with Christ, who will return to earth with a heavenly army and conquer His enemies (Rev 19:11-21). The informed Christian reader of Luke's parable would have no trouble in seeing the comparison which is implied.

> "Sit at My right hand, till I make Your
> enemies Your footstool" (Ps 110:1; see Luke
> 20:41-44 and parallels; Heb 1:13).

His enemies were doomed. Their efforts to frustrate His claims (Luke 19:14) could only end in their own destruction (Luke 19:27). Meanwhile, his servants had been told, "Do business till I come" (Luke 19:13).

Here lay the central point of the parable. The interadvent period which the parable proclaimed could be used to advantage. It was a time for investment. More than that, it was a time for investment directly related to the coming kingdom of God. Therefore, Zacchaeus needed to hear the parable at this crucial moment in his life. But so did everyone else in the audience as well.

What was there to invest? For each servant it was a mina—a piece of money. Zacchaeus, the tax-collector, could appreciate a story about money. And it was no insignificant piece of money at that. It was an amount which an ordinary working man might accumulate only after about three months of labor. Yet, in the light of the potential return, a mina was not very much after all.

Each servant received the same *amount—one* mina. This suggests that our Lord was thinking of the one thing all His servants have in common: their life's potential. Whatever may be their differences in aptitude or situation, all had a life that could be invested with all its potentialities for Him. The echoes of His great saying about saving or losing one's life are thus not difficult to detect in the background of this story.

But though each of the ten servants *began* with the same amount, they do not all end with the same amount. This fact became evident on the day of accounting. Accordingly we read:

> "And so it was that when he returned, having
> received the kingdom, he then commanded
> these servants, to whom he had given the
> money, to be called to him, that he might

know how much every man had gained by trading" (Luke 19:15).

There is no mistaking here the Judgment Seat of Christ. This is a judgment of servants which, in this parable, is set in sharp contrast to the later judgment of enemies. The enemies of the King are slain (Luke 19:27); none of the servants are.

Given the parabolic form of our Lord's instruction, it is not hard to see in the death of these enemies a reference to the Judgment of the Great White Throne which terminates in "the second death" for the unsaved (Rev 20:11-15). But this judgment is removed by a thousand years from the advent of the King. No believer in Christ need fear such a judgment. It is something into which believers cannot go (John 5:24).

But the day of accounting for *servants* is clearly another thing. Their use of their life—the investment of their mina—must be reviewed. And all do not fare equally well.

Sharing the Kingdom

The first servant has invested his mina with remarkable profit. Its value has increased 1,000 percent. He now has ten minas to present to his Lord (Luke 19:16). His reward is according to his work (Rev 22:12). The King replies:

> "Well done, good servant; because you were faithful in a very little, have authority over ten cities" (Luke 19:17).

This was a splendid recompense. For the prudent investment of a sum earnable in a relatively short span of time, this diligent servant is elevated to a role of high authority in the new King's domain. He receives ten cities.

Zacchaeus must not miss this truth. The Guest whom he had received under his roof was the future King of all mankind. If Zacchaeus invested his life and his resources as fully as his initial commitments suggested he might, he could actually share the power of God's coming kingdom. And he could share it on a scale that was commensurate with his own dedication to the King.

The second servant has not used his life's potential as well. Still, he has earned a significant return on his Lord's investment. He has earned five minas. To him the King replies, "You also be over five cities" (Luke 19:19).

A thought-provoking response indeed. This time there was no "well done" as there had been for the first servant. There had been no explicit reproof either. And there was a significant reward. Clearly, this servant was a "middle man" whose life merited neither unqualified praise nor sweeping rebuke. Zacchaeus should ponder this. His commitment to generosity had been wonderfully open-handed. Let him beware lest a tendency to retreat from this should diminish the ultimate value of his investment.

Why should he aim for only five cities? Why not aim for the unstinting praise of his new-found Lord and Master?

But there was another servant. He had done nothing with his mina, except to wrap it in a cloth and hide it (Luke 19:20). His excuse for this was his fear of the severity of his Master. His was a Master who did not concern Himself only with His own activities. He was concerned with that of others as well. He expected to collect what he had not personally deposited and to reap what He had not personally sown. Clearly, He was a demanding Lord (Luke 19:22).

To this timid figure the King replies:

> "Out of your own mouth I will judge you, you wicked servant. You knew that I was an austere man, collecting what I did not deposit and reaping what I did not sow. Why then did you not put my money in the bank, that at my coming I might have collected it with interest?" (Luke 19:22-23).

The excuse made by the unproductive servant was invalid. His fearful recognition that his Lord expected gains from the efforts of others should have driven him to the appropriate activity. But it had not. Like Paul, he knew "the terror of the Lord," but unlike Paul this did not spur him to service (2 Cor 5:11).

His Master now turns solemnly to those standing around Him (this is no private audience, but a public one). His words are sobering:

> "And he said to those who stood by, 'Take the mina from him, and give it to him who has ten minas.' (But they said to him, 'Master, he has ten minas.') For I say to you, that to everyone who has will be given; and from him who does not have, even what he has will be taken away from him" (Luke 19:24-26).

Life's opportunity had been lost. The mina was gone. It was put into the hands of the faithful servant whose opportunities, now represented by *ten* minas, are augmented even further.

The wicked, slothful servant had nothing to show for the opportunity he had been given. So even the opportunity itself is taken away from him. A kingdom had come where the possibilities for serving the King were richer and more varied than anything one had ever known before. The man who had served well with his one mina now found a fresh and challenging door opened to him. He could now serve his Master more fully by ruling ten cities for Him.

The unfaithful servant found that same door closed—decisively and completely.

No doubt it would be embarrassing. But it would be much more than that. In that moment when a servant of Christ might long more genuinely than ever for the chance to do something significant for his Savior, the golden portal into such service was barred forever. The Christian was face to face with the Master who loved him—and whom he had failed. The cost in wasted potential was staggering.

Zacchaeus could think about that if he were ever tempted to renege on his new commitment to generosity. A return to selfish living was the most imprudent step he could possibly contemplate. To do that would be to wrap his mina in a handkerchief. To do that would be to throw his life completely away.

8
To Receive a Kingdom

In a real sense, the King had denied his unfaithful servant. He had *denied* him approval and given him rebuke instead. He had denied that servant the opportunity to serve and had given the opportunity to another instead.

This truth had deeply ingrained itself in the thinking of the early church, and found expression in a nicely crafted "faithful saying" designed to admonish Christians. Paul spoke of it in his second letter to Timothy:

> This is a faithful saying: For if we died with Him, we shall also live with Him. If we endure, we shall also reign with Him. If we deny Him, He also will deny us. If we are faithless, He remains faithful; He cannot deny Himself (2 Tim 2:11-13).

Much Christian truth is wrapped up in these pithy, memorable expressions. Very neatly they balance Christian certitudes with Christian responsibilities.

To one who knew Pauline thought, as Timothy certainly did, it was clear that all Christians had died in spiritual union with Christ and were thus destined to live with Him. Truly, they could already do so as their oneness with Him was realized in personal experience (Rom 6:1-14; Gal 2:20). But their eternal future was sure: they would "live together with Him" (1 Thess 5:9-10).

Equally certain was the truth formulated at the conclusion of the faithful saying. If we Christians were "faithless," this in no way affected His loyalty to us. Every guarantee that had been made to us in grace would still be ours, regardless of our lack of faith or fidelity. (The Greek word for "faithless" covers both possibilities.) "The gifts and the calling of God" were still "irrevocable" (Rom 11:29).

For Him to act otherwise toward us, whatever form our faithlessness might take, was unthinkable. Our Lord always remained faithful to us precisely because anything else would be an act that *denied* His own nature and character. As the prophet had said long ago:

> Righteousness shall be the belt of His loins,
> And faithfulness the belt of His waist (Isa 11:5).

But between these pillars of certainty ("We shall also live with Him" and "He remains faithful") lay alternatives that were fully conditional. The conditional elements were: "If we endure," "If we deny," and "If we are faithless."

Since it was quite conceivable that we could be "faithless," it was also conceivable that we might not "endure." But if we did not endure, neither could we reign with Him. In like fashion, a failure to endure could become a form of denial.

There was, in fact, more than one way of "denying" one's Master. The denial could take a verbal form and involve an unwillingness to confess Him and identify with Him before men. Or one could deny Him by works that were unsuited to a Christian profession (Titus 1:16).

In either case our denial would be appropriately recompensed by His denial of us. Not, of course, a rejection of our status before Him as redeemed and justified people. *That kind* of denial would touch the question of His own faithfulness.

But the kind of denial experienced by the unfaithful servant in the parable of the ten minas was all too solemn a possibility. This was not a rejection of this man's position in the family of God. It was rather a rejection of his role *as a servant*. Since that role had not been carried out during his earthly life, it could not be carried out in the kingdom either.

In short, the unproductive servant was not allowed to reign with His Lord. That priceless privilege of service was denied to him. He was judged according to his works.

Heirs of the Kingdom

It should be obvious that the faithless servant of our Savior's parable was not an heir of the kingdom of God. It *should* be—but to many it is not.

Here again the shadow cast by the eclipse of grace has darkened our understanding of many Scriptures that would otherwise be clear and plain to us. To many of the Lord's people, when one speaks of "inheriting" the kingdom one is only talking about *getting into it*.[32]

Few equations are more gratuitous and superficial. Why should "inherit" equal "enter"? There is no good reason. Purely on the grounds of ordinary usage, "entering a house" or even "living there" are not the same as "inheriting a house." The latter speaks of ownership in a way that the former does not.

Nor was Biblical usage any different. In normal Old Testament usage an "inheritance" referred especially to

---

[32] Although it is very common to equate "entering" the kingdom with "inheriting" it, this equation is not universally made. See the extended discussion of the difference in Kenneth F. Dodson, *The Prize of the Up-Calling* (Grand Rapids: Baker Book House, 1969), 121-42. In the Septuagint the expression "to inherit a/the kingdom" apparently does not occur. The closest analogy to this seems to be 1 Maccabees 2:57, "David, because he was merciful, inherited the throne of the kingdom for ever." See *The Oxford Annotated Apocrypha*, ed. by Bruce M. Metzger (New York: Oxford University Press, 1977), 226. But it should be pointed out that the very similar idea, "to inherit the land," is frequent in the sense of "to possess (own) the land." Moreover, the difference between "entering" and "inheriting" the land can be seen in 1 Esdras 8:83 ("'The land which you are entering to take possession of [Greek, inherit] it is a land polluted...'") and in Neh 9:15 (" And told them to go in to possess [Greek, inherit] the land..."). In these texts the action of "entering" the land is antecedent to, and for the purpose of, "taking possession" of the land. The actions involved are *not* synonymous.

property that one owned, particularly what was passed down through a family or a tribe.

For example, the property that had belonged to Zelophehad of the tribe of Manasseh—which is called his "inheritance" (Num 36:2)— had been passed to his five daughters in the absence of any sons. But their "inheritance" was safeguarded for the tribe of Manasseh by the Mosaic stipulation that the daughters must marry within their own tribe. Hence Moses laid down a rule that was binding on all the tribes and safeguarded the tribal properties:

> "So the *inheritance* of the children of Israel shall not change hands from tribe to tribe, for every one of the children of Israel shall keep the *inheritance* of the tribe of his fathers. And every daughter who possesses an *inheritance* in any tribe of the children of Israel shall be the wife of one of the family of her father's tribe, so that the children of Israel each may possess the *inheritance* of his fathers. Thus no *inheritance* shall change hands from one tribe to another, but every tribe of the children of Israel shall keep its own *inheritance*" (Num 36:7-9, emphasis added).

"Inheritance" and "property," then, were often convertible ideas. To inherit was thus to "own" or "possess."

There was nothing strange about the concept of "living" in a land where one had no "inheritance" or property. Thus the Old Testament speaks frequently of the "strangers" who "sojourned" among the people of Israel. If a "stranger" underwent circumcision he could even be treated as a "native of the land" (Exod 12:48-49), but the Old Testament does not speak of such people as having an "inheritance," since property rights were assigned to the Israelite tribes themselves.

Similarly, the Levites are expressly forbidden to own property in the land:

> Then the Lord said to Aaron: "You shall have no *inheritance* in their land, nor shall you have any portion among them; I am your portion and your *inheritance* among the children of Israel" (Num 18:20, emphasis added).

Shortly afterwards, we read:

> "For the tithes of the children of Israel, which they offer up as a heave offering to the Lord, I have given to the Levites as an *inheritance*; therefore I have said to them, 'Among the children of Israel they shall have no *inheritance*'" (Num 18:24, emphasis added).

From all this it is clear that, while "inheritance" is a multifaceted concept in the Old Testament, one could easily speak of people living within Israel's territory without their having an "inheritance" there.

In the same way, there is no difficulty at all in speaking of people who *live* in the kingdom of God but who do not *inherit* that kingdom. Indeed, we *must* so speak as is proved by a decisive statement of Paul. In his famous discussion of the resurrection, the Apostle writes:

> Now this I say, brethren, that flesh and blood *cannot inherit* the kingdom of God (1 Cor 15:50, emphasis added).

In the context this can only mean that mortals who do not possess transformed or resurrected bodies are barred from *inheriting* God's kingdom. But this cannot be synonymous with being prohibited from *living there*. Otherwise one could not account for the great, unregenerate multitude which follows Satan in his final rebellion at the end of the thousand years. This host, in fact, is all too mortal, for they are "devoured" by the fire that descends on them from heaven (Rev 20:7-10).

But obviously, not every untransformed human being in the kingdom will join this rebellion. After a thousand years, a multitude of regenerate mortals will have believed in the King (cf. Mic 4:1-3). But these mortal men and women are only *inhabitants* of the kingdom. They are not its *heirs*, as Paul's words make clear.

Paul does not intend to say that human beings in mortal bodies cannot *live* in God's kingdom. Rather, in line with the very basic sense of "inheritance" as that which one "owns" or "possesses," Paul means that only people in immortal bodies can *possess* this kingdom. And that's different.

Of course, neither does Paul say that *all* transformed or resurrected people inherit the kingdom of God. That is not true either. What he does affirm is that this inheritance cannot be attained by mere mortal "flesh and blood."

The heirs of the kingdom are its *owners*, not merely its residents or citizens. And they are, without exception, glorified people who have acquired immortality. Immortality is thus a condition, but not the only condition, for inheriting God's kingdom.

Meritorious Heirship

It is perfectly true that all Christians are God's heirs precisely because they are God's children. This fact is plainly stated by Paul (Rom 8:17a). But the Biblical conception of heirship is not the facile, simplistic notion that is so often suggested.

Without question, all Christians will inherit resurrection life. That is their birthright, as Jesus Himself affirmed:

> "And this is the will of Him who sent Me,
> that everyone who sees the Son and believes
> in Him may have everlasting life; *and I will
> raise him up at the last day*" (John 6:40,
> emphasis added).

Of course, this immortality consists in a sinless and glorious likeness to our Lord Jesus Christ. Thus Paul declared:

> For whom He foreknew, He also predestined
> to be conformed to the image of His Son, that
> He might be the firstborn among many brethren. Moreover whom He predestined, these
> He also called; whom He called, these He also
> justified; and whom He justified, these He
> also glorified (Rom 8:29-30).

These are impressive words and, as often stated, there is no break in this chain. Those who are predestined to conformity to Christ are not only called and justified, but ultimately glorified as well. This is the child of God's inalienable inheritance.

But Paul's words also show that the Lord Jesus Christ is viewed as "the firstborn among many brethren" (Rom 8:29). And every Jew instructed in the Old Testament law of inheritance knew well that the firstborn son received a *double portion* of his father's inheritance (Deut 21:15-17). The idea that one son might inherit more than another son was thus commonplace in Jewish thought.[33]

If we ask who owns or possesses God's kingdom, the primary answer must be: Jesus, God's Son, does. Accordingly, speaking of David—and of David's greater Son—God says:

> "Also I will make him *My firstborn*, the
> highest of the kings of the earth" (Ps 89:27,
> emphasis added).

Likewise, the angel Gabriel proclaimed to Mary:

---

[33] For a good summary of the rights and role of the firstborn son in Old Testament thought, see Erich Sauer, *In the Arena of Faith* (London: Paternoster Press, 1955), 127-31. For the view that firstborn rights may be forfeited by unfaithful Christians (who are nevertheless eternally saved), see G. H. Lang, *Firstborn Sons: Their Rights and Risks*, 2nd ed. (London: Oliphants, 1943). Lang thought, however, that failing Christians would be excluded from the millennial kingdom. See also our footnote 46 on p. 478.

> "He will be great, and will be called the Son of the Highest; and the Lord *God will give Him* the throne of His father David. And He will reign over the house of Jacob forever, and of His kingdom there will be no end" (Luke 1:32-33, emphasis added).

According to the Davidic covenant, David's son was to become *God's* son (2 Sam 7:14). The author of Hebrews applies this promise to Christ (Heb 1:5) and immediately afterward (Heb 1:6) calls Him the *firstborn*. His throne, in fact, is eternal (Heb 1:8-9).

Thus the *Son* is the Heir *par excellence*. Of course, His *divine* Sonship is eternal. But in terms of His Davidic *Kingship*, His Sonship had a point at which it began. This is quite clearly indicated in Psalm 2:6-7:

> "Yet I have set my *King*
> on My holy hill of Zion."
>
> "I will declare the decree:
> The Lord has said to Me
> 'You *are* My *Son*,
> *Today* I have begotten you'" (emphasis added).

Therefore, to this *Royal Son* God also said:

> "Ask of Me, and I will give *You*
> The nations *for* Your *inheritance*,
> And the ends of the earth *for* Your *possession*"
> (Ps 2:8, emphasis added).

The kingdom will be *His* inheritance and *His* possession. When God "set" His King on His "holy hill of Zion," He was duly recognizing Him as the Royal Son who has a right to reign. On the "Today" of His ascension, God said to Him, "Sit at My right hand, till I make Your enemies Your footstool" (Ps 110:1). When the time comes for Him to "ask" (Ps 2:8), God will give Him His kingdom—a worldwide dominion over all the earth (Ps 2:8-9). In that way, He will take possession of His *royal inheritance.* Until then, He sits on heavenly Mt. Zion (see Heb 12:22) waiting for that day to come (Heb 10:12-13).

Can Christians enter *into* this inheritance? Can they become *joint-heirs* (see Rom 8:17b) with the King?[34] They certainly can. But it is also obvious that this is a *meritorious* heirship, and not one conferred by grace alone: "If we endure, We shall also reign with Him" (2 Tim 2:12). The Scriptures bear powerful and repeated testimony to this truth. As we have seen already, the productive servants in our Lord's parable of the minas received ten and five cities respectively. The unproductive servant received none.

Similarly in the letters to the seven churches, the risen Christ conditions the sharing of His royal power on obedience and victorious living. So we read:

> "And he who overcomes, and keeps My works
> until the end, to him I will give power over
> the nations— 'He shall rule them with a rod
> of iron; they shall be dashed to pieces like the
> potter's vessels'" (Rev 2:26-27).

And again:

> "To him who overcomes I will grant to sit
> with Me on My throne, as I also overcame and
> sat down with My Father on His throne" (Rev 3:21).

Even in that grand scene which is described in the Book of Revelation, after our Lord has triumphantly returned to reign, we still encounter the theme of heirship. For there the

---

[34] Romans 8:17 distinguishes the two kinds of heirship as clearly as any text. The concept of joint-heirship is communicated by Paul through a sequence of words using the Greek prefix *sun-*, which is roughly equivalent to our prefix co-. We may paraphrase the text for purposes of clarity as follows: "And if we are children, we are also heirs—on the one hand heirs of God, and on the other hand co-heirs with Christ, providing that we co-suffer that we may also be co-glorified." The distinction is nicely picked up by Dodson, *Prize,* 134-35 (see footnote 33 on p. 381).

rulers of the world to come are described as having a "part" (NKJV)—that is, a "portion"—in the first resurrection (Rev 20:6). But the Greek word for "portion" can signify a *share* in an inheritance.

It is, in fact, this very word which the Prodigal Son used when he asked for his inheritance ahead of time. We could translate as follows:

> "And the younger of them said to his father: 'Father, give me the *share* of the wealth that is to become mine.' So he divided his assets between them" (Luke 15:12, Greek emphasis added).

In the Greek translation of the Old Testament, a synonym for the Greek word used in Luke 15:12 and Rev 20:6 often translates a Hebrew word that refers to a portion in the sense of an "inheritance." This is clear, for example, in the text quoted earlier:

> "You shall have no inheritance in their land, nor shall you have any *portion* among them; I am your *portion* and your inheritance..." (Num 18:20, emphasis added).[35]

The words of the Apostle John are rich with significance when he writes:

> And I saw thrones, and they sat on them, and judgment was committed to them. And I saw the souls of those who had been beheaded for their witness to Jesus and for the word of God, who had not worshipped the beast or his

---

[35] The Greek word *meros* (Rev 20:6; Luke 15:12) is used once in the Septuagint (Prov 17:2) to translate the Hebrew word *nahal* (inheritance, possession). The word *meris* is the one usually used in the Greek Old Testament to render *heleq* (portion), although *meros* stands for *heleq* once (Eccl 5:18). *Meris* is rare in the New Testament (5 times, all in Luke and Paul), while *meros* is common (about 40 times). It is highly probable that for New Testament writers other than Luke and Paul *meros* has largely replaced *meris* in the sense of "portion" (= inheritance).

> image, and had not received his mark on their foreheads or on their hands. And they lived and reigned with Christ a thousand years (Rev 20:4).

Here the theme of merit is unmistakable. The faithful martyrs of the Great Tribulation are rewarded with a *share* in Christ's royal power. What John wrote next has been widely misread. His words are:

> Blessed and holy is he who has *part* [a *portion*] in the first resurrection. Over such the second death has no power, but they shall be priests of God and of Christ, and shall reign with Him a thousand years (Rev 20:6, emphasis added).

It would be wrong to read these words in a vacuum. The text *need not* be construed as saying that certain people simply "take part" in the first resurrection. On the contrary, John's vivid statements must be read against the background of our Lord's parable of the minas and against the background of all the other Scriptures already noted.

What we have here is co-heirship with Christ. In this splendid sphere of existence which is called "the first resurrection," there are those especially blessed because they have a *portion*, an *inheritance*, there. And that *inheritance* or *portion* is described as an immortality which entails priestly and kingly duties.

So these are the servants whose minas have multiplied into vibrant opportunities for further activity for their Lord. They are the joint-heirs of God's firstborn Son, and this is their *portion*—this is their *role*—in the world to come.

Kingly Character

Since the superlative privilege of reigning with Christ is contingent on our faithfulness to Him, it follows that the joint-heirs are people whose personalities have been molded by a spirit of obedience. It is not surprising that the Scripture lays down character qualifications for those who aspire to possess a royal role in the kingdom of God.

Thus, as Jesus opened the Sermon on the Mount with instructions for His disciples (Matt 5:1-2), He said:

> "Blessed are the poor in spirit, for theirs is the kingdom of heaven" (Matt 5:3).

One beatitude later He declares:

> "Blessed are the meek, for they shall inherit the earth" (Matt 5:5).

And He concludes this segment of His message with the words:

> "Blessed are those who are persecuted for righteousness' sake, for theirs is the kingdom of heaven" (Matt 5:10).

The kingdom, says Jesus, *belongs to* disciples whose lowly and submissive spirits seem impoverished in a world of arrogance and pride. It *belongs to* His followers who are persecuted because of their righteous lives. And the earth will someday be the property—the inheritance—of the meek.[36]

There is no hint in such words that the kingdom *belongs to* men as a gift of divine grace. Eternal life belongs to men that way—but not the kingdom.

The heir of the kingdom must reflect the spirit of His Lord. His deeds and actions must be congruent with the

---

[36] Totally misconceived is the statement of Margaret Pamment that, "The Beatitudes offer encouragement and consolation, and they indicate the characteristics of those who will enter the kingdom, and thereby the conditions of entry" (Margaret Pamment, "The Kingdom of Heaven According to the First Gospel," *New Testament Studies* 27 [1981]:213). The premise of this statement is wrong and so is the conclusion. Matthew in no way indicates that such character traits are conditions for *entering* the kingdom. But, clearly, the kingdom belongs to those with such qualifications: Matthew 5:3 and 10 "frame" the Beatitudes. Verses 11-12 speak in terms of *reward*.

standards of his Master. When this is not so, heirship is forfeited. The writer of Hebrews made this plain when he warned his readers to take care "lest there be any fornicator or profane person like Esau, who for one morsel of food sold his birthright" (Heb 12:16).

The Greek expression rendered "birthright" here signifies Esau's special inheritance rights as Isaac's firstborn son. Being a man of low moral standards and little spirituality, he was willing to part with his rights for a temporary, physical gratification. "Beware," the author means, "that none of you do likewise."[37]

In a similar fashion, the Apostle Paul cautioned his Christian brethren against the forfeiture of heirship through immoral living. He wrote pointedly about this to the Corinthians:

> Do you not know that the unrighteous *will not inherit* the kingdom of God? Do not be deceived. Neither fornicators, nor idolaters, nor adulterers, nor homosexuals, nor sodomites, nor thieves, nor covetous, nor drunkards, nor revilers, nor extortioners *will inherit* the kingdom of God. And such were some of you. But you were washed, but you were sanctified, but you were justified in the name of the Lord Jesus and by the Spirit of our God (1 Cor 6:9-11, emphasis added; see also Gal 5:19-21; Eph 5:5-6).

It is unfortunate that these words have been so widely misconstrued. When the thought of "inheriting" the kingdom is reduced to a mere synonym for "entering" it, the force of the warning is largely lost.

The unsavory descriptions in Paul's list of vices had fit many of the Corinthians in their unsaved days. But God had mercifully washed their past away as He sanctified and

---

[37] See the treatment of Esau by Erich Sauer, *Arena*, 126-127, 152-53, 161-62.

justified them by His saving grace. Their past no longer stood as a barrier to heirship in God's kingdom.

But the present could, and this is Paul's point. "The unrighteous will not inherit the kingdom of God," he insists, and he has just charged them with behaving unrighteously:

> No, you yourselves *do wrong* [Gk = act unrighteously] and cheat, and you do these things to your brethren! (1 Cor 6:8, emphasis added).

But not only that, there was a case of incest in the Corinthian church (1 Cor 5:1) and the apostle will shortly urge them to "flee immorality" (1 Cor 6:18; see vv 12-20). Their present conduct imperiled their heirship.

This does not mean that if a believer commits one of these sins he is forever barred from reigning with Christ. Should he fall, God's cleansing and restoring grace can be his again (1 John 1:9) and he can cease to be a person like that.

But suppose Christ comes and finds me walking in unjudged sins of this kind? Suppose I am, at His coming, an adulterer or a thief or a drunkard or any of the other things mentioned here? In that case, the Scripture is plain. I am the kind of person who cannot inherit the kingdom of God. But these spiritual conditions, as deplorable as they are, do not jeopardize the Christian's *entrance* into God's kingdom. That remains a gift of God's matchless grace.

Be Ready!

No wonder then that the Scriptures lay such stress on how Christ finds us when He comes back. We have already read John's words:

> And now, little children, abide in Him, that when He appears, we may have confidence and not be ashamed before Him at His coming (1 John 2:28).

And Peter also admonishes us:

> Therefore, beloved, looking forward to these things, be diligent *to be found by Him* in peace, without spot and blameless (2 Pet 3:14, emphasis added).

But the most solemn warning of all was issued by the King Himself. On one occasion the Lord Jesus had spoken at length concerning the events surrounding His second advent. In the midst of this great exposition of future things—we call it the Olivet Discourse (Matthew 24–25)—the Son of God had inserted a parable designed to warn and challenge His servants.

He began the parable this way:

> "Who then is a faithful and wise servant, whom his master made ruler over his household, to give them food in due season? Blessed is that servant whom his master, *when he comes*, will find so doing. Assuredly, I say to you that he will make him ruler over all his goods" (Matt 24:45-47, emphasis added).

Here again is co-heirship with the coming King. The servant who is faithfully performing his duties, *when his Master arrives*, is elevated to a position with sweeping authority: "He will make him ruler over all his goods."

But another outcome for this servant's career looms as a somber possibility:

> "But if that evil servant says in his heart, 'My master is delaying his coming,' and begins to beat his fellow servants, and to eat and drink with the drunkards, the master of that servant *will come on a day when he is not looking* for him and at an hour that he is not aware of, and will cut him in two and appoint him his *portion* with the hypocrites. There

shall be weeping and gnashing of teeth" (Matt 24:48-51, emphasis added).

Naturally, we must not suppose, as many have done, that our Lord speaks here of an unsaved man. He is still talking about the same individual whom he has just described as a potential[38] ruler over His goods. The words, "But if that *evil* servant...," make this plain.

Moreover, this wicked slave is *not* an unbeliever at all. He actually believes in the coming of his Lord but has persuaded himself that this coming will be postponed: "My master is delaying his coming." But this was his fatal error. No longer moved by a sense of watchfulness, his lifestyle degenerates rapidly. He begins to mistreat his Christian brethren (his "fellow servants") and then to indulge himself with intemperate and base behavior. He eats and drinks with the drunkards.[39]

In this lamentable state of soul, the servant is utterly unprepared for his Master's arrival and for the day of accounting that follows. Indeed, his Judge cuts him to pieces.

Of course, Jesus was dealing here in metaphor. The English rendering ("cut him in two") is too precise. The underlying Greek verb can signify "to cut something up," and it should be evident that this expression is a figure of speech. Not even unsaved people will ever be *literally* cut to pieces. How much less *Jesus'* own servants.

But the day of accounting is nonetheless dreadful for the unfaithful servant of Christ. The "terror of the Lord" will

---

[38] Editor's note: The reason why Zane put *potential ruler* instead of simply *ruler* is because he understood the statement in verse 47 to be conditioned on perseverance. As long as a believer is faithfully serving Christ, the Lord will make him a ruler in the life to come. But if he ceases following Christ, then he will forfeit what would have been his, though, of course, he remains eternally secure.

[39] One should compare the warning of Paul against similar conduct in 1 Thess 5:4-8.

be, for such a man, only too real. And the instrument by which his failed life will be judged is sharp indeed:

> For the word of God is living and powerful, and sharper than any two-edged sword, piercing even to the division of soul and spirit, and of joints and marrow, and is a discerner of the thoughts and intents of the heart. And there is no creature hidden from His sight, but all things are naked and open to the eyes of Him *to whom* we *must give account* (Heb 4:12-13, emphasis added).

No doubt, for the kind of man whom our Lord's parable describes, the Judgment Seat of Christ will seem like an exquisitely painful surgery on his soul. The sharp, two-edged sword of the divine Word will "bring to light the hidden things of darkness and reveal the counsels of the heart" (1 Cor 4:5). Surely the agony of exposure will be indescribably acute.[40]

But in addition to that, there is no co-heirship with Christ. Instead—and the irony is powerful—there *is* co-heirship with hypocrites. For He will "appoint him his *portion* with the hypocrites. There shall be weeping and gnashing of teeth."

This servant had become a hypocrite. *Not* a hypocrite in the sense that he only pretended to be a Christian. Such a thought is totally extraneous to this text. Instead, he had occupied the position and role of a servant of Christ, and had ended by serving only himself. His role was ostensibly

---

[40] A very similar parable is found in Luke 12:42-46. It is followed, in verses 47-48, by a reference to the flogging of disobedient servants. Those who were ignorantly disobedient receive fewer lashes of the whip than those who disobeyed while knowing their Master's will. Here, too, we should conclude that metaphor is at work. The lashes can then refer to the stinging rebukes which the Lord will give to unfaithful servants. No doubt these will be deeply felt by those servants precisely because they are now holy and fully sensitive to their Master's feelings about them.

to feed his Lord's household, but instead he beat his fellow-servants and indulgently fed himself. And that was hypocrisy. Profound regret was its rightful legacy.[41]

Tragically, there is no reason to think that there will not be many such hypocrites standing at the Judgment Seat of Christ. Like the fearful servant in the parable of the minas they will hear their Lord's stinging rebuke, and it will be as though a two-edged sword pierced their innermost being. They will experience deep shame. They will weep and gnash their teeth.

Not forever, of course. Indeed, perhaps only for a short time. For ultimately God will wipe away every tear from their eyes (Rev 21:4). But those who cannot conceive of a Christian grieving deeply over an unfaithful life, and sorrowing profoundly over a lost heirship, are not being realistic. In fact, it is precisely the glorified saint, free at last from the deluding influences of sin, who will likely be most moved with unutterable sadness over a life that has been poorly invested for God.

To Receive a Kingdom

The nobleman in the Savior's parable went into a far country "to receive for himself a kingdom and to return" (Luke 19:12, see v 15). This statement was easily recognized as a reference to the acquisition of kingly authority. A virtually identical expression ("to receive a/the kingdom") is used in this very sense in the Septuagint (the Greek translation of the Old Testament).[42]

While the nobleman was away, His servants served Him. As they did so, they too were "receiving a kingdom."

---

[41] In the similar parable of Luke 12:42-46, instead of the designation "the hypocrites," we find the Greek words *tōn apistōn*. These words should be rendered "the unfaithful," as the context shows, rather than as "the unbelievers" (NKJV).

[42] The phrase in Luke 19:12, 15 uses the Greek verb *lambanō* whereas the Septuagint expression used the synonym *paralambanō*. For references, see footnote 43 following.

Their service constituted them "partners" with the coming King, and "co-heirs" with God's firstborn Son. But their service needed to go on right to the very end.

Should they turn from this service at any time, there was the danger that they would be overtaken suddenly by their Master's return.

This would be a calamity of unspeakable magnitude. They needed to cling to God's strength and rely on His grace, to keep on serving Him well. They needed to be aware of God's awesome holiness which, like an all-devouring flame, could reduce man's pretensions and hypocrisy to ashes. They needed to understand that they must someday meet their God in the Person of His Son and, with Him as their Judge, submit their lives to the fiery trial of His all-knowing gaze (cf. 1 Cor 3:11-15). It is understandable that at the climax of his powerful Epistle, the author of Hebrews writes:

> Therefore, since we are *receiving a kingdom* which cannot be shaken, let us have grace, by which we may *serve God* acceptably with reverence and godly fear. For our God is a consuming fire (Heb 12:28-29, emphasis added).[43]

---

[43] As is well known, the author of Hebrews is steeped in the Greek Old Testament. Here he uses a Septuagintal phrase (*paralambanein basileian*) which meant "to obtain the power of kingship." See the Septuagint rendering of the following passages (references are to the English text): Daniel 5:31, 6:28; 7:18; Bel and the Dragon (Apocrypha) 1; 2 Maccabees (Apocrypha) 4:7; 10:11. The original readers of Hebrews knew precisely what the author meant. One might even suspect an allusion to Dan 7:18.

9
The Darkness Outside

A time of great joy awaits the Heir of all things. For the present, He has gone into the "far country" of heaven to receive His kingdom. At God's appointed time He will return to reign and to rejoice.

The anticipation of this joy to come is nowhere more beautifully expressed than in the words of the writer of Hebrews, as he urges his readers to consider the Lord Jesus Christ,

> ...the author and finisher of our faith, who *for the joy that was set before Him* endured the cross, despising the shame, and has sat down at the right hand of the throne of God (Heb 12:2, emphasis added).

We are not left to imagine what kind of joy the inspired author of Hebrews has in mind, since he has spoken of it plainly in the opening chapter of this epistle. There, quoting the ancient psalmist, he writes of God's Son:

> "Your throne, O God, is forever and ever;
>
> A scepter of righteousness is the scepter of Your kingdom.
>
> You have loved righteousness and hated lawlessness;
>
> Therefore God, Your God, has anointed You
> *With the oil of gladness more than Your companions*"

(Heb 1:8-9, quoting Ps 45:6-7, emphasis added).

As the larger context of the psalm discloses, the first half of it (vv 1-9) describes a King who is fully triumphant over His enemies, whose throne is eternally established, and whose kingly joy is shared by His "companions" (or "partners"; Gk = *metachoi*).

The final half of the Psalm (Ps 45:10-17) describes a beautiful, regal woman to whom the King is evidently to be married. She is accompanied by virgins, her own companions (v 14), and she is challenged to forget her paternal home as she becomes the wife of the King (vv 10-11). Thus the psalm as a whole presents the splendor and festivity of a royal wedding.[44]

In this lovely poem, the psalmist no doubt foresees that future day of surpassing joy, when Messiah's eternal kingdom is established on earth and when the King celebrates His wedding. The royal bride whom the King marries is evidently not Jewish (Ps 45:10); and, in the light of New Testament teaching, this bride can now be understood to represent the largely Gentile Church (see Eph 5:25-32). From the time of the King's return, the church will live with Him forever as His queen.

This magnificent subject (the "good theme" of Ps 45:1) naturally finds a significant place in the teachings of Jesus Himself. After all, He *personally* was the King whose special joy in that day would exceed the joy of all others. But He would also have companions, or partners, to share this joy with Him (Heb 1:9). And these companions, or partners, must understand on what terms they could enter into the joy of their Lord, and what demands this privilege placed upon them right here and now.

To attain that joy, the King Himself had endured the cross and despised the shame (Heb 12:2). He now sat at the

---

[44] Craigie comments, "With respect to form, Psalm 45 is basically a *royal psalm*; specifically, it is described in the title (v 1) as a *love song*, and the substance indicates that the love song should be interpreted as a *wedding song*... There are no precise parallels to this type of psalm elsewhere in the Psalter..." (Peter C. Craigie, *Psalms 1-50*, Word Biblical Commentary [Waco, TX: Word Books, 1983], 337, emphasis his). No doubt the great beauty and uniqueness of the psalm both contributed to its influence on New Testament thought.

right hand of the throne of God awaiting the very subjugation of His enemies which the psalmist had so graphically portrayed (Heb 12:2; 10:12-13; Ps 45:3-5). It was precisely because He had loved righteousness and hated wickedness that His God had anointed Him with the oil of gladness more than His companions (Ps 45:7; Heb 1:9).

That was *His* reward! It would be no different for His companions. For although they could not love righteousness as perfectly as He did, nor hate wickedness as completely as He did, they could nevertheless follow His example and share His joy to a significant degree.

And that was co-heirship. It was to share royal dignity and prerogatives—and royal joy—with the King. So bright and luminous was such a prospect, that to be excluded from this experience might well be described as a kind of banishment into darkness, where such shining happinesses were beyond one's capacity to attain, or even to comprehend.

To put it another way, to be excluded from this honor was like being expelled from a royal wedding celebration.

The Man with No Wedding Garment

To make this truth vivid and real to men, Jesus once told a parable about a man who accepted a wedding invitation but failed to come properly dressed for the occasion. He was ignominiously put out into the dark. This parable has caused significant perplexity among Christian readers, mainly because its parabolic nature has not been kept clearly in mind.

Then, too, the problem has been compounded by the fact that in much of the Evangelical world God's rich grace has suffered significant eclipse. Parables such as this one are not read with the simplicity that a firm grasp of the Christian gospel ought to make possible. This multiplies the likelihood that their real message will go unheard.

The opening statement of the Savior's parable announces that "the kingdom of heaven is like a certain king who arranged a marriage for his son" (Matt 22:2). The invitations are then sent out and are refused. This is followed by a fresh round of invitations which are likewise spurned, but also the king's servants are mistreated and killed (22:3-6). The king then sends out his armies, kills these murderers, and burns up their city (22:7).

How skillfully does our Lord paint the sad history of the Jewish rejection of God's purposes. The kingdom He Himself preached to them (Matt 4:17) they were in the process of refusing. Their city, Jerusalem, was destined to be burned to the ground by the Roman armies, which God used as His instrument of judgment.

But the rich and special joys of the wedding celebration were not to be abandoned just because some had spurned them. The king's son must have companions. So the servants of the king are now sent on a wider circuit which this time included the highways beyond the city. These servants are urged to invite all whom they found (22:8-9). This they do without regard to character or attainment, so that we read:

> "So those servants went out into the highways and gathered together all whom they found, both bad and good. And the wedding hall was filled with guests" (Matt 22:10).

Of course, as our Lord had pointed out to the rich young ruler, in the full sense of the word, "no one is good but One, that is, God" (Mark 10:18). Nevertheless, from a human point of view, Paul could speak of a "good man" (Rom 5:7), and the two named converts of the Evangelist Philip—Simon Magus and the Ethiopian eunuch (Acts 8:9-40)—were opposites of the kind suggested in this parable. One was steeped in sorcery, the other was steeped in Scripture. But both, on scriptural testimony, became Christians (8:13, 38). The "bad" and the "good" were gathered in.

In like manner, the invitation to experience the special joys of the kingdom of God—the call to co-heirship with

Jesus Christ—is not confined to those with the special qualities which men find attractive and admirable. Instead, it is an invitation that has already overleaped the barriers of Judaism and proceeds along the highways of larger humanity, seeking only hearers that are willing to come, whether they be "bad" or "good."

But it is to the wedding supper itself, and not merely to the kingdom as such, that the call is extended. That certainly implies a saving belief in the message about the King's Son. But it involves more than that. It involves also a willingness to be His disciple, to love righteousness and hate wickedness as He did, to take up our own cross as He took up His.

In short, it involves a willingness to enter the kingdom prepared for its special privileges. It means coming to the wedding properly dressed.

What follows in the parable no doubt reaches its central point:

> "But when the king came in to see [or, observe] the guests, he saw a man there who did not have on a wedding garment. So he said to him, 'Friend, how did you come in here without a wedding garment?' And he was speechless" (Matt 22:11-12).

Naturally, some have thought that the garment lacked by the man in question was a "robe of righteousness" which the king would have given him freely. But the parable itself does not suggest this. Indeed, it seems not to have been the custom in those days.[45] The invitation to attend was freely given, but the one who accepted the call took it upon himself to obtain and wear suitable attire.

This man had failed to carry out an obligation which his acceptance of the King's invitation placed upon him. It is surely not hard for the Christian reader to detect in the

---

[45] See Joachim Jeremias, *The Parables of Jesus*, revised ed. (New York: Charles Scribner's Sons, 1963), 65.

appearance of the king, who then "observes" the assembled guests, another clear reference to the day of accounting which lies ahead for every Christian. In that day our garments—our life and its works—will come under God's scrutiny and evaluation.

To be sure, we have also accepted an invitation to *live* in God's kingdom. That destiny can be ours by simple faith alone and is never subject at all to divine review. But to set foot on the pathway of Christian living is to hear God's call to the highest privileges which eternity affords. It is to respond to the challenge to become joint-heirs with the King and to enter richly into His special joys. But before the celebration begins, there must come the review.

The next words are solemn:

> "Then the king said to the servants, 'Bind him hand and foot, take him away, and cast him into outer darkness; there will be weeping and gnashing of teeth.' For many are called, but few are chosen" (Matt 22:13-14).

Solemn, yes, but not so grim as they are usually made out to be. Most Christian readers identify the "outer darkness" as a description of hell.[46] They would be surprised

---

[46] It is right for G.H. Lang to say of the "outer darkness" that, "Few expressions have been treated with more laxity and liberty than this, though, seeing its solemnity, it should have received very exact study" (G.H. Lang, *The Parabolic Teaching of Scripture* [Grand Rapids: Eerdmans, 1956], 305). His point is well taken and his general discussion of the term is outstanding (305-308). Most of the observations made by the present writer are anticipated by Lang. See also, "The Outer Darkness," *The Star of Hope* 7 (Southern Hebrew Mission: August-September, 1964):1-4 (but the accuracy of some of the references found in this article is open to question). It needs to be pointed out that many of those who have not taken "the outer darkness" as a description of eternal damnation have thought that the failing servant of Christ was to be excluded from the millennial kingdom. But this involves a misperception of the imagery employed and contradicts the promise of 1 Thess 5:9-10, which guarantees to the watchful and unwatchful the privilege of living together with Christ. See Zane C. Hodges, "The Rapture in 1 Thessalonians 5:1-11," in *Walvoord: A Tribute*, ed. by Donald K.

to learn that the Greek phrase employed here is used only three times, all in Matthew (8:12; 22:13; 25:30), and nowhere else in the New Testament. It is true that Peter and Jude describe hell in terms of abysmal darkness (2 Pet 2:4, 17; Jude 13), but Matthew's words take a form distinctive to his Gospel. They might be idiomatically rendered "the darkness outside."[47]

Here one must keep firmly in mind that we are dealing with a parable filled with symbolic elements. The man's hands and feet are bound, our Lord reports. But no one takes this binding literally, even if it is thought that an unsaved man is in view. Indeed, the wedding garment he lacks is not literal, nor for that matter is the wedding supper itself.

The Savior's parable is a magnificent metaphor. It visualizes the kingly joys of God's Son under the familiar Old Testament image of a wedding celebration (see again Psalm 45). The invited guests are called to participate in these joys, and their wedding garments are symbols of their successful efforts to prepare themselves for these.

But the man who lacked the garment was unprepared for such special privileges. His activities in the kingdom of God thus come under severe restriction as his hands and feet are bound. Like the servant who hid the mina (Luke 19:26), the man is not allowed to be *active* for his Lord in the experience of joint heirship. The "darkness outside" is a powerful, evocative image for the exclusion he experiences as a result.

There is no suggestion here of punishment or torment. The presence of remorse, in the form of weeping and

---

Campbell (Chicago: Moody Press, 1982), 67-79. For more recent discussion on the relation of unfaithful Christians to the Rapture, see Zane C. Hodges, *Jesus God's Prophet: His Teaching About the Coming Surprise* (Dallas: Kerugma, 2006), 33-43.

[47] Thayer correctly observes: "the darkness outside the limits of the lighted palace..." (Joseph Henry Thayer, *A Greek-English Lexicon of the New Testament* [New York: American Book Company, 1889], 226).

gnashing of teeth, does not in any way require this inference.[48] Indeed, what we actually see in the image itself is a man soundly "trussed up" out on the darkened grounds of the king's private estate, while the banquet hall glows with light and reverberates with the joys of those inside.[49] That is what we actually see. *And that is all.*

But that is enough. We do not need to embellish the parable with the lurid colors of eternal damnation. There is no fire and brimstone on the king's handsome estate, no worms of corruption creeping out from under the boulders of his well-kept grounds. This is what has been read into the story. But it isn't there. A parable has its natural limits and these we must be careful not to breach.

Nor are we to deduce that the failing Christian will spend an anguished eternity in some darkened corner of God's kingdom with nothing meaningful at all to do. That, too, would be a grotesque distortion of our Lord's teaching.

No, it is enough to say that the failing Christian has missed a splendid experience of co-reigning with Christ, with all the multiplied joys which that experience implies. It is enough to affirm that he undergoes a significant exclusion from the "light and gladness, joy and honor" (see Esth 8:16) which the co-heirs experience with Christ. Whatever else eternity holds for him, he has at least missed *that*.

If he can view such a loss with equanimity now, our Lord makes it clear that he will not view it that way hereafter: "There will be weeping and gnashing of teeth." (The Gk = "Weeping and gnashing of teeth will be there.") The servant who is "tied up" in the darkness outside the wedding hall will be deeply remorseful over the loss he has suffered. In that situation, he weeps and gnashes his teeth.

---

[48] See G.H. Lang, *Parabolic Teaching*, 306. He points out, in connection with "weeping and gnashing of teeth," that Orientals are very demonstrative in their expression of grief. The phrase only sounds extreme to reserved Westerners.
[49] Ibid.

Therefore, the unfaithful Christian, like the ill-dressed guest, has missed the wedding supper just as surely as did those who spurned the invitation to begin with. So he joins the crowded ranks of the many who are called to co-heirship and misses the elite number of the few who actually attain it. And that is certainly worth weeping about.

The Unprofitable Servant

The rude guest who came to the wedding improperly attired is but another of our Lord's effective portraits of a failing servant of God. In him we glimpse again the servant who hid his mina (Luke 19:20-26), or the one who concluded that his Lord's coming was delayed and who slipped into a belligerent and self-indulgent style of living (Matt 24:48-51).

Thus we are not surprised when such a man emerges in a parable strikingly similar to the one about the minas. The story is found near the end of the Savior's great exposition of prophetic truth, called the Olivet Discourse. It is traditionally known as the parable of the talents (Matt 25:14-30).

Here, as before, we encounter the Master's trip into a far country and a commitment of money into the hands of the servants who are left behind (Matt 25:14). The talent was a substantially larger amount of money than the mina, and was a unit of monetary reckoning whose value was always high. Unlike the previous parable, the servants are not viewed as equal, but as charged with responsibilities appropriate to their ability to carry them out (Matt 25:15). This, of course, is simply another side of Christian accountability. The day of assessment will evaluate our performance in terms of the God-given capacity to perform. We will be measured in terms of our own abilities, not in terms of the abilities of others.

The servant in the parable who had the maximum ability and hence, the maximum responsibility (five talents)—performs well in his Lord's absence. He multiplies his Lord's investment 100 percent, gaining five more talents, and is suitably rewarded:

> "Well done, good and faithful servant; you were faithful over a few things, I will make you *ruler over many things.* Enter into *the joy of your lord*" (Matt 25:21, emphasis added).

It seems plain that co-heirship with the King is once again in view. This faithful man, despite what by common standards seemed a huge amount of money, is told that until now he has actually been the guardian of only a small sum: a "few things." His new position, by comparison, dwarfs his previous responsibility: "I will make you ruler over *many*" things. This pronouncement is followed at once by an invitation to *enter into* the King's personal joy.

It is an encouraging feature of this form of our Savior's parable that the second servant, though less competent than the previous one (he has received only two talents), has nevertheless maximized his own opportunities as well. He is able to give his Master also a 100 percent return—two additional talents. His commendation and reward are *identical* with those of his more capable brother (Matt 25:23). He, too, becomes a joint-heir with access to his Lord's joy at precisely the same level as the ten-talent man.

Obviously, such could have been the experience of the servant with one talent as well if he had but gained a mere additional talent. But he had not. And with words fully reminiscent of the reasonings of the servant who wrapped his mina in a handkerchief, this sad failure of a man digs up the buried money and returns it to his Lord.

The King's response to him stands in total contrast to His response to the faithful servants. Whereas they had received His warm *commendation* ("Well done, good and faithful servant"), this man receives His ringing *condemnation*:

> "You wicked and lazy servant, you knew that I reap where I have not sown, and gather

where I have not scattered seed. So you ought
to have deposited my money with the bankers,
and at my coming I would have received back
my own with interest" (Matt 25:26-27).

There is certainly nothing here to suggest an unbeliever. This was a man with real responsibility given to him by his Master, and the fundamental charge is that he had not acted on the knowledge of his Master's character which he himself admitted that he had. That the Judgment Seat of Christ is before us in this scene is an observation that ought not to require making.

It follows that the failing servant is denied the opportunity to rule—not merely only over many things, but over anything at all. Whereas *promotion* to additional responsibility had come to the previous servants, *demotion* from responsibility comes to him:

"Therefore take the talent from him, and give
it to him who has ten talents. For to everyone
who has, more will be given, and he will have
abundance; but from him who does not have,
even what he has will be taken away" (Matt
25:28-29).

Once more there is the tragedy of deprivation. Once more there is the equivalent of the bound hands and feet. And once more there is "the darkness outside":

"And cast the unprofitable servant into the
outer darkness. There will be weeping and
gnashing of teeth" (Matt 25:30).

At this point, of course, most readers lose touch with the obvious overall thrust of the parable and think at once of hell. But it is after all a parable! There are no literal sums of money—whether ten talents, four, or one—to be laid down at the feet of the Judge, either at the Judgment Seat of Christ or at the Great White Throne. Instead, as in the parable previously considered, we are in the presence of metaphor.

"The darkness outside" is the reverse of "the joy inside." The faithful servants *enter into* the joy of their Lord. The unfaithful servant is *excluded from* that joy. The image of the wedding celebration (Matthew 22) hovers in the background of the reader's mind and permits him to interpret the imagery properly.

The judgment of the two kinds of servants is thus skillfully contrasted. The faithful servants experience *commendation, promotion,* and *access to joy.* The unfaithful servant experiences *condemnation, demotion,* and *exclusion from joy.* The former reign joyfully with the King. The latter does not.

The Supreme Reward

No doubt eternity holds many special joys and many special rewards for the people of God. Even a cup of cold water given in the name of a disciple "shall by no means lose" its due reward (Matt 10:41-42). God never forgets anything that has been truly done for Him (Heb 6:10).

But the stress which the recorded teaching of Jesus lays upon the privilege of ruling with Him makes it plain that this is the highest reward of all. And for this, much more is required than an occasional good deed here and there. Certainly, when the Apostle Paul describes for us the fire that will test our life's work, his image is well-chosen for its impressive flexibility. Thus he can write:

> For no other foundation can anyone lay than that which is laid, which is Jesus Christ. Now if anyone builds on this foundation with gold, silver, precious stones, wood, hay, straw, each one's work will become clear; for the Day will declare it, because it will be revealed by fire; and the fire will test each one's work, of what sort it is. If anyone's work which he has built on it endures, he will receive a reward.

> If anyone's work is burned, he will suffer
> loss; but he himself will be saved, yet so as
> through fire (1 Cor 3:11-15).

The value of this apostolic instruction can hardly be praised too much. Suppose a man's works are utterly burned up, is his salvation threatened because of that? "No!" says Paul. "He himself will be saved." But the fiery ordeal of the Judgment Seat of Christ, through which he must pass, will not easily be forgotten.

But Paul's metaphor also permits us to visualize a man who builds largely with wood, hay, and straw, yet manages a pearl or a diamond here and there. The conflagration on the day of reckoning will be considerable, but there will also be something left to reward. And God, we may be certain, will do so with the generosity which is so much a part of His nature.

But a life largely constructed of perishable materials is obviously not what our Lord requires of His co-heirs. In such servants the Savior seeks an accounting in which His investment in them reaps a profit. This is evident particularly from the parables about the minas and the talents. Hence, a life "saved," rather than a life left in ruins, is what He demands of those who would enter into His royal authority and joy.

And those believers who fail to attain that kind of experience are like runners in a race who are disqualified for the crown. Such was the possibility that even Paul himself confronted seriously and sought earnestly to avoid (1 Cor 9:24-27).[50]

But if it was a race, obviously staying power was part of the process. It was necessary to reach the finish line, for only there was the crown of victory dispensed. Hence, amid the hardships and fatigue which the contest entailed, one

---

[50] Sauer summarizes these truths well: "Justification is a gift of free grace, but the measure of glorification depends upon personal devotion and steadfastness in the race" (Erich Sauer, *Arena*, 162).

needed always to keep this truth in mind: "If we *endure*, We shall also reign with Him" (2 Tim 2:12). Or, as the Son of God Himself had put it so effectively:

> "And he who overcomes, and *keeps My works until the end*, to him I will give power over the nations—'He shall rule them with a rod of iron; They shall be dashed to pieces like the potter's vessels'—*as I also have received from My Father*" (Rev 2:26-27, emphasis added).

These are the joint-heirs. They are the servants of Christ who endured to the end and share the kingly prerogatives the Father has given to His Son. They are the King's companions in unspeakable, eternal joy (Heb 1:9).

What a brilliant and glorious prospect. Here is a bright anticipation that offers the fulfillment of man's deepest aspirations. Indeed, through that unique mastery of words which the Lord Jesus so clearly possessed, this truth became a hope which shone before His followers like a distant banquet hall gleaming with light and echoing with the joy of a wondrous wedding celebration.

And once that scene has been truly glimpsed, who would want to be left in "the darkness outside"?

10

The Overcomers

No earthly banquet was ever so splendid. No roster of assembled guests was ever so impressive. The co-heirs of King Jesus are the elite of human history. To be numbered among them is the highest honor—and greatest victory—which any man or woman can achieve.[51]

But what is it that really makes an overcomer? What are the secrets of his victorious life? Some of these secrets have already come before us in the various Scriptures pertaining to this theme. But some deserve special stress from passages which have not yet been considered.

Spiritual victory is not an accident. It is the outworking of the fundamental truths and principles which permeate the Word of God. The would-be overcomer needs to grasp these principles firmly. He needs to live these truths out in daily life.

Abundant Faith

Without exception, the overcomer is a man or a woman of great faith.

It was apparently not long after completing his famous Sermon on the Mount (Matt 5–7) that Jesus encountered a Gentile with remarkable faith (Matt 8:5-13). He was a Roman centurion whose servant was desperately sick. But so great was this man's confidence in the word of Jesus that he was able to say to Him:

> "Lord, I am not worthy that You should come under my roof. But only speak a word, and my servant will be healed. For I also am a man

---

[51] Compare the hymn, "When He Shall Come," by Almeda J. Pearce.

> under authority, having soldiers under me.
> And I say to this one, 'Go,' and he goes; and
> to another, 'Come,' and he comes; and to my
> servant, 'Do this,' and he does it" (Matt 8:8-9).

Clearly, here was a man with supreme confidence in the *authority* of the word of Jesus. But it was precisely this note of authority that had astonished His audience on the Mount (Matt 7:28-29). Nevertheless, one could not effectively build his life (his "house") on Jesus' words (see Matt 7:24-27) unless he had confidence like that of the centurion in Jesus' authority.

No wonder the centurion's words elicit from Jesus not only high praise but His very first recorded reference to the banquet of co-heirship:

> When Jesus heard it, He marveled, and said
> to those who followed, "Assuredly, I say to
> you, I have not found such great faith, not
> even in Israel! And I say to you that many
> will come from east and west, and sit down
> [recline] with Abraham, Isaac, and Jacob in
> the kingdom of heaven. But the sons of the
> kingdom will be cast into outer darkness [the
> darkness outside]. There will be weeping and
> gnashing of teeth" (Matt 8:10-12).

It is unmistakable that our Lord's great metaphor about the wedding supper shimmers in the background of these words. The imagery will later be developed more fully by the master Teacher of men, but it is here already in embryonic form.

Abraham, Isaac, and Jacob are *reclining* in the kingdom of heaven. The word used for this was quite commonly employed to describe someone reclining at a table to eat food. One begins to visualize some great chamber or room in which these Old Testament worthies are assembled to dine with many others from the east and west. Since great banquets were normally held in the ancient Middle East at night, by inference one can conceive of "the darkness outside" as the region just beyond the brightly lighted hall where the festivities take place.

Unlike the discourses in Matt 22:1-14 and 25:14-30, which are clearly parables, Matt 8:11-12 does not have the form of a parable. We can therefore understand it as referring to a *literal* banquet attended only by the co-heirs. As the banquet is about to begin, those present in the banquet hall who are not entitled to attend are asked to leave (= "cast out"). As the "disqualified" walk outside into the darkness of the night, weeping and mourning can be heard. The Greek expression literally reads, "weeping and gnashing of teeth will be there" (v 12).

The concept of a literal banquet for the co-heirs seems to be verified in Heb 12:23 where the Greek can be more literally rendered: "[you have come] to the festal gathering and assembly of first born *persons*." The Greek term translated "first born" is *prōtotakōn* which clearly alludes to the first born inheritance rights (*prōtotokia*) that Esau "sold" for "one meal" (Heb 12:16). The "first born ones" would then be the King's "companions," or "partners," in His kingdom (Heb 1:8-9; see the discussion on pp. 473-475 of this book).

Clearly, in this first use of the expression "the darkness outside" (a phrase found only in Matthew), our Lord's teaching about this "festal gathering" sets the background for the parables in Matthew 22 and 25. The literal occasion (found in chapter 8) is elevated in 22 and 25 to the level of a powerful metaphor describing access to—or exclusion from—co-heirship with the King.

And one thing is clear: the guest list at this "festal assembly" is impressive. It includes the three patriarchs of the Jewish race, who in their own right were men of great faith (see Heb 11:8-16). And it includes Gentiles—like this centurion—who will come from the far corners of the earth to celebrate with the illustrious heroes of days gone by.

But almost equally impressive is the roster of the excluded: "But the sons of the kingdom will be cast into the darkness outside" (emphasis added).

The "sons of the kingdom"? What a surprise. Yet in quoting this expression from the lips of Jesus, Matthew employs a phrase which (like "the darkness outside") is found only in his Gospel. Indeed, its only other occurrence in the entire New Testament is in the Savior's interpretation of the wheat and the tares, as reported in Matt 13:36-43. "The good seed"—the wheat—"are the sons of the kingdom," said Jesus, "but the tares are the sons of the wicked one" (Matt 13:38).

So it was not that "the sons of the kingdom" did not belong in the kingdom. They *did* belong there, as the tares did not. But they did not belong at the same *banquet* as Abraham, Isaac, and Jacob unless—like the centurion—they were people of great faith.

These words were directed at Jews. It was not that Jesus had not found *faith* in Israel. He had found it there. But He had not found *"such great faith"* in Israel. He had not found faith like that which He had just now encountered in this centurion.

The crowds on the Mount who had listened to Jesus' sermon *"were astonished"* at His authority (Matt 7:28). The centurion *believed* it!

Yes, faith got a man into God's kingdom and made him a son of that kingdom. But *great* faith could get him into the banquet. And there were Jewish sons of the kingdom who would miss that banquet (while Gentiles from many quarters were admitted) unless their faith could be stretched beyond its present restricted limits. Precisely for this reason, the Roman centurion was a striking challenge to all to trust Christ's word completely and to construct one's life on the bedrock of His unshakable authority.

Great faith was thus often found in unlikely persons, like this Gentile. And for that reason, it was often found also among the poor.

Indeed, it was James, the Lord's own natural half-brother, who was later to write:

> Listen, my beloved brethren: Has God not chosen the poor of this world to be *rich in faith* and *heirs of the kingdom* which He promised to those who love Him? (Jas 2:5, emphasis added).

James' readers had been making a mistake. They had been honoring the rich and slighting the poor (2:1-4). What a miscalculation that was. More often than not it was the Christian of little means who had a wealth of faith and thus was destined to become a co-heir with Jesus Christ, a co-possessor of His kingdom.

It was hard for a man who trusted in riches even to *enter* God's kingdom (Mark 10:24). And that took only a simple act of faith. But what of the lofty demands which devoted discipleship made on the would-be heir? That required *much* faith. And material destitution was often fertile soil for that kind of faith. The man who must trust God for the next meal will soon find he can trust Him for everything else as well. But material well-being was often—though not always—hard, resistant ground in which faith, if it existed there at all, thrived poorly.

Not surprisingly Jesus Himself said to disciples who knew the meaning of earthly poverty: "Blessed are you poor, For yours is the kingdom of God" (Luke 6:20). If one must choose it would be far better to have little material wealth and an abundance of faith in God. After all, God's kingdom *belonged* to people like that. No doubt a rich Christian could attain to co-heirship, but—James' words imply—their numbers were few.

Devotion to Christ

But another trait also marked the heir of God's kingdom. God had promised that kingdom, said James, "to those who love Him" (Jas 4:5). And great faith in God flourished naturally in an atmosphere of love for God.

In fact, as Jesus Himself made clear, love for Him stood at the root of a life of obedience (John 14:21-24), which in turn is the life of faith (Gal 2:20). Not surprisingly it was to disciples who had proved their devotion to Him that Jesus said:

> "But you are those who have continued with Me in My trials. And I bestow upon you a kingdom, just as My Father bestowed one upon Me, that you may eat and drink at My table in My kingdom, and sit on thrones judging the twelve tribes of Israel" (Luke 22:28-30).

This is co-heirship described here in literal terms rather than in parable. The apostles had been loyal to Jesus during His earthly trials (all except unregenerate Judas who may already have left the room). The reward for this fidelity was a kingdom in which they would have distinct spheres of royal authority.[52] They were to serve as the King's regents over the twelve tribes of Israel. So prestigious and honorable was such a role that, when the King sat down to eat in His royal palace at the head table, these men would be privileged to sit there with Him.

"You…have continued with Me," said Jesus, knowing full well that before the night was over they would all forsake Him and flee. But he also foresaw their restoration and future usefulness (see Luke 22:31-32). He had given them a splendid appointment, which their subsequent apostolic careers fully ratified and confirmed. These men really loved Him (John 21:15-19). And because they did, they endured. Hence, they shall also reign with Him.

---

[52] Over a century ago, A. B. Bruce artfully interpreted the Lord's words in this way: "Ye have done nobly, and noble shall be your reward…" Alexander Balmain Bruce, *The Parabolic Teaching of Christ* (New York: A.C. Armstrong & Son, 1892), 493.

Kindness to Christ's Brethren

But who can love the King, without also loving those who belong to the King? Thus the future co-heirs are marked by their kindness to Christ's brethren, however costly or dangerous such kindness may be.

Nowhere is this more clearly seen than in the co-heirs who come before the King immediately after the trying days of the Great Tribulation. In a passage often referred to as the judgment of the sheep and the goats, we are told how the living Gentiles are gathered before the King's glorious throne and separated into two differing groups (Matt 25:31-33).

The sheep, who stand at the King's right hand, are saluted as heirs of the kingdom:

> "Come, you blessed of My Father, *inherit the kingdom* prepared for you from the foundation of the world: for I was hungry and you gave Me food; I was thirsty and you gave Me drink; I was a stranger and you took Me in; I was naked and you clothed Me; I was sick and you visited Me; I was in prison and you came to Me" (Matt 25:34-36, emphasis added).

Once again, as in *all* the New Testament texts that deal with inheriting the kingdom, the stress on merit and good works, or good character, is plain and unmistakable. The kingdom is not inherited by faith alone, it is only entered that way.

The goats are wicked people who have done none of the good things that the sheep have done. They are sent away into everlasting punishment (Matt 25:46). They are unsaved.

There is no middle ground in this exceptional scene. There are no failing servants of Christ. But the reason for that has been explained earlier in the Olivet Discourse. The Great Tribulation is a period of such unparalleled, globe-spanning catastrophe that it threatens the extinction of the entire human race. Accordingly, Jesus affirmed:

> "And unless those days were shortened, no flesh *would be saved*; but for the elect's[53] sake those days will be shortened" (Matt 24:22, emphasis added).

But, as if that were not enough, this stressful era will be a time when evil reigns supreme. The Beast and the False Prophet, who are energized by Satan himself, dominate the world politically and economically (Rev 13:1-8). As a result, many believers will succumb to the pressures of worldwide lawlessness and *will not be saved* from the ravishing judgments of the Great Tribulation.[54] Their lives will be swept away with millions of others. Their "houses" will collapse!

Jesus tells us this when He says:

> "And then many will be offended, will betray one another, and will hate one another. ...And because lawlessness shall abound, *the love of many will grow cold. But he who endures to the end shall be saved*" (Matt 24:10-13, emphasis added; connect "saved" here with "saved" in v 22).

---

[53] Editor's note: "The elect" here is Israel, God's *chosen* (or elect) people. If every living person died in the Tribulation, God's promises to Abraham would fail since there would be no Jewish people in natural bodies to populate the Promised Land in the Millenium.

[54] It may be pointed out that Matt 24:13, or its parallels in 10:22 and Mark 13:13, played a role in Augustinian theology (see his *On the Gift of Perseverance*, chapter 2). According to Augustine, perseverance to the end is a divine gift necessary for "final salvation." He states that "it is uncertain whether anyone has received this gift so long as he is still alive" (chapter 1). Thus, for Augustine, there could be no assurance of one's election before death. Indeed, all who insist on perseverance to the end as a sign of genuine faith must likewise abandon the doctrine of assurance. Augustine, however, held that one could possess eternal life and lose it (*Perseverance*, chapter 1). So in his view a man could be a true Christian for a time, yet not elect!

The sheep are Gentile believers whose love did not "grow cold," despite the arctic spiritual temperatures all around them. They have been careful for the well-being of the King's brethren, who are perhaps chiefly the Jewish missionaries who will spread the gospel during those climactic days (cf. Rev 12:17; 14:1-7; Matt 24:14).[55] Hated and hunted by the Beast, forbidden to buy or sell without his mark, these traveling servants of God will be utterly dependent on the aid of courageous believers. The unsaved world, deluded by the prevailing Satanic deceptions, will want nothing to do with such men.

Some of these brethren unquestionably are martyred, but will be raised to reign with Christ (Rev 20:4). Others, though perhaps surviving, will experience hunger, thirst, nakedness, sickness, or imprisonment. But the Gentile believers have ministered to them in situations like that, and in doing so (to their surprise) they have ministered directly to the King! For it was the King who confronted the world of that day through the preaching of these, His brethren. It was therefore the King to whom men responded.

The co-heirs have passed the test. They have endured to the end, and their lives have been saved out of the wreckage of a ruined world (see again Matt 24:12). But something more awaits them, for finally we read of them:

> "And these [the goats] will go away into everlasting punishment, but the righteous into eternal life" (Matt 25:46).

---

[55] Ladd holds that the "brethren" of this parable are Jesus' disciples who preach the good news about the kingdom of God. This is similar to, but obviously not identical with, the view taken by the present writer. See George Eldon Ladd, "The Parable of the Sheep and the Goats in Recent Interpretation," in *New Dimensions in New Testament Study* (Grand Rapids: Zondervan, 1974), 197-99. Ladd, of course, does not hold to a pre-tribulation rapture of the Church. Of course, young children below the age of accountability are not in view in Matthew 25. Perhaps they will grow up in, and repopulate, the kingdom (see Matt 19:14).

It must be remembered that "flesh and blood cannot inherit the kingdom of God; nor does corruption inherit incorruption" (1 Cor 15:50). At the moment of their encounter with the King, the sheep are people of flesh and blood. Their physical lives have been saved, but to enter into their heirship they must also be transformed. Hence, as this scene concludes, they enter *eternal life*.

Of course, they *already had it* by faith in the King. What happens here is that the heirs become immortal. They become possessors of resurrection life itself. No doubt the transformation will be instantaneous for them, as it will be for living Christians at the Rapture of the Church (1 Cor 15:51-53; 1 Thess 4:15-18), but the transformation is still essential. If they could not enter the resurrection state of everlasting incorruption, neither could they inherit the incorruptible kingdom of God.

But they do inherit the kingdom, and deservedly so. They have stood loyally with the servants of Christ during history's most trying times. Can any who aspire to heirship do less?

Watchfulness

If the great trilogy of Christian virtues is considered, all three are markedly prominent in the King's joint-heirs. *Faith* they possess richly, *love* they exercise vigorously toward Christ, toward His servants, and toward all (Gal 6:10). But *hope* also is a watchword of their earthly lives.

In a remarkable discourse with His own disciples, which is recorded only by Luke (12:22-53), Jesus condenses into brief scope an impressive number of themes that are related to coheirship with Himself. In public, He had just told the parable about the rich fool who laid up treasure for himself and was not rich toward God (Luke 12:16-21). It was then that He turned specifically to His disciples (Luke 12:22).

His disciples, Jesus warns, must be careful not to worry about their material needs. They must learn rather to trust

God for these (Luke 12:22-30). Their first priority must be the kingdom of God. Indeed they are to *seek* it (Luke 12:31). Why? The answer is impressive:

> "Do not fear, little flock, for it is your Father's good pleasure to *give you the kingdom*" (Luke 12:32, emphasis added).

Seek the kingdom, says Jesus, because God wants to *give it to you*.[56] He wants you to be co-heirs! But this truth has practical applications at the level of material life, for Jesus adds:

> "Sell what you have and give alms; provide yourselves money bags which do not grow old, a treasure in the heavens that does not fail, where no thief approaches nor moth destroys. For where your treasure is, there your heart will be also" (Luke 12:33-34).

It was excellent advice. (It was *not* a legalistic demand, as Peter's words to Ananias sufficiently show: Acts 5:4.) The disciple who truly seeks to acquire the kingdom must be preoccupied with heavenly, rather than earthly, treasure. He must handle the transient things of this life so that they abundantly enrich the life to come. Such is the pathway of the joint-heirs.

There follows these challenging words a fresh parable of Jesus which, though similar to others, is in some ways remarkably unique. In it, He says:

> "Let your waist be girded and your lamps burning; and you yourselves be like men who wait for their master, when he will return from the wedding [wedding banquet], that when he comes and knocks they may open to him immediately. Blessed are those servants

---

[56] Compare in the Greek Old Testament the references to "giving" someone a kingdom: for example, 2 Sam 16:8; 2 Chron 21:3; Dan 2:37; 7:27. The references are to the English text.

whom the master, when he comes, will find watching. Assuredly, I say to you that he will gird himself and have them sit down [recline] to eat, and will come and serve them" (Luke 12:35-37).

Perhaps none of the Savior's utterances about co-heirship are more deeply touching than this one. In this fresh articulation of that great theme, the wedding supper is viewed as *past*, and the Master as returning *from it*. This is significant and instructive.

In those parables in which Master and servants take part together in the wedding festivities the stress falls obviously on the thought of their shared experiences. The King thus has *companions* who *enter into* His personal joy. This is a rich and important truth.

But the parable under consideration looks at things differently. The metaphor of the wedding banquet is employed with that flexibility which is so useful in figures of speech. It is as though the King's joy has been realized. Now that it has, the time has come for His servants to rejoice as well.

The servants have been watchful for their Lord's return from the wedding banquet. Girded for service, and keeping their lamps alight during the darkest hours of the night, they have listened eagerly and attentively for His arrival. They are ready to respond instantly to His knock.

This must be rewarded. So, in a lovely reversal of roles, the Master becomes a Servant to His servants. For now it is He who girds Himself and directs them to recline at a table to eat. Then He personally serves their food, for this is their banquet. This is *their* time of joy!

Through the skilled imagery of the Savior, the King's banquet has become the *slaves'* banquet. Their devotion to Him—their unremitting watchfulness—have brought them a splendid experience of personal fulfillment. All their personal hungers are now satisfied as their Lord graciously ministers like a waiter serving the very finest of foods.

Such is the *hope* which undergirds the watchful anticipation of the co-heirs. During their time of waiting, the spirit of their service has been: "Lord, what can I do for You?" Hence the spirit of their reward will be: "What can I, your Lord, do for *you*?"

Let there be no mistake about it. Watchfulness is an indispensable key to the overcoming life which leads to co-heirship with the King. But watchfulness is always sustained by hope.

Conclusion

Naturally there are other passages that might well be considered in connection with the theme of spiritual victory and reward. One readily thinks of the splendid promises made to the overcomers in our Lord's letters to the seven churches of Asia (Revelation 2 and 3).

Although a detailed consideration of these promises lies outside the design of this book, a few words need to be said about them. Under the shadow cast by the eclipse of grace, the overcomers of Revelation 2 and 3 have often been thought to describe all those who attain final salvation from hell. Thus the promises are regarded as presenting the destiny of every saved individual.

This general view is commonly presented in one of two distinctly diverse ways. On the one hand are those who think that a true Christian can be eternally lost if he fails to achieve the status of an overcomer. On the other hand are those who teach that all who are truly saved to begin with will overcome.

When carefully considered both views have one significant feature in common. Both insist that there is no final salvation from hell apart from good works. When our Lord spoke of him "who overcomes, and keeps My works to the end," (Rev 2:26) He must (in these views) have been speaking of *all* who would ultimately escape damnation. Accordingly, those who did not keep His works to the end would go to hell. How far this conclusion is from the teaching of the New Testament as a whole will hopefully be quite evident to the reader of this book.

It is true that the Apostle John affirms that "whatever is born of God overcomes the world" and goes on to say that "our faith" is "the victory that has overcome the world" (1 John 5:4). Moreover, he adds: "Who is he who overcomes the world, but he who believes that Jesus is the Son of God?" (1 John 5:5).

Neither statement is in any way synonymous with the statements of Revelation 2 and 3. They are not only found in wholly different books, but also in contexts different from each other. To appeal to the letter of First John to interpret the promises in Revelation simply because similar expressions are used, is totally invalid. All good interpretation takes place *in context*.

What the Apostle clearly wishes to affirm in First John is that the very act of believing in Christ is a singular—and permanent—victory over the unbelieving world around us. Moreover, this victory is the reason why obedience to God's commands is not a burden to the believer (1 John 5:3-4; see Matt 11:28-30). But this is very different from saying that the Christian has no other battles to fight or that victory in every spiritual conflict is assured. When the text in First John is used to affirm thoughts like this, it is clearly being misused.

Indeed, conflict confronts Christians in a multitude of shapes and forms. In Revelation 2 and 3, the problems described in each church have their own distinctive character and nature. The victory won by the overcomer at Pergamos, for example, does not take exactly the same form as that of the overcomer at Thyatira. For that matter, no two Christian lives are exactly the same in terms of their struggles or their triumphs. The Risen Christ is Lord of each unique Christian assembly and of each unique person within that assembly.

In all the diversity which the conditions in the seven churches of Asia reflect, there is manifest struggle and the hope of victory through grace. These letters do not present victory as a *certainty*, but rather as an *aspiration* which each individual should pursue. The Savior's words are never to *them* who overcome, but rather to *him* who overcomes. Victory is not a *collective* right, but an *individual* attainment.

Clearly, the promises to the overcomers are rewards for obedience to the commands of the Lord of the Church. As one writer has pointedly observed, "A command that everyone keeps is superfluous, and a reward that everyone receives for a virtue that everyone has is nonsense."[57]

Two promises in particular have been thought to impinge on the eternal salvation of the overcomer. These are the ones made in the letters to Smyrna and Sardis. To those in Smyrna it is said, "He who overcomes shall not be hurt by the second death" (Rev 2:11); and to those in Sardis:

> "He who overcomes shall be clothed in white garments, *and I will not blot out his name from the Book of Life*; but I will confess his name before My Father and before His angels" (Rev 3:5, emphasis added).

---

[57] J. William Fuller, "'I Will Not Erase His Name from the Book of Life' (Revelation 3:5)," *Journal of the Evangelical Theological Society* 26 (1983):299. He goes on to say, "Surely the burden of proof is on the shoulders of those who would argue that the warnings are not genuinely addressed to true believers as they seem to be and that the promises are genuinely addressed to all believers (as they seem not to be). Hence the 'overcomer' is the individual Christian who enjoys special benefits in eternity for refusing to give up his faith in spite of persecution during life on earth" (299). Of course, this general view of the "overcomers" of Revelation 2 and 3 has a long and respectable exegetical history. See, for example. J. N. Darby, *Synopsis of the Books of the Bible*, 5: *Colossians-The Revelation* (Kingston-On-Thames: Stow Hill Bible and Tract Depot, 1949 printing):380; William Kelly, *Lectures on the Book of Revelation*, new ed. (London: G. Morrish, n.d.), 36; Walter Scott, *Exposition of the Revelation of Jesus Christ*, 4th ed. (London: Pickering & Inglis, n.d.), 64-65.

Both statements can be held to employ a figure of speech called "litotes," which is extremely common in literature and in everyday speech. Litotes is a way of making a positive affirmation by negating its opposite. The presence of litotes is often signaled by obvious understatement. For example, litotes occur in statements like: "that test was no snap" (= "it was hard"); "he's no superman" (= "he's weak"); "it's not a walk in the park" (= "it's tough"); "she's no miser" (= "she's generous"), etc.

The author of Hebrews uses litotes when he writes, "For God is not unjust to forget your work and labor of love" (Heb 6:10). It can be assumed that the reader already *knows* that God is never unjust or forgetful. The reader therefore correctly infers that the writer means something like: "God will keep your labor of love in mind and will stand by you accordingly."

Since the Christian readers of the letter to Smyrna could be presumed to understand that no believer experiences the second death, the statement in Rev 2:11 immediately suggests litotes (unfortunately, this *cannot* be assumed for the modern reader). Jesus promises that the overcomer will certainly suffer no hurt from the second death. But this sharply understates what must be the destiny of the victorious Christian. Hence the reader is left with a tantalizing inference like: "The experience of the overcomer is *radically free* from the second death."
This inference is very natural in the light of the immediately preceding words:

> Be faithful until death, and I will give you the crown of life (Rev 2:10).

This can mean: "Die for Me, if need be, and you will enjoy the *crowning experience* of life." Hence, in the promise to the overcomer, Jesus is saying something like this: "Though physical death may touch you here, the second death cannot touch you hereafter. Your experience will be much too wonderful for that."[58]

In a similar fashion, the words, "I will not blot out his name from the Book of Life" (Rev 3:5), at once suggest the understatement of a litotes. No Christian will have his name blotted from that book. His eternal identity rests on the fact that he is an individual whose name is written in heaven (Luke 10:20). And that is just the point. The litotes should be taken along with the following statement in the same verse: "but I will confess his name before My Father and before His angels." The whole verse implies: "Your everlasting name is *supremely secure*. For, as you stand clothed in a victor's garments, I will acknowledge that name in the august presence of My Father and before the holy angels."[59]

Abundant and triumphant life, superlative and everlasting honor, are thus the rewards held out to the struggling Christians at Smyrna and Sardis. The use of litotes in both of these promises is a way of imparting, through understatement, the delicate suggestion that the experience will excel the description that is given of it.

When someone says, "If you do this, you won't regret it," he means, "You will be very pleased with the reward." But he leaves the reward *unspecified*. Just so, our Lord is saying to the overcomers, "You will triumph greatly over the second death," and "Your name will possess a superlative

---

[58] Tatford clearly thinks in terms of litotes when he writes of the promise of Rev 2:11, "True life lay beyond. In no wise should he be touched by the second death and the very form of the expression but emphasizes the certainty of that truer and fuller life" (Frederick. A. Tatford, *Prophecy's Last Word* [London: Pickering & Inglis, 1947], 46).

[59] Tatford again interprets through litotes when he writes of Rev 3:5, "Practically every city of that day kept a role or register of its citizens... one who had performed some great exploit deserving of special distinction, was honoured by having his name inscribed in golden letters in the citizens' roll. Our Lord's emphatic statement, therefore, implies not merely that the name of the overcomer shall not be expunged, but per contra that it shall be inscribed in golden letters in the heavenly roll" (Tatford, *Prophecy's Last Word*, 62-63). His whole discussion here is worth reading.

permanence before God." But tantalizingly, the two litotes leave the details of each reward *unspecified*—and thus all the more challenging.

So rewards they most assuredly are, as are all of the risen Savior's promises to overcomers. And thus there is a sense in which this final book of the Biblical canon, through these challenging calls to victory, effectively punctuates the teaching of the entire New Testament on the subject of spiritual conflict and eternal rewards.[60] The figure who emerges from these portraits is a conqueror, just as Jesus was *the* Conqueror. The rewarded one is a victor worthy of co-heirship with the greatest Victor in human history.

And this is precisely the principle which is emphasized in the seventh and final promise to the overcomers:

> "To him who overcomes I will grant to sit with Me on My throne, as I also overcame and sat down with My Father on His throne. He who has an ear, let him hear what the Spirit says to the churches" (Rev 3:21-22).

---

[60] Alexander Patterson weaves together many strands of truth when he writes about the Judgment Seat of Christ, "Not a service done for Christ loses its reward. 'For his sake' is the criterion by which everything is to be judged. The sacrifices of the believer are then shown and rewarded. It is then the Beatitudes are completely fulfilled. Then those who have laid up treasure in heaven receive it with manifold interest. All losses are made good. Then it is the promises are fulfilled, made 'to him that overcometh.' It is then the righteous 'shine forth as the sun in the kingdom of their Father.' At this time the faithful servants are rewarded for good use of their pounds and talents....The rewards are of glory, power, and privilege. The glory, as has been shown by Paul, differs as one star differs from another. The power, as the ruler over ten cities is superior to the ruler over one city. Among the privileges seems to be nearness to the person of Christ. There were two who asked that they might sit on his right hand and left. Christ said this was to be given to those for whom it was prepared... In the distribution of rewards it is not against one that he came in at the eleventh hour" (Patterson, *The Greater Life and Work of Christ*, 316). This beautiful résumé of rewards truth was written in the nineteenth century. How little of it is understood in the twenty-first!

Such then is the call to joint-heirship. Such is the challenge of New Testament living. Its essence is superbly captured by a great hymn of the faith which needs to be sung in our day with increased appreciation:

> Am I a soldier of the cross,
> A follower of the Lamb,
> and shall I fear to own his cause,
> Or blush to speak His name?
>
> Must I be carried to the skies
> On flowery beds of ease,
> While others fought to win the prize,
> And sailed through bloody seas?
>
> Sure I must fight, if I would reign;
> Increase my courage, Lord.
> I'll bear the toil, endure the pain,
> Supported by Thy Word.[61]
>
> In the name of Christ the King,
> Who has purchased life for me,
> Through grace I'll win the promised crown,
> Whate'er my cross shall be.

The message in these words is Biblical to the core. Accordingly, it simply remains that "he who has an ear" should "hear what the Spirit says to the churches"!

---

[61] "Am I a Soldier of the Cross?" by Isaac Watts, written in 1724 and published circa 1726.

Epilogue

Even though Frank had dampened his spirits a bit, Jim continued to go to the group Bible study to learn all he could about rewards.

As an increasing number of passages in the New Testament were opened up to him, Jim saw the challenge of Christian living more clearly. He understood more deeply what the Bible meant when it said, "If we endure, we shall also reign with Him."

"I think I'll try to help Frank understand these things a little better," Jim said to himself. "I think he'll be thrilled when he realizes what it means to be an overcomer."

So the next day at work, on their break, the two Christian friends talked further about the meaning of Christian victory. It was the first of many such chats in the months that followed.

These were good days for Jim. He knew, of course, that struggles and trials lay along the path he had chosen. He was determined to trust God whenever these came. But the road was bright as he looked ahead—because it ended on a throne.

That was a healthy perspective to have. And if Jim could keep his heart focused on that, the shadows cast by the eclipse of grace would not darken his pathway anymore.

Scripture Index

Genesis
1:26 445
2:23 183
15:6 183
15:7-8 317
19:17 ..... 171, 407
32:30 .... 171, 407

Exodus
12:48-49 456
17:14 322
34:9 317

Leviticus
12:6-8 107
20:24 317
25:46 317

Numbers
16:5 232
16:14 317
18:20 ..... 457, 462
18:21 317
18:24 457
21 160
21:8-9 160
26:52-55 317
36:2 456
36:7-9 456

Deuteronomy
12:12 317
21:15-17 459
27:9-26 238
32:22-24 197

Joshua
2 185
2:20 185
17:14 317

Judges
2:6 317

Ruth
4:5 317

1 Samuel
19:9 239
19:11 ..... 171, 407

2 Samuel
7:14 460
12:13 227
16:8 497

1 Kings
11:1-10 327
21:2-3 317

2 Chronicles
14:13 242
20:7 183
21:3 497

Nehemiah
9:15 455

Esther
8:16 480

Job
33:28 407
42:15 317

Psalms
2:6-7 460
2:6-9 317
2:8 460
2:8-9 460
3:8 267
8 445
8:4-8 445
14:3 417
18:3 267
18:35 267
18:46 267
18:50 267
24 445
31:7 407
33:6 48
33:9 48
34:8 236
35:3 267
37:39 267
38:22 267
44:4 267
45 .... 474, 479
45:1 474
45:1-9 473
45:3-5 475
45:6-7 473
45:7 475
45:10 474
45:10-11 474
45:10-17 474
45:14 474
51 227
72:13 407
78:21 197
89:27 459
109:31 407
110:1 ..... 447, 460
136:3 57
136:7 57

Proverbs
10:27 .... 97, 172, 243
11:19 ...... 97, 172, 175, 229, 243

Proverbs ...
12:28 172
13:14 .... 97, 173
17:2 462
19:16 173

Ecclesiastes
5:18 462

Isaiah
9:18-19 197
11:5 454
41:8 183
44:3-5 293
53:10-12 400

Jeremiah
15:14 197
48:6 ...... 171, 407

Lamentations
4:6 239
4:9 239

Ezekiel
37:5-10 293

Daniel
2:37 497
5:31 471
6:28 471
7:18 471
7:27 497

Amos
1:4 197
1:7 197
1:10 197
1:12 197

Micah
4:1-3 458

Habakkuk
2:3-4 241

Haggai
2:9 242

Zechariah
14:16-19 402

Malachi
3:17 242

Matthew
1:18-25 52
3:15 400
4:12-17 399
4:13 43
4:17 476
4:25 401
5:1 .... 400, 401
5:1-2 .... 94, 464
5:1-3 107
5:2 400
5:3 .... 111, 464
5:3-12 401
5:5 464
5-7 ..... 399–406, 401, 487
5:10 464
5:11-12 .... 92, 464
5:13-16 401
5:17–7:12 402
5:17-18 .. 402, 403
5:19 .... 402, 403
5:20 ...... 400, 403
5:21-48 403
5:22 402
5:44 178
6:3-4 436
6:6 436
6:17-18 436
6:19-21 .... 108, 412, 425
6:20 413
6:24 117
7:11 92
7:12 .... 394, 402
7:13-14 394
7:13-23 398
7:13-27 .... 393, 404
7:15 395
7:16 395
7:16-20 395
7:21-23 ..393, 396
7:24 101
7:24-27 ..93, 100, 404, 488
7:26 101
7:28 490
7:28-29 ...93, 488
8:5-13 487
8:8-9 488
8:10-12 488
8:11-12 489
8:12 ...... 479, 489
10:22 494
10:39 414
10:41-42 484
11:2 231
11:3 231
11:28-30 500
12:12 178
12:33-35 395
13:35 224
13:36-43 490
13:38 490
13:55 52
16:17 234
16:24-25 408
16:25 .... 268, 414
19:14 495
19:16 416
19:19 419
19:19-26 418
19:22 415

Scripture Index

19:27 425
19:29 252
21:38 355
22 .... 484, 489
22:1-14 489
22:2 476
22:3-6 476
22:7 476
22:8-9 476
22:10 476
22:11-12 477
22:13 479
22:13-14 478
24:10-13 494
24:12 495
24:13 494
24:14 495
24:22 494
24–25 467
24:37-38 304
24:45-47 467
24:48-51 ...... 468, 481
25 .... 489, 495
25:14 481
25:14-30 ...... 481, 489
25:15 481
25:21 482
25:23 482
25:26-27 483
25:28-29 483
25:30 .... 479, 483
25:31-33 493
25:34-36 493
25:46 .... 493, 495
26:8 242
27:20-25 79
28:19-20 196
38-39 224

Mark
1:14-15 399
3:4 171
3:21 53
6:1-6 44
6:3 51
6:4 51
8:34-35 .... 408, 411
8:36-37 411
8:37 441
8:38 ...... 128, 441
10:13-15 420
10:17 415
10:18 ...... 417, 476
10:19 419
10:20 419
10:21 .... 419, 420, 421
10:23 .... 112, 424
10:24 .... 422, 491
10:24-25 112
10:25 424
10:26 424
10:27 .... 113, 425
10:28 425
10:29-30 426
10:30 253
10:31 428
12:7 317
13:13 494
14:4 242
16:9-20 302
16:16 .... 302, 302–303, 303
16:17-18 302

Luke
1:32-33 .... 137, 460
2:21-24 107
2:42 419
3:20 399
3:23 44
4:16-24 44
5:7 244
6:9 171
6:20 ..... 107, 111, 114, 491
6:27 178
8:1-15 63
8:5 65
8:6 65
8:7 66
8:8 66
8:10 67
8:11 67
8:11-15 63
8:12 67
8:13 .... 69, 105
8:14 71
8:15 72
9:18 76
9:18-26 75
9:19 77
9:20 77
9:22 .... 78, 79
9:23 .... 79, 84
9:23-24 408
9:23-26 75
9:24 82
9:25 .... 84, 86, 88
9:26 86
9:56 171
9:59-62 71
10:1 82
10:20 ...... 82, 503
11:1 76
11:1-4 305
11:4 .... 298, 305
12:1-3 435
12:15 411
12:16-21 ...... 412, 496
12:19 412
12:19-20 412

Luke ...
12:20 412
12:22 496
12:22-30 497
12:22-31 412
12:22-53 496
12:31 .... 412, 497
12:32-34 ...... 114, 412, 425
12:33 413
12:33-34 497
12:35-37 498
12:42-46 ...... 469, 470
12:47-48 469
14 .... 190, 189–200, 191, 192
14:9 355
14:26 190
14:26-27 189
14:28-30 190
14:31-32 190
14:33 189
15:12 462
15:18-19 386
15:21 386
17:26-27 304
17:33 243
18:9-14 400
18:11 367
18:19 366
18:30 253
19:2 444
19:8 443
19:9-10 443
19:11 ..... 443, 446
19:11-27 .... 310, 310–313
19:12 .... 446, 470
19:12-13 311
19:13 447
19:14 ..... 349, 447
19:15 ..... 448, 470
19:16 448
19:17 ..... 311, 448
19:19 ..... 311, 449
19:20 449
19:20-26 481
19:22 449
19:22-23 449
19:22-24 311
19:24-26 450
19:26 479
19:27 .... 447, 448
20:41-44 447
22:28-30 492
22:31-32 492

John
1:12 ..... 127, 191, 199, 398
1:12-13 298
1:18 429
1:29 ...... 231, 329
1:34 231
1:35-40 120
1:35-51 399
1:38-39 196
1:40-51 214
2:1-11 45
2:11 ...... 191, 214, 399
2:12 43
2:19-22 194
2:23 193
3 .... 160, 161, 163, 294
3:1-21 399
3:3 .. 87, 116, 298
3:4 194
3:5 .... 293, 293–295, 294, 295
3:7 166
3:8 293
3:14-15 .... 159, 161, 332
3:15 191
3:15-16 398
3:16 ...... 161, 191, 303, 338, 401
3:17 302
3:18 191
3:24 399
3:31-32 194
3:36 ..... 191, 279, 388, 398
4 34
4:1 399
4:1-2 ..... 196, 299
4:1-26 399
4:1-29 17
4:7 17
4:9 17
4:10 .... 17, 18, 36, 78, 124, 125, 155, 156, 392
4:11 194
4:11-12 18
4:12 .... 20, 194
4:13 69
4:13-14 ... 19, 156, 321, 359, 433
4:14 .... 19, 20, 48, 124, 199
4:15 20
4:16 21
4:17 21
4:17-18 41
4:18 .... 21, 157
4:19-20 21
4:21 23
4:21-22 22
4:22 23
4:23 22
4:24 22
4:25 .. 23, 77, 156

4:26 ..23, 78, 156	6:39 383	8:41 ....52, 193, 194
4:27 26	6:39-40 427	8:42 193
4:27-39 25	6:40 ...... 191, 458	8:44 193
4:27-42 399	6:47 ...... 191, 192, 362, 368, 387	8:48 194
4:28-29 157	6:50-51 359	8:52 194
4:29 ...28, 41, 48, 139	6:54 199	8:57 194
4:31 26	6:56 196	8:59 194
4:31-32 25	6:64 119	9:35 191
4:32 ....26, 31	7:3-5 53	9:36 191
4:33 27	7:15 44	9:41 235
4:34 .... 27, 29, 31	7:17 413	10:4-5 199
4:35 ....29, 38	7:25 269	10:9 ......302, 394
4:36 ....30, 31	7:35 194	10:10 ..... 251, 427
4:37-38 30	7:38 191	10:14 ..... 199, 397
4:39 42	7:38-39 294	10:25-26 200
4:39-54 41	7:39 ...... 191, 298, 302	10:26 199
4:40 33	8 .... 191–194, 206	10:27 ....198, 199
4:41-42 41	8:13 193	10:27-28 ......198, 198–200, 199, 200
4:42 ..42, 63, 163	8:13-59 193	
4:48 46	8:19 194	10:27-30 359
4:49 46	8:20 193	10:42 .... 191, 194
4:50 46	8:22 194	11:11-13 194
4:51 .... 47, 58	8:25 194	11:25 .... 191, 371
4:52 47	8:27 194	11:25-26 ....359, 369, 389, 427
5:24 ..... 152, 174, 192, 193, 199, 200, 208, 226, 271, 303, 321, 361, 368, 417, 429, 436, 448	8:30 ..... 191, 192, 193, 194	11:26 .... 191, 389
	8:30-31 ....193, 194	11:27 ....369, 389
	8:30-32 ....193, 194	11:45 .... 191, 194
		12:24-26 410
		12:25 408
	8:31 ...... 192, 193, 194, 196	12:42 193
5:25 417		12:44 191
5:34 302	8:31-32 ....102, 192, 194	12:46 191
6 34		13:23 429
6:29 ...... 163, 191	8:33 ......193, 194	13:23-25 120
6:34 194	8:33-47 193	13:35 227
6:35 .... 34, 191, 192, 199	8:34 102	14:6 ...... 219, 227, 395
	8:39 ......193, 194	
6:35-40 359	8:40 193	14:7 213
6:37 199		14:8 214
6:37-40 .... 192, 321, 433		14:9 214
6:38-40 309		

John ...
14:10 214
14:19-24 285
14:21-24 .... 215, 492
15 .... 196, 197, 198, 206, 227
15:1-7 196
15:1-8 285
15:4 197
15:5 197
15:6 197
15:7 197
15:8 197
15:14 184
17:3 ...... 204, 213, 397
17:4 29
19:26 429
19:26-27 .... 54, 120
19:30 29
20:30-31 ...... 163, 369, 389, 392, 398, 423
20:31 ... 157, 297, 388
21:7 429
21:15-19 492
21:20 429
70-71 119

Acts
1:14 55
2 .... 298, 301, 302, 303
2:36 297
2:37 297
2:38 .... 296, 296–299, 297, 298, 299, 300, 306, 349, 349–352, 351, 352
2:40 299
2:41 301
2:41-42 196
2:44-45 91
2:47 301
5:4 497
7:5 317
8 .... 301, 303
8:1 55
8:9-40 476
8:12 354
8:12-17 301
8:13 476
8:38 476
9:3-5 299
9:5 35
9:6 299
9:9 299
9:11 299
9:17-20 299
10 301
10:33 178
10:43-44 301
10:43-48 298
10:47-48 301
11:14-18 301
13:10 224
14:22 284
15 .... 146, 148
15:1 .... 145, 210
15:5 146
15:11 147
15:13-21 55
15:24 ... 145, 146, 147, 210
16:30 155
16:31 ..... 155, 387
16:34 155
19 .... 301, 303
19:1-7 .... 300, 300–301
19:2 300
19:3 300
19:5-6 300
19:10 35
20:20-21 35
20:27 35
22 301
22:6-8 299
22:10 299
22:16 ..... 299, 300
25:16 242
26:9-20 35
26:12-15 299

Romans
1:5 .... 278, 278–279
1:8 275
1:16 286
1:18–3:10 272
1:20-25 234
2 .... 270, 272
2:5 270
2:6-7 270
2:6-10 436
2:7 .... 270, 269–273, 271, 272, 436
2:10 .... 270, 269–273, 271, 272
2:12 436
2:13 .... 270, 269–273, 272, 273, 436
3 273
3:4 328
3:8 279
3:9 272

3:9-19 272
3:12 ...... 271, 417
3:19-20 .... 147, 436
3:20 ..... 270, 272, 403
3:21-22 134
3:21-26 .... 273, 298, 400
3:22 286
3:23 436
3:24 125
4:1-8 324
4:2 180
4:3 364
4:4 .... 364, 365
4:4-5 ..... 364, 432
4:5 .... 249, 290, 363
4:6 184
4:19-21 182
4:20-22 162
5:1 347
5:1-2 275
5:7 476
5:15-18 .... 250, 298
5:18 271
6 277
6:1-14 453
6:18 .... 102, 235
6:20-22 235
6:23 250
7 221
7:11 228
7:20 222
7:20-25 222
7:25 222
8 222
8:3-4 147
8:9 .... 245, 301
8:9-11 286
8:10 229

8:11 253
8:12-13 .... 276, 277
8:13 ...... 153, 172, 229
8:14 .... 275, 275–277, 276
8:15 276
8:16 374
8:16-17 .. 128, 307
8:17 ...... 130, 309, 310, 458, 461
8:29 ..... 308, 327, 459
8:29-30 459
8:30 ...... 308, 383
8:33-34 174
8:34 374
8:38-39 383
9:19-20 177
10:1-4 403
11:6 ..... 168, 252, 364, 365
11:29 ... 129, 192, 298, 453
13:11 354
14:1 284
14:9-12 430
14:10-12 .... 255, 260, 311
14:11 434
15:26 .... 209, 262
15:27 209
16:13 427
16:26 .... 278, 278–279

1 Corinthians
1 295
1:4-9 ..... 259, 261
1:8 .... 259, 259–261, 261
1:9 261

1:13-16 295
1:17 .... 295, 295–296
2:6 254
2:12 374
3 260
3:11-15 .... 260, 311, 405, 471, 485
3:12 433
3:12-15 174
3:15 ...... 260, 311, 312, 321
4:5 .... 311, 435, 469
5:1 466
5:1-2 134
5:1-13 315
5:4-5 246
5:5 354
6:6 314
6:7-8 314
6:8 .... 134, 314, 466
6:9 314
6:9-10 .. 313–318, 314, 315, 316
6:9-11 .. 134, 318, 465
6:11 ...... 134, 315, 318
6:12-20 .... 315, 466
6:15 .... 135, 315
6:15-20 203
6:18 466
6:19 203
6:19-20 .... 135, 315
6:20 ...... 203, 275
9:23 209
9:24-27 .... 154, 485

1 Corinthians ...
9:27 ..... 153, 286, 383, 405
10:12 ..... 247, 324
11:18-19 211
11:28 286
11:32 246
12:13 ... 296, 301, 304
13:12 442
14:20 254
15 355
15:1 257
15:1-2 256
15:1-11 354
15:2 .... 257, 256–258, 258, 353, 353–356, 354, 355
15:3-4 79
15:7 54
15:12 355
15:13 355
15:14 ..... 258, 355
15:17 ..... 258, 355
15:29 295
15:35-36 177
15:42-43 308
15:50 .... 457, 496
15:51-53 496
15:58 355
16:13 ..... 284, 286

2 Corinthians
1:1-2 283
1:13-14 283
1:15–2:2 281
1:21 283
1:24 286
3:2-3 283
3:6-9 147
4:2 282

4:3-4 .... 148, 159, 233
4:3-6 323
4:6 .... 167, 234, 299
5:7 286
5:9 311
5:10 .... 174, 253, 255, 260, 430, 434
5:11 ...... 311, 434, 438, 450
6:9 246
6:14-16 283
7:6-16 281
8:5 374
8:7 283
8:9 112
9:15 334
10:7-12 281
11:12-15 281
11:23-29 286
12:4 320
12:20-21 281
13 280
13:1 281
13:2-4 281
13:2-6 281
13:3 281
13:4 ...... 281, 282
13:5 .... 280, 280–289, 281, 282, 284, 285, 286, 287, 288, 289
13:6 287
13:13 209

Galatians
1 332
1:8 149
1:8-9 326
1:11-12 400

2:4-5 391
2:20 ..... 222, 223, 286, 453, 492
3:2-5 250
3:7 444
3:19-24 403
3:21 147
4:1-2 276
4:1-7 275
5:3 146
5:16-26 318
5:18 276
5:19-21 .... 318, 465
6:7-9 250
6:8 ...... 250–253, 345–348,
6:10 496

Ephesians
1:3 198
1:7 305
1:12-14 245
1:13-14 383
1:18 236
2 ..... 37, 275, 354
2:1 235
2:5 353
2:6 305
2:8 .. 35, 125, 353
2:8-9 ...... 37, 158, 264, 271, 353, 363
2:8-10 ..... 33, 159
2:9 36
2:10 .... 37, 158
4:1 .... 135, 203, 279
4:18 235
5:5-6 465
5:25-32 .. 137, 474
6:12 149

Scripture Index

Philippians
1:3-6 262
1:6 .... 262, 263
1:19-20 264
1:27-30 .. 265–266
2:12-13 .... 263, 263–266
2:14-16 266
2:15 266
3:10 310
3:20-21 .... 308, 442
4:3 269
4:10-19 262

Colossians
1:10 135
1:21-23 .... 253, 253–256, 355
1:22 ..... 254, 255, 259
1:22-23 255
1:23 ...... 254, 255
1:28 254
1:28-29 255
2:6-7 285
2:8 253
2:16-23 253
3:12 203
3:13 203
22-23 255

1 Thessalonians
1:10 304
2:12 135
4:15-18 496
5:1-11 304
5:4-8 468
5:9-10 ... 453, 478

1 Timothy
1:18-20 256
1:19-20 246

1:20 ...... 246, 281
3:10 254

2 Timothy
1:10 416
2:10-12 310
2:11-13 453
2:12 ..... 309–310, 461, 486
2:12-13 128
2:13 ...... 129, 328
2:17 247
2:17-18 232
2:17-19 256
2:19 ...... 232, 233
2:20-21 233
2:25 246

Titus
1:6-7 254
1:13 .... 278, 284
1:16 .... 278, 454
2:2 284
2:12 246
3 275
3:4-7 ..... 264, 301
3:5 249
3:8 405

Hebrews
1:5 460
1:6 460
1:8-9 .... 460, 473, 489
1:9 .... 245, 474, 475, 486
1:13 447
2:5 .... 243, 319, 445
2:8-9 445
2:9 236
2:10 445
2:11 241

3 244–245
3:1 .... 236, 244, 245
3:6 .... 237, 245
3:12 245
3:12-15 237
3:14 .... 244, 245
4:12-13 469
4:14-16 246
5:11 243
5:14 254
6 235–238
6:4 .... 236, 237
6:4-5 ..... 235, 236
6:4-6 237
6:6 238
6:7 238
6:7-8 ..... 238, 247
6:8 238
6:9 .... 243, 321
6:10 ...... 484, 502
6:11 243
6:11-12 237
8:1 243
10 238–243
10:10 240
10:12-13 461, 475
10:14 240
10:19 245
10:23 238
10:23-25 237
10:25 .... 239, 244
10:26 239
10:26-27 ...... 238, 239
10:26-39 238
10:27 .... 239, 242
10:28 243
10:28-29 239
10:29 239
10:30-31 241
10:30-36 241
10:32 236

Hebrews ...
10:32-34 241
10:32-36 243
10:35 .... 237, 241
10:37 241
10:38 ...241, 242, 243
10:39 ....242, 243
11:6 413
11:8-16 489
11:17-19 182
11:31 185
12:2 ..... 473, 474, 475
12:16 .....465, 489
12:22 461
12:23 489
12:28-29 471
13:8 368
13:9 147
13:10 244
13:15-16 244
13:18 243
13:22 245

James
1 171
1:1 55
1:1-18 51
1:2 ....56, 95, 166
1:3-4 56
1:5-7 56
1:13-18 96
1:15 ...... 104, 171, 172, 229, 243
1:16 166
1:16-18 51
1:17 57
1:17-18 .... 61, 166
1:18 ....58, 59, 63, 95, 96, 98, 102, 103, 170, 173, 361, 377
1:19 166
1:19–2:26 91
1:19-21 98
1:21 ..... 172, 173, 174, 185, 242
1:21–2:26 .... 173, 173–174, 174
1:21-22 ... 91, 171
1:22-25 ..101, 173
1:23 ...... 101, 135
1:24 101
1:25 ..... 103, 173, 174
1:26–2:13 173
1:26-27 173
1:27 .... 55, 175
2 ..165–188, 168, 186, 387
2:1 .... 166, 173, 437
2:1-4 ..... 114, 491
2:1-13 173
2:2-3 437
2:2-6 175
2:5 .... 107, 115, 166, 491
2:8 ....173, 178
2:8-9 437
2:10 436
2 :12 174
2:12 ...... 174, 437
2:12-13 430
2:13 ...... 174, 437
2:14 ...... 166, 168, 169, 170, 171, 174, 185, 188, 342
2:14-16 .... 170, 341–344
2:14-17 175
2:14-26 ....
168–184, 174, 188, 339, 341, 365
2:15-16 .... 174, 175, 188
2:17 ...... 168, 170, 175
2:18 ...... 169, 170, 177
2:18-19 .... 176, 176–178, 177
2:19 ...... 177, 343
2:20 ......170, 176, 177, 179
2:20-23 179
2:20-24.. 179–184
2:21 ...... 181, 342
2:21-23 179
2:22 ......170, 179, 181
2:23 ..... 104, 181, 343
2:24 ..... 126, 179, 180
2:24-26 .... 184, 184–186, 185
2:26 .... 91, 104, 165, 170, 186, 339
3:1 166
3:10 166
3:12 166
4:5 492
5:19-20 172
5:20 ......171, 172, 243

1 Peter
1:5 268
1:6-9 268
1:7 268
1:9 268

Scripture Index

1:10-11 268
1:23-25 377
2:1-3 236
3:17-22 296
3:18–4:6 304
3:18-19 303
3:18-22 303
3:21 ..... 296, 303, 303–304, 304
4:15 227
5:8-9 285
5:10 86

2 Peter
1:11 312
2:4 479
2:17 479
3:13 59
3:14 467
3:18 149

1 John
1:1 208
1:1-3 210
1:1-4 360
1:1-5 226
1:1-8 222
1:2 .... 227, 228
1:3 .... 208, 209, 212, 213, 360
1:3-4 230
1:5 209
1:5-7 216
1:5-10 .. 207, 209, 360
1:7 .... 209, 287, 298
1:8 .... 216, 217, 218, 220
1:9 .... 216, 227, 298, 305, 306, 466

2:1 .... 207, 208, 360
2:2 329
2:3 .... 204, 358
2:3-6 215
2:5-6 197
2:6 358
2:7-10 358
2:12-14 .... 202, 203, 206
2:15-16 203
2:15-17 .. 203, 212
2:18 ...... 204, 205, 225
2:18-25 360
2:18-27 212
2:19 ...... 210, 211
2:20 210
2:21 206
2:22 204
2:22-23 212
2:24 ...... 206, 358
2:24-27 210
2:24b 206
2:25 ..... 205, 206, 208, 213, 228
2:25-27 205
2:26 ..... 205, 207, 208, 360
2:27 222
2:28 ...... 442, 466
3:1-9 224
3:2 .... 135, 442
3:5 219
3:6 .... 216, 217, 219, 220, 221, 222, 223
3:8 223
3:9 .... 135, 216, 217, 219, 220, 223, 224
3:10 .... 224, 225
3:10b-15 229

3:11 ...... 226, 227, 228
3:12a 226
3:12b 226
3:13 226
3:13-14 226
3:14 .... 226, 228
3:14-15 227
3:14b 226
3:15 .... 227, 228
4:1-3 212
4:1-6 212
4:4 .... 210, 226
4:4-6 ..... 210, 226
4:5 .... 204, 210, 226
4:6 226
4:7 .... 212, 216, 230
4:7-8 215
4:7-21 212
4:10 330
4:10-11 439
4:11 216
4:17 430
4:17-18 438
5:1 .... 157, 163, 297, 370, 377, 389
5:1-12 .... 207, 358
5:3-4 500
5:4-5 323
5:5 .... 207, 500
5:5-12 207
5:5-13 207
5:8 294
5:9-10 162
5:9-12 .. 207, 208, 360
5:10 .... 360, 377
5:11 361
5:11-12 361
5:12-13 361

1 John ...
5:13 ...... 206, 207, 208, 213, 358, 359, 360, 361
5:16 219
5:18 .... 224, 323
5:20 227

Jude
13 479

Revelation
1:9 121
1:17 439
2 ... 319, 320, 323
2–3 ...... 499, 500, 501
2:5 324
2:7 320
2:10 ...... 321, 324, 502
2:11 .... 320, 320–322, 321, 322, 501, 502, 503
2:15 324
2:16 324
2:26 ...... 324, 499
2:26-27 .... 129, 317, 461, 486
2 and 3 500
3 ... 319, 320, 323
3:3 324
3:4 324
3:5 .... 321, 320–322, 322, 323, 501, 503
3:21 ..... 130, 318, 461
3:21-22 504
12:5 402
12:17 495
13:1-8 494
14:1-7 495
19:11-21 446
19:15 402
20:4 ...... 463, 495
20:6 ...... 462, 463
20:7-10 .. 402, 457
20:11-15 .... 402, 448
20:12 .... 271, 436
21:1 .... 327, 403
21:1-4 122
21:1-8 119
21:4 470
21:5 123
21:5-8 119
21:6 ..... 123, 124, 125
21:7 ...... 125, 126, 130
21:8 ..... 131, 132, 136, 327
22:12 ... 430, 432, 448
22:16 136
22:16-17 119
22:17 .... 119, 125, 137, 145, 157, 160, 191, 420

Subject Index

A

Abraham 424, 443–444, 488–490

Acceptance 385–386, 403, 446, 477–478

Antinomian .. 385

Approval 441, 446, 453

Assurance 384, 421, 494

B

Believe 151–155, 249, 362, 368–378, 387–391, 477

C

Calvin ... 162–163, 273, 288–289, 336–345

Calvinism 385

Commitment 157, 192, 195, 386–391

Confess 306, 320–322, 501–502

Confidence ... 182, 237, 241, 245, 487–488

Cross 54, 79–90, 256–257, 329–334, 362–367, 409

Crown ... 321, 383, 485, 502–505

D

Day of Judgment 397, 430–440

Deny 128–129, 278, 453–455

Disapproved 287, 383

Discipline 244, 246–247

Disqualified 153–154, 281–290, 383, 485, 489

Doubt 231, 370

E

Election 233, 494

Endure 69, 309, 453–454, 484–486, 492–494

Eternal Life 30–36, 151–156, 163, 165-167, 201–208, 251–252, 270–272, 293–306, 359–363, 369–371, 415–428, 429–439, 441-442

Eternal Security 309, 357

Eternity 30, 478–480, 484

Everlasting Life 20, 161, 250, 387–388

F

Faith ....
33–35, 67–72,
91–106, 109–110,
113–118, 146–
148, 158–187,
237–250,
283–290, 339,
341–346, 361–
378, 487–492

**Faithful,
Faithfulness** ....
311, 448–455,
463–472,
482–484

Fear ....
148, 438–440,
448–450

Fruit 29–30,
63–74, 197–198,
238, 345, 395,
410

G

Garment ....
477–479,
501–502

Gift 17–24,
26–27, 33–37,
57–62, 69–74, 78,
92–98, 113–117,
124–140, 155–
158, 166–167,
250–252,
296–302

Glory ....
84–87, 268–270,
308–311, 330

Gospel ... 113–115,
145–150, 151,
157–159, 230,
233–234,
256–258,
325–326, 331–
332, 354–355,
368, 391–393,
424–426

Grace ....
33–37, 133–136,
147–149, 158–
160, 166–169,
274–275, 326–
329, 364–365,
424–425

**Great White
Throne** 271,
402, 448, 483

H

Heaven ... 122, 365

Heir 115–117,
126–130, 307–
324, 455–466,
491–496

Holiness 147, 312,
330

Honor 85, 441,
503

I

**Inherit,
Inheritance** .....
116–117, 125–
128, 133–136,
308–309, 314–
318, 455–466,
496

J

Joy ....
82–84, 473–474,
480–486

Judge ....
174, 271–272,
429–440,
434–435

Judgment 152,
174, 238–243,
270–273, 361,
429–442, 448

Judgment Seat ..
260–261, 430–
436, 469–470,
483–485

**Justification,
Justify** 104,
125, 134–135,
179–185, 249–
250, 270–273,
287–290, 296–
299, 341–345,
363–366, 383–
384, 403–405,
465

Subject Index

K

Kingdom ..66–67, 81–88, 107–117, 126–137, 310–320, 396–403, 418–424, 447–473, 488–497

L

Law 101–103, 146–149, 173, 221–222, 250–252, 270–276, 400–403, 418

Lordship Salvation ... 161, 163, 290, 357

Love 115–118, 212–216, 224–230, 419–420, 437–439, 491–496

M

Mature .. 181, 254, 438–439

O

Obedience 146, 173–175, 179–183, 214–215, 278–279, 359

Outer Darkness ... 478, 483, 488–489

Overcomer 127–130, 320–323, 487–505

P

Partners 244–245, 471–473

Paul 35–38, 127–130, 134–135, 148–149, 153–159, 166–173, 179–184, 232–233, 249–292, 295–303, 308–320, 353–355, 457–466

Persecution ... 55, 95, 426

Perseverance 256–257, 312

Praise 88, 268, 435, 449

Promise 157–158, 162–163, 205–209, 331–333, 502–504

R

Rebuke 278, 284, 453, 470

Redemption 305, 319, 383

Reign 128, 137–138, 309–310, 453–455, 460–463, 484–485, 492–495

Repentance 237, 386–387

Resurrection 182, 258, 308, 349, 354–355, 369–370, 427, 457–463, 496

Reward 34, 241, 251–252, 322–323, 345, 426–438, 482, 503–504

Righteousness ... 98–99, 134–136, 224–226, 249, 273, 336, 363–367, 399–400, 403–404, 431–432, 475

Rule 310–311, 317–319, 402, 450, 484–486

Ruler 415, 467–468

S

Salvation ..22–23, 34–37, 146–150, 151–163, 165–166, 189–193, 252–258, 263–275, 290, 301–303, 313–316, 329–335, 357–371, 383–388

Saving Faith 151–152, 192, 249–250, 335, 366–373, 377, 386–393

Shame 89, 128–129, 441–442

Sin 216–224, 235–243, 326–327

Soul 99, 147, 171–172, 241–242, 268–269, 407–408, 411, 468–469

Suffering 85, 128–131, 265–268, 309–310, 409

T

Treasure 108–111, 114, 412–415, 421–427, 497

U

Unregenerate 34, 194, 404, 457

V

Victory .. 153–154, 318, 323–324, 499–501, 504

W

Wages 30, 31, 364, 432

Works 36–39, 102–105, 151–161, 165–188, 252–255, 270–278, 288–290, 335–339, 341–346, 363–367, 429–439